MW00575145

THE
ECONOMICS
RELIGION
OF

THE
ECONOMICS
OF RELIGION

Editor

Robert M Sauer

Royal Holloway, University of London, UK

World Scientific

NEW JERSEY · LONDON · SINGAPORE · BEIJING · SHANGHAI · HONG KONG · TAIPEI · CHENNAI · TOKYO

Published by

World Scientific Publishing Co. Pte. Ltd.

5 Toh Tuck Link, Singapore 596224

USA office: 27 Warren Street, Suite 401-402, Hackensack, NJ 07601

UK office: 57 Shelton Street, Covent Garden, London WC2H 9HE

Library of Congress Cataloging-in-Publication Data

Names: Sauer, Robert M., editor.

Title: The economics of religion / editor, Robert M. Sauer,
  Royal Holloway, University of London, UK.

Description: New Jersey : World Scientific, [2023] |
  Includes bibliographical references and index.

Identifiers: LCCN 2023000833 | ISBN 9789811273131 (hardcover) |
  ISBN 9789811273148 (ebook) | ISBN 9789811273155 (ebook other)

Subjects: LCSH: Economics--Religious aspects. | Religion--Economic aspects.

Classification: LCC HB72 .E2746 2023 | DDC 306.3--dc23/eng/20230109

LC record available at https://lccn.loc.gov/2023000833

British Library Cataloguing-in-Publication Data

A catalogue record for this book is available from the British Library.

For any available supplementary material, please visit
https://www.worldscientific.com/worldscibooks/10.1142/13328#t=suppl

Desk Editors: Nimal Koliyat/Lai Ann/Sylvia Koh

Typeset by Stallion Press
Email: enquiries@stallionpress.com

Preface

In their recent book, *The Wealth of Religions: The Political Economy of Believing and Belonging,* Rachel M. McCleary and Robert J. Barro suggest that the modern economics of religion literature derives much of its inspiration from two giants of intellectual history — Adam Smith and Max Weber. Adam Smith, one of the founding fathers of contemporary economics, observed in his famous 1776 treatise, *The Wealth of Nations,* that religiosity is influenced by the extent of regulation in the "market" for religion. For example, in countries where there is a state-sponsored religion, one can expect less overall religiosity than if the market were competitive and religions had to compete to increase their membership. In this sense, religion is similar to all other goods and services supplied in a market economy.

In a similar spirit, Max Weber, one of the founding fathers of contemporary sociology, also proposed in his famous 1905 book, *The Protestant Ethic and the Spirit of Capitalism,* that religiosity and economic principles were strongly interconnected phenomena. In particular, Weber thought that Protestant religious beliefs about the importance of work, savings and trustworthiness played an important role in sparking the Industrial Revolution and accelerating economic growth. He believed that religious commitment to hard work and honesty formed character traits that coalesced into a form of human capital. The increased human capital and productivity deriving from these religious beliefs was a key factor in unleashing the unprecedented economic growth in the West during the eighteenth and nineteenth centuries.

This edited volume contains original contributions by eminent scholars in the field of the economics of religion. They can all be squarely placed within the Smith–Weber paradigm. The chapters also illuminate new directions for research in this relatively young, intellectually exciting and rapidly growing multidisciplinary field of scientific inquiry.

About the Editor

Robert M. Sauer is a Professor of Economics at Royal Holloway, University of London and the Editor-in-Chief of the *European Economic Review*, the *European Economic Review Plus*, and the *Journal of Economics, Management and Religion*.

His research focuses on immigration, labor force dynamics, entrepreneurship, volunteerism and the economics of religion. He has published his work in *Econometrica*, the *Journal of Political Economy*, the *Review of Economic Studies*, the *International Economic Review* and the *Journal of Labor Economics*, among many other scientific journals.

In addition, he has published numerous essays and opinion pieces on contemporary economic and social issues in the popular press and have appeared on podcasts to discuss them.

His previous academic appointments include the Hebrew University of Jerusalem, Tel Aviv University, Brown University and the University of Bristol. He completed a PhD in economics at New York University in 1995.

Contents

https://doi.org/10.1142/9789811273148_0001

Chapter 1

Cultural Transmission and Religion

Alberto Bisin[*,§], Jean-Paul Carvalho[†,¶], and Thierry Verdier[‡,‖]

*Department of Economics, New York University,
19th West Fourth Street, 6th Floor, NY 10012, USA
†Department of Economics, University of Oxford,
Manor Road Building, Manor Road Oxford OX1 3UQ, UK
‡Paris School of Economics, 48 Boulevard Jourdan,
75014 Paris, France
§alberto.bisin@nyu.edu
¶jean-paul.carvalho@economics.ox.ac.uk
‖thierry.verdier@psemail.eu

Abstract

Based on population dynamics models, the literature on cultural transmission has studied the formation and diffusion of religious traits
through evolutionary and bottom-up forces such as parental socialization. This chapter provides a bird's eye view of this approach and
its main extensions. We also emphasize two additional dimensions
of the cultural dynamics of religious preferences. The first is cultural
blending and religious syncretism, namely the fusion of diverse religious beliefs and practices. The second highlights the importance of

1

purposeful and centralized authorities, such as religious leaders and institutions, that influence the cultural dynamics of religious beliefs and preferences.

Keywords: Religion, Cultural Transmission, Belief Systems

1. How are Religious Beliefs and Preferences Produced?

The basic building blocks of economic models are beliefs, preferences and constraints (Henrich *et al.*, 2005). Given enough information about person i's choices, we could characterize her beliefs and preferences and, under certain consistency conditions, anticipate her choices under a different set of constraints. But that would not tell us why person j's choices would differ from i's, why i's choices at date t differ from her own choices at date $t + 1$, or how i's choices are influenced by her identity, political affiliation and exposure to role models and "influencers." Consider for example the curious association between the decision to wear a mask during the COVID-19 pandemic and one's political affiliation. These questions require us to go further and investigate how beliefs and preferences are produced.

Bowles (1998) sets out the ways in which fixed preferences limit economic theory:

> But the scope of economic inquiry is thereby truncated in ways which restrict its explanatory power, policy relevance, and ethical coherence. If preferences are affected by the policies or institutional arrangements we study, we can neither accurately predict nor coherently evaluate the likely consequences of new policies or institutions without taking account of preference endogeneity. (Bowles, 1998: p. 75)

When it comes to religion, many important questions force us to think about the origins, persistence and change in religious belief and preferences. For example, suppose we wish to know why group A exhibits higher rates of religious participation than group B, or why individual i converted to religion k, or why religious belief rose in country C.

Religion is an ideal training ground for theories of belief and preference formation. Belief in supernatural agents has been found in every known human society. Religious organizations are among the most ubiquitous and long-lived human institutions. Religious participation also has important consequences for economic decisions (Iannaconne, 1998), including education (Becker and Woessman, 2009; Meyersson, 2014), fertility (McQuillan, 2014) and labor market participation (Berman, 2000; Carvalho, 2013). In addition, there is extensive survey data on religious belief, identity and participation from sources such as the *World Values Survey* and The Association of Religion Data Archives (ARDA), as well as a large body of anthropological data on religious belief and participation in small-scale societies gathered in sources such as Murdock's *Ethnographic Atlas*.

This chapter focuses on religious belief and preference formation through *cultural transmission*. Before proceeding, however, let us mention three other approaches (see also Bowles, 1998):

(1) *Religious Capital*: Iannaconne (1998) models the accumulation of "religious capital" over an individual's lifetime. This religious "appreciation capital" can be thought of as intensity of religious belief or attachment to a religious group, among other things. In this view, religious belief and preferences are cultivated by participation in religious activities. Religious participation contributes to religious capital. In turn, a larger stock of religious capital means a higher preferred level of religious participation. McBride (2015) explores the implications for religious organizations. Even strict religious groups tolerate free-riding by newcomers in anticipation of future contributions, as newcomers accumulate religious capital. The accumulation of religious capital is consistent with two empirical regularities: (i) the best predictor of an individual's religious affiliation and participation is their parents' religious affiliation and participation and (ii) people who switch religions tend to join groups with similar theology and practices (Iannaconne, 1998).

(2) *Motivated Beliefs*: In economics, the term "belief" is typically used to denote a probability distribution over states of the world, which can be updated based on empirical evidence. Such beliefs are instrumental in that forming correct beliefs furthers some other objective. When it comes to religion, however, beliefs are largely non-empirical and often ends in themselves. In this sense, the formation of religious beliefs is motivated.

In his famous study of the Trobriand Islanders, Malinowski (1925) points to the anxiety-reducing benefits of ritual:

> It is most significant that in the Lagoon fishing, where man can rely completely upon his knowledge and skill, magic does not exist, while in the open-sea fishing, full of danger and uncertainty, there is extensive magical ritual to secure safety and good result.

Similarly, religious belief can be cultivated for its psychological benefits and be part of the "psychological immune system" (Benabou and Tirole, 2002). Fruehwirth *et al.* (2019) find that religious exposure significantly reduces depression in adolescence. Binzel and Carvalho (2017) present a model in which individuals can respond to unfulfilled aspirations by either working harder to catch up or "dropping out" and immersing themselves in religion. Economic shocks can thus lead to sharp rises in religious participation and these religious awakenings can persist long after the economic shock has subsided. Consistent with this, Bentzen (2019) presents evidence of a sharp rise in religiosity after natural disasters. In addition, Chen (2010) finds that communal Qur'an study and Islamic school attendance in Indonesia rose following the 1997–1998 financial crisis.

(3) *Socially Adaptive Beliefs*: Forms of religious belief that solve social dilemmas can evolve through processes such as cultural group selection (Gintis, 2003; Henrich, 2004). Sosis and Ruffle (2003) conduct experimental games in religious and secular kibbutzim and find that religious males are significantly more cooperative than secular males. Levy and Razin (2012) show how belief in supernatural punishment in social dilemmas emerges in equilibrium and boosts cooperation, especially within religious groups. Analyzing a database of nineteenth century utopian communes, Sosis (2000) shows that religious communes are more cooperative and longer lived than secular ones. In addition, Norenzayan (2013) proposes that "Big Gods" who monitor and punish transgressions evolved to support large-scale cooperation as societies scaled up. Skaperdas and Vaidya (2020) argue that the move to Big-God religions was a key factor in the development of the modern state.

Based on population dynamics models, the cultural transmission literature on the formation and diffusion of religious traits has focused on evolutionary and bottom-up forces driving the persistence or homogenization of religious beliefs in a society. This chapter provides a bird's eye view of this approach and its main extensions. We also emphasize two additional dimensions that bring interesting issues in the cultural dynamics of religious preferences. The first one relates to cultural blending and religious syncretism, namely the fusion of diverse religious beliefs and practices. The second one highlights the importance of purposeful and centralized authorities such as religious leaders and institutions that influence the cultural dynamics of religious beliefs and preferences.

The chapter is structured as follows. In Section 2, we present the baseline model of cultural transmission with two cultural traits and introduce endogenous socialization à la Bisin and Verdier (2001). In Section 3, we outline several extensions of this setup and their connection to the cultural dynamics of religious traits. Further extending the model to multi-trait cultural transmission, Section 4 considers the important issue of cultural blending and its application to syncretism of religious traits. Section 5 focuses on the interaction between institutions and cultural transmission, covering in particular recent works analyzing the influence and impact of religious leaders and organizations in the diffusion and persistence of religious traits, as well as the role of religion in the building up of political legitimacy and state power. Section 6 offers a conclusion briefly discussing avenues for future research.

2. The Bisin–Verdier Model of Cultural Transmission

Mathematical models of cultural transmission were pioneered by evolutionary biologists Cavalli-Sforza and Feldman (1981), anthropologists/ biologists Boyd and Richerson (1985) and economists Bisin and Verdier (2000, 2001). Religion is an intensely social phenomenon (Iannaconne, 1998), making cultural transmission — the transmission of traits from person to person — a good fit for modeling the formation of religious beliefs and preferences. This contrasts with religious capital models in which appreciation capital is privately accumulated over an individual's lifetime. Social transmission is important both for the distribution of religious traits in a population and choices such as religious participation and education that govern social transmission.

Let us begin with a baseline model of cultural transmission.

2.1 *Intergenerational cultural transmission*

The population is a continuum of agents. Individuals have either cultural trait *a* or *b*, which can be two different religions, or two different levels of religiosity with *a* types being religious and *b* types being secular.

The population dynamics are highly simplified. We assume that reproduction is asexual and that each parent has one child. Hence the population is stationary and normalized to *L* = 1. We consider cultural transmission to be the result of *direct vertical* (parental) socialization and *oblique socialization* in society at large. More precisely, each parent (asexually) produces one child, socializes them and then dies. With probability τ_i, a parent with trait $i \in \{a, b\}$ successfully passes on her trait to her child. For the moment, assume each τ_i is exogenous. With probability $1 - \tau_i$ however the child remains "unsocialized." He then becomes subject to a second stage of socialization by the social environment of his parent (i.e., oblique transmission). Specifically, he is matched at random with someone from his parent's generation (i.e., oblique transmission) and acquires their trait.

Let *q* equal the share of *a* types in the population. The cultural transmission mechanism is then represented by the following system of equations for P^{ij}, the transition probability that a child from a family with trait *i* is socialized to trait *j*:

$$P_{aa} = \tau_a + (1 - \tau_a)q, \; P_{ab} = (1 - \tau_a)(1 - q), \tag{1}$$

$$P_{ba} = (1 - \tau_b)q, \; P_{bb} = \tau_b + (1 - \tau_b)(1 - q). \tag{2}$$

Take for instance trait *a*. The probability P_{aa} for a child of a family of type *a* to be socialized to that trait includes two terms: the direct vertical socialization probability τ_a plus the indirect oblique socialization probability $(1 - \tau_a)q$ reflecting the fact when he is not successfully socialized by the family in the first stage (with probability $1 - \tau_a$), he is socialized by a similar type *a* from the population at large with probability *q*. Conversely, the probability P_{ab} for a child to acquire the other trait *b* reflects the fact that the child was not successfully socialized by his parent (with probability $1 - \tau_a$) and was exposed to an oblique role model of type *b* from society at large (with probability $1 - q$).

Using the law of large numbers and continuous time, this process of cultural socialization results in the following cultural dynamic, describing the diffusion of trait *a* in the population:

$$\dot{q} = \underbrace{(1-q)P_{ba}}_{\text{inflow}} - \underbrace{qP_{ab}}_{\%\text{outflow}}$$

$$= (1-q)(1-\tau_b)q - q(1-\tau_a)(1-q)$$

or

$$\dot{q} = q(1-q)(\tau_a - \tau_b). \tag{3}$$

Equation (3) is actually a simple version of the replicator dynamics in evolutionary biology for a two-trait population dynamic model.[1] $(\tau_a - \tau_b)$ can be interpreted as the relative "cultural fitness" of trait a compared to trait b. It is a simple matter to see that:

> Generically, beginning in any interior state $q(0) \in (0,1)$, the cultural dynamic ends up in a monomorphic equilibrium ($q = 1$ if $\tau_a > \tau_b$ or $q = 0$ if $\tau_a < \tau_b$).[2]

Hence the melting pot result of cultural homogenization.

Given the persistent diversity we observe, how can a polymorphic cultural equilibrium be generated? One way to generate long-run persistence of cultural diversity can be obtained by introducing the possibility of cultural transmission rates which are frequency dependent.

For instance, Boyd and Richerson (1985) consider situations where the commonness or rarity of a trait affects the probability of its transmission more (or less) than proportionally. Typically when individuals are predisposed to adopt the behavior of a larger group, this frequency-dependent bias generates conformity. On the opposite, when individuals tend to adopt more than proportionally traits that are associated with smaller groups, there is an anti-conformist bias.[3] It is then a simple matter

---

[1] In terms of Cavalli-Sforza and Feldman (1981) and Boyd and Richerson (1985) terminology, this model reflects a cultural transmission process that is equivalent to a linear transmission model characterized by "direct biased" transmission $\tau_a - \tau_b$ between the two cultural variants a and b of our trait.

[2] If $\tau_a - \tau_b$, $q(t) = q(0)$ for all t.

[3] Boyd and Richerson (1985) and Henrich and Gil-White (2001) also identify as "indirect bias" the situation where individuals may also use a cue about one trait (wealth, prestige)

to see that the "melting pot" homogenization result still prevails under conformity bias. On the contrary, an anti-conformist bias preserves cultural diversity in the population.[4]

In the cultural evolution literature, the nature of frequency-dependent bias is assumed to be fixed in the short run and to be subject to genetic evolution in the long run. In particular, it is generally argued that it can be genetically adaptive for individuals to develop frequency-dependent bias such as conformity and indirect bias associated with prestige (Boyd and Richerson, 1985: Henrich and Gil-White, 2001; Panchanathan, 2010). Such co-evolutionary explanations of frequency-dependent transmission rates however necessitate selective forces spanning over long periods of time (many thousands of years). For our purpose of the cultural transmission of religious traits, these genetic processes should probably be best considered as fixed and therefore can hardly explain cultural phenomena of religious resistance/resilience or disappearance due to changes in the social and economic environment under much shorter time scales. As we will see in Section 2.2, bringing a "short/medium" term social-economic evolutionary perspective allows cultural transmission rates to be endogenously frequency dependent.

2.2 *An economic model of cultural transmission*

2.2.1 *Endogenous socialization*

Let us now introduce some economics. We bring two important features to the previous framework. The first element is that transmission rates across generations can be the result of costly and purposeful actions by socializing agents. The second feature (related to the first one) is the

---

to choose which role model to observe in order to acquire information about another trait.

[4]Formally, the direct socialization probabilities may be written as

$$\tau_a = f_a(q), \tau_b = f_b(1-q),$$

where a conformity bias is captured by the fact that $f_i(.)$ is an increasing function of its argument and $f_i(0) = 0$. Conversely, an anti-conformist bias is reflected by a decreasing function $f_i(.)$, with $f_i(1) = 0$. The cultural relative fitness $\tau^a - \tau^b = \Theta(q)$ is now a function reflecting the "frequency-dependent bias" associated to the cultural variant a.

With a conformity bias, the cultural dynamic converges again monotonically to a monomorphic equilibrium $q = 0$ or $q = 1$, while with an anti-conformity bias, it converges monotonically to the polymorphic state $q^* \in (0,1)$ satisfying the condition $\Theta(q^*) = 0$.

question of the motivation for agents to undertake such costly socialization efforts.

Bisin and Verdier (2001) introduce agency into the previous model of cultural transmission. In particular, they allow a choice of socialization effort, thereby making the transition probabilities endogenous. Parents can choose how intensively to socialize their children, at some cost, through (1) teaching, (2) school choice, (3) residential choice, (4) homogamy, and other costly actions.

To model socialization choice, parents need to have preferences over the traits that their children can acquire. Bisin and Verdier take an approach they call *imperfect empathy*: parents evaluate their children's behavior based on their own preferences. Formally, a parent with trait i gets a payoff of V_{ij} if her child acquires trait j, where $V_{ii} > V_{ij}$ whenever $i \neq j$.

A parent with trait a in state q has payoff function:

$$U^a(q) = \underbrace{[\tau_a + (1-\tau_a)q]}_{P_{aa}} V_{aa} + \underbrace{(1-\tau_a)(1-q)}_{P_{ab}} V_{ab} - c(\tau_a). \tag{4}$$

She chooses socialization effort τ_a at cost $c(\tau_a)$ to maximize this function.[5] A parent with trait b in state q has payoff function:

$$U^b(q) = \underbrace{[\tau_b + (1-\tau_b)(1-q)]}_{P_{bb}} V_{bb} + \underbrace{(1-\tau_b)q}_{P_{ba}} V_{ba} - c(\tau_b). \tag{5}$$

Before deriving optimal socialization efforts let us define the notion of "cultural intolerance." Type i's cultural intolerance is denoted by Δ_i, where

$$\Delta_a = V_{aa} - V_{ab} \text{ and } \Delta_b = V_{bb} - V_{ba}.$$

The first-order conditions for a type and b type are, respectively,

$$(1-q)\Delta_a = c'(\tau_a) \text{ and } q\Delta_b = c'(\tau_b), \tag{6}$$

and population dynamics are given by (3) except that now τ_i is endogenous and given by (6). We have the following proposition.

---

[5] $c(\tau)$ is supposed to be an increasing convex function with the Inada conditions: $c(0) = c'(0) = 0$ and $\lim_{\tau \to 1} c(\tau) = \lim_{\tau \to 1} c'(\tau) = +\infty$.

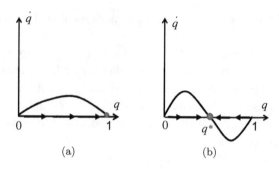

Figure 1:   Cultural Transmission Models. (a) Cultural Dynamics, Cavalli Sforza-Feldman (1981) (Case: $\tau_a > \tau_b$). (b) Cultural Dynamics, Bisin and Verdier (2001) (Cultural substitution)

Proposition 1 (Bisin and Verdier, 2001). *Optimal socialization effort varies in the following manner:*

(i) τ_i *is strictly increasing in "cultural intolerance"* Δ_i, *(ii)* τ_a *is strictly decreasing in q, (iii)* τ_b *is strictly increasing in q, (iv)* $\tau_a > \tau_b$ *if and only if* $q < \frac{\Delta_a}{\Delta_a + \Delta_b}$, *(v) From any interior state* $q(0) \in (0,1)$, *the dynamic converges to* $q^* = \frac{\Delta_a}{\Delta_a + \Delta_b}$.

First, higher degrees of cultural intolerance mean more intensive socialization. Second, the smaller a cultural group the more it expends on socialization effort. Third, cultural group i socializes more intensively than group j if its share of the population q is less than its relative cultural intolerance, $\Delta_i/(\Delta_i + \Delta_j)$. If the cultural intolerances are the same across groups, then the minority group will exert greater socialization effort. Otherwise, an intolerant majority can expend more on socialization than a more tolerant minority. Consequently, a *polymorphic* cultural distribution emerges from almost every initial state whenever cultural intolerance is positive for each type.

Introducing endogenous socialization effort in (1) qualitatively changes the population dynamics. It generates an *endogenous* anti-conformist bias that maintains cultural diversity in the population. Figures 1(a) and 1(b) illustrate the starkly different population dynamics in the leading models proposed by Cavalli-Sforza and Feldman (1981) and in the benchmark model of Bisin and Verdier (2001).

As pointed out by Bisin and Verdier (2001), the cultural transmission mechanism described in (1) satisfies the property of *cultural substitution*, by which role models inside the family (direct vertical transmission) act as *cultural substitutes* to role models outside the family (oblique or horizontal transmission).[6] In such a case, parents have less incentives to socialize their children the more widely dominant are their values in the population. Consequently, as a trait begins to die out in the society at large, parents with that trait socialize more intensively, and this in turn keeps the cultural dynamic away from the boundaries $q = 0$ and $q = 1$. Conversely, when parental role models act as *cultural complements* to other social role models, parental socialization effort if larger the more frequent their trait is in the population, providing therefore a transmission force pushing towards cultural homogeneity.[7]

In general, both cultural substitution and complementary effects may be present in the way role models (parental and social) tend to interact to influence children. The relative strength of these effects then shapes the cultural dynamic in society, eventually leading to the existence of multiple long-run possible cultural steady states towards which the society converges, depending on its initial conditions.

Summarizing, the endogenous cultural transmission model in Bisin and Verdier (2000, 2001) allows for population dynamics of the distribution of cultural traits which converge to a heterogeneous distribution. This can explain the observed resilience of ethnic and religious traits.

There is evidence for the endogenous socialization hypothesis. Cohen-Zada (2006) finds that rates of religious schooling for religious minorities in the United States are decreasing in their population share. Bisin and Verdier (2000) present an alternative model of socialization with sexual reproduction in which homogamy increases the likelihood that one's child acquires one's cultural trait. The results are similar. Bisin *et al.* (2004) present evidence consistent with both socialization and homogamy channels from the United States. Using General Social Survey (GSS) data and examining variation across US states from 1972 to 1996, they find that religious minorities socialize more intensively and exhibit higher rates of homogamy than majorities. Calibrating the model and simulating the population dynamics, they show that minority religion shares stabilize at higher levels than predicted by linear extrapolations.

---

[6]Denote $q_i \in [0, 1]$, the frequency of trait $i \in \{a, b\}$ in the population (i.e., $q_a = q$, $q_b = 1 - q$). Bisin and Verdier (2001) formally define *cultural substitution* as τ_i of a parent of type $i \in \{a, b\}$· (for any $\Delta_i > 0$, $\tau_i (q_i, \Delta_i)$ is a continuous, strictly decreasing function in q_i, and moreover, $\tau_i (1, \Delta_i) = 0$.)

[7]Bisin and Verdier (2001) provide examples of such transmission processes.

While the evidence offered by Bisin *et al.* (2004) and Cohen-Zada (2006) is consistent with a cultural substitution effect between direct and oblique socialization, Patacchini and Zenou (2011) on the other hand present evidence of complementarity in the UK. This suggests that the type of relationship between direct and oblique religious socialization is probably dependent on population conditions and therefore consistent with a multiple steady-state model.

3. Generalizations

One advantage of the economic model of cultural transmission we outline above is the fact that it is versatile enough to allow extensions along several dimensions important for the evolution of religious traits, such as fertility decisions, spatial or social segregation, identity formation and more generally, the possibility of socioeconomic interactions. We turn to these extensions below.

3.1 *Endogenous fertility and cultural transmission*

There is a considerable body of literature in the social sciences that highlights the association between religion and fertility. For instance, it is well known that even controlling for income and education, religious people have more children on average than secular people (Blume, 2009; Frejka and Westhoff, 2008). Historical studies of Western Europe also suggest that fertility declines are often related to differences in religious affiliation and involvement (Anderson, 1986; Derosas and van Poppel, 2006). Studies in the United States highlight as well religious differences in fertility, mainly between Catholics and Protestants (Bouvier and Rao, 1975; Gutmann, 1990; Parkerson and Parkerson, 1988). In developing societies, religious fertility differentials have also been commonly observed, with a particular focus on Muslim-Christian fertility differences (Bailey, 1986; Johnson and Hanks, 2006; Heaton, 2011; Dharmalingam and Morgan, 2004; Jayasree, 1989; Johnson, 1993; Knodel *et al.*, 1999; Morgan *et al.*, 2002). Regardless of denominational affiliation, people expressing higher religiosity usually tend to have higher fertility and lower contraceptive use (Brewster *et al.*, 1998; Goldscheider and Mosher, 1991; Philipov and Berghammer, 2007; Hayford and Morgan, 2008; Zhang, 2008), or tend to favor formal marriage over cohabitation, which in turn, leads to higher fertility (Berghammer, 2012).

Importantly enough, when it is determined as an endogenous choice of parents, fertility decisions naturally interact with socialization decisions if for no other reason than that socialization costs naturally increase with the number of children to socialize. Consider then our previous model of cultural transmission and extend it to allow for some parental choice of reproductive pattern. Specifically, let $n_i \geq 0$ denote the number of children chosen by parents with trait i, at cost $m \cdot N_i$ (where m is the cost of raising one child). Assuming for simplicity that socialization costs are linear in n_i, and therefore that parents of type i choose $\tau_i \in [0, 1]$ and $n_i \geq 0$ to maximize

$$n_i(P_{ii}V_{ii} + P_{ij}V_{ij}) - n_i c(\tau_i) - m \cdot n_i, \qquad (7)$$

where P_{ii} and P_{ij} are as in (1). The dynamics of the distribution of traits in the population is then determined by

$$\dot{q} = q(1-q)\frac{(\tau_a v_a - \tau_b v_b)}{v_a q + (1-v_a)(1-q)},$$

where $v_i = \frac{n_i}{n_a + n_b}$ and τ_i are determined at equilibrium for $i \in \{a, b\}$.

Bisin and Verdier (2001) point out that the choice of reproduction patterns tends to introduce a cultural complementarity force in the cultural transmission process (i.e., $n_a(q)$ is increasing in q and $n_b(1 - q)$ increasing in $1 - q$). As a matter of fact, parents endowed with a more frequent trait have a higher chance, everything else being equal, to get their children sharing their trait through society's socialization. Such an outcome is perceived by these paternalistic parents as increasing the quality of children, motivating higher fertility rates and consequently more effective cultural transmission of their trait in the population. When fertility interacts with direct socialization more generally, total socialization costs increase with the number of children, and hence parents, when choosing direct children socialization, incur a classic quantity/quality (of children) trade-off. In such a case, as Bisin and Verdier (2001) show, the quantity/quality trade-off is sufficient to re-establish the dynamics associated to cultural substitution, over-riding the cultural complementarity due to endogenous fertility.

Bar-El *et al.* (2013) consider numerical simulations of a version of the previous model to investigate the evolution of secularization in a society. In their framework, the presence of both cultural complementarity and cultural substitution effects eventually leads to multiple steady-state levels of secularization in the population. Also, around a stable steady state, the model predicts a non monotonic parabolic dependence of the current level of secularity on the past level of secularity.[8] The authors provide suggestive evidence of this parabolic relationship using data from the International Social Survey Program (ISSP 1998 National Identity module: Religion II) that collects information on attitudes, religious beliefs and religiosity measures (private prayer habits and Church attendance) in 32 countries.

Bar-Gill and Fershtman (2016) extend the Bisin and Verdier model of cultural transmission with endogenous fertility to the case where paternalistic preferences for transmitting one's own trait are not separable across children. Individuals from different cultures may have different intolerance to having only some of their children adopting different cultural identities. In such a situation, the conversion of one child affects the paternalistic motives associated with another child. They consider two opposite situations: one in which the emphasis is on having at least one child that remains loyal to the parents' religious group (described as a "survivalist type"); the other in which the emphasis is on having all the children maintaining the group's religious trait (described as a "zealot type"). In this context, individuals' fertility decision and their direct socialization effort crucially depend on their degree of zealousness. In this context, they show that integration policies aimed at promoting the cultural conversion of minority groups to the trait of the majority may be ineffective and even result in more resilient and larger minority groups. For instance, whenever individuals are of the "survivalist" type, an integration policy may induce higher fertility rates as individuals may switch from having one child with a high (and costly) direct socialization level to having two children with much lower direct socialization level. This change may result in a larger minority size whenever the effect of higher fertility is stronger than the effect of lower direct socialization.

---

[8]Up to some level, an increase in secularization in the past increases secularization in the present, while above this level, one finds a negative relation between secularization in the past and the present.

3.2 *Self-segregation, isolation and network homophily*

Sociologists and social psychologists have widely acknowledged the fact that people have significant contact with others like themselves, and that social interactions are characterized by homophily (that is, the fact that contact between similar people occurs at a higher rate than among dissimilar people) (McPherson *et al.*, 2001). Concerning religious characteristics, this implies that people of different faiths tend to form relatively isolated communities socially or spatially to preserve the persistence of their cultural values. Extreme examples run from the case of the Hutterite and Amish communities who strongly emphasize separation from non-Amish world (including even a reluctance to adopt modern conveniences such as electricity) (Kraybill and Bowman, 2001) to the Haredi (ultra-Orthodox) Jews whose communal self-awareness is found in the clear tendency to avoid the larger society and form sizable enclaves in major cities around the globe, including New York and London (Flint *et al.*, 2013; Shilhav, 1993; Valins, 2003). In such examples, expression of religious lifestyles motivates voluntary territorial separation, which allows religiously based lives to remain cut off from external influences and safeguards the younger generation from the perceived threats of secular culture. More generally, religious homophily (often correlated to ethnic homophily) is recognized as significant (Fischer, 1977, 1982; Marsden, 1988; Kalmijn, 1998; Hu *et al.*, 2019), especially among individuals with high religiosity (Windzio and Wingens, 2014; Smith *et al.*, 2014, 2016; Leszczensky and Pink, 2017).

From a cultural transmission perspective, this dimension implies that socialization at large with society is unlikely to be fully random. In particular the matching process through which children get socialized may be partly controlled by their parents (or other role models) through their choice of schools, neighborhood (where to live), associations or clubs (where to go), and so on. Also, children themselves may choose peer connections in a non-random way, reinforcing or mitigating the bias that parents produced in the first place.

In the benchmark socialization model that we introduced, oblique transmission occurred through random matching with society at large. One may however extend this framework to include the possibility that the cultural composition of society children get exposed to is at least partly under the control of parents. Abstracting from specific details of the contact process, the transmission probabilities could be generally written as

$$P_{ii} = \tau_i + (1-\tau_i)Q_i,$$
$$P_{ij} = (1-\tau_i)(1-Q_i), \tag{8}$$

where the composition of the social environment of the child, Q_i, is itself a function of the population shares q^i and a costly parental intervention, say, s^i. In such a case, the effective "technology" of parental socialization is multi-dimensional, involving various margins of transmission: time, effort and social or spatial segregation decisions. Examples of models along these lines are analyzed in Bisin and Verdier (2001) and Saez-Marti and Sjogren (2008). The marriage segmentation model analyzed in Bisin and Verdier (2000) is also an example of segregation strategies that affect cultural transmission. Other examples consider explicitly a social network structure and analyze how the topology of social connections matters for the cultural dynamics (Buechel *et al.*, 2014; Panebianco, 2014; Panebianco and Verdier, 2017; Verdier and Zenou, 2017).

An interesting relevant extension in the context of the cultural transmission of religion is Patacchini and Zenou (2016). It develops a theoretical framework in which parents' involvement in religious activities as well as the peers' influence on the children are the key ingredients in explaining religious outcomes. Contrary to the benchmark model of Bisin and Verdier (2001) where peer effects are conceived as an average intra-group externality that affects identically all the members of a given group, peer effects are only supported by the structure of active bilateral connections or dyads that constitute the social network in which individuals are embedded. In their model, the convexity or concavity of the parental socialization cost function crucially affects whether there is cultural substitutability or cultural complementarity between parental socialization intensity and peers' influence. They test their model using a very detailed dataset of adolescent friendship networks in the United States (the National Longitudinal Survey of Adolescent Health (AddHealth)). Interestingly, they find that, for religious parents, the higher is the fraction of religious peers, the more the effort put in by parents in transmitting their religiosity, indicating cultural complementarity. For non-religious parents, they obtain the reverse result of cultural substitutability, suggesting that the technology of socialization can be strongly trait dependent (religious versus non-religious).

3.3 *Religious identity and cultural transmission*

The economic model of cultural transmission can also be extended to incorporate insights from the economics of identity formation (Akerlof and Kranton, 2000). This might be particularly relevant for the issue of religious identity. As such, religious identity is anchored in a system of guiding beliefs and symbols and refers to how individuals develop their personal sense of religious meaning and/or spirituality over the course of their lifetimes. Social psychologists and sociologists acknowledge that religion serves a uniquely powerful function in shaping psychological and social processes (Ysseldyk *et al.*, 2010; Coyle and Lyons, 2011). Also, it is widely recognized that the formation of religious identity typically occurs within family and community contexts (Goodman and Dyer, 2020), although it is also admitted that some dimensions of its transmission relate both to genetic and cultural factors (White *et al.*, 2011).

As for other types of social identity (race, gender or political), the formation of religious identity can be analyzed through two somewhat opposite lenses. A first perspective argues that group identity is driven by a motive for inclusiveness and *cultural conformity*, and therefore, that identity is reduced by assimilation and contact across cultures.[9] The alternative view suggests that cultural minorities are motivated in keeping their own distinctive heritage to generate a sense of positive *distinctiveness* or *cultural distinction*[10] from individuals who are part of that group.[11] When identity formation is characterized by cultural distinction, social interactions across groups might induce the formation of oppositional or radical identities on the part of specific groups. In the context of religious

---

[9]*Assimilation theories*, in political science and sociology (Gordon, 1964; Moghaddam and Solliday, 1991), *contact theory* in social psychology (Allport, 1953) are the prominent theories of this line of thought.

[10]*Cultural distinction*, as defined here, is a property of individual preferences. It is related but distinct from *cultural substitution* (see Section 2), which is a property of socialization mechanisms.

[11]These ideas have been expressed by the theories of *multiculturalism* (Glazer and Moynihan, 1970). At a broader level, this view is also related to the *social identity theory* in social psychology (Tajfel, 1981; Turner, 1982; Abrams and Hogg, 1988).

identities, this may explain the existence of religious radicalization and its associated social frictions.

For instance, Bisin *et al.* (2011) present a model where an individual's identity is a personal choice that depends on the cultural composition of the neighborhood in which he is raised and his personal negative experiences related to interacting with individuals not sharing his own cultural trait. This dimension is embedded into a cultural transmission model in which parents decide how much to invest in socializing their children to their own trait, anticipating the possible peer effects favoring society's influence and their children's future identity choice. The analysis shows that both cultural substitution and cultural distinction jointly induce resilience and persistence of minoritarian traits, therefore preserving cultural diversity in the long run. Interestingly, the prevalence of an oppositional (radical) culture in a minority group can be sustained when there is enough cultural segmentation in terms of role models, the size the group is significant enough, the degree of radicalization it implies is high enough, and the socioeconomic opportunity cost of the actions it prescribes is small enough.

Using data on ethnic preferences and attitudes provided by the Fourth National Survey of Ethnic Minorities in the UK, Bisin *et al.* (2016) find evidence that might be consistent with intense ethnic and religious identity mostly formed as a cultural distinction mechanism. Consistently, they document that such identities might be more intense in mixed than in segregated neighborhoods.

3.4 *Cultural transmission and social interactions*

In the cultural transmission models we described so far, parental socialization depends on the parents' relative value of having a child with the same cultural trait as theirs, Δ_i, which we referred to as the *cultural intolerance* of trait i. In fact, the Δ_is have been treated as exogenous preference parameters in the frameworks we surveyed up to this point. In many contexts of interest, however, this is too restrictive an assumption. The endogeneity of Δ_i can originate in many different environments. For instance, when individuals interact in markets, their indirect utility may depend on economic variables such as prices and incomes or policy outcomes that depend on the type of society and therefore the distribution of cultural traits that prevails in such society. Similarly, in the contexts of strategic and matching interactions, the payoffs that an individual may obtain is likely to be influenced by the distribution of cultural traits in the population. In the religious context, it is clear that the degree of religious intolerance of an individual towards other people not sharing his worldview may be influenced (positively or negatively) by the behavior of these individuals and the frequency of their encounters. Also, in a religious community, the Δ_i may be manipulated (opportunistically or not) by community leaders reacting to the social environment in which this community is embedded. In all these situations, it is therefore reasonable to expect cultural intolerance, Δ_i, to be endogenous.

While the implications of the endogeneity of ΔV^i for socialization and population dynamics need to be derived case by case, a reduced form analysis is useful to clarify what to look for in the applications. Suppose, for instance, that each individual (parent or child) chooses $x \in X$ to maximize $u_i(x, q_i)$ for $x_i \in \{a, b\}$, with $x_i = \arg \max_{x \in X} u_i(x, q_i)$ the optimal behavior associated with trait i. Under *paternalism*, direct parental socialization for types i depends on $\Delta_i(q_i) = u_i(x_i, q_i) - u^i(x_j, q_i)$. The first fundamental implication of the endogeneity of Δ_i is the following:

> When cultural intolerance Δ_i depends on qi, paternalism does not necessarily imply that $\Delta_i(q_i) \geq 0$.

In fact, socialization to the parents' trait might put the children at a disadvantage in the child social environment, represented by q_i. While *paternalism or cultural intolerance* is manifested as a preference on the part of parents for sharing their cultural traits with their children, such a preference depends on the economic and social conditions which parents expect for their children. Different economic and social conditions could, in principle, lead parents to socialize their children to a trait different than their own.

Furthermore, when cultural intolerance is endogenous, the dynamic system for the evolution of cultural traits can be written as

$$\dot{q} = q(1-q)[\tau_a(q, \Delta_a(q)) - \tau_b(1-q, \Delta_b(1-q))].$$

While full *cultural substitution* (after integrating the fact that the paternalistic motives $\Delta_i(q_i)$ are frequency dependent) is still sufficient to guarantee population dynamics which converge to cultural heterogeneity, an additional condition on $\Delta_i(q_i)$ is necessary to produce direct socialization maps $\tau_i(q_i) = \tau_i(q_i, \Delta_i(q_i))$ satisfying such property. Bisin and Verdier (2010) denote this assumption as *strategic substitution*.

Strategic substitution: The social environment is characterized by strategic substitution if

$$\frac{\partial}{\partial q_i} \Delta_i(q_i) < 0.$$

It is easy to see then that if direct and oblique socialization mechanisms are culturally substitutes then the following holds:

> In a social environment characterized by strategic substitution, from any interior state $q \in (0, 1)$, the cultural dynamic converges to a cultural polymorphism q^*, where $0 < q < 1$.

Strategic substitution guarantees that cultural minorities will face relatively larger gains from socialization, independent of the socialization mechanism. In the case of strategic complementarity, on the contrary, cultural minorities face smaller (even possibly negative) socialization gains. Therefore, depending on the strength of cultural substitution in this case, cultural heterogeneity might or might not be preserved.

In the context of religious traits, $\Delta_i(q_i)$ may depend on the distribution of traits in the population when the nature of the religious trait matters for socioeconomic interactions between individuals in society. This happens, for instance, when the person endowed with that trait is subject to various types of socioeconomic discrimination in areas such as the labor market, access to education or entrepreneurial capital or choices of housing location. An example of this which has recently attracted quite some attention by social scientists concerns the issue of socioeconomic integration of Muslim minorities in western countries (Adida *et al.*, 2016). The way $\Delta_i(q_i)$ might vary with q_i depends on the circumstances. For instance, in many social contexts, an increase in q_i may reduce the degree of social and economic discrimination of individuals endowed with that trait. Indeed a larger set of individuals sharing trait i also means more possibilities to trade and interact within that set, reducing therefore the need to interact with others and, in turn, the cost of socioeconomic discrimination by the rest of society.[12] Given such reduced discrimination, the perceived

---

[12]Likewise, in the context of labor markets when employers' hiring is based on a group-based statistical inference of some non-observable individual characteristic, a higher frequency q_i of individuals' sharing the group trait i may generate additional variation in the

economic cost to transmit the trait intergenerationally is also reduced, increasing therefore the paternalistic motive $\Delta_i(q_i)$ that parents have to transmit their trait. In such a case, there is *strategic complementarity*, which in itself tends to promote a force towards assimilation and a reduction of long-run religious diversity.

Conversely, an increase in the frequency of a religious group q_i may also induce a lower paternalistic motive $\Delta_i(q_i)$ when discrimination has an endogenous taste or identity component. Indeed in such a case, a higher value of q_i may increase the frequency of intergroup contacts. In the context of *cultural distinction*, this triggers negative reactions of other groups to reaffirm their differences. Such reactions may imply in turn increased actions of discrimination and social segmentation against individuals of group i and consequently a lower paternalistic motive $\Delta_i(q_i)$ for the trait to be transmitted. The resulting *strategic substitution* effect leads smaller minority groups to have higher incentives to transmit their traits, driving therefore in itself a force for the preservation of religious diversity.

Other channels through which $\Delta_i(q_i)$ may be endogenously determined reflect the idea that cultural transmission does not occur in an institutional vacuum. Indeed, rather than having only families, oblique and peer contacts as decentralized agents of socialization, the cultural dynamic of religious traits often benefits from various institutional organizations (such as community organizations, churches, sects and leaders) that help coordinate and monitor the efforts of a group to maintain over generations the prevalence of its religious characteristics. We turn to some of these dimensions in Section 5.

4. Multiple Religious Traits, Cultural Blending and Syncretism

An important feature of cultural evolution is the phenomenon of cultural blending, namely the fact that, through social contacts and interactions, individuals endowed with different cultural traits create new traits mixing the characteristics of their initial cultures. In linguistics and cultural anthropology, this process is also referred as creolization (Cohen, 2007;

---

individual characteristic, reducing the relevance of the statistical inference based on the group observable trait i. This in turn may reduce the significance of statistical discrimination.

Stewart, 2016) or hybridization (Nederveen Pieterse, 1994), the mechanism through which creole languages and cultures emerge.

In the context of religions, the analog is religious syncretism, namely the fusion of diverse religious beliefs and practices. Examples of religious syncretism abound in historical times and parts of the world. Historically, the fusion of cultures brought by the conquest of Alexander the Great and then the Roman Empire, tended to bring together a variety of religious and philosophical views that resulted in a strong tendency toward religious syncretism. A well-known example is Gnosticism, a religious dualistic system mixing elements from Eastern mystery religions, Judaism, Christianity and Greek philosophical concepts, and which originated in the late first century AD in non-rabbinical Jewish sects and early Christian sects (Albrile, 2005). In the same vein, emanating from Islam, the Barghawatas in Morocco mixed Sunni, Shi'ite and Kharijite Islamic concepts with elements of astrological and traditional Berber mythology (Le Tourneau, 1986), or the Abangan in Java provided through their Kejawen (Javanism) an amalgam of Islamic beliefs, and other animistic, Buddhist and Hindu aspects (Geertz, 1976). In East Asian societies, notable syncretization of Buddhism with local beliefs includes the Three Teachings, or Triple Religion, that harmonizes Mahayana Buddhism with Confucian philosophy and elements of Taoism, and Shinbutsu-shūgō (Dumoulin, 1976). Similarly various forms of cultural creolization involve religious syncretic dimensions, such as Caribbean Vodou (combining elements of Western African, native Caribbean and Roman Catholic beliefs), Jamaican Rastafari (mixing features from the Bible, Pan-Africanism, Hinduism and Caribbean culture), or Brazilian Candomblé (syncretism between traditional Yoruba religion of West Africa and Roman Catholicism).

How can religious blending and/or emergence of new religious forms be analyzed through the lens of our cultural transmission framework? The natural way to do this is to enrich the space of possible cultural dimensions that can be transmitted.

4.1 *Syncretism and the n-trait Model*

A first step in this direction is to extend the Bisin–Verdier framework to *n* traits (Bisin *et al.*, 2009; Montgomery, 2010). Interestingly, this will also confirm its deep relationship to evolutionary game theory. Specifically, based on Montgomery (2010), we will see that when cultural intolerances are given an appropriate interpretation, the Bisin–Verdier cultural dynamic is the standard replicator dynamic.

Consider again that agents form a continuum. Cultural traits are denoted by $i \in \{1, \ldots, n\}$. Each parent (asexually) produces one child, socializes them and then dies. A parent with trait i will have a child with trait $j \neq i$ with probability

$$P_{ij} = (1-\tau_i)q_j \qquad (9)$$

and a child with trait i with probability

$$P_{ii} = \tau_i + (1-\tau_i)q_i. \qquad (10)$$

In discrete time, the share of trait i is given by

$$q_i(t+1) = \sum_j q_j(t)P_{ji}. \qquad (11)$$

Substituting (9) and (10) into (11) and taking the continuous-time limit, we find

$$\dot{q}_i = q_i\left[\tau_i - \sum_j q_j\tau_j\right] \qquad (12)$$

for all $i = 1, \ldots, n$.

Clearly, when the τ's are exogenous, the dynamic converges from every interior state to a monomorphic distribution centered on trait $\arg\max_i\{\tau_i\}_{i=1}^n$. So let us proceed along the lines of Bisin and Verdier (2000) except with n traits and a quadratic socialization cost:

$$\max_{\tau_i} \sum_j P_{ij}V_{ij} - \frac{1}{2}(\tau_i)^2, \qquad (13)$$

where V_{ij} is an i type's payoff from having a child with trait j.

The first-order condition is

$$\tau_i^* = \sum_j q_j\Delta_{ij},$$

where Δ_{ij} is an i type's intolerance toward j.

Substituting into the dynamic (12), we have

$$\dot{q}_i = q_i \left[\sum_j q_j \Delta_{ij} - \sum_j q_j \sum_j q_k \Delta_{jk} \right] \tag{14}$$

for all $i = 1, \ldots, n$.

Interpret Δ_{ij} as the payoff from playing strategy i against j. This links the dynamic system (14) to evolutionary game theory (Smith, 1982; Young, 1998; Sandholm, 2010). More specifically, (14) is the replicator dynamic operating on random matching to play the $n \times n$ game composed of the payoffs Δ_{ij}. The replicator dynamic can arise from natural selection, imitation and reinforcement learning (see the Appendix). Thus, there is a deep connection between the cultural transmission framework and other evolutionary processes. Moreover, we can exploit a large body of results about the replicator dynamic to study cultural evolution.

Specifically, suppose that $\Delta_{ij} = \Delta_i$ for all $j \neq i$ (and $\Delta_{ii} = 0$), that is, each group is intolerant of all other traits to an equal degree. Then, this is a *strictly stable* game. There is a unique Nash equilibrium (distribution of traits), $q_i = \frac{1}{n}$, which is globally asymptotically stable and every trajectory of the replicator dynamic in the interior of the n-dimensional simplex converges to this state. Once again we have persistent diversity.

- *The three-trait example applied to religious syncretism.*

Our extended setup may provide some insight into the conditions under which religious syncretism emerges and persists. The simplest way to do so is to consider a three-trait version of this model in which the first two traits (1 and 2) are two specific religious traits and trait 3 is a mixture of them. Denote by q_1, q_2 and q_3 the frequencies of traits 1, 2 and 3, respectively, with $q_1 + q_2 + q_3 = 1$. Following Montgomery (2010), the "cultural payoff" matrix of the evolutionary game associated with the cultural transmission process is

$$\Delta = \begin{Bmatrix} 0 & \Delta_{12} & \Delta_{13} \\ \Delta_{21} & 0 & \Delta_{23} \\ \Delta_{31} & \Delta_{32} & 0 \end{Bmatrix},$$

where Δ_{ij} is the "cultural intolerance" of trait i for trait j.

To be more specific, we are interested in religious syncretism in which two religions 1 and 2 give rise to a mixed trait 3. Assume first that religions 1 and 2 are symmetric in the sense that they have the same degree of intolerance with respect to each other: $\Delta_{21} = \Delta_{12} = \theta > 0$. In the context of syncretism, it appears natural to also assume that these "pure" religions 1 and 2 are less intolerant towards the syncretic mixed trait than towards each other: $\Delta_{13} = \Delta_{23}\ \lambda\theta$, with $\lambda < 1$. Conversely, the syncretic trait is also more tolerant towards each of the "pure" religious traits 1 and 2 than they may be towards the syncretic trait: $\Delta_{31} = \Delta_{32}\ \mu\theta$, with $\mu < \lambda$ to reflect the fact that the syncretic trait is less exclusive than each of the pure religions.

Consider then the situation where religions 1 and 2 coexist in a cultural steady state and syncretism has not yet appeared. In such a case, we are back to the standard two-trait model of Bisin–Verdier, and we have (because of the symmetry) the long-run cultural steady state

$$q_1^* = 1 - q_2^* = \frac{1}{2}$$

and the expected payoff π^* (or expected cultural fitness in the cultural dynamics interpretation) of the two religious traits is

$$\pi^* = \frac{1}{2}\cdot\theta.$$

When is it that syncretism between religions 1 and 2 appear? For this, consider the "cultural fitness of trait 3" at the previous cultural steady state with the population equally divided between the pure traits 1 and 2. Then, the syncretic trait 3 has a chance to diffuse in the population if and only if its expected cultural fitness at this population state is larger than the cultural fitness of any of the two other religious traits, namely

$$q_1^*\Delta_{31} + q_2^*\Delta_{32} > \pi^*.$$

In this simple case, this condition reduces to $\mu > \frac{1}{2}$, that is, the syncretic trait can only diffuse when it embodies enough "exclusivity" towards the two already present traits. Now, after such cultural invasion of the mixed trait, where does the cultural dynamics go? And specifically do we observe in the long run the presence of the three religious traits with $q_i^* > 0$ for $i \in \{1, 2, 3\}$ (that is an interior religious polymorphism)?

Considering general asymmetric situations for the structure of the cultural payoff matrix Δ, Montgomery (2010) defines the following quantities:

$$\Psi_1 = \Delta_{12}\Delta_{23} + \Delta_{13}\Delta_{32} - \Delta_{23}\Delta_{32},$$
$$\Psi_2 = \Delta_{21}\Delta_{13} + \Delta_{23}\Delta_{31} - \Delta_{13}\Delta_{31},$$
$$\Psi_3 = \Delta_{31}\Delta_{12} + \Delta_{32}\Delta_{21} - \Delta_{12}\Delta_{21}$$

and shows that the cultural dynamics converges towards an interior religious polymorphism with $q_i^* > 0$ for $i = 1$, 2 and 3 if and only if $\psi_i > 0$ for $i \in \{1, 2, 3\}$. In such a case, the interior long-run frequencies are given by

$$q_i^* = \frac{\Psi_i}{\Psi_1 + \Psi_2 + \Psi_2} \quad \text{for } i \in \{1,2,3\}. \tag{15}$$

For our simple symmetric context, this collapses to $\psi_1 = \psi_2 = \lambda\theta^2 > 0$ and $\psi_3 = (2\mu - 1)\theta^2 > 0$. The first conditions are automatically satisfied, while the last one is again $\mu > \frac{1}{2}$. Hence, once it is able to diffuse, the syncretic trait stabilizes at a positive frequency but it cannot displace the two pure religious traits. Applying (15) to our simple example provides the long-run cultural polymorphism:

$$q_1^* = q_2^* = \frac{\lambda}{2\lambda + 2\mu - 1} \quad \text{and} \quad q_3^* = \frac{2\mu - 1}{2\lambda + 2\mu - 1}.$$

Interestingly, when $\mu < \lambda$, the long-run fraction of syncretic individuals is always less than 1/3 $\left(\text{as } q_3^* < \frac{2\lambda-1}{4\lambda-1} < \frac{1}{3}\right)$. A syncretic trait may survive if it is sufficiently exclusive (i.e., $\mu > 1/2$) but cannot diffuse very widely in the population when it faces alternative strong and exclusive "pure" religions.

4.2 The continuous-trait model

While cultural blending and its religious analogy, syncretism can be analyzed in a setup with a discrete number of traits, a more natural way to think about the issue is to allow for some continuous mixing of traits. In this respect, there is a well-established tradition in evolutionary biology and anthropology that considers continuous-trait models of cultural transmission. These models typically postulate a dynamic of cultural traits, which is driven by exogenous linear mixing (Cavalli-Sforza, 1973; Otto *et al.*, 1994). More specifically, consider a population of N dynasties in which reproduction is asexual and that each parent has one child. Let $R^i(t) \in (0, \infty)$ denote the value of the cultural trait of a representative individual of dynasty i at time t. Assume that transmission from one generation to the next results from cultural blending from two sources: vertical transmission and oblique transmission from the rest of society. Specifically, $R^i(t)$ evolves according to the following process:

$$R_i(t+1) = \tau_i \cdot R_i(t) + (1 - \tau_i) O_i(t), \qquad (16)$$

where $\tau_i \in (0, 1)$ represents the weight of vertical socialization by parents of type i, and $O_i(t)$ is the pattern of oblique role-model influence to which a child of dynasty i might be exposed. Conveniently, $O_i(t)$ can be defined as a weighted average of the various models in society:

$$O_i(t) = \sum_{j=1}^{j=N} \gamma_{ij} R_j(t),$$

with $\Gamma = [\gamma_{ij}]_{i,j}$ is a row stochastic matrix reflecting the social connectivity of oblique influence across the different dynasties. Denoting $R(t) = (R_j(t))_{i=1,N}$ the N-dimensional vector of the cultural trait, the cultural dynamics can then be written in matrix form:

$$R(t+1) = \mathbf{X} \cdot R(t),$$

where $\mathbf{X} = \mathbf{T} + (\mathbf{I} - \mathbf{T})\Gamma$ is a row stochastic matrix, $\mathbf{I}$ the identity matrix of dimension N and $\mathbf{T}$ a diagonal matrix of dimension N where the ith diagonal element is τ^i. In some sense, $\mathbf{X}$ reflects the force of the cultural inheritance blending process resulting from the interaction between vertical and oblique transmission. Brueckner and Smirnov (2007, 2008) consider this transmission framework when the vertical influence weights τ^i are exogenous. They show that, when the matrix $\mathbf{X}$ is irreducible and noncyclic, the evolutionary process is fully homogenizing and leads to a "melting-pot" equilibrium, in which the value of the cultural trait is the same across the population. Cyclicity of the matrix **X**, on the other hand, preserves the possibility of long-term heterogeneity.

Another mechanism through which cultural diversity may be preserved, even in the presence of linear cultural blending, is the presence of learning errors in the process of cultural transmission. To see this, consider for instance that the continuous trait $R^i(t)$ in dynasty i evolves according to the following stochastic process:

$$R_i(t+1) = \tau \cdot R_i(t) + (1-\tau)\bar{R} + \varepsilon_i(t),$$

where $\varepsilon_i(t)$ reflects a learning error term reflected by an independently and identically distributed random shock with zero mean and constant variance σ^2, and $\tau \in (0, 1)$ is now a common weight of vertical socialization.[13] It is then a simple matter to see that the average trait in the population $E_i\,(R_i(t))$ converges towards $\bar{R}$, while the variance of the trait $V(t) = E_i[(R_i(t) - E_i(R_i(t)))^2]$ converges towards $\sigma^2/(1 - \tau)$. With no learning noise (i.e., $\sigma^2 = 0$), as usual, cultural blending reduces variation in each generation until it is all gone. With positive learning mistakes, the population comes to rest at a positive amount of cultural variation, reflecting the balance between two forces: the homogenization effect of blending inheritance and the maintenance of variation due to error in learning.

In the religious context, the previous models suggest that syncretism (and full-trait blending) is prevented to emerge only because of specific features of the social interaction context (cyclicity of the social influence matrix **X**) or because of fundamental learning errors. From the simple three discrete trait example provided in Section 4.1, one may wonder how these conclusions are robust to endogenous cultural transmission efforts.

In the spirit of the Bisin–Verdier framework, some related models consider this possibility and allow for endogenous economic choices of the τ^i values (Vaughan, 2010; Büchel *et al.*, 2014; Panebianco, 2014). In order to ensure long-run cultural convergence, they impose however additional structure on the interacting matrix Γ. In particular, when a child's trait is a weighted average of his parent's trait and the mean value of the

---

[13]More complex and interesting models along these lines are discussed in Boyd and Richerson (1985).

trait in the society, cultural blending prevents the long-run cultural heterogeneity result of Bisin and Verdier (2001). Indeed, in such linear weighting models, direct vertical socialization and oblique socialization interact in such a way that there is a standard mean reverting linear process, leading naturally to cultural homogeneity in the long run. From the point of view of religious traits, this blending view of cultural transmission should favor syncretism rather than polarization.

An interesting model investigating the issue of cultural hybridization and syncretism in a continuous trait setup is Kuran and Sandholm (2008). The paper considers two interrelated mechanisms of cultural influences: behavioral adaptations driven by payoffs to coordination, and preference changes shaped by socialization and self-persuasion. Preferences and behaviors vary continuously. Importantly, the setup posits a two-speed formulation whereby gradual changes in preferences are accompanied by immediate behavioral adjustments that maintain equilibrium play. Using techniques from evolutionary game theory, the model analyzes the set of conditions under which cross-cultural contacts across cultural groups promote cultural hybridization and homogenization, and characterizes both the ultimate composition of the hybrid culture and the speed of cultural change. The model suggests some interesting political economy implications of cultural blending and religious syncretism. Because cultural groups and religious communities are not homogeneous with respect to their relevant cultural trait, the costs and benefits of cultural adjustment are not shared equally. Significant cultural conflicts may arise therefore within and across cultural groups. Also, communities benefit from having other communities adjust their behaviors.

With a proper probabilistic structure of cultural transmission however, cultural diversity may still depend on the notion of cultural substitution between vertical role models and other influences. Cheung and Wu (2018) provide, in this respect, an elegant extension of the Bisin and Verdier (2001) to this kind of setting.

Specifically, they consider a population of unit mass, where each agent in the population has a trait from set $T = [0, 1]$. The population state is a distribution of traits over T and thus is described by a probability measure over T. Denote by Δ_{zy}: $= V_{zz} - V_{zy}$ the cultural intolerance a z-parent has towards trait $y \in T$. Assume that V_{zy} is continuous in z and y, and hence Δ_{zy} is continuous in z and y. $\Delta_{zy} \in [0, 1]$ for any $z\, y \in T$, and $\Delta_{zy} = 0$ only if $y = z$. Describing a population state over T by its probability distribution μ,[14] one may define the aggregate cultural intolerance of a z-parent at population state μ by

$$\Delta_z(\mu) = \int_{y\in T} \Delta_{zy}\mu(dy).$$

Denoting by $\tau_z(\mu)$ the socialization rate exerted by a z-parent at population state μ, the cultural evolutionary dynamic is then characterized by the following differential equation for all (integrable) subset of traits A:

$$\dot{\mu}(A) = \underbrace{\int_{y\in A}\int_{z\in T\backslash A}(1-\tau_z(\mu))\mu(dz)\mu(dy)}_{\text{inflows}} - \underbrace{\int_{y\in A}\int_{z\in T\backslash A}(1-\tau_y(\mu))\mu(dy)\mu(dz)}_{\text{outflows}}.$$

(17)

The rate of change $\dot{\mu}(A)$ in the mass of agents with traits in set A is equal to the "inflow" of children whose parents' traits are not in set A but who themselves adopt traits in set A, minus the "outflow" of children whose parents' traits are in set A but who themselves adopt traits not in set A. It is a simple matter to see that Equation (17) rewrites as

$$\dot{\mu}(A) = \int_{y\in A}\int_{z\in T}[\tau_y(\mu) - \tau_z(\mu)]\mu(dy)\mu(dz).$$

Now, at state μ, a z-parent solves the following maximization problem:

$$\max \tau_z V_{zz} + (1-\tau_z)\int_{y\in T}V_{zy}\mu(dy) - c(\tau_z),$$

which in the standard quadratic cost function case $c(\tau_z) = \tau_z^2/2$, yields

$$\tau_z(\mu) = V_{zz} - \int_{y\in T}V_{zy}\mu(dy) = \int_{y\in T}\Delta_{zy}\mu(dy) = \Delta_z(\mu).$$

---

[14]More rigorously, let B be the Borel σ-algebra on T. Denote by $M^+(T)$ the space of probability measures on (T, B). A population state is a distribution of traits over T and is described by a probability measure $\mu \in M^+(T)$.

From this, the cultural dynamic with continuous traits takes the following form:

$$\dot\mu(A) = \int_{y\in A}\int_{z\in T}[\Delta_y(\mu) - \Delta_z(\mu)]\mu(dy)\mu(dz)$$
$$= \int_{y\in A}\Delta_y(\mu)\mu(dy) - \mu(A)\int_{z\in T}\Delta_z(\mu)\mu(dz).$$

As with Montgomery (2010) for discrete traits, Cheung and Wu note again the important connection with evolutionary game dynamic on continuous sets of strategies (Oechssler and Riedel, 2001). Indeed consider the population game where a unit mass of agents are randomly matched in pairs to play a two-player symmetric game with continuous strategy set T and payoff function Δ_{yz} (i.e., the single match payoff of an agent playing strategy y against an opponent playing strategy z). Defining then $F_y(\mu)$ the expected payoff of an agent playing pure strategy $y \in T$ at population state μ as

$$F_y(\mu) = \int_{z\in T}\Delta_{yz}\mu(dz) = \Delta_y(\mu)$$

and noting that $\mu(T) = 1$, the cultural dynamic can be rewritten as

$$\dot\mu(A) = \mu(A)\left[\frac{\int_{y\in A}F_y(\mu)\mu(dy)}{\mu(A)} - \frac{\int_{z\in T}F_z(\mu)\mu(dz)}{\mu(T)}\right].$$

The cultural dynamic of continuous traits is then equivalent to an imitative dynamic with continuous strategies (Oechssler and Riedel, 2001). Using sophisticated measure theory tools for such dynamic systems, Cheung and Wu show that cultural substitutability is again essential for the preservation of long-run cultural heterogeneity. Furthermore, when one parameterizes an agent's cultural intolerance towards another agent Δ_{zy} as an increasing function of their cultural distance $|z - y|$, they highlight that the curvature of the cultural intolerance function plays an important role in determining the long-run cultural phenomena. In particular, when the cultural intolerance function is convex, only the most extremely polarized state distribution with mass points at the extreme traits $z = 0$ and $z = 1$ is a stable limit point of the cultural dynamics.

In the context of transmission of religious traits, this result suggests that radicalization in religious attributes rather than syncretism tends to occur when the perceived distance between these associated attributes increasingly generates some degree of intolerance and exclusivity in the transmission process across individuals.

5. Institutions and Cultural Transmission

So far, we presented cultural transmission models that take a strong evolutionary and bottom-up perspective on the diffusion and evolution of religious beliefs and preferences. A central issue neglected by this approach is the fact that some important entities (religious organizations and clubs, churches, community leaders, states) participate actively in the process of religious socialization and, as such, are able to internalize some of the dynamic implications of the cultural transmission of religious traits in the society. Hence, on top of the evolutionary and purely decentralized dimensions of cultural transmission as reflected so far by vertical and oblique socialization, there also exist coordinated and forward looking aspects related to purposeful and centralized authorities and organizations. In this section, we cover a recent strand of the literature that incorporates these features. First, we examine the effect of religious leaders on the previously decentralized process of cultural transmission. Second, we analyze religious clubs in conjunction with other socializing institutions such as the media and education system. Finally, we review work on the co-evolution of culture and institutions, with a focus on the political economy of religious organizations.

5.1 *Religious leaders*

Religious leaders have always played a tremendously important role in the transmission and diffusion of religious beliefs and religious attributes across the world. Some regarded as prophets, such as Abraham and Moses in Judaism, Muhammad in Islam or Guru Nanak in Sikhism, diffused the world of God because of their privileged relationship with him. Others, like Siddhārtha Gautama in Buddhism, Peter and Paul in Christianity, Gurus of Sikhism, or Foundation members of Islam and the early Caliphs, founded or helped found a faith community or spread a religion or a belief-system. Some religious leaders, such as Martin Luther King Jr., Saint Theresa, Mahatma Gandhi or the Dalai Lama, became role models from the way their lifestyle exemplified the values of the faith community. More commonly, religious leaders, like clergy, imams, gurus, priests, rabbis and lamas, are individuals who play an active role in the contemporary faith community.

An emerging economic literature has started to analyze more closely how including religious leaders matters for the cultural dynamics of religious traits (Verdier and Zenou, 2015, 2018; Hauk and Mueller, 2015; Carvalho and Koyama, 2016; Carvalho *et al.*, 2017; Prummer and Siedlarek, 2017; Chen *et al.*, 2019; Carvalho and Sacks, 2020).[15]

From the perspective of our framework for cultural transmission, religious leaders bring three new analytical features. First, cultural leaders have their own motivations and objectives related to the diffusion of their religion. Because of this, they can take actions that promote or discourage the transmission of their religious trait in the society. In particular, because of the legitimacy they draw in their community, religious leaders can inculturate and manipulate directly or indirectly the paternalistic motives Δ_i of their believers, affecting therefore the dynamic sustainability of their religion in the population.

Second, also because of their privileged position, cultural leaders have the capacity to internalize group-related effects of cultural transmission for their community. In particular, they may incentivize and coordinate collective action by their followers, changing again endogenously the payoffs of acquiring or maintaining the religious trait they promote in the population. Their forward-looking perspective means they internalize the dynamic externalities associated with the diffusion of cultural and religious attributes.

Finally, cultural leaders tend to compete across communities, or within their own community, to acquire and maintain their privileged positions. From a conceptual point of view, the process of cultural transmission of religion is therefore not only determined by decentralized parental and oblique transmission motives (i.e., the "demand side" of cultural transmission) but also by the competitive context in which cultural leaders "offer" incentives and motivations for cultural diffusion (i.e., the market structure of the "supply side" of cultural transmission).

To illustrate, consider for instance the framework of Hauk and Mueller (2015), building upon Bisin and Verdier (2001), which introduces the possibility for leaders to manipulate the paternalistic motives Δ_i of parents to transmit their trait. They assume that cultural leaders can be either

---

[15] See also Prummer (2019) for an insightful survey focusing on cultural leaders.

intrinsically motivated by proselytism (i.e., maximize the number of people their religion is successfully distributed to), or alternatively they can enjoy rents (pecuniary or not) associated with the overall level of religious transmission exerted in their community. Assume that a cultural leader promotes religious trait *a*. Focusing on steady states of the cultural dynamics, this means that a proselytist leader is interested in maximizing

$$q^* = \frac{\Delta_a}{\Delta_a + \Delta_b},$$

while a rent-seeker leader would like to maximize (assuming quadratic costs of socialization) something proportional to

$$q^* \tau_a^* = q^*(1 - q^*)\Delta_a = \left(\frac{\Delta_a}{\Delta_a + \Delta_b}\right)^2 \Delta_b.$$

As is easily noted, the cultural leader always has an incentive to raise as much as possible the perception of cultural differences Δ_a of ingroup members. Indeed, this motivates parents to socialize their children to that trait. An increase in this difference can be achieved in two ways: through the provision of cultural values (raising V_{aa}) or through claims of "religious superiority" making the alternative trait (other religion or secularism) appear inferior (lowering V_{ab}). Both strategies generate symmetric outcomes from the point of view of the religious leader, regardless of his objective function (proselytism or rent seeker). For ingroup parents of type *a*, things however are different. Parents indeed have to live with a chance that their children change religion. High values of V_{aa} mean that high perceived benefits drive parental socialization efforts, while low values of V_{ab} imply that parents inculturate their children mostly out of fear.

While it seems natural to think that religious leaders have some influence on their ingroup believers, one may also think that they may undertake actions to affect the perception that outgroup members have about their ingroup. This would be done in our setting by changing Δ_b through some manipulation of V_{ba}. In the case of a proselytist leader from group *a*, clearly his interest is in reducing Δ_b through an increase in V_{ba} that makes his religious trait *a* look more attractive to individuals from group *b*. Surprisingly enough, when the leader is of a rent-seeking type, he may not necessarily be interested in making his religious trait look good. Actually, he might want to increase Δ_b by lowering V_{ba}, the cultural perception of the outgroup towards the ingroup, something Hauk and Mueller describe as *cultural alienation*. The reason is based on the *cultural substitution* effect already mentioned by Bisin and Verdier. Indeed, as Δ_b increases, the outgroup members socialize more intensively their children to keep their trait (i.e., trait b). This in turn leads the population of ingroup believers to become more minoritarian in the population (i.e., q^* goes down). By the cultural substitution effect, they consequently intensify in turn their own socialization effort τ_a^*. This effect on parental socialization may countervail the reduced size of the ingroup, so that the rents that the leader receives $q^*\tau_a^*$ may actually increase. In such a case, the religious leader prefers to have a small ingroup of believers who are intensively active in the religious education of their children, something which is the source of the rents he enjoys. Overall the analysis indicates that religious leaders have incentives to amplify disagreement about their religious values, and that the population does not always benefit from such actions.

Religious leaders are certainly motivated not only to spread their beliefs, but also to care about the economic well-being of their community members. Prummer and Siedlarek (2017) incorporate both features in the leader's objective function. In this setup, leaders influence the beliefs and attitudes of community members by establishing rules and religious norms. Departing from the Bisin and Verdier approach, they consider a continuous value framework, implying that religious leaders care about the *intensive margin* with which their religious trait is displayed. Importantly, the leader can only indirectly affect the economic well-being of his community members, which depends on the economic outcomes that are induced in the market by the norms the believers follow. The leader then eventually faces the following trade-off. On the one hand, he would want his community to identify faithfully with the values of the religious norms he supports. On the other hand, such norms are not necessarily well adapted to market behavior, and he would nevertheless like his community to be economically integrated and wealthy. Prummer and Siedlarek (2017) show that three possible outcomes arise out of this trade-off. The leader may select the most extreme level of religiosity, or he may support some intermediate level, or finally, he may completely refrain from encouraging any display of religious behavior. Which outcome emerges, depends on the economic environment and the interplay between earnings and religious beliefs in the leader's objective function.

The previous analyzes studies the optimal manipulation by cultural leaders at the cultural steady state but do not consider the dynamic transition path to that steady state. The latter exercise requires developing a dynamic framework where forward looking leaders fully take into account the effects of their manipulation of religious values on the cultural diffusion of their religious trait. Verdier and Zenou (2018) provide such a framework. More specifically, they consider a situation where leaders provide community public goods that affect positively the paternalistic motive of their believers to transmit their trait to their children.

Formally, consider a cultural leader for group a who provides an amount G^a of a public good specific to trait a. If, for example, we consider traits a and b as "religious" and "secular," then G^a will be a religious public good (a church, religious center or a mosque). Assume now that the provision of G^a increases the paternalistic motive of a parent of type a to transmit his trait to his children such that $\Delta_a = \Delta_a^0 + vG^a$ with $v > 0$ a positive constant. Following the same lines as in our benchmark model in Section 2.2, the cultural dynamic now rewrites as

$$\dot{q}_t = q_t(1-q_t)[\tau_a - \tau_b],$$

where

$$\tau_a = (1-q_t)(\Delta_a^0 + vG_t^a) \text{ and } \tau_b = q_t\Delta_b,$$

where we allow *a priori* the provision of G_t^a to be time varying. Consider also that the technology to produce the public good G^a has constant marginal cost c up to a capacity constraint $\bar{G}$, so that $G^a \in [0, \bar{G}]$. While capturing the essential features of a convex production technology, this assumption is convenient to fully characterize the transitional dynamics of the socialization mechanism under cultural leadership.

Note that when the leader is never active ($G^a = 0$), the cultural dynamic converges towards the steady state

$$q(0) = \frac{\Delta_a^0}{\Delta_a^0 + \Delta_b},$$

while when the leader is providing constantly the maximum public good provision $G^a = \bar{G}$, the cultural dynamic converge towards

$$q(\bar{G}) = \frac{\Delta_a^0 + v\bar{G}}{\Delta_a^0 + v\bar{G} + \Delta_b},$$

which obviously is the largest possible long-run diffusion of trait a in society.

To analyze the role of a perfect forward-looking religious leader, Verdier and Zenou (2018) assumes that the utility of a leader for group a is given by

$$\int_0^\infty e^{-\rho t}(W^a q_t - c G_t^a)\, dt, \tag{18}$$

where ρ is the discount rate and where the religious leader's rents $W^a q^a$ increase with the size q of group a. Also, to highlight in the purest way the role of the leader on cultural diffusion, they assume that the initial state of the population is exactly the cultural steady state $q(0)$ when there is no leader intervention.

The equilibrium pattern of public good provision G_t^{a*} of the religious leader is then the solution of the following optimal control problem:

$$\max_{0 \leq G_t^a \leq \bar{G}^a} \int_0^\infty e^{-\rho t}(W^a q_t - c G_t^a)\, dt$$

$$\text{s.t. } \dot{q}_t = q_t(1 - q_t)[(1 - q_t)(\Delta_a^0 + v G_t^a) - q_t \Delta_b] \tag{19}$$

$$\text{s.t. } q_0 = q(0) \text{ given.}$$

Because of the linear dependence of the problem on the control G_t^a, this optimization problem is of a bang-bang nature. Applying a characterization method based on a "Most Rapid Approach Path" formulation of the problem,[16] Verdier and Zenou (2018) show that the optimal cultural trajectory of this problem has the property that it approaches as rapidly as possible some point q^* and stays there forever, given the constraint that q^* can be reached using the control $G^a \in [0, \bar{G}]$. The characterization of the state point q^* (and the associated control function $G^{a*}(t)$) clearly depends on the shape of the objective function of the leader and the initial state $q(0)$ of the population.

Specifically, Verdier and Zenou (2018) show that the cultural leader can only be active when the marginal religious rent W^a is above a certain threshold $\overline{W}$. Second, even when such circumstances are satisfied (i.e., when $W^a > \overline{W}$), they show that the degree of activity of the religious leader varies in a nonmonotonic way with the initial size $q(0)$ of his

---

[16]The associated Hamiltonian is not concave in G_t^a, qt, and therefore the first-order approach is generally not sufficient to characterize optimal trajectories.

ingroup a. Specifically, there is a range (q_L, q_H) such that the leader is active and does influence the cultural diffusion of his religious trait only when $q(0)$ falls within that range. Typically, when the initial size $q(0)$ of group a is less than the first threshold q_L, it is not profitable for the cultural leader to promote more socialization than what parents of the ingroup already do. The system stays therefore at its initial steady state $q(0)$. Similarly, when vertical socialization by parents is strong enough to generate a cultural steady state with a steady-state size group $q(0)$ larger than the second threshold q_H, then it does not either pay to the leader to promote more socialization to his ingroup members. Families indeed already do enough of a good job that the leader need not spend additional resources to stimulate more cultural transmission.

When however the group size is intermediate (i.e., $q(0) \in (q_L, q_H)$), the cultural leader is active to push forward cultural dynamics in the direction of a higher steady state than would prevail without his intervention (i.e., $q(0)$). When the steady-state value at permanent full capacity $q(\bar{G})$ is less than the threshold q_H (above which the leader stops being active), then the dynamic system converges asymptotically towards $q(\bar{G})$ with a religious leader permanently active at this full capacity. When conversely, the cultural dynamic with full capacity reaches in finite time the threshold q_H, then the leader reduces endogenously his provision of public good just to ensure that cultural evolution remains critically at this threshold long-run steady state q_H.[17]

The model allows for discussion of some interesting comparative dynamics along the transition path of cultural evolution. Importantly, the analysis indicates that a shift in a parameter determining the context in which the religious group evolves has different short run versus long-run effects in terms of the socialization activity of the group. Typically, there will always be some over-reactions or under-reactions compared to the long-run effect that can be expected. These transitory dynamics have important policy implications in terms of the reaction of minority religious community associations to changes in their environment.

Finally, Verdier and Zenou (2018) extend the framework presented above to the case of competition between two perfectly forward-looking

---

[17] In other words, the optimal trajectory for the leader is to be active to full capacity (i.e., $G^a(t) = \bar{G}^a$) up to the moment where the ingroup size reaches the level min $[q_H, q(\bar{G})]$. Whenever that occurs in finite time T (i.e., when $q_H < q(\bar{G})$), the leader ensures that the cultural steady state stays at q_H by choosing a "singular" interior policy $G^a(t) = G^F < \bar{G}$.

religious leaders with their respective ingroups a and b.[18] The leaders may differ in terms of their discount factor ρ. When both evaluate the future in the same way, then there is a symmetric dynamic equilibrium where both select the same levels of public goods and their effort at influencing the cultural dynamics simply cancel each other out: the long-run cultural steady state is the same as if no leaders were present. If, however, one leader is more patient than the other, then the less patient leader does not provide any public good and remains inactive. Interestingly, differences in time-discount factors across leaders can be interpreted as differences in institutional stability. In such a case, a leader who is part of an organization that has a strong base can naturally be more forward looking. This higher institutional stability translates into a higher capacity to influence the cultural diffusion of his religious trait, at the expense of other outgroups with less institutional stability. A plausible application of the setting concerns the case where the more patient leader has ingroups with a strong and stable religious commitment, whereas the less patient leader is a secular leader, facing the political uncertainty of elections and support. The model suggests that the secular leader may then refrain from opposing the more patient, religious leader. This may be indicative of why extremist leaders may face too little opposition in democratic societies.

Using a similar "Most Rapid Approach Path" approach, Almagro and Andrés-Cerezo (2020) also explore, in the context of nation-building, how a forward-looking leader (i.e., a central state) may promote the diffusion of a cultural trait (national identity) on its territory. The key control variable in this context is the share of a fixed resource that is allocated to the provision of a public good specifically attached to the national identity trait. Homogenization of the population towards such trait is constrained by political unrest, electoral competition and the intergenerational transmission of local identities within the family. Different from Verdier and Zenou (2018), the zero-sum character of the conflict over resources pushes the cultural dynamic toward homogeneous steady states and extreme levels of allocations of the public good. A common feature is the fact that the long-run distribution of cultural traits in the society is highly dependent on initial conditions.

---

[18]The issue of religious competition between leaders is also tackled by Verdier and Zenou (2015, 2018) as well as Hauk and Mueller (2015). Verdier and Zenou (2015) consider two leaders who myopically invest in their own cultural trait, while Hauk and Mueller (2015) focus on competition once the cultural dynamics are already at their steady states.

Carvalho and Sacks (2017) is another study considering explicitly the transition dynamics of religious traits' diffusion. Specifically, they discuss the conditions under which a forward-looking religious leader is willing and able to radicalize a community, transitioning it from an inclusive and liberal community to an exclusive and strict club. They identify two mechanisms which are critical to radicalization, prestige-biased cultural transmission and niche construction. Both are important in cultural evolutionary theory (Henrich and Gil-White, 2001; Odling-Smee et al., 2003) but largely ignored in economics. Prestige bias occurs when actively religious members of the community have greater visibility and prestige, giving them disproportionate influence over cultural transmission. Niche construction occurs when a leader can induce blanket discrimination against community members, and thereby shield the religious club from outside pressures. In both cases, the religious leader begins by forming a small but extreme club, using it to radicalize the community over time through cultural transmission and niche construction. Religious competition, however, rules out these dynamic radicalization strategies.

5.2 Religious clubs and other socializing institutions

There are potentially severe *free rider* and *externality* problems associated with cultural transmission. It is natural that organizations emerge to deal with these problems. Carvalho (2016) analyzes how religious clubs regulate the process of cultural transmission. In addition, social transmission in the Bisin–Verdier framework is replaced by institutional transmission of a "mainstream trait," for example through the education system or mainstream media. See also Carvalho and Koyama (2014) for a model of education choices when the education system transmits a mainstream cultural trait.

Organizations cultivate cultural traits through (i) rules of participation in cultural activities and (ii) excluding nonmembers from social interactions. For example, regarding (i), communal prayer, scriptural study and religious sacrifice can convert someone into a believer in an organization's doctrine. The exclusivity condition (ii) means that a cultural trait can be viewed as a *club good*, which is a central subject of the economics of religion (Iannaccone, 1992; Berman, 2000; McBride, 2008).

Consider a society consisting of a finite set of risk-neutral individuals I, partitioned into two (nonempty) communities I_a and I_b (e.g., secular and religious).

There are two cultural traits $k \in \{a, b\}$. Let a be the "mainstream" trait and b be the alternative trait. For example, a could be the official religion of a society, or it could be a secular belief system. There are two risk-neutral organizations (or groups), with organization A (B) cultivating trait a (b).

Each $i \in I_\theta$ receives a payoff of $V_{\theta k}$ from acquiring trait k, where $V_{aa} - V_{ab} \equiv \Delta_a > 0$ and $V_{bb} - V_{ba} \equiv \Delta_b > 0$. Hence, we refer to members of I_a as mainstream types and members of I_b as alternative types.

Let c be an individual's (privately known) cost of joining an organization, which is determined by an independent draw from the distribution F. It is assumed that $F(0) = 0$ and F is twice differentiable and strictly log-concave on $(0, \infty)$.

The timing of the game is as follows:

- DATE 0 (*Strictness*): Each organization $\ell \in \{A, B\}$ announces its strictness, s_ℓ, which is the minimum level of participation required of its members.
- DATE 1 (*Membership*): Each individual i can choose to become a member of an organization, $m_i = \ell \in \{A, B\}$, or be unaffiliated, $m_i = n$. M_ℓ is the set of organization ℓ members and $N = I - M_A \cup M_B$ is the set of unaffiliated agents.
- DATE 2 (*Participation*): Each member $i \in M_\ell$ chooses participation level $x_i \geq s_\ell$ in group ℓ's activities, at cost x_i^2. Unaffiliated agents are excluded: x_i 0 for all $i \in N$.
- DATE 3 (*Cultural Transmission*): Group and institutional transmission occurs and the final distribution of traits is determined.

The likelihood $i \in M_\ell$ acquires the trait cultivated by ℓ through group transmission is the average level of participation among ℓ members:

$$\bar{x}_\ell \equiv \frac{1}{|M_\ell|} \sum_{i \in M_\ell} x_i.$$

If group transmission fails, institutional transmission occurs and i acquires the mainstream trait a with a probability of one.

The expected payoff to a (θ, c)-type agent i who joins organization ℓ cultivating trait k is

$$u_i = V_{\theta k} \bar{x}_\ell + V_{\theta a}(1 - \bar{x}_\ell) - x_i^2 - c.$$

The probability that $i \in N$ acquires the mainstream trait a is one, so the payoff when unaffiliated is $V_{\theta a}$.

Each organization ℓ maximizes aggregate participation in its activities:

$$X_\ell = \sum_{i \in M_l} x_i.$$

For example, it could be that organizations are paternalistic, maximizing the welfare of their members but not internalizing their cost of participation. Alternatively, religious organizations might have financial and political interests in the tangible products of participation, including cultural power, public good provision and political opposition.

This leads to the following result:

(Carvalho, 2016) *Recall the cultural intolerance of I_b members is $\Delta_b \equiv V_{bb} - V_{ba}$. There exists a unique SPE of this game. In this equilibrium:*

(i) *All a-type individuals remain unaffiliated: $I_a \subset N$,* (ii) *Organization A attracts no members: $M_A = \theta$,* (iii) *For all $i \in M_B$, the participation rule binds: $x_i^* = s_B^*$,* (iv) *For organization B, strictness is $s_B^* \in \left(\frac{1}{2}\Delta_b, \Delta_b\right)$ and expected membership size is $\left| M_B^* \right| \in \left(0, |I_b|\right)$.*

Intolerance Δ_b can be reinterpreted as "cultural tension," which is an important concept in the sociology of religion. According to Stark and Finke (2000, p. 143), "All religious groups can be located along an axis of tension between the group and its sociocultural environment," where tension is defined in terms of "distinctiveness, separation and antagonism." Here, tension dictates strictness and total participation:

(Carvalho, 2016) *In the subgame, perfect equilibrium of the game, organization B's strictness s^*_B and total participation X^*_B are strictly increasing in Δ_b.*

The lessons from introducing clubs and other socializing institutions are as follows:

- Organizations that form will tend to be ones cultivating oppositional culture.
- Stricter organizations will have doctrines far from the mainstream worldview.
- Groups cultivating oppositional cultural traits will have an advantage in collective action.

Now, suppose we extend this game to an infinite horizon with discrete time, letting the share of mainstream types $|I_a^t|/|I|$ equal the share of agents who acquired trait a in the previous period q^{t-1}. This is consistent with imperfect empathy and the desire of parents to have children acquire their own cultural trait. The asymptotic behavior of such a dynamic would be $\lim_{t\to\infty} q^t = 1$. That is, the alternative trait would be driven to extinction through the force of institutional transmission.

From the Carvalho (2016) setup that connects religious doctrine and participation, the implications for religion are as follows. Religious groups that are marginalized in mainstream society should generate the most intensive participation. If, for example, we rank all Protestant denominations by their doctrinal tension with the mainstream secular worldview, denominations with higher doctrinal tension should have more intensive participation. This is roughly what we see. However, the long-run prediction is that such groups die out due to institutional transmission of the secular worldview from the state, media and public education system. This can be avoided if alternative religions could obtain some control over institutional transmission, possibly through the collective action which they are able to generate, or insulate themselves from it through socialization within the family.

5.3 *Political economy, cultural transmission and religious legitimacy*

The connections between religion and political economy have been widely acknowledged by social scientists and more recently by economists in different contexts (Cosgel and Miceli, 2009; Platteau, 2011; Cosgel *et al.*, 2012; Chaney, 2013; Auriol and Platteau, 2017; Rubin, 2017; Barro and McCleary, 2019; Carvalho *et al.*, 2020). Economic and political developments affect religiosity and the diffusion of beliefs in a society. In turn, the extent of religious participation and beliefs influence economic performance and political institutions. Typically, a religion by providing (or not) legitimacy to state powers reduces (or increases) the transactions costs of law enforcement and authority, while conversely, state powers try to regulate positively (through the establishment of state religions) or negatively (through secularism and laicity) the extent of religious influence on public matters. Mediating this connection between the political and the spiritual spheres is the prevalence of religious beliefs in the population, itself the endogenous result of inculturation processes (transmission and conversion), and public policies favoring (or not) their diffusion in society.

To highlight these connections between political economy and religion, one may take our cultural transmission perspective and develop a framework analyzing the dynamic interaction of political institutions and religious culture. A starting point for this is Bisin and Verdier (2017) who formalize the evolution of institutions and culture and study their joint dynamics. We then see how this framework can be fruitfully applied to the issue of religious legitimacy in some specific historical and political economy contexts (Bisin *et al.*, 2019, 2020).

5.3.1   *The joint evolution of culture and institutions*

Bisin and Verdier (2017) formalize the evolution of institutions and culture and study their joint dynamics. There are two building blocks. The first block describes the mechanism of institutional change. Here in line with Acemoglu and Robinson (2000, 2006), institutions are conceptualized as mechanisms through which social choices are delineated and implemented. More specifically, institutional change represents an effective commitment mechanism on the part of the political elites to imperfectly and indirectly internalize the lack of commitment and the externalities which plague social choice problems. The second block is just the Bisin–Verdier cultural transmission framework outlined in Section 2.

To illustrate, consider a simple society constituted by two groups $i \in \{E, S\}$ (*E* for *elite* and *S* for the rest of *society*), with distinct cultural traits, objectives and technologies. At each period *t*, let us describe in a relatively abstract way a societal policy game which is played between private individuals and a hierarchical public authority (the state) controlling socioeconomic policies. Individuals in each group $i \in \{E, S\}$ are characterized by an objective function $V^i = U^i(a^i, \mathbf{p}, \mathbf{A})$ that depends on the "cultural" type *i* of the individual, private actions a^i by that individual, a policy vector $\mathbf{p}$ implemented by the state during the period and some aggregator measure of socioeconomic outcomes $\mathbf{A} = \mathbf{A}(\mathbf{a}, \mathbf{p}, \mathbf{q})$ that captures the interactions between the private agents and the public authorities. $\mathbf{A}$ naturally depends on the aggregate vector $\mathbf{a}$ of actions by individuals of the two groups, the public policy vector $\mathbf{p}$ and the distribution of cultural types in the population (captured by the frequency distribution $\mathbf{q}$ of types in society).

Collective decisions on socioeconomic policies are made in accordance with the distribution of political power between the two groups encoded and represented by institutions. Specifically, the institutional system is characterized by weights β^E and $\beta^S = 1 - \beta^E$ associated with the two groups E and S in the decision making problem of the state with respect to the policy vector $\mathbf{p}$. A given institutional setup $\beta_t = (\beta_t^E, \beta_t^S)$ in period t induces a set of policies $\mathbf{p}^*$ $(\beta_t, \mathbf{q}_t)$ and actions $\mathbf{a}^*$ $(\beta_t, \mathbf{q}_t)$, as the equilibrium of the societal policy game between individuals and the public authority. Importantly, the equilibrium outcomes $\mathbf{p}^*$ and $\mathbf{a}^*$ also depend on the distribution of cultural traits $\mathbf{q}_t$ prevailing in the population during period t.

With respect to institutional change, Bisin and Verdier (2017) note that the key issue about societies is the fact that they are characterized by economic and political externalities that are not fully accounted for by private and public decisions. Externalities typically arise because of socioeconomic or political imperfections associated with the existence of various frictions going from asymmetric/incomplete information, matching problems, limited rationality and cognitive biases, strategic behaviors associated with market power, private opportunism and lack of political commitment. In any of these situations, the equilibrium outcomes $\mathbf{a}^*$ $(\beta_t, \mathbf{q}_t)$ and $\mathbf{p}^*$ $(\beta_t, \mathbf{q}_t)$ of the societal policy game do not fully internalize their impacts on aggregate social outcomes $\mathbf{A} = \mathbf{A}(\mathbf{a}, \mathbf{p}, \mathbf{q})$, and as a result, inefficient policies and social allocations are implemented.

Taking a simple mechanism design approach, the institutional structure corresponding to a power structure β_t at any point in time might then have an incentive to change the distribution of political power in the future to internalize the externalities responsible for the inefficiencies at equilibrium. This is a fundamental driver of institutional change in society. Similar to the governance theory of organizations (Coase, 1937; Williamson, 1996), it induces as a general principle that the political group most likely to internalize the externality is the group receiving more residual decision rights along the institutional dynamics, i.e., the group having a higher political weight in the state policy choice problem.

As schematically illustrated in Figure 2, for any cultural population profile at a given time t, $\mathbf{q}_t$, this mechanism provides a mapping from the institutional system at t, β_t, into the one at $t + 1$, β_{t+1}.

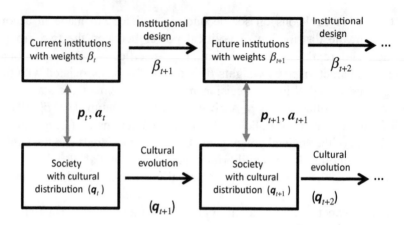

Figure 2:   Joint Dynamics of Culture and Institutions

As mentioned, the second part of the framework is the cultural transmission block. In this respect the Bisin–Verdier cultural transmission setup is augmented by the fact that the degree of paternalistic motivations for cultural transmission now depend on the equilibrium outcome of the societal policy game $\Delta_i = \Delta_i (\mathbf{a}^*, \mathbf{p}^*)$. Under cultural substitution, parental socialization is generally stronger for cultural minorities and, *ceteris paribus*, for the group which is relatively favored at the equilibrium outcome $(\mathbf{a}^*, \mathbf{p}^*)$ of the policy game. These considerations determine the cultural dynamic of the profile of society $\mathbf{q}_t$ over time. Given that $(\mathbf{a}^*, \mathbf{p}^*)$ are themselves function of the institutional weights β_t, the diffusion of cultural traits across generations are consequently also influenced by the status of the institutional system, β_t. This mechanism induces a mapping from $\mathbf{q}_t$ into $\mathbf{q}_{t+1}$, which represents the cultural dynamic.

The politico-economic and cultural structures of society are then characterized by the joint dynamics of institutions and culture $(\beta_t, \mathbf{q}_t)$ as described in Figure 2. This system eventually reaches a long-run steady state (β^*, q^*). Importantly, the joint dynamics may reinforce or hinder each other in response to shocks, depending on whether culture and institutions are dynamic complements or substitutes. To get an intuition on this, consider for instance the case of complementarity and take an exogenous shock to the system that makes more salient the existence of an externality or a political commitment issue. Such a shock triggers an institutional response aimed at internalizing the externality and/or committing policy choices. This institutional response implies augmenting the political weight to the group who gains relatively more from a policy change that helps correct the externality and/or the commitment issue. When the strength of this institutional response is positively related to the frequency of the cultural traits carried by that group, and that such more empowered group has in turn a higher success at diffusing those specific traits, then complementarity between institutions and culture prevails. Over time, institutional and cultural dynamics reinforce each other and therefore act as dynamic complements.

5.3.2 *Religious legitimacy*

The previous logic can be fruitfully applied to the study of religious legitimacy and its implications in terms of institutional and cultural change in a society. For this, define an elite as legitimate when the people believe in its right to rule. Such a belief is ingrained into a set of values and normative statements describing how society should be organized. While some legitimacy principles can be derived from rational premises, legitimacy often takes its roots in the existence of internalized values and worldviews provided by specific organizations or individuals. Given the nature of the beliefs and values that they promote, religious institutions and their members (priests, clerics, etc.) are important agents contributing to the construction of legitimate orders which elites can leverage for their authority and policy making.

In the context of religious legitimacy, Bisin *et al.* (2019) highlight three basic principles driving the joint evolution between institutions and culture:

(1) Legitimacy helps (secular) elites to affirm their authority and reduce the transactions costs associated with the implementation of their policy choices.
(2) The capacity of the religious clerics to supply legitimacy to the elite relies fundamentally on how religious values promoted by the clerics are disseminated in society.
(3) The diffusion of religious values is in turn facilitated by institutions that entrust more political power to the clerics.

The first item is at the source of specific institutional changes which determine an evolution of the distribution of political power between the elite and those supplying the legitimacy: the religious clerics. The second item implies that institutional changes associated with legitimacy depend on the cultural profile of society in terms of religious beliefs and values. Finally, the last item indicates that the institutional system reflecting the structure of power between elite and religious clerics impacts strongly on the dynamics of cultural diffusion of religious values in the population.

In a recent work, Bisin *et al.* (2020) discuss the implications of these different elements for the emergence of religious legitimacy and the associated joint evolution of culture and institutions. For this, they consider a society composed of a political elite, clerics and civil society (merchants, workers, popular masses, etc.). The political power of the religious clerics reflects their relative control of policies and reforms. It relates, for instance, to their control of the judicial administration, the local police and taxation. It is also linked to their presence in key institutions providing social services to the population. Clerics care about the provision of a religious good, e.g., places of worship or of religious study, which they control and they extract (material or immaterial) rents from.

The interaction between rulers, clerics and civil society involves a number of externalities and commitment issues not internalized by individual decisions. For instance, the religious good constitutes a public good for individuals in society, in that it facilitates individual participation in religious activities. In turn, participating in religious activities results in psychological and emotional benefits, as a consequence of a (perceived) closer relationship with the divine. Favoring a more intense participation in religious practices, the religious good provided for by the clerics legitimizes the political control of the elites, e.g., reducing at the margin the psychological cost associated with taxation and other forms of extraction. Less directly, participating in religious activities may also increase the scope of social interactions between religious individuals. This can have positive effects on productivity, since it potentially improves prosocial attitudes, e.g., coordination and cooperation; also, it promotes informal information networks in principle very useful in trading and other economic activities. At the same time though, religious beliefs and restrictions may also increase the costs of economic activities and transactions. Religious regulations on occupational choices in labor markets, restrictions on credit markets at a positive interest rate, or prohibitions of adoption of new technologies are typical examples distorting the allocation of resources away from efficiency.

In this environment, the public provision of the religious good controlled by the clerics will generally not internalize these social externalities, and depending on the state of society and its organizational features, can be inefficiently low or high. Because of commitment issues, the elites controlling political power may not internalize the public good aspect of the religious good. Also, they may not internalize fully how such religious good and the legitimacy it provides allows them to extract more (and more efficiently) resources from society. Consequently, when the legitimacy effect is sufficiently strong, institutional change pushes for a shift in the structure of power towards religious clerics. In turn, clerics exercise this power by providing the religious good in larger quantities, which in turn favors religious practices and activities, propagating beliefs within the population that justify the ruling and extractive capacity of the political elite.

Bisin *et al.* (2020) show that this mechanism of political empowerment of religious clerics has important consequences in terms of institutional trajectory and cultural change. In particular, since clerics care about the provision of religious services, their prevalence in society should increase religious parents' direct inculturation efforts, that is, vertical socialization. Religious legitimacy then makes culture and institutions complements: institutional change devolving political power to the clerics reinforces the incentives of the religious members of society to transmit their values, while in turn, a higher fraction of religious individuals augments the political incentive to credibly change the institutional structure so as to empower the clerics.

Interestingly, the dynamic complementarity between institutional change and diffusion of religious values gives rise to multiple stationary states in the joint dynamics. On the one hand, the system may converge towards a *strong religious state* characterized by the wide diffusion of religious norms and influential clerics imposing religious restrictions that facilitate the extractive power of political rulers (eventually at some cost in terms of economic efficiency). On the other hand, one may have a *secular state* where religious norms do not diffuse, clerics become steadily less influential on economic and political aspects of social life, and civil society (merchants, workers or popular masses) eventually gain control over production and redistribution. As can be expected in such situations, history matters in the sense that the joint evolution of religious values and institutions crucially depends on the initial conditions. Following the analytical implications of this setup, Bisin *et al.* (2020) discuss how the historical divergence between the Christian West and the Muslim East can be understood in terms of the political economy relationships between political elites and religious elites, and the process of building up political legitimacy in the two respective regions.

In a similar vein, but focusing this time on the role of the Reformation in the secularization of the West, Cantoni *et al.* (2018) propose a conceptual framework in which the introduction of religious competition shifts the way religious authorities provide legitimacy to rulers in exchange for control over resources, and consequently the balance of power between secular and religious elites. Using original microdata, they document an important, unintended consequence of the Protestant Reformation: a reallocation of resources from religious to secular purposes. Indeed as secular authorities acquired enormous amounts of wealth from monasteries closed during the Reformation, this transfer of resources had significant consequences. In Protestant regions it shifted the allocation of upper-tail human capital, with graduates of Protestant universities increasingly studying secular subjects and taking thereafter secular, especially administrative, occupations rather than church-sector-specific positions. They also show that this process affected the sectoral composition of fixed investment. Particularly in Protestant regions, new construction shifted from religious toward secular purposes, especially the building of palaces and administrative buildings, which reflected the increased wealth and power of secular lords.

6. Conclusion

This chapter has surveyed the literature on cultural transmission and its application to religion. The study of religion makes clear that preferences are endogenous and must be brought within the scope of economic analysis. The central theoretical framework of Bisin and Verdier (2000, 2001) connects the bottom-up evolutionary dynamic approach to the diffusion of cultural traits to the standard microeconomic choice approach of socialization decisions on the part of families. The model is flexible enough to incorporate various features important for the formation and transmission of religious traits such as endogenous fertility, homophily, religious identity, spatial and social segregation. We highlighted how generalizations of this setup to n discrete traits and continuous traits can also bring interesting and new insights on the genesis of important religious phenomena, such as syncretism.

Importantly, we emphasize that this setup is versatile enough to allow the inclusion of more centralized forces of religious change. These include churches, religious clubs, community leaders, the media, the education system, or other state and private institutions. Introducing these top-down entities qualitatively changes the cultural dynamics of religious beliefs. Further, it opens up a set of new and interesting issues. In this chapter, we touched upon the role of coordination and competition between these centralized entities, and how that may matter for the diffusion or radicalization of religious beliefs. We also outlined some of the political economy and institutional implications associated to the provision of religious legitimacy.

Other dimensions may certainly be worth exploring. One of them for instance relates to demography and how religious leaders and organizations may strategically influence marriage and fertility norms to promote the persistence and diffusion of their religious beliefs. This strategy also connects to important political economy implications, as illustrated for instance by "revenge of the cradle" and other pronatalist policies promoted for example by Roman Catholics in Northern Ireland, or Haredi (ultra-Orthodox) groups in Israel.

Future empirical work is also likely to present new avenues for extending the model. In this respect, one potentially fruitful line of research could be to design cultural transmission models of religious beliefs with and without leaders and analyze how they give different and interesting empirical implications across religions and denominations.

In the end, we hope this survey encourages further theoretical and empirical work on cultural transmission and its application to the many open questions in the study of religion.

References

Abrams, D. and Hogg, M. (1988). *Social Identifications: A Social Psychology of Intergroup Relations and Group Processes*, London: Routledge.

Acemoglu, D. and Robinson, J. (2000). "Why Did the West Extend the Franchise? Democracy, Inequality, and Growth in Historical Perspective," *The Quarterly Journal of Economics*, 115, 1167–1199.

Acemoglu, D. and Robinson, J. (2006). *Economic Origins of Dictatorship and Democracy*, Cambridge: Cambridge University Press.

Adida, C., Laitin, D. and Valfort, M.A. (2016). *Why Muslim Integration Fails in Christian-Heritage Societies*, Cambridge, MA: Harvard University Press.

Akerlof, G. and Kranton, R.E. (2000). "Economics and Identity," *The Quarterly Journal of Economics*, 115(3), 715–753.

Albrile, E. (2005). "Gnosticism: History of Study," in *MacMillan Encyclopedia of Religion*, J., Lindsay (ed.). New York, NY: MacMillan.

Almagro, M. and Andrés-Cerezo, D. (2020). "The Construction of National Identities," *Theoretical Economics*, 15, 763–810.

Allport, F. (1953). "The Effects of Segregation and the Consequences of Desegregation: A Social Science Statement," *Journal of Negro Education*, 22(1), 68–76.

Anderson, B.A. (1986). "Regional and cultural factors in the decline of marital fertility in Western Europe," in *The Decline of Fertility in Europe*, A.J. Coale and S.C. Watkins (eds.), pp. 293–313. Princeton: Princeton University Press.

Auriol, E. and Platteau, J.P. (2017). "Religious Co-option in Autocracy: A Theory Inspired by History," *Journal of Development Economics*, 127(C), 395–412.

Bailey, M. (1986). "Differential Fertility by Religious Group in Rural Sierra Leone," *Journal of Biosocial Science*, 18(1), 75–85.

Bar-El, R., García-Muñoz, T., Neuman, S. and Tobol, Y. (2013). "The Evolution of Secularization: Cultural Transmission, Religion and Fertility-Theory, Simulations and Evidence," *Journal of Population Economics*, 26(3), 1129–1174.

Bar-Gill, S. and Fershtman, C. (2016). "Integration Policy: Cultural Transmission with Endogenous Fertility," *Journal of Population Economics*, 29(1), 105–133.

Barro, R.J. and McCleary, R. (2019). *The Wealth of Religions: The Political Economy of Believing and Belonging*, Princeton, NJ: Princeton University Press.

Becker, S. O. and Woessmann, L. (2009). "Was Weber Wrong? A Human Capital Theory of Protestant Economic History," *The Quarterly Journal of Economics*, 124(2), 531–596.

Benabou, R. and Tirole, J. (2002). "Self-confidence and Personal Motivation," *The Quarterly Journal of Economics*, 117(3), 871–915.

Bentzen, J. (2019). "Acts of God? Religiosity and Natural Disasters across Subnational World Districts," *The Economic Journal*, 129(622), 2295–2321.

Berghammer, C. (2012). "Family Life Trajectories and Religiosity in Austria," *European Sociological Review*, 28(1), 127–144.

Berman, E. (2000). "Sect, Subsidy, and Sacrifice: An Economist's View of Ultra-Orthodox Jews," *The Quarterly Journal of Economics*, 115(3), 905–953.

Binzel, C. and Carvalho, J.-P. (2017). "Education, Social Mobility, and Religious Movements: The Islamic Revival in Egypt," *The Economic Journal*, 127(607), 2553–2580.

Bisin, A., Topa, G. and Verdier, T. (2004). "Religious Intermarriage and Socialization in the United States," *Journal of Political Economy*, 112(3), 615–664.

Bisin, A., Topa, G. and Verdier, T. (2009). "Cultural Transmission, Socialization and the Population Dynamics of Multiple-Trait Distributions," *International Journal of Economic Theory*, 5(1), 139–154.

Bisin, A. and Verdier, T. (2000). "'Beyond the Melting Pot': Cultural Transmission, Marriage, and the Evolution of Ethnic and Religious Traits," *The Quarterly Journal of Economics*, 115(3), 955–988.

Bisin, A. and Verdier, T. (2001). "The Economics of Cultural Transmission and the Dynamics of Preferences," *Journal of Economic Theory*, 97(2), 298–319.

Bisin, A. and Verdier, T. (2010). "The Economics of Cultural Transmission and Socialization," in the *Handbook of Social Economics*, J. Benhabib, A. Bisin and M. Jackson (eds.). San Diego, CA: North Holland.

Bisin, A. and Verdier, T. (2017). "On the Joint Evolution of Culture and Institutions," NBER Working Paper No. 23375.

Bisin A., Patacchini, E., Verdier, T. and Zenou, Y. (2011). "Cultural Persistence and the Persistence of Oppositional Identities," *European Economic Review*, 55, 1046–1071.

Bisin A., Patacchini, E., Verdier, T., and Zenou, Y. (2016). "Bend It Like Beckham: Ethnic Identity and Integration," *European Economic Review*, 90, 146–164.

Bisin A., Rubin, J., Seror, A. and Verdier, T. (2020). "Culture, Institutions and the Long Divergence between Western Europe and the Middle East," Mimeo: NYU.

Bisin A., Seror, A. and Verdier, T. (2018). "Religious Legitimacy and the Joint Evolution of Culture and Institutions," in *Advances in the Economics of Religion*, J.-P. Carvalho, S. Iyer and J. Rubin (eds.), pp. 321–332. Palgrave: Macmillan.

Blume, M. (2009). "The Reproductive Benefits of Religious Affiliation," in *The Biological Evolution of Religious Mind and Behavior*, E. Voland and W. Schiefenhoevel (eds.), pp. 117–126. Berlin, Germany: Springer.

Bouvier, L.F. and Rao, S.L.N. (1975). *Socio-Religious Factors in Fertility Decline*. Cambridge: Ballinger.

Bowles, S. (1998). "Endogenous Preferences: The Cultural Consequences of Markets and Other Economic Institutions," *Journal of Economic Literature*, 36(1), 75–111.

Boyd, R. and Richerson, P.J. (1985). *Culture and the Evolutionary Process*, Chicago, IL: University of Chicago press.

Brewster, K.L., Cooksey, E.C., Guilkey, D.K. and Rindfuss, R.R. (1988). "The Changing Impact of Religion on the Sexual and Contraceptive Behavior of Adolescent Women in the United States," *Journal of Marriage and the Family*, 60(2), 493–504.

Brueckner, J. and Smirnov, O. (2007). "Workings of the Melting Pot: Social Networks and the Evolution of Population Attributes," *Journal of Regional Sciences*, 47(2), 209–228.

Brueckner, J. and Smirnov, O. (2008). "Social Networks and the Convergence of Population Attributes: A Generalization," *Journal of Regional Sciences*, 48(2), 359–365.

Buechel, B., Hellmann, T. and Pichler, M.M. (2014). "The Dynamics of Continuous Cultural Traits in Social Networks," *Journal of Economic Theory*, 154, 274–309.

Cantoni D., Dittmar, J. and Yuchtman, N. (2018). "Religious Competition and Reallocation: The Political Economy of Secularization in the Protestant Reformation," *The Quarterly Journal of Economics*, 133(4), 2037–2096.

Carvalho, J.-P. (2013). "Veiling," *The Quarterly Journal of Economics*, 128(1), 337–370.

Carvalho, J.-P. (2016). "Identity-based Organizations," *American Economic Review: Papers and Proceedings*, 106, 410–414.

Carvalho, J.-P. and Koyama, M. (2014). "Resisting Education," Working Paper, University of California, Irvine.

Carvalho, J.-P. and Koyama, M. (2016). "Jewish Emancipation and Schism: Economic Development and Religious Change," *Journal of Comparative Economics*, 44(3), 562–584.

Carvalho, J.-P., Koyama, M. and Sacks, M. (2017). "Education, Identity, and Community: Lessons from Jewish Emancipation," *Public Choice*, 171(1–2), 119–143.

Carvalho, J.-P. and Sacks, M. (2020). "Radicalization," working paper, University of California, Irvine.

Cavalli Sforza, L.L. and Feldman, M. (1973). "Cultural Versus Biological Inheritance: Phenotypic Transmission from Parent to Children," *American Journal of Human Genetics*, 25(6), 618–637.

Cavalli-Sforza, L.L. and Feldman, M.W. (1981). *Cultural Transmission and Evolution: A Quantitative Approach*, Princeton University Press.

Chaney, E. (2013). "Revolt on the Nile: Economic Shocks, Religion, and Political Power," *Econometrica*, 81(5), 2033–2053.

Chen, D.L. (2010). "Club Goods and Group Identity: Evidence from Islamic Resurgence during the Indonesian Financial Crisis," *Journal of Political Economy*, 118(2), 300–354.

Chen, T., McBride, M. and Short, M.B. (2019). "Dynamics of Religious Group Growth and Survival," *Journal for the Scientific Study of Religion*, 58(1), 67–92.

Cheung, M.W. and Wu, J. (2018). "On the Probabilistic Transmission of Continuous Cultural Traits," *Journal of Economic Theory*, 174, 300–323.

Coase, R. H. (1937). "The Nature of the Firm," *Economica*, 4(16), 386–405.

Cohen, R. (2007). "Creolization and Cultural Globalization: The Soft Sounds of Fugitive Power," *Globalizations*, 4(3), 369–384.

Cohen-Zada, D. (2006). "Preserving Religious Identity through Education: Economic Analysis and Evidence from the US," *Journal of Urban Economics*, 60(3), 372–398.

Cosgel, M. and Miceli, T. (2009). "State and Religion," *Journal of Comparative Economics*, 37, 402–416.

Cosgel, M., Miceli T. and Rubin J. (2012). "The Political Economy of Mass Printing: Legitimacy, Revolt, and Technology Change in the Ottoman Empire," *Journal of Comparative Economics*, 40(3), 357–371.

Coyle, A. and Lyons, E. (2011). "The Social Psychology of Religion: Current Research Themes," *Journal of Community and Applied Social Psychology*, 21(6), 461–467.

Derosas, R. and van Poppel, F. (2006). *Religion and the Decline of Fertility in the Western World* Dordrecht: Springer.

Dharmalingam, A. and Morgan, S.P. (2004). "Pervasive Muslim–Hindu Fertility Differences in India," *Demography*, 41(3), 529–554.

Dumoulin, H. and Maraldo J.C. (1976). *Buddhism in the Modern World*, The University of Virginia: Macmillan.

Fischer, C.S. (1977). *Networks and Places: Social Relations in the Urban Setting*, New York: Free Press.

Fischer, C.S. (1982). *To Dwell among Friends*, Chicago: Univ. Chicago Press.

Flint, S., Benenson, I., Alfasi, N. and Bakman, Y. (2013). "Between Friends and Strangers: Schelling-Like Residential Dynamics in a Haredi Neighborhood in Jerusalem," in *Emergent Phenomena in Housing Markets*, L. Diappi (ed.), pp. 103–126.

Frejka, T. and Westhoff, C.F. (2008). "Religion, Religiousness and Fertility in the US and Europe," *European Journal of Populations*, 24, 5–31.

Fruehwirth, J.C., Iyer, S. and Zhang, A. (2019). "Religion and Depression in Adolescence," *Journal of Political Economy*, 127(3), 1178–1209.

Geertz, C. (1976). *The Religion of Java*, Chicago, IL: University of Chicago Press.

Gintis, H. (2003). "The Hitchhiker's Guide to Altruism: Gene-culture Coevolution, and the Internalization of Norms," *Journal of Theoretical Biology*, 220(4), 407–418.

Glazer, N. and Moynihan, D.P. (1970). *Beyond the Melting Pot: The Negroes, Puerto Ricans, Jews, Italians and Irish of New York City*, Cambridge, MA: MIT Press.

Goldscheider, C. and Mosher, W.D. (1991). "Patterns of Contraceptive Use in the United States: The Importance of Religious Factors," *Studies in Family Planning*, 22(2), 102–115.

Goodman, M.A. and Dyer, W.J. (2020). "From Parent to Child: Family Factors that Influence Faith Transmission," *Psychology of Religion and Spirituality*, 12(2), 178–190.

Gordon M.M. (1964). *Human Nature, Class, and Ethnicity*, New York: Oxford University Press.

56   *A. Bisin et al.*

Gutmann, M.P. (1990). "Denomination and Fertility Decline: The Catholics and Protestants of Gillespie County Texas," *Continuity and Change*, 5(3), 391–416.

Hauk, E. and Mueller, H. (2015). "Cultural Leaders and the Clash of Civilizations," *Journal of Conflict Resolution*, 59(3), 367–400.

Hayford, S.R. and Morgan, S.P. (2008). "Religiosity and Fertility in the United States: The Role of Fertility Intentions," *Social Forces*, 86(3), 1163–1188.

Heaton, T.B. (2011). "Does Religion Influence Fertility in Developing Countries?" *Population Research and Policy Review*, 30(3), 449–465.

Henrich, J. (2004). "Cultural Group Selection, Coevolutionary Processes and Large-Scale Cooperation," *Journal of Economic Behavior & Organization*, 53(1), 3–35.

Henrich, J., Boyd, R., Bowles, S., Camerer, C., Fehr, E., Gintis, H., McEl-reath, R., Alvard, M., Barr, A., Ensminger, J. *et al.* (2005). "'Economic man' in cross-cultural perspective: Behavioral experiments in 15 small scale societies," *Behavioral and Brain Sciences*, 28(6), 795–815.

Henrich, J. and Gil-White, F. J. (2001). "The Evolution of Prestige: Freely Conferred Deference as a Mechanism for Enhancing the Benefits of Cultural Transmission," *Evolution and Human Behavior*, 22(3), 165–196.

Hu J., Zhang Q.M. and Zhou T. (2019). "Segregation in Religion Networks," *EPJ Data Science*, 8(6) 1–11.

Iannaccone, L.R. (1990). "Religious Practice: A Human Capital Approach," *Journal for the Scientific Study of Religion*, 29(3), 297–314.

Iannaccone, L.R. (1992). "Sacrifice and Stigma: Reducing Free-Riding in Cults, Communes, and Other Collectives," *Journal of Political Economy*, 100(2), 271–291.

Iannaccone, L.R. (1998). "Introduction to the Economics of Religion," *Journal of Economic Literature*, 36(3), 1465–1495.

Jayasree, R. (1989). *Religion, Social Change and Fertility Behaviour: A Study of Kerala*. New Delhi: Concept Publishing.

Johnson, N.E. (1993). "Hindu and Christian Fertility in India: A Test of Three Hypotheses," *Social Biology*, 40(1–2), 87–105.

Johnson-Hanks, J. (2006). "On the Politics and Practice of Muslim Fertility: Comparative Evidence from West Africa," *Medical Anthropology Quarterly*, 20(1), 12–30.

Kalmijn, M. (1998). "Intermarriage and Homogamy: Causes, Patterns and Trends," *Annual Review of Sociology*, 24, 395–421.

Knodel, J., Gray, R.S. and Peracca, S. (1999). "Religion and Reproduction: Muslims in Buddhist Thailand," *Population Studies*, 53(2), 149–164.

Kraybill, D. and Bowman, C. (2001). *On the Backroad to Heaven: Old Order Hutterites, Mennonites, Amish, and Brethren*. Baltimore: John Hopkins University Press.

Kuran, T. and Sandholm, W. (2008). "Cultural Integration and Its Discontent," *Review of Economic Studies*, 75, 201–228.

Leszczensky, L. and Pink, S. (2017). "Intra- and Inter-group Friendship Choices of Christian, Muslim, and Non-religious Youth in Germany," *European Sociological Review*, 33(1), 72–83.

Le Tourneau, R. (1986). "Barghawāta," in *Encyclopaedia of Islam*, P. Bearman, Th. Bianquis, C.E. Bosworth, E. van Donzel and W.P. Heinrichs (eds.), Vol. I, 2nd Edition, p. 1044. Leiden, Netherlands: Brill Publishers.

Levy, G. and Razin, R. (2012). "Religious Beliefs, Religious Participation, and Cooperation," *American Economic Journal: Microeconomics*, 4(3), 121–151.

Malinowski, B. (1925). *Science, Religion, and Reality*, New York: Macmillan.

Marsden, P.V. (1988). "Homogeneity in Confiding Relations," *Social Networks*, 10, 57–76.

McBride, M. (2008). "Religious Pluralism and Religious Participation: A Game Theoretic Analysis," *American Journal of Sociology*, 114(1), 77–106.

McBride, M. (2015). "Why Churches Need Free-Riders: Religious Capital Formation and Religious Group Survival," *Journal of Behavioral and Experimental Economics*, 58, 77–87.

McPherson, M., Smith-Lovin, L. and Cook, J.M. (2001). "Birds of a Feather: Homophily in Social Networks," *Annual Review of Sociology*, 27, 415–444.

McQuillan, K. (2004). "When Does Religion Influence Fertility?" *Population and Development Review*, 30(1), 25–56.

Meyersson, E. (2014). "Islamic Rule and the Empowerment of the Poor and Pious," *Econometrica*, 82(1), 229–269.

Moghaddam, F.M. and Solliday, E.A. (1991). "Balanced Multiculturalism and the Challenge of Peaceful Coexistence in Pluralistic Societies," *Psychology and Developing Societies*, 3, 51–71.

Montgomery, J.D. (2010). "Intergenerational Cultural Transmission as an Evolutionary Game," *American Economic Journal: Microeconomics*, 2(4), 115–136.

Morgan, S.P., Stash, S., Smith, H.L. and Mason, K.O. (2002). "Muslim and Non-Muslim Differences in Female Autonomy and Fertility: Evidence from Four Asian Countries," *Population and Development Review*, 28(3), 515–537.

Nederveen Pieterse, J. (1994). "Globalization as Hybridisation," *International Sociology*, 9(2), 161–184.

Norenzayan, A. (2013). *Big Gods: How Religion Transformed Cooperation and Conflict*, Princeton, NJ: Princeton University Press.

Odling-Smee, F.J., Laland, K.N. and Feldman, M.W. (2003). *Niche Construction: The Neglected Process in Evolution*, Princeton, NJ: Princeton University Press.

Oechssler, J. and Riedel, F. (2001). "Evolutionary Dynamics on Infinite Strategy Spaces," *Economic Theory*, 17, 141–162.

Otto S.P., Christiansen, F.B. and Feldman, M.W. (1994). "Genetic and Cultural Inheritance of Continuous Traits," Morrison Institute for Population and Resource Studies, Working Paper 0064, Stanford University.

Panchanathan, K. (2010). *The Evolution of Prestige-biased Transmission Center for Behavior*, Mimeo: University of Missouri.

Panebianco, F. (2014). "Socialization Networks and the Transmission of Interethnic Attitudes," *Journal of Economic Theory*, 150, 583–610.

Panebianco, F. and Verdier, T. (2017). "Paternalism, Homophily and Cultural Transmission in Random Networks," *Games and Economic Behavior*, 105(C), 155–176.

Parkerson, D.H. and Parkerson, J.A. (1988). "Fewer Children of Greater Spiritual Quality: Religion and the Decline of Fertility in Nineteenth-Century America," *Social Science History*, 12(1), 49–70.

Patacchini, E. and Zenou, Y. (2011). "Neighborhood Effects and Parental Involvement in the Intergenerational Transmission of Education," *Journal of Regional Science*, 51(5), 987–1013.

Patacchini, E. and Zenou, Y. (2016). "Social Networks and Parental Behavior in the Intergenerational Transmission of Religion," *Quantitative Economics, Econometric Society*, 7(3), 969–995.

Philipov, D. and Berghammer, C. (2007). "Religion and Fertility Ideals, Intentions and Behaviour: A Comparative Study of European Countries," *Vienna Yearbook of Population Research*, pp. 271–305. Vienna, Austria: Vienna Institute of Demography at the Austrian Academy of Sciences.

Platteau, J.P. (2011). "Political Instrumentalization of Islam and the Risk of Obscurantist Deadlock," *World Development*, 39(2), 243–260.

Prummer, A. and Siedlarek, J.-P. (2017). "Community Leaders and the Preservation of Cultural Traits," *Journal of Economic Theory*, 168, 143–176.

Rubin, J. (2017). *Rulers, Religion, and Riches: Why the West Got Rich and the Middle East Did Not*, New York: Cambridge University Press.

Sáez-Martí, M. and Sjögren, A. (2008). "Peers and Culture," *Scandinavian Journal of Economics*, 110(1), 73–92.

Sandholm, W.H. (2010). *Population Games and Evolutionary Dynamics*, Cambridge, MA: MIT press.

Shilhav, Y. (1993). "The Emergence of Ultra-Orthodox Neighborhoods in Israeli Urban Centers," in *Local Communities and the Israeli Polity: Conflict of Values and Interests*, E. Ben-Zadok (ed.), pp. 157–187. Albany, NY: Sunny Press.

Skaperdas, S. and Vaidya, S. (2020). "Why Did Pre-modern States Adopt Big-God Religions?" *Public Choice*, 182(3–4), 373–394.

Smith, J.M. (1982). *Evolution and the Theory of Games*, Cambridge, UK: Cambridge University Press.

Smith, S., Maas, I. and van Tubergen, F. (2014). "Ethnic Ingroup Friendships in Schools: Testing the By-product Hypothesis in England, Germany, the Netherlands and Sweden," *Social Networks*, 39, 33–45.

Smith, S., McFarland, D. and van Tubergen, F. (2016). "Ethnic Composition and Friendship Segregation: Differential Effects for Adolescent Natives and Immigrants," *American Journal of Sociology*, 121, 1223–1272.

Sosis, R. (2000). "Religion and Intragroup Cooperation: Preliminary Results of a Comparative Analysis of Utopian Communities," *Cross-Cultural Research*, 34(1), 70–87.

Sosis, R. and Ruffle, B.J. (2003). "Religious Ritual and Cooperation: Testing for a Relationship on Israeli Religious and Secular Kibbutzim," *Current Anthropology*, 44(5), 713–722.

Stark, R. and Finke, R. (2000). *Acts of Faith: Explaining the Human Side of Religion*, Berkeley, CA: University of California Press.

Stewart, C. (2016). *Creolization History, Ethnography, Theory*. Walnut Creek, CA Coast Press, pp. 1–25.

Tajfel, H. (1981). *Human Groups and Social Categories: Studies in Social Psychology*, Cambridge: Cambridge University Press.

Taylor, P.D. and Jonker, L.B. (1978). "Evolutionary Stable Strategies and Game Dynamics," *Mathematical Biosciences*, 40(1–2), 145–156.

Turner, J.C. (1982). "Towards a Cognitive Redenition of the Social Group," in *Social Identity and Intergroup Relations*, H. Tajfel (ed.), pp. 15–44. Cambridge: Cambridge University Press.

Valins, O. (2003). "Stubborn Identities and the Construction of Socio-Spatial Boundaries: Ultra-Orthodox Jews Living in Contemporary Britain," *Transactions of the Institute of British Geographers*, 28(2), 158–175.

Vaughan, D. (2010). "To be or not to be : Conformity, Social Interactions and the Transmission of Preferences," Mimeo: NYU.

Verdier, T. and Zenou, Y. (2017). "The Role of Social Networks in Cultural Assimilation," *Journal of Urban Economics*, 97, 15–39.

Verdier, T. and Zenou, Y. (2015). "The Role of Cultural Leaders in the Transmission of Preferences," *Economics Letters*, 136, 158–161.

Verdier, T. and Zenou, Y. (2018). "Cultural Leader and the Dynamics of Assimilation," *Journal of Economic Theory*, 175, 374–414.

White, C., Baimel, A. and Norenzayan, A. (forthcoming). "How Cultural Learning and Cognitive Biases Shape Religious Beliefs," *Current Opinion in Psychology*, 40, 34–39.

Williamson, O.E. (1996). *The Mechanisms of Governance*, New York: Oxford University Press.

Windzio, M. and Wingens, M. (2014). "Religion, Friendship Networks and Home Visits of Immigrant and Native Children," *Acta Sociologica*, 57, 59–75.

Ysseldyk, R., Matheson, K. and Anisma, H. (2010). "Religiosity as Identity: Toward an Understanding of Religion From a Social Identity Perspective," *Personality and Social Psychology Review*, 14(1), 60–71.

Young, H.P. (1998). *Individual Strategy and Social Structure: An Evolutionary Theory of Institutions*, Princeton, NJ: Princeton University Press.

Zhang, L. (2008). "Religious Affiliation, Religiosity, and Male and Female Fertility," *Demographic Research*, 18, 233–262.

Appendix: The Replicator Dynamic

In this Appendix, we derive the replicator dynamic taking the biological approach of interpreting payoffs as *reproduction rates* of strategies. Because payoffs are frequency dependent, this extends the notion of survival of the fittest from an exogenous environment to an interactive setting.

Evolutionary game theory is the study of bounded rational populations of agents who may (or may not) evolve or learn their way into equilibrium by gradually revising simple, myopic rules of behavior. Strategies that do better, given what everyone else is doing, proliferate. Following this approach, we could also show that the replicator dynamic emerges from a variety of learning protocols including imitation and reinforcement learning (Sandholm, 2010).

Once again the population consists of a continuum of agents. Consider a population game with a set of (pure) strategies $S = \{1, \ldots, n\}$, with typical members i, j and s. The mass of agents programmed with strategy i is m_i, where $\sum_{i=1}^{n} m_i = m$.

Players do not choose strategies through deliberation. Rather, they are *programmed* with a strategy, and strategies with higher payoffs proliferate.

Let $q_i = \frac{m_i}{m}$ denote the share of players programmed with strategy $i \in S$ and $q = (q_i)$ $i \in S$ be the full distribution.

The set of population states (or strategy distributions) is $Q = \{q \in [0,1]^n : \sum_{i \in S} q_i = 1\}$. That is, Q is the unit simplex in $\mathbb{R}^n$.

The set of vertices of Q are the pure population states — those in which all agents choose the same strategy. These are the standard basis vectors in $\mathbb{R}^n$:

$$e_1 = (1,0,0, \ldots), e_2 = (0,1,0, \ldots), e_3 = (0,0,1, \ldots), \ldots$$

A *continuous* payoff function $F: Q \to \mathbb{R}^n$ assigns to each population state a vector of payoffs, consisting of a real number for each strategy. $F_i: Q \to \mathbb{R}$ denotes the payoff function for strategy i.

Consider the expected payoff to strategy i if i is matched with another strategy drawn uniformly at random from the population to play the following *two-player* game:

	1	2	$\cdots$	n
i	$u(i, 1)$	$u(i, 2)$	$\cdots$	$u(i, n)$

The expected payoff to strategy i in state q is

$$\begin{aligned} F_i(q) &= q_1 u(i, 1) + q_2 u(i, 2) + \ldots + q_n u(i, n) \\ &= \sum_{j=1}^{n} q_j u(i, j) \\ &= \sum_{j=1}^{n} q_j F_i(e_j). \end{aligned}$$

The average payoff in the population is

$$\begin{aligned} \bar{F}(q) &= q_1 F_1(q) + q_2 F_2(q) + \ldots + q_n F_n(q) \\ &= \sum_{i=1}^{n} q_i F_i(q). \end{aligned}$$

Note that this is the same as the payoff from playing the mixed strategy q against itself.

To derive the replicator dynamic, suppose that payoffs represent *fitness* (rates of reproduction) and reproduction takes place in continuous time. This yields a continuous-time evolutionary dynamic called the *replicator dynamic* (Taylor and Jonker, 1978). The replicators here are pure strategies that are copied without error from parent to child. As the population state q changes, so do the payoffs and thereby the fitness of each strategy.

Let the rate of growth of strategy i be

$$\frac{\dot{m}_i}{m_i} = [\beta - \delta + F_i(q)],$$

where β and δ are "background" birth and death rates (which are independent of payoffs). This is the interpretation of payoffs as fitness (reproduction rates) in biological models of evolution.

What is the rate of growth of q_i, the *population share* of strategy i? By definition, $q_i = \frac{m_i}{m}$. Hence $\ln(q_i) = \ln(m_i) - \ln(m)$, which means

$$\frac{\dot{q}_i}{q_i} = \frac{\dot{m}_i}{m_i} - \frac{\dot{m}}{m}$$

$$= [\beta - \delta + F_i(q)] - \sum_{j=1}^{n} q_j [\beta - \delta + F_j(q)]$$

$$= F_i(q) - \bar{F}(q).$$

That is, the growth rate of a strategy equals the excess of its payoff over the average payoff.

The following results are immediate:

- Those sub-populations that are associated with better than average payoffs grow and *vice versa*.
- The sub-populations associated with pure best replies to the current population state $q \in Q$ have the highest growth rate.
- Support invariance: $\dot{q}_i = q_i[F_i(q) - \bar{F}(q)]$, so that if $m_i = 0$ at T, then $m_i = 0$ for all $t > T$.

Again, though we have derived the replicator dynamic based on a biological interpretation of payoffs as reproduction rates, the replicator dynamic also emerges at the population level from a variety of learning protocols including imitation and reinforcement learning (Sandholm, 2010).

Chapter 2

Did Seismic Activity Lead to the Rise of Religions?

Jeanet Sinding Bentzen[*,‡] **and Eric R. Force**[†,§]

Department of Economics, University of Copenhagen, Denmark
†*Department of Geosciences, University of Arizona, USA*
‡*jeanet.bentzen@econ.ku.dk*
§*ejforce@aol.com*

Abstract

We document a link between religiosity and natural disasters — earthquakes in particular. Using modern data from surveys, we first show that religiosity has increased in the aftermath of disasters such as earthquakes. As emotional effects can be analytically disentangled from those of physical destruction, we suggest that religious coping is the most potent link; people use their religion for comfort and explanation to match the otherworldly aspect of seismic destruction. Second, we show that the major religions of the modern world emerged in a remarkably tight band along seismically active plate-tectonic boundaries, suggesting the persistence of this link. Third, we show that the majority of known immediate cultural responses to historic earthquakes have been religious rather than secular. We conclude that religion tends to emerge as a response to the unanswerable questions posed by earthquakes, and other natural disasters, and as a provider of comfort to survivors. Earthquakes may thus have played a pivotal role for millennia in the emergence and persistence of religion.

Keywords: Religiosity, Major Religions, Coping, Natural Disasters, Earthquakes

1. Introduction

For most of our history and throughout most of the globe, religion has played a surprisingly central role in human lives.[1] Only recently has the importance of religion dwindled in some societies, while it continues to influence most aspects of life in others. A puzzle of the social sciences remains why religion emerged in the first place. A second puzzle is why religion has not declined in importance in most parts of the world today as the secularization hypothesis otherwise suggests.[2] This chapter aims to improve our understanding of these puzzles.

To do so, we combine two insights from the literature. First, people across the globe become more religious when earthquakes and other natural disasters hit (Bentzen, 2019a; Sibley and Bulbulia, 2012). The reason is that people use religion to cope with the adversity caused by disaster, in keeping with the religious coping hypothesis (Pargament, 2001). Even the corona pandemic has instigated people across the globe to pray (Bentzen, 2020). Second, thousands of years ago, all the major religions emerged particularly close to boundaries between tectonic plates and the majority of past great earthquakes have led to some religious response (Force, 2015, 2018). Residing in areas with much tectonic activity historically most likely instigated a larger need for explaining of the world, compared to living in calmer areas. The belief in God often satisfied this requirement (e.g., Hall, 1990; Van De Wetering, 1982). While we do not have detailed data on people's religious beliefs in the past, we instead draw on numerous examples of ancient societies engaging in direct religious responses to earthquakes. For instance, all explanations of earthquakes in the ancient Judaic world built on religion; God's anger in particular.

Combining these two insights leads to our hypothesis that providing comfort and explanation form important reasons for the emergence of the

---

[1] For example, Murdock (1965), Brown (1991) and Peoples *et al.* (2016).

[2] The secularization hypothesis predicts that religiosity falls as societies modernize. It has received mixed support, though. Norris and Inglehart (2011) show that while religion has become less important in many Western countries it has increased in importance in other parts of the world, leading to a net increase in the number of people with traditional religious views during the past 50 years. See also Stark and Finke (2000) and Iannaccone (1998) for discussions and Becker *et al.* (2017) for an empirical investigation of the influence of education on the secularization process.

world's major religions and for why they continue to hold such a strong position in most contemporary societies. In particular, we argue that earthquakes (and other natural disasters) played a crucial role in the emergence of religion thousands of years ago and at the same time help explain why religion retains center stage in many societies today. While modernization may tend to reduce religiosity, the continued existence of natural disasters may help explain why average global religiosity is not falling. As we shall see, religious coping can also be exploited by rulers with an interest in using religion for power purposes, which further anchors the role of religion in society.

Studies have found correlations between religiosity and various socioeconomic outcomes such as health, fertility choices, gender roles, productivity, labor force participation and education choices.[3] Understanding religious origins and continued impact may help understand the socioeconomic consequences of religion.

2. What Explains Religion?

In this section, we review existing explanations of differences in religiosity and the emergence of religion. The two are not necessarily intertwined: Factors that led to the emergence of religion thousands of years ago may not be the same factors that make people more religious today. We argue, though, that some factors may explain both the emergence of religion historically and the differences in religiosity today.

Social scientists have applied microeconomic theory to explain why some individuals, societies, or groups are more religious than others.[4] By religiosity, we mean both the degree of participation in religious activities and the strength of beliefs in religious concepts. The notion of religiosity is to be distinguished from types of religious denominations, such as Christianity versus Islam. The work explaining why some are more religious than others began with the model by Azzi and Ehrenberg (1975), where individuals allocate their time and goods among religious and

---

[3]See Guiso *et al.* (2003), Scheve and Stasavage (2006), McCleary and Barro (2006), Gruber and Hungerman (2008), Campante and Yanagizawa-Drott (2015), and Bentzen and Sperling (2020) for empirical investigations or Iannaccone (1998), Lehrer (2004) and Kimball *et al.* (2009) for reviews.

[4]See reviews by Iannaccone (1998) and Iyer (2016).

secular commodities to maximize their lifetime and afterlife utility. Within this framework, the reasons for differences in religiosity can be grouped into demand and supply side factors (e.g., Finke and Stark, 2005).

One supply-side explanation of differences in religiosity is that religious congregations compete for followers, thus increasing the quality and quantity of the religious services provided. The larger supply in turn would improve the match rate between potential follower and religion, thus increasing the likelihood that people take up religion (e.g., Finke and Stark, 2005; Olson, 2011). Bryan *et al.* (2020) collaborated with an evangelical Protestant anti-poverty organization to randomly offer poor households in the Philippines an education program based on "theology and values." In support of the supply-driven explanation of religiosity, the researchers found significant increases in religiosity in areas "treated" with the religious program. Across Africa, Nunn (2010) found that descendants of people who experienced greater missionary contact are more likely to identify themselves as Christians today. In a modern Western country, the USA, Bentzen and Sperling (2020) exploited the faith-based initiatives as quasi-exogenous shocks to the supply of religious organizations. They found that the initiatives led to an increase in the number of religious organizations and a rise in churchgoing, religious beliefs, and associated attitudes such as skepticism toward homosexuals and science. Instead of competing with other religious congregations, a potentially important competitor from the viewpoint of the particular congregation could be secular organizations (e.g., Hungerman, 2005, 2010). In support, Gruber and Hungerman (2008) show that the legalization of retail activity on Sundays led to lower church attendance and church donations across the US states.

The supply-side theories are arguably not that great at explaining the emergence of religion, as they assume the prior existence of religion and from that explain differences in religiosity by differences in the availability of this religion.

Turning to the demand-side, demand-side explanations of differences in religiosity emphasize factors that elevate the demand for religion, in turn increasing the extent of religious engagement (e.g., Norris and Inglehart, 2011). One demand-side theory that has received widespread empirical support is the idea that individuals use their religion to cope with stress, uncertainty and events that are otherwise difficult to explain. This is termed the religious coping hypothesis, a theory to which we will return in Sections 3–5. Another demand-side theory is the secularization hypothesis, which claims that religion will die out as countries develop. This, however, has received mixed support in the data.[5]

The demand-side explanations of differences in the degree of religiosity can plausibly also contribute to our understanding of the emergence of religion: Religion would be more likely to emerge when the demand for religion is higher. This would be the case when the particular population demands comfort and explanation to a larger extent, for instance.

The model by Azzi and Ehrenberg (1975) views differences in religiosity as a product of the supply and demand for religion seen from the viewpoint of the populace. An important part of the literature instead views differences in religiosity and religious institutions as products of the *rulers'* demand for religion. In particular, a line of research focuses on the use of religion for power legitimacy and social control. This research goes far back, at least to Marx (1844), including a list of research within political science (e.g., Djupe and Calfano, 2013; Hertzke *et al.*, 2018; Jelen, 2006) and economics (Belloc *et al.*, 2016; Bentzen and Gokmen, forthcoming; Chaney, 2013; Kuran, 2012; Platteau, 2017; Rubin, 2017). Belloc *et al.* (2016) document that transition to democracy across Medieval Italian cities was less likely when an earthquake had recently hit, but only in cities, where the political and religious leader was the same person. They argue that the earthquake increased religiosity due to religious coping, which could be exploited by the religious ruler who would then have a higher chance to withstand the movement towards democracy. Across 1,265 societies spread across the globe, Bentzen and Gokmen (forthcoming) document that all types of societies have used religion for power legitimization at some point. In fact, certain types of gods, Big Gods, were more likely to develop in societies that could benefit more from religious power legitimacy. They further document that these societies are more likely to remain autocracies today, have a larger share of current state laws that are religious laws, and are more religious. This theory thus potentially explains both differences in contemporary religiosity and the emergence

---

[5]Rather, religion seems to be on the rise in many societies, which some see as a rejection of the secularization hypothesis (e.g., Iannaccone, 1998; Finke and Stark, 2005; Norris and Inglehart, 2011). Some scholars have viewed rising religiosity in the US as a counter example of the secularization hypothesis. However, Voas and Chaves (2016) document that religiosity in the US has declined over the past decades when cohort effects are accounted for.

of religion historically. The theory also illustrates how religious coping can be exploited by rulers to entrench their powers.

One may conjecture that differences in religiosity arise due to differences in the type of religious affiliation.[6] For instance, Muslims are more religious than Protestants, on average. In turns out, though, that this explains only a rather small share of differences in religiosity. Bentzen (2019b) finds that differences in terms of religious denominations explain a miniscule part of differences in religiosity in a sample of nearly 500,000 individuals across the globe. This also means that theories explaining the differential emergence of Islam or Protestantism do not explain contemporary differences in religiosity (something which they do not claim to do either).

Turning to theories aiming specifically at explaining the emergence of religion, evolutionary theories dominate. One important theory states that religion evolved as a solution to large-scale cooperation problems (e.g., Norenzayan, 2013). According to this theory, beliefs in an almighty punishing god solved the problem of free-riding in pre-modern societies; God was believed to punish deviants, thus inducing cooperation. Inhabitants in societies that developed punishing gods were better able to cooperate, and thus more likely to survive and multiply. Eventually, evolution selected societies that held beliefs in punishing gods. As time went by, the invention of formal policing institutions reduced the need for God as such an institution, thus reducing the importance of religion. This theory, therefore, cannot explain why religion did *not* die out as modern institutions emerged and thus cannot explain current differences in religiosity. This is not a critique of the theory *per se*; the theory explains the emergence of religions based on moralizing so-called Big Gods — not contemporary differences in religiosity.[7]

Another influential evolutionary theory was set forth by cognitive anthropologist Pascal Boyer. Boyer (2008) takes religious ideas to be a subset of the ideas we are able to hold and argues, based on cognitive science, that ideas are more likely to attract our attention if they are

---

[6] Scholars have documented various socioeconomic differences between Protestants and Catholics or between Christians and Muslims (e.g., Andersen *et al.*, 2017; Becker and Woessmann, 2009; Weber, 1905; Rubin, 2017).

[7] Moralizing gods is one aspect of religion, preceded by thousands of years with animistic religions and spirituality. Whether Big Gods or complex societies came first is still being debated, cf. for instance Whitehouse *et al.* (2019) and Beheim *et al.* (2019).

interesting. This happens when they violate our intuitive expectations to a limited degree that still allows us to make inference. Culturally successful ideas, then, are those with a prominent counterintuitive feature that attracts our attention and at the same time have a rich inferential potential. Most religious rituals and beliefs are arguably somewhat counterintuitive and at the same time are handy explanations for the social environments in which they emerge. This theory is not meant to explain *differences* in either emergence of religion or current differences in religiosity, as it does not focus on differences across societies or individuals. Rather, it focuses on something ingrained in all societies and individuals.

The remainder of this chapter will describe and explore in more detail the theory of religious coping. We will use this theory to deepen our understanding of the emergence of religion and of differences in religiosity across contemporary societies. We are not claiming that religious coping is the only explanation. We are only claiming that it is *one* important explanation.

3. Religious Coping

The religious coping hypothesis states that individuals draw on religious beliefs and practices to understand and deal with unbearable and unpredictable situations.[8] Religion may provide comfort, it may be a way to make sense of events that are otherwise difficult to explain, or it may provide a sense of control in these situations.[9] Indeed, when asked, religious survey respondents stated that one of the main purposes of religion is to provide buffering against life stressors.[10] Examples of religious coping are seeking a closer relationship with God, praying or finding a reason for the event by attributing it to an act of God. When adversity hits in the modern world, only some of the few very religious would believe that God was directly responsible for the event. That is, most would not engage in the type of religious coping where religion provides an *explanation* for the event, though such coping was quite common in the past, as

---

[8] For example, Pargament (2001), Cohen and Wills (1985), Park *et al.* (1990) and Williams *et al.* (1991). The terminology "religious coping" is taken from the psychology literature, but other labels have been used in the literature. For instance, religious buffering, the religious comfort hypothesis and psychological social insurance.

[9] For example, Geertz (1966) and Pargament *et al.* (2000).

[10] For example, Clark (1958) and Pargament (2001).

we shall see. Instead, most people using religion for coping in the modern world would use it for comfort and support when adversity hits — much like meditation or other recreational activities.[11] However, disasters — including earthquakes — are sometimes attributed to divine retribution even in the modern world. For instance, a Gallup survey conducted in the aftermath of the great 1993 Mississippi River floods asked Americans whether the recent floods were an indication of God's judgment upon the sinful ways of the Americans. Around 18 percent answered in the affirmative (Steinberg, 2006). A more recent example of direct attribution of disaster to acts of God is evident in the title of a sermon by Pastor Robert Jeffress at an Evangelical Christian megachurch in Dallas, which asks "Is the Coronavirus a Judgement from God?" Indeed, a Pew Research Center survey from March 2020 revealed that more than half of Americans had prayed to end the coronavirus (Pew, 2020). Bentzen (2020) extends the analysis to the world and documents that half of the global population had prayed in an attempt to end the coronavirus. As we will see in Section 5, this tendency to attribute disaster to acts of God has its roots in the past, even in ancient history.

Numerous empirical studies document that individuals hit by various adverse life events, such as cancer, heart problems, death in close family, alcoholism, divorce or injury are more religious than others.[12] In addition, prayer is often chosen by hospitalized patients as a coping strategy above seeking information, going to the doctor or taking prescription drugs (Conway, 1985). This literature faces the major challenge that being hit by adverse life events is most likely correlated with unobserved characteristics (such as lifestyle), which in turn may matter for the individual's inclination to be religious.

Norenzayan and Hansen (2006) addressed the endogeneity concern in four different controlled experiments of a total of 288 participants from North America. In lack of exogenous variation in adverse life events, they exploited exogenous variation in thoughts of death. For instance, they primed half of the participants with thoughts of death by asking them questions such as "What will happen to you when you die?" After the experiments, the participants primed with thoughts of death

---

[11] Vail *et al.* (2010) argues that, compared to secular beliefs, religious beliefs are particularly useful for mitigating death anxiety as they are all encompassing, rely on concepts that are not easily disconfirmed, and promise literal immortality.

[12] See, e.g., Ano and Vasconcelles (2005) and Pargament (2001) for reviews.

were more likely to reveal beliefs in God and to rank themselves as being more religious. In the remaining experiments, they found similar effects for other supernatural beliefs. While solving the endogeneity issue, conclusions based on 288 participants — mainly students — from North America cannot necessarily be extended to the world at large. The study cannot tell us whether elderly from California or students from Pakistan would respond in the same way. Yet, the theory is that religious coping is not something peculiar to Christianity. For instance, Pargament (2001) notes that (p. 3), "While different religions envision different solutions to problems, every religion offers a way to come to terms with tragedy, suffering, and the most significant issues in life."[13] Performing lab experiments for a representative global population is rather tedious and costly.[14] Instead, one can exploit the presence of a natural experiment to obtain random variation in the extent to which individuals experienced unpredictable adverse events.

4. Natural Disasters and Religiosity Today

Natural disasters form such a natural experiment, as they are adverse shocks and most of them are quite unpredictable. As opposed to other natural disasters, such as seasonal storms, earthquakes are particularly unpredictable — and they are better measured than most other disasters. Indeed, the belief that natural disasters carried a deeper message from God was the rule rather than the exception before the Enlightenment (e.g., Hall, 1990; Van De Wetering, 1982). Later, the famous 1755 Lisbon earthquake has been compared to the Holocaust as a catastrophe that transformed European culture and philosophy.[15] Penick (1981) documented that the US states hit by massive earthquakes in 1811 and 1812 saw church membership increase

---

[13] See also Feuerbach (1957), Freud (1927) and Marx (1867) for similar statements, generalizing across all religions.

[14] Other scholars have performed similar experiments to the Norenzayan and Hansen experiment for non-Christian students (e.g., Vail *et al.*, 2012), confirming the results.

[15] See review by Ray (2004). In addition to being one of the deadliest earthquakes ever, it struck on a church holiday and destroyed many churches in Lisbon, but spared the red light district. Accordingly, many thinkers associate the earthquake with the decline in religiosity across Europe afterward. According to religious coping theory, shocks can instigate leaving God or embracing him. Empirics show that the latter is most common (e.g., Pargament, 2001).

by 50 percent in the following year, compared to an increase of only 1 percent in the remaining states. More recently, Sibley and Bulbulia (2012) found that conversion rates increased more in the Christchurch region after a large earthquake hit the region in 2011, compared to the remaining four regions of New Zealand. Other disasters may have left an imprint on religiosity. For instance, Ager *et al.* (2016) find that church membership rose in counties affected by the Mississippi river flood of 1927.

Bentzen (2019a) exploited earthquakes, tsunamis and volcanic eruptions as shocks that hit the globe at large. The remainder of this section reviews this research. While the studies reviewed thus far focus on a single country or a subset of individuals within one country, Bentzen identifies the impact of natural disasters on religiosity across the world. This enables testing of whether the religious coping hypothesis holds across all major religions, countries and socio-economic groups, on average. To do so, Bentzen uses measures of religiosity provided by the World Values Survey and European Values Study, which are surveys of a total of 500,000 individuals from 109 countries interviewed over the period 1981–2014.[16] The surveys contain multiple questions related to religiosity. The persons responsible for the surveys document that six particular measures span global religiosity (Inglehart and Norris, 2003). Bentzen conducts the analysis for these six questions, which are "How important is God in your life?," "Are you a religious person?," "How often do you attend religious services?," "Do you get comfort and strength from religion?," "Do you believe in God?," and "Do you believe in a life after death?" These questions were answered by up to a total of 396,211 individuals interviewed in up to 105 different countries.[17]

One caveat of conducting a global analysis is that different measures of religiosity most likely do not compare across different religions and countries. It may not be possible to compare the religiosity of a Muslim from Indonesia with the religiosity of an American Protestant. Instead, Bentzen compares religiosity of the American Protestant only to other

---

[16]The surveys are constructed so that they can be appended and all measures are comparable across the two surveys.

[17]The different questions were not raised in all waves and in all countries. Of the six questions, the question raised to the fewest people was "Do you believe in a life after death?" answered by 268,859 respondents in 82 different countries. The question asked to the largest number of respondents was "How often do you attend religious services?" answered by 396,211 persons in 105 different countries.

American Protestants and the Muslim Indonesian to other Muslim Indonesians. To do so, Bentzen exploits that the surveys contain information on the subnational district of the respondents to allow conducting within-country and within-religion analysis. The advantages of doing within country analysis, instead of having to compare across countries is that differences in individuals' understanding of the questions across countries is not a problem and also that unobserved country-level factors can be accounted for, such as national institutions and culture.

Bentzen (2019a) combines the survey data with data on the risk of natural disasters and data for actual earthquakes that hit the globe during the past decades.[18] In the first part of the analysis (the cross-section analysis), Bentzen finds that individuals living in districts more frequently hit by earthquakes, volcanic eruptions or tsunamis are more religious than those living in areas hit by fewer disasters. The main analysis focuses on earthquakes, as data on earthquakes is more precise than other disasters and since earthquakes are comparatively much more unpredictable.[19] Figure 1 illustrates the relation between earthquake risk and religiosity.[20,21]

---

[18] The data on earthquake risk measures the risk of being hit by an earthquake of a certain size within the next 50 years. The data on earthquake events measure the exact location of actual earthquakes of various strengths. Larger earthquakes increase religiosity more.

[19] The US Geological Survey (USGS) notes that earthquakes still cannot be predicted (https://www2.usgs.gov/faq/categories/9830/3278) and so does the study by Hough (2002). See also the following post about our ability to forecast storms and their paths, as opposed to our inability to forecast earthquakes: https://www.tripwire.com/state-of-security/risk-based-security-for-executives/risk-management/hurricanes-earthquakes-prediction-vs-forecasting-in-information-security/.

[20] In Figure 1, religiosity is measured by answers to the question "How important is God in your life?" which is the preferred measure of religiosity among the six measures, due to the much higher number of observations and the two main theoretical considerations that (a) intrinsic religiosity should be more affected than extrinsic religiosity such as churchgoing and (b) that the intensive margin (how strongly you believe) is more likely to be affected than the extensive margin (whether or not you believe). Earthquake risk is measured by 5,000 kms minus the distance to high-risk earthquake zones. Using distances to measure earthquake risk instead of the average across earthquake zones has the advantage that the mechanisms behind the relation between earthquake risk and religiosity can be disentangled, cf. Section 4.1.

[21] Compared to the figures in Bentzen (2019), Figure 1 excludes districts that are located more than 1,500 km from a high-risk earthquake zone. The rationale is that being located 100 km closer to a high-risk earthquake zone arguably does not matter much if you are

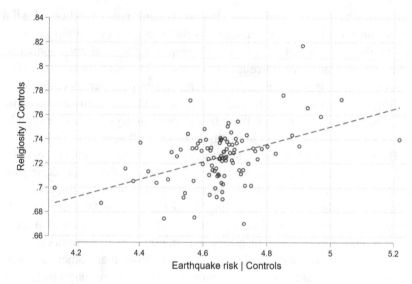

Figure 1:   Relation between Religiosity and Earthquake Risk

Notes: Binned scatterplot between religiosity measured by importance of God and earthquake risk measured by 5,000 km minus the distance to high-risk earthquake zones. The figure is based on a regression across 186,944 individuals, controlling for age, age squared, gender, marital status, absolute latitude, distance to the coast, dummies for recent earthquakes, year fixed effects, and country fixed effects. The stippled line represents this regression. The slope is significantly different from zero at the 1 percent level. The sample is restricted to regions within a 1,500 km radius of high-risk earthquake zones. Observations are binned into 100 equally sized bins.

The stippled line shows the linear regression line between the two variables, including baseline controls. The relation is clear: Individuals living in districts with higher earthquake risk are more religious.

Figure 2 illustrates that the effect is rather homogenous across the different major religions. The figure shows the impact of earthquake risk on religiosity for the world on average and for each major religious denomination separately. Religiosity increases for Christians (both Protestants and Catholics), Muslims, Hindus, and others, but is statistically indistinguishable from zero for Buddhists. The large standard errors for Hindus and Buddhists reflect that these are not well represented in the sample.[22] Thus, the analysis does not allow concluding whether the insignificance for

---

already located 1,500 km from high-risk earthquake zones. Other factors than earthquakes are more important for shaping religion in these regions.

[22] The sample for which information on the religious denomination of the respondent drops to 88,000 individuals living in 580 districts across the world. Of these, 62 districts include

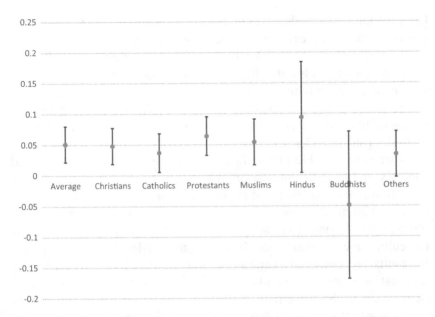

Figure 2:   Impact of Disaster Risk on Religiosity across Religious Denominations

Notes: The figure shows the parameter estimate (indicated by the dot) on earthquake risk in a regression of religiosity, accounting for country-fixed effects and a dummy equal to one if one or more earthquakes hit during the past year across 88,000 individuals in 580 districts across the world. The first parameter estimate is calculated for the full sample, the second is calculated using a sample restricted to Christians, the third is further restricted to Catholics, fourth is Protestants, fifth Muslims, sixth Hindus, seventh Buddhists, and the last estimate is estimated on a sample restricted to other religions. The vertical lines represent the 95 percent confidence intervals.

Buddhists is due to imprecise estimates caused by few Buddhists in the sample or due to Buddhists not using religion for coping. In later research, Bentzen (2020) used Google search shares for prayer to document that people from all major religions have prayed to cope with the corona crisis.[23] However, Buddhists and Hindus seem to use their religions more for celebration of religious holidays than for coping with adversity. Bentzen (2019a) further documents that earthquakes increase religiosity to the same extent on all continents, and across all income and education groups.

---

at least one respondent identifying as Hindu and 89 districts are inhabited by at least one respondent identifying as Buddhist.

[23] Again, the estimates for the rise in prayer search shares for Hindus and Buddhists are quite imprecise. The rise is only significant at the 8 percent and 17 percent level, respectively.

Thus, the impact of earthquakes on religiosity is not particular to any religious denomination, region, or socioeconomic group.

In addition to being statistically significant, the impact of earthquake risk on religiosity is also of a significant magnitude: A one standard deviation increase in earthquake risk increases religiosity by 3 percentage points. This coincides in magnitude to the fall in religiosity over the past 30 years. Put differently, the size of the effect amounts to 80 percent of the well-established gender difference in religiosity.[24] Similar results obtain for other unpredictable major disasters such as volcanic eruptions and tsunamis, and for different measures of earthquake risk (Bentzen, 2019a).

A first-order concern is that important factors have been left out of the analysis, biasing the results. The main analysis includes country-fixed effects, which means that country-level characteristics such as institutions and culture are accounted for. However, district-level factors may bias the results. Hypothetically, earthquakes may be more likely to occur along the coast, as some tectonic plate boundaries are close to the coast (e.g., Figure 4).[25] At the same time, religiosity may differ across individuals living close to the coast and those living inland for other reasons than coping. In that case, omitting distance to the coast in the regression would create a spurious relation between earthquakes and religiosity. To account for these omitted factors, Bentzen does two things: First, she adds relevant controls to the analysis and next she exploits the time-varying feature of the data, which enables inclusion of district-fixed effects. Regarding the former, the analysis includes a control for distance to the coast, country fixed effects, absolute latitude, recent actual earthquakes, population density, light intensity, the share of arable land, average temperature, average and variance of precipitation, district area and a dummy equal to one if the district is often hit by earthquakes, as well as individual-level confounders, such as age, gender, marital status, income, education, employment status and various measures of other cultural values.

[24] It is a well-known finding that women are more religious than men (e.g., Miller and Hoffmann, 1995).

[25] To simplify, collisional/transpressional plate-tectonic boundaries are sufficiently close to coastlines to produce related earthquake damage there, if one plate margin consists of oceanic crust and the other consists of continental (including island-arc) crust. This is the case in a significant share of the earth's surface (e.g., Figure 4), particularly the western coasts of the Americas, some shores of the Mediterranean and Black Seas, those parts of eastern shores of Asia where island arcs face Pacific plates, etc.

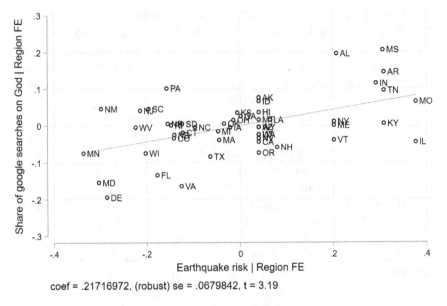

coef = .21716972, (robust) se = .0679842, t = 3.19

Figure 3: Earthquake Risk and Google Searches for Religious Terms

Notes: The figure documents the relation between earthquake risk (measured by 5,000 km minus the distance to high-risk earthquake zones) and religiosity measured by Google searches for God as a share of all Google searches. The line represents the regression line across 50 US states, including region-fixed effects for the four major US regions. The slope is significantly different from zero at the 1 percent level.

Bentzen proceeds to show that the results are not particular to the survey-based measures of religiosity. Google searches for religious terms are also higher in areas with higher earthquake risk, cf., Figure 3. This analysis is conducted across US states, where internet penetration is equally high. The share of Google searches for God, Jesus, Pray and Bible is higher in states with higher earthquake risk, even accounting for region fixed effects, income, distance to the ocean and absolute latitude.

While the analysis thus far has documented that religiosity is higher in areas where earthquakes more often hit, the next part of the analysis identifies the effect on religiosity of an actual earthquake. Unfortunately, the same individuals are not followed over time. Instead, Bentzen exploits that a third of the respondents are interviewed in subnational districts that were interviewed more than once. This enables constructing a so-called synthetic panel, where the districts are the panel dimension. In a difference-in-difference analysis, Bentzen finds that district-level religiosity increases when an earthquake hit in between the years of interview, in keeping with the religious coping hypothesis. In particular, the religious become more religious, whereas those without a religion do not start believing.[26] Furthermore, an earthquake in a district that is otherwise rarely hit increases religiosity more than an earthquake in a district that is often hit. This is consistent with the theory that religion is used mainly to cope with unpredictable events, while people tend to use problem-focused coping to cope with more foreseeable stressful events, such as an approaching job interview.[27] Religion belongs to emotion-focused coping that deals with the emotional distress caused by a situation, while problem-focused coping aims at altering the situation more actively.

Average religiosity increases by 7.6 percentage points when an earthquake hits. This is twice as much as the fall in global religiosity over the past 30 years. Put differently, the rise amounts to increasing religiosity from the level in the median district to the level in the district at the 80th percentile. As expected, this rise in religiosity diminishes after a while, but a residual remains, which is passed on through generations. This persistent impact is investigated in the fourth part of the analysis, which identifies whether higher religiosity is transmitted across generations. This transmission is theoretically plausible: In a model of cultural transmission, parents will choose to transmit a particular cultural trait to their children if this grants utility to either parents or children (e.g., Bisin and Verdier, 2001). Empirical evidence suggests that religiosity may be such a trait: Religion is likely to improve mental health, life satisfaction, abilities to cope with adverse life events and deter deviant behavior.[28] Bentzen (2019a) investigates this empirically by combining data on earthquake risk with a dataset containing information on children of migrants currently living in Europe, but whose parents came from various countries across the globe.[29] The data reveal that children of immigrants whose

---

[26] The result is robust to adding country-by-year fixed effects, individual and district level controls, and consistent with the idea that nothing correlated with religiosity is causing the earthquakes, future earthquakes have no impact on current levels of religiosity.

[27] Lazarus and Folkman (1984), Park *et al.* (1990), Norris and Inglehart (2011) and Sosis (2008).

[28] For instance Miller *et al.* (2014), Clark and Lelkes (2005) and Lehrer (2004). See also reviews by Smith *et al.* (2000) and Pargament (2001).

[29] This analysis is based on the European Social Survey. The methodology used is termed epidemiological approach by Fernandez (2011).

parents came from countries with high earthquake risk are more religious than those from low earthquake risk areas, independent of actual earthquake risk and level of religiosity in their current country of residence. It seems that living in high-earthquake risk areas instigates a culture of religiosity that is passed on to future generations like many other cultural values.

4.1 *The proposed mechanism*

Identifying an effect of earthquakes on religiosity does not confirm the religious coping hypothesis in itself. Alternative explanations for why religiosity increases in the face of disasters could potentially be that people go to church for material aid, that people move in the face of disasters, or that disasters also affect development or other cultural values, in turn affecting religiosity. Bentzen (2019a) documents that the main reason for the impact of disasters on religiosity is religious coping.

To disentangle these alternative explanations from the religious coping hypothesis, Bentzen (2019a) sets up testable predictions for the religious coping hypothesis versus alternative explanations. First, religious coping involves a response to the psychological distress, while most of the alternative explanations involve a response to the physical losses caused by disaster. To substantiate that the rise in religiosity reflects a response to the psychological damaged caused by disaster, Bentzen excludes districts that are directly hit by earthquakes from the analysis.[30] What is left in the analysis are districts that are not physically hit, but that neighbor the damaged districts. The results are unchanged: Religiosity rises more in districts located close to districts that are hit, compared to districts located further away. The rationale is that people in surrounding areas may have friends and family members in these areas and may therefore suffer psychologically without suffering material losses. This indicates that the explanation has to involve psychological losses rather than material losses.

Furthermore, if the effect is simply driven by people going to church for material needs, church going should rise when an earthquake hits. On

---

[30] When using distances to high-risk zones as the main measure of earthquake risk, the main variation comes from *outside* the regions that are most severely hit. This enables removing the districts that are hit, and thus enables discounting alternative explanations based on the physical damage caused by earthquakes.

the other hand, the literature on religious coping finds that people mainly use their intrinsic religiosity (ones' personal relation to God) to cope with adversity, and to a lesser extent their extrinsic religiosity (going to church).[31] Likewise, depressed individuals tend to prefer solitude to socializing as a coping strategy. Similarly, Bentzen's results reveal that only intrinsic religiosity increases in response to a recent earthquake, while church going is not affected. In addition, Google searches for God, Jesus, Bible and Pray are higher in states with high earthquake risk, while searches for Church are not.

If the results had reflected that religion is used for obtaining material needs from the church, one would expect other disasters to have similar effects on religiosity, as long as they pose the same material losses. The degree of predictability of the disaster should not matter much in such responses. On the other hand, the religious coping hypothesis predicts that individuals use religion more when faced with adverse *unpredictable* events versus predictable ones (e.g., Norris and Inglehart, 2011; Sosis, 2008; Park *et al.*, 1990). That is, foreseeable events, such as an approaching feared exam or even an approaching devastating storm, are more likely to ignite problem-focused coping, which involves altering the source of the stress.[32] Thus, the religious coping hypothesis predicts larger effects for unpredictable disasters, while the "physical insurance" hypothesis predicts similar effects as long as material losses are similar. Major geophysical and

---

[31] For example, Johnson and Spilka (1991), review by Pargament (2001). Koenig *et al.* (1988) found that the most frequently mentioned coping strategies among 100 older adults dealing with three stressful events were faith in God, prayer and gaining strength from God. Social church-related activities were less commonly noted. Similarly, a medical study by Miller *et al.* (2014) found that individuals for whom religion is more important in their lives experienced reduced depression risk (measured by cortical thickness), while frequency of church attendance was not associated with thickness of the cortices.

[32] See also Mattlin *et al.* (1990) on how practical everyday problems are less likely to trigger religious coping compared to large bad events. Skinner (1948) found that something similar to this reaction to unpredictability extends into the animal world. He found that pigeons subjected to an unpredictable feeding schedule were more likely to develop inexplicable behavior, compared to the birds not subject to unpredictability. Since Skinner's pioneering work, various studies have documented how children and adults in analogous unpredictable experimental conditions quickly generate novel superstitious practices (e.g., Ono, 1987). While these types of superstitious behavior are not necessarily directly comparable to religiosity, the studies are somewhat informative to the religious coping literature.

meteorological disasters can be grouped in terms of predictability. For instance, meteorologists have a much easier time predicting storms than seismologists have in predicting earthquakes. Also, earthquakes can be grouped into more or less surprising ones based on recurrence frequency, where the latter hit areas frequently hit in general. Consistent with the religious coping literature, Bentzen finds that surprising disasters increase religiosity more than less surprising ones for equal amount of damage. For instance, elevated risk of earthquakes, tsunamis and volcanic eruptions increase religiosity, while storm risk does not. Storms result in comparable material and personal losses, and thus should instigate the same effect on religiosity if the explanation was physical insurance. In contrast, earthquakes in areas frequently hit by earthquakes affect religiosity less than earthquakes in areas otherwise rarely hit. Thus, this part of the analysis also supports religious coping as the main explanation.

In addition, if religion is a matter of physical needs, one would expect that the effect is larger for poorer individuals, since they are more likely to be in need for material support. On the contrary, both poor and rich can be in need for stress relief, and income should not matter for how much earthquakes increase religiosity. The data support the latter relation.

Turning to another alternative explanation, one could conjecture that the results are caused by atheists moving out in the face of disaster. In that case, one would not expect that the short-term effect on religiosity abates with time. Explaining this tendency with population movements would mean that atheists move out in the immediate aftermath of the earthquake, but then choose to move into the district again after 6–12 years, only to move out again when the next earthquake hits, an unlikely scenario. On the other hand, the fall in religiosity after a while is reconcilable with the idea that religion provides stress relief, reducing the need for religion after a while.

If the effect is purely due to a direct impact on income, the effect should vanish or at least fall drastically when accounting for development. This proved not to be the case: The impact is unchanged when accounting for personal or regional income or education levels. Last, if religiosity is just part of the characteristics of a different type of people emerging in earthquake areas, the effect should fall when controlling for cultural characteristics, such as trust, independence, thriftiness or preferences for hard work. This is also not the case.

To sum up, the data do not support the alternative explanations involving physical insurance, direct economic loss, migration/selection, or a special culture evolving in high-risk areas. Nevertheless, we cannot rule out that each set of results is partly due to some of these explanations. However, the only explanation that can explain all results across all four analyzes (cross-section, Google searches, difference-in-difference analysis, and cross-generational analysis) is religious coping.

5. Earthquakes and Religion in History

If earthquakes have strengthened religious beliefs in the contemporary world, it would certainly seem plausible that it has done so in the past. In this section, we show that strong religious responses to earthquakes have been characteristic of our past, taking forms that commonly changed religions and thereby changed the cultures harboring them. Our presentation is in two parts: First, we show that the origination of new religions through the millennia tends to occur where earthquakes are most severe and frequent. Of course, other factors may correlate both with seismic activity and religion. Therefore, we proceed to the second part to describe links between individual earthquakes in historical eras and their religious responses.

While the main type of religious coping today probably consists of religion providing comfort and support, the evidence that we present from the past is based in large part on attributing disasters to God's anger. Attributions of an earthquake to a punishing God not only provides a way to understand the disaster but it is also a potential way to perceive control of future earthquakes through more virtuous/religious behavior. Of course, that might also be more comforting and, in that sense, the functions of comfort, meaning-making and control become intermingled. All of these types of religious coping were most likely at play in our past, but our evidence emphasizes attributing earthquakes to messages from God. Again, we do not claim that earthquakes (and other disasters) are the sole explanation for the emergence of religion. But we do claim that they are one explanation.

5.1 *The origination of complex religions*

The locales of origination of new complex religions through history could be a clue to perceived inadequacy of preceding simpler religions by their cultures. Here we compare the origination sites of today's most populous religions to seismic activity of those sites via their plate-tectonic

Table 1:   Plate Tectonic Positions of World Religions' Originating Sites

Rank and Name	Adherents (Million)	Originating Site	Distance to Boundary (km)	Plate Boundary
1. Christian	2400	Jordan Valley	0	Af-Ar
2. Muslim	1800	Mecca	100	Af-Ar
3. Hindu	1150	Hastinapura[a]	100	In-Ea
4. Buddhist	521	Kushinagar[b]	110	In-Ea
5. Tao/Confucian	394	Zhou[c]	300	—
6. Sikh	30	Kartarpur	0	In-Ea
7. Judaism	14.4	Jordan Valley	0	Af-Ar
8. Bahai	7	Acre/Haifa	60	Af-Ar
9. Jain	4.2	Patna	160	In-Ea
10. Shinto	4.0	Kyoto	500	PO-Ea
11. Cao Dai	4.0	Tay Ninh	1,300	In-Ea

Notes: Omitted from the Wikipedia list are irreligious, ethnic/indigenous, African indigenous, spiritism and neopagan, i.e., religious categories that are composite and have no single origin. Similarly, Zorastrianism is omitted from calculations due to lack of definite origination site. Plate boundaries Af indicate African plate boundary; Ar – Arabian; In – Indo-Australian; Ea – Eurasian; PO – Philippine and Okhotsk plates.
[a] Hastinapura is taken for the coalescence of the religious traditions that became Vedic Hinduism.
[b] Bodh Gaya is the traditional inspiration site but most sites pertinent to origination such as Kushinagar are about 110 km away.
[c] Confucianism and other traditional Chinese religions are thought to have been codified in Zhou times in their capital. The distance listed is that to the Altyn Tagh-Qinling fault system, a proto-plate boundary as discussed in Force (2015). Otherwise, the listed distance would be about 1,500 km.

positions. Table 1 compares today's religions numbering adherents over a million (from Wikipedia 2018) with the tectonic environments of the originating sites for each, listed as distance to the nearest plate-tectonic boundary, cf. Figure 4.

Taking an unweighted arithmetic average of site-distances from Table 1 gives 239 km, a remarkably small average distance on a globe with thousands of kilometers of distance available for founding religions. Indeed these originating sites form a cluster around tectonic boundaries that represent only 5.6 percent of the available land in the eastern hemisphere alone.[33] We can calculate the chance that this distribution is

[33] Even if the distance for Confucian/Tao had been listed as 1,500 km, the average would still be only 251 km.

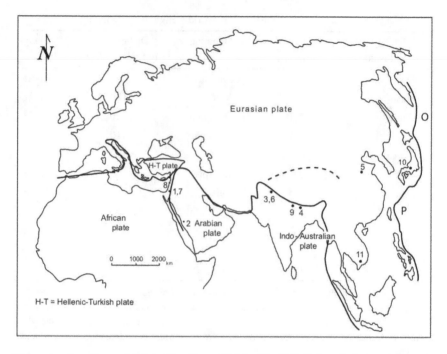

Figure 4:   Locations of Originating Sites of Major World Religions Relative to Tectonic Plate Boundaries

Notes: The numbers refer to the religions in Table 1. The tectonic boundaries are marked by heavy lines. P and O are Philippine and Okhotsk plates, respectively. Dashed line is the Altyn Tagh-Qinling fault system.

random. This probability would be 0.056^{11} or 1.7×10^{-14} (one in several trillion). So regardless of the causes, there is a strong spatial association of active plate tectonic boundaries with religious origination.

Perusing Table 1 also gives one the impression that religions with the most adherents originated closest to tectonic boundaries. An average weighted by number of adherents is called for. Dividing the product of adherents and distance by the number of religions gives 75.7 km for the average adherent-distance for originating sites, a much smaller distance confirming that religions with the most adherents tended to originate closest to plate-tectonic boundaries. It is clear from Table 1 and Figure 4 that the northern margin of the Indian plate and the western margin of the Arabian plate were the locus of origination of disproportionately many religions, and those with many adherents.

The observation connecting religious origination sites with plate-tectonic environment is a simple one,[34] which may have complex causes. For instance, the major religions also emerged in areas that became the origin of early complex societies. Perhaps complex societies first emerged in these areas and then later came the major religions.[35] In that case, the reason for the emergence of religion is not religious coping, but rather some link involving complex societies, which themselves tend to follow tectonic boundaries (Force and McFadgen, 2010). This explanation, though, would have to explain why complex societies emerged close to tectonic boundaries. While we cannot rule out such alternative explanations in this dataset, we turn to another source of information that documents a direct link between earthquakes and religion in our past.

In particular, our goal is to identify whether the spatial association with earthquakes is with religion rather than some other cultural variable that makes the apparent relation with religion indirect. Previous research has shown a relation between seismicity and cultural character in the ancient world (Force and McFadgen, 2010; Force, 2015) and through history (e.g., deBoer and Sanders, 2005; Hough and Bilham, 2006; Nur and Burgess, 2008; Robinson, 2016).[36] The question of whether physical factors — other than tectonic activity — explain the ancient cultural distribution has been addressed most systematically by Force (2015). Force included separate analyzes of climate, soils, rivers, transportation potential, mineral resources, and topography. He found that cultural response was required to produce the observed distributions for all but one factor, potable water especially fault-related springs. The next step calls for a demonstration that religious factors predominate among cultural factors in response to earthquakes.

5.2 Case histories of religious responses to earthquakes through history

Seismic events have occurred all through human history, but human responses of most have gone unrecorded. We have found 52 cases for

---

[34] Originating by Henry Spall of the US Geological Survey in the 1980s.

[35] Indeed, this is what Whitehouse *et al.* (2019) documented. However, Beheim *et al.* (2019) document the reverse when correcting the data.

[36] These all enter the Force (2020) list.

which description of cultural and religious response to earthquakes has been sufficient to distinguish religious from non-religious responses (described in Force, 2020). This of course is a small fraction of recorded earthquakes for which only deaths and damage to palaces and religious structures appear in the records (e.g., Ambraseys, 2009). Our analysis requires response descriptions by historians/journalists, of which there are relatively few. Our 52 earthquakes were mostly quite damaging, but our sample necessarily was by description rather than earthquake magnitude. The analysis here is a compilation of case studies and provides evidence that religious responses are most common but shows a variety in character that varies among time periods, especially in attribution of earthquakes to acts of God.

The listed earthquakes are historic, ranging in age from 464 BC to AD 2011. Most presented earthquakes were very destructive, but in a few cases modest earthquakes produced notable responses. The lists show that religious responses to earthquakes outnumber other cultural responses by 35 to 11. Six additional responses are composite; in these, religious reactions are immediate, but precede other responses. The ratio of religious to other cultural responses decreases somewhat into the modern era, perhaps because more cultural avenues became available.

Religious responses to earthquakes have included proclamation of divine appearances, warnings and retribution (sometimes with priestly manipulation), of change to religious observance (sometimes leading to different subsistence and military strategies), and of religion-based increase of nationalism. The types of non-religious responses include civic reorganization, revolution and improved earthquake preparation (Force, 2020).

It should be noted parenthetically here that sudden volcanic events, a somewhat similar type of tectonic occurrence, produces somewhat similar cultural responses (e.g., Balmuth, 2005; Grattan and Torrence, 2007). The most nearly parallel compilation to ours lists a total of 41 religious responses to volcanic events and 11 non-religious responses, the latter only occurring post-1900 (Chester and Duncan, 2007, 2009). Details of the volcanic responses differ; for example, veneration of the volcano can play a part, in contrast to an apparent lack of veneration for earthquakes themselves.

In the following, we provide some examples of religious, non-religious, and composite responses to earthquakes. First, ancient Hellenic and Judaic literature records cultural and religious responses to earthquakes. The Hellenic responses changed over time from religious as recorded in poetry and drama, to non-religious as recorded in historical and philosophical works, with the latter predominating as of about 500 BC. In ancient Judaic literature, the treatment of earthquakes was never anything but religious. Later examples of religious responses vary; in the western world earthquakes were commonly a consequence of sin as preached by John Wesley in England, the Mathers in New England, and Mary Baker Eddy in San Francisco over a period of several hundred years (de Boer and Sanders, 2004; Rozario, 2007; Winchester, 2006). An illustrative example of religious response is that from the New Madrid, Missouri earthquakes of 1811–1812 (de Boer and Sanders, 2004), which saw nearby church membership increase much more than in farther states (Penick, 1981). Religious responses in Japan to earthquakes in AD 1257, 1855, and 1923, involved the Lotus sect, religious imagery of earthquakes, and increased Shinto militarism respectively (de Boer and Sanders, 2004; Robinson, 2016).

Perhaps the most consequential religious response to earthquakes described in Force (2020) is that in the ancient Judaic world, exemplified by response to an earthquake of 760–750 BC known archaeologically (Dever, 1992). This earthquake was "predicted" in nebulous terms by prophet Amos (Amos 1:1), who also proclaimed that God would appear at such times. These appearances coupled earthquakes with God's retribution for hundreds of years (Freedman and Welch, 1994) and with earthquakes being used as a threat by seven subsequent prophets (Isaiah, Jeremiah, Ezekiel, Joel, Nahum, Haggai, and Zechariah). The Christian New Testament continues this treatment of earthquakes, resulting in a linkage of earthquakes as divine punishment that is occasionally invoked throughout the Judeo-Christian world (reviewed by Chester and Duncan, 2009). Dread of earthquakes and their supposed divine retribution set a pattern of "god-fearing" religion in modern Western culture, a pattern that now extends well beyond earthquakes.

Lisbon in 1755 gives us a glimpse of religious and other cultural responses unfolding sequentially. A severe earthquake offshore shook much of western Europe, and was particularly damaging in Lisbon, which also suffered a related tsunami. Jesuit fathers attributed the earthquake to retribution for the sinful behavior of the citizens, and redoubled the Inquisition. The Marquis of Pombal, however, acquired enough power to rebuild the city — and banish the Jesuits from Portuguese possessions. This earthquake also had long-term philosophical repercussions, beginning with Voltaire, his Candide being an example (e.g., de Boer and Sanders, 2004; Robinson, 2016).

Even in the modern world, religious responses to earthquakes may be the more immediate (Force, 2020). The Managua earthquake of 1972 prompted general priestly attribution to sinful behavior, but catalyzed the lengthy Sandinista revolt once this stage passed. Four other composite responses provide insight into sequential composite responses that may actually be the norm. These encompass an immediate somewhat instinctive religious response, commonly orchestrated and/or manipulated by a priestly class, followed by longer-term cultural responses that may themselves be religious (such as reform) or quasi-religious (such as building a better temple). Other long-term responses may be civic, political, artistic, and/or scientific, but such cultural changes have been catalyzed and accelerated by earthquakes. In this way, earthquakes have forced the pace of cultural change via religious pathways.

An interesting example of non-religious responses from antiquity comes from Sparta in Greece, where the consequences of an earthquake in ca. 464 BC were described by classical authors. It permitted the revolt of serfs captured in Sparta's wars, leading eventually to the Peloponnesian wars (reviewed, e.g., by de Boer and Sanders, 2004). In the modern world an example comes from Mexico City in 1985, where the entrenched bureaucracy of the ruling party was unable to cope with recovery after an earthquake. A coalition of citizens formed a new alignment to deal with damage and rebuilding, eventually becoming a political party (Davis, 2005).

These 52 examples show that direct and immediate religious responses to earthquakes are characteristic. These may initiate religious reform or even new religions. Such religious responses commonly precede other cultural development.

To sum up, ancient origination sites of major religions preferentially cluster around areas of greater seismic activity, providing a suggestion of a link to seismicity from earliest religious histories. Recorded histories from antiquity to the present era show that religious responses to earthquakes far outnumber those that are non-religious; some responses are sequential, with religious response being more immediate versus more long-term non-religious ones. The religious responses include religious reform, consistent with the distribution of religious origination. Prior to an understanding of natural causes of earthquakes, religious responses included fear of God's causing them — a response occasionally seen even today.

6. Conclusion

Why did religion emerge in our distant past? Why has it not dwindled as societies modernized? And why are some societies more religious than others today? These questions have posed major puzzles within the social science. We point to religious coping as one explanation: People used religion as a way of explaining matters that were otherwise difficult to comprehend and as a way of obtaining stress relief. The role of religion as a coping tool may have led to the emergence of religion, and may also explain why religion has not vanished with modern science and why some societies are more religious than others: They may have a larger demand for religious coping.

We provide support for this explanation using three types of data. First, earthquakes, tsunamis and volcanic eruptions have increased religiosity within all of the major religions, on all continents, and for individuals at all levels of income and education. The reason can be pinned down to being psychological rather than material. Second, the major religions of the world emerged in an unusually tight band near fault lines associated with plate-tectonic boundaries. Third, the majority of cultural responses to past earthquakes have been religious. This indicates that disasters — and earthquakes in particular — have instigated people to use their existing religion or even invent new religions throughout human history. This understanding of the causes of religion may later help understand its consequences for various socioeconomic confounders.

Acknowledgment

Bentzen is the main person responsible for Sections 2–4, while Force is the main person responsible for Section 5. We thank Kenneth I. Pargament and Ara Norenzayan for comments on this chapter.

References

Ager, P., Hansen, C. W. and Loenstrup, L. (2016). "Church Membership and Social Insurance: Evidence from the American South," *University of Southern Denmark Discussion Papers on Business and Economics No. 7/2016.*

Ambraseys, N. (2009). *Earthquakes in the Mediterranean and Middle East: A Multidisciplinary Study of Seismicity up to 1900.* Cambridge: Cambridge University Press.

Andersen, T. B., Bentzen, J., Dalgaard, C.-J. and Sharp, P. (2017). "Pre-Reformation Roots of the Protestant Ethic," *The Economic Journal*, 127(604) 1756–1793.

Ano, G. G. and Vasconcelles, E. B. (2005). "Religious Coping and Psychological Adjustment to Stress: A Meta-Analysis," *Journal of Clinical Psychology*, 61(4), 461–480.

Azzi, C. and Ehrenberg, R. (1975). "Household Allocation of Time and Church Attendance," *Journal of Political Economy*, 83(1), 27–56.

Balmuth, M. S., Chester, D. K. and Johnston, P. A. (2005). *Cultural Responses to the Volcanic Landscape*, Boston, MA: Archaeological Institute of America.

Becker, S. O., Nagler, M. and Woessmann, L. (2017). "Education and Religious Participation: City-level Evidence from Germany's Secularization Period 1890–1930," *Journal of Economic Growth*, 22(3), 273–311.

Becker, S. O. and Woessmann, L. (2009). "Was Weber Wrong? A Human Capital Theory of Protestant Economic History," *The Quarterly Journal of Economics*, 124(2), 531–596.

Beheim, B., Quentin A., Bulbulia, J., Gervais, W. M., Gray, R., Henrich, J., Lang, M. *et al.* (2019). "Treatment of Missing Data Determines Conclusions Regarding Moralizing Gods," PsyArXiv, May 2.

Belloc, M., Drago, F. and Galbiati, R. (2016). "Earthquakes, Religion, and Transition to Self-Government in Italian Cities," *The Quarterly Journal of Economics*, 131(4), 1875–1926.

Bentzen, J. S. (2019a). "Acts of God? Religiosity and Natural Disasters Across Subnational World Districts," *The Economic Journal*, 129(622), 2295–2321.

Bentzen, J. S. (2019b). "Why are Some Societies More Religious Than Others?" in *Advances in the Economics of Religion*, J.-P. Carvalho, J. Rubin and S. Iyer (eds.). London: Palgrave, International Economics Association.

Bentzen, J. S. (2020). "In Crisis, We Pray: Religiosity and the COVID-19 Pandemic," COVID Economics, Centre for Economic Policy Research Press issue 20, May 20, 52–108.

Bentzen, J. S. and Gokmen, G. (forthcoming). "The Power of Religion," *Journal of Economic Growth*.

Bentzen, J. S. and Sperling, L. L. (2020). "God Politics: Religion, Attitudes, and Outcomes," CEPR Discussion Paper DP14380.

Bisin, A. and Verdier, T. (2001). "The Economics of Cultural Transmission and the Dynamics of Preferences," *Journal of Economic Theory*, 97(2), 298–319.

Boyer, P. (2008). *Religion Explained*. London: Random House.

Brown, D. E. (1991). *Human Universals*. Philadelphia: Temple University Press.

Bryan, G. T., Choi, J. J. and Karlan, D. (2020). "Randomizing Religion: The Impact of Protestant Evangelism on Economic Outcomes," *The Quarterly Journal of Economics*, 1(88), 293–380.

Campante, F. and Yanagizawa-Drott, D. (2015). "Does Religion Affect Economic Growth and Happiness? Evidence from Ramadan," *The Quarterly Journal of Economics*, 130(2), 615–658.

Chaney, E. (2013). "Revolt on the Nile: Economic Shocks, Religion, and Political Power," *Econometrica*, 81(5), 2033–2053.

Chester, D. K. and Duncan, A. M. (2007). "Geomythology, Theodicy, and the Continuing Relevance of Religious Worldviews in Response to Volcanic Eruptions," in *Living under the Shadow*, J. Grattan and R. Torrence (eds.), pp. 203–224. Walnut Creek (CA): Left Coast Press.

Chester, D. K. and Duncan, A. M. (2009). "The Bible, Theodicy, and Christian Responses to Historic and Contemporary Earthquakes and Volcanic Eruptions," *Environmental Hazards*, 8, 304–332.

Clark, A. and Lelkes, O. (2005). "Deliver Us from Evil: Religion as Insurance," *Papers on Economics of Religion*, 603, 1–36.

Clark, W. H. (1958). "How Do Social Scientists Define Religion?" *The Journal of Social Psychology*, 47(1), 143–147.

Cohen, S. and Wills, T. A. (1985). "Stress, Social Support, and the Buffering Hypothesis," *Psychological Bulletin*, 98(2), 310–357.

Conway, K. (1985). "Coping with the Stress of Medical Problems among Black and White Elderly," *The International Journal of Aging and Human Development*, 21(1), 39–48.

Davis, D. E. (2005). "Reverberations: Mexico City's 1985 Earthquake and Transformation of the Capitol," in *The Resilient City*, L. J. Vale and T. J. Campanella (eds.), pp. 255–280. Oxford: Oxford University Press.

de Boer, J. Z. and Sanders, D. T. (2004). *Earthquakes in Human History: The Far-Reaching Effects of Seismic Disruptions*, Princeton, Oxford: Princeton University Press.

Dever, W. G. (1992). "A Case-Study in Biblical Archaeology — The Earthquake of ca. 760 BCE," *Eretz-Israel*, 23, 27–35.

Djupe, P. and Calfano, B. (2013). *God Talk: Experimenting with the Religious Causes of Public Opinion.* Philadelphia: Temple University Press.

Fernandez, R. (2011). *Does Culture Matter?* The Netherlands: North-Holland.

Feuerbach, L. (1957). *The Essence of Christianity.* New York: Barnes & Noble Publishing.

Finke, R. and Stark, R. (2005). *The Churching of America, 1776–2005: Winners and Losers in Our Religious Economy.* New Brunswick: Rutgers University Press.

Force, E. R. (2015). *Impact of Tectonic Activity on Ancient Civilizations: Recurrent Shakeups, Tenacity, Resilience, and Change.* Lanham, MD: Lexington Books.

Force, E. R. (2018). "Religious Paths between Seismic Activity and Cultural Evolution," Geological Society of America, Phoenix Annual Meeting Abstracts.

Force, E. R. (2020). Supplementary information for the chapter "Did Seismic Activity Lead to the Rise of Religion?" (J. S. Bentzen and E. R. Force, *Handbook on Economics and Religion*), https://works.bepress.com/eric_force/19/.

Force, E. R. and McFadgen, B. G. (2010). "Tectonic Environments of Ancient Civilizations: Opportunities of Archaeoseismological and Anthropological Studies," *Geological Society of America Special Paper*, 471, 21–28.

Freedman, D. N. and Welch, A. (1994). "Amos's Earthquake and Israelite Prophesy, in Scripture and Other Artifacts," in *Scripture and Other Artifacts*, M. D. Coogan, J. C. Exum and L. E. Stager (eds.). Louisville: Westminster and John Knox Press.

Freud, S. (1927). *The Future of an Illusion*. Ontario: Broadview Press.

Geertz, C. (1966). "Religion as a Cultural System," in *The Interpretation of Cultures: Selected Essays*, M. Banton, (ed.). London: Tavistock.

Grattan, J. and Torrence R. (2007). *Living Under the Shadow — The Cultural Impacts of Volcanic Eruptions*. Walnut Creek, CA: Left Coast Press.

Gruber, J. and Hungerman, D. M. (2008). "The Church Versus the Mall: What Happens When Religion Faces Increased Secular Competition?" *The Quarterly Journal of Economics*, 123(2), 831–862.

Guiso, L., Sapienza, P. and Zingales, L. (2003). "People's Opium? Religion and Economic Attitudes," *Journal of Monetary Economics*, 50(1), 225–282.

Hall, D. D. (1990). *Worlds of Wonder, Days of Judgment: Popular Religious Belief in Early New England*. Harvard: Harvard University Press.

Hertzke, A. D., Olson, L. R., Den, D., Kevin, R. and Fowler, R. B. (2018). *Religion and Politics in America: Faith, Culture, and Strategic Choices*. London: Routledge.

Hough, S. E. (2002). *Earthshaking Science: What We Know (And Don't Know) about Earthquakes*. Princeton: Princeton University Press.

Hough, S. E. and Bilham, R. G. (2006). *After the Earth Quakes: Elastic Rebound on an Urban Planet*. New York: Oxford University Press.

Hungerman, D. M. (2005). "Are Church and State Substitutes? Evidence from the 1996 Welfare Reform," *Journal of Public Economics*, 89(11), 2245–2267.

Hungerman, D. M. (2010). "Rethinking the Study of Religious Markets," in *The Oxford Handbook of the Economics of Religion*, R. M. McCleary, (ed.). pp. 257–275. Oxford: Oxford University Press.

Jelen, T. G. (2006). "Religion and Politics in the United States: Persistence, Limitations and the Prophetic Voice," *Social Compass*, 53(3), 329–343.

Iannaccone, L. R. (1998). "Introduction to the Economics of Religion," *Journal of Economic Literature*, 36(3), 1465–1495.

Inglehart, R. and Norris, P. (2003). *Rising Tide: Gender Equality and Cultural Change around the World*. Cambridge: Cambridge University Press.

Iyer, S. (2016). "The New Economics of Religion," *Journal of Economic Literature*, 54(2), 395–441.

Johnson, S. C. and Spilka, B. (1991). "Coping with Breast Cancer: The Roles of Clergy and Faith," *Journal of Religion and Health*, 30(1), 21–33.

Kimball, M. S., Mitchell, C. M., Thornton, A. D. and Young-Demarco, L. C. (2009). "Empirics on the Origins of Preferences: The Case of College Major and Religiosity," Tech. Rept. *National Bureau of Economic Research*.

Koenig, H. G., George, L. K. and Siegler, I. C. (1988). "The Use of Religion and Other Emotion-Regulating Coping Strategies among Older Adults," *The Gerontologist*, 28(3), 303–310.

Kuran, T. (2012). *The Long Divergence: How Islamic Law Held Back the Middle East*. Princeton: Princeton University Press.

Lazarus, R. S. and Folkman, S. (1984). *Stress, Appraisal, and Coping*. Berlin: Springer Publishing Company.

Lehrer, E. L. (2004). "Religion as a Determinant of Economic and Demographic Behavior in the United States," *Population and Development Review*, 30(4), 707–726.

Marx, K. (1844). "Contribution to the Critique of Hegel's Philosophy of Right," *Deutsch-Französische Jahrbücher*, 7(10), 261–271.

Marx, K. (1867). *Capital: A Critique of Political Economy*. London: The Penguin Group.

Mattlin, J. A., Wethington, E. and Kessler, R. C. (1990). "Situational Determinants of Coping and Coping Effectiveness," *Journal of Health and Social Behavior*, 31(1), 103–122.

McCleary, R. M. and Barro, R. J. (2006). "Religion and Economy," *The Journal of Economic Perspectives*, 20(2), 49–72.

Miller, A. S. and Hoffmann, J. P. (1995). "Risk and Religion: An Explanation of Gender Differences in Religiosity," *Journal for the Scientific Study of Religion*, 34(1), 63–75.

Miller, L., Bansal, R., Wickramaratne, P., Hao, X., Tenke, C. E., Weissman, M. M. and Peterson, B. S. (2014). "Neuroanatomical Correlates of Religiosity and Spirituality: A Study in Adults at High and Low Familial Risk for Depression," *JAMA Psychiatry*, 71(2), 128–135.

Murdock, G. P. (1965). *Culture and Society: Twenty-Four Essays*. Pittsburg: University of Pittsburgh Press.

Norenzayan, A. and Hansen, I. G. (2006). "Belief in Supernatural Agents in the Face of Death," *Personality and Social Psychology Bulletin*, 32(2), 174–187.

Norenzayan, A. (2013). *Big Gods: How Religion Transformed Cooperation and Conflict*. Princeton: Princeton University Press.

Norris, P. and Inglehart, R. (2011). *Sacred and Secular: Religion and Politics Worldwide*. Cambridge: Cambridge University Press.

Nunn, N. (2010). "Religious Conversion in Colonial Africa," *American Economic Review*, 100(2), 147–152.

Nur, A. and Burgess, D. (2008). *Apocalypse: Earthquakes, Archaeology, and the Wrath of God*. Princeton: Princeton University Press.

Olson, D. (2011). "Toward Better Measures of Supply and Demand for Testing Theories of Religious Participation," in *The Oxford Handbook of the Economics of Religion*, R. M. McCleary, (ed.). Oxford: Oxford University Press.

Ono, K. (1987). "Superstitious Behavior in Humans," *Journal of the Experimental Analysis of Behavior*, 47(3), 261.

Pargament, K. I. (2001). *The Psychology of Religion and Coping: Theory, Research, Practice*. New York: Guilford Press.

Pargament, K. I., Koenig, H. G. and Perez, L. M. (2000). "The Many Methods of Religious Coping: Development and Initial Validation of the RCOPE," *Journal of Clinical Psychology*, 56(4), 519–543.

Park, C., Cohen, L. H. and Herb, L. (1990). "Intrinsic Religiousness and Religious Coping as Life Stress Moderators for Catholics versus Protestants," *Journal of Personality and Social Psychology*, 59(3), 562.

Penick, J. L. (1981). *The New Madrid Earthquakes*. Missouri: University of Missouri.

Peoples, H. C., Duda, P. and Marlowe, F. W. (2016). Hunter-Gatherers and the Origins of Religion," *Human Nature*, 27(3), 261–282.

Pew Research Center (2020). "Most Americans Say Coronavirus Outbreak Has Impacted Their Lives, Social and Demographic Trends," March 30.

Platteau, J.-P. (2017). *Islam Instrumentalized*. Cambridge: Cambridge University Press.

Ray, G. (2004). "Reading the Lisbon Earthquake: Adorno, Lyotard, and the Contemporary Sublime," *The Yale Journal of Criticism*, 17(1), 1–18.

Robinson, A. (2016). *Earth-Shattering Events: Earthquakes, Nations, and Civilizations*. London: Thames and Hudson.

Rozario, K. (2007). *The Culture of Calamity: Disaster and the Making of Modern America*. Chicago: University of Chicago Press.

Rubin, J. (2017). *Rulers, Religion, and Riches: Why the West Got Rich and the Middle East Did Not*. Cambridge: Cambridge University Press.

Scheve, K. and Stasavage, D. (2006). "Religion and Preferences for Social Insurance," *Quarterly Journal of Political Science*, 1(3), 255–286.

Sibley, C. G. and Bulbulia, J. (2012). "Faith after an Earthquake: A Longitudinal Study of Religion and Perceived Health before and after the 2011 Christchurch New Zealand Earthquake," *PloS One*, 7(12), e49648.

Skinner, B. F. (1948). "'Superstition' in the Pigeon," *Journal of Experimental Psychology*, 38(2), 168.

Smith, B. W., Pargament, K. I., Brant, C. and Oliver, J. M. (2000). "Noah Revisited: Religious Coping by Church Members and the Impact of the 1993 Midwest Flood," *Journal of Community Psychology*, 28(2), 169–186.

Sosis, R. (2008). "Pigeons, Foxholes, and the Book of Psalms," in *Evolution of Religion*, Bulbulia *et al.* (eds.), pp. 103–109. Oxford: Oxford University Press.

Stark, R. and Finke, R. (2000). *Acts of Faith: Explaining the Human Side of Religion*. California: University of California Press.

Steinberg, T. (2006). *Acts of God: The Unnatural History of Natural Disaster in America*, Oxford: Oxford University Press.

Vail, K. E., Rothschild, Z. K., Weise, D. R., Solomon, S., Pyszczynski, T. and Greenberg, J. (2010). "A Terror Management Analysis of the Psychological Functions of Religion," *Personality and Social Psychology Review*, 14(1), 84–94.

Vail III, K. E., Arndt, J. and Abdollahi, A. (2012). "Exploring the Existential Function of Religion and Supernatural Agent Beliefs among Christians, Muslims, Atheists, and Agnostics," *Personality and Social Psychology Bulletin*, 38(10), 1288–1300.

Van De Wetering, M. (1982). "Moralizing in Puritan Natural Science: Mysteriousness in Earthquake Sermons," *Journal of the History of Ideas*, 43, 417–438.

Voas, D. and Chaves, M. (2016). "Is the United States a Counterexample to the Secularization Thesis?" *American Journal of Sociology*, 121(5), 1517–1556.

Weber, M. (1905). *The Protestant Ethic and the Spirit of Capitalism*. London: Penguin Books.

Whitehouse, H., François, P., Savage, P. E. *et al.* (2019). "Complex Societies Precede Moralizing Gods Throughout World History," *Nature*, 568, 226–229.

Williams, D. R., Larson, D. B., Buckler, R. E., Heckmann, R. C. and Pyle, C. M. (1991). "Religion and Psychological Distress in a Community Sample," *Social Science C Medicine*, 32(11), 1257–1262.

Winchester, S. (2006). *A Crack in the Edge of the World: America and the Great California Earthquake of 1906*, New York: Harper.

https://doi.org/10.1142/9789811273148_0003

Chapter 3

Evaluating the Long-Term Development Impact of Christian Missions

Valeria Rueda

University of Nottingham and CEPR, Nottingham, UK
valeria.rueda@nottingham.ac.uk

Abstract

Since the late 2000s, Christian missions have been extensively researched in the fields of long-run comparative economic history. This chapter surveys the main findings of this literature. On the one hand, missionary work went beyond evangelization, as in many cases, missions engaged in activities that today we would consider to be of the realm of international development work, such as education and healthcare. Missionary investments in these sectors have been consistently associated with long-run development benefits, especially in terms of human capital accumulation. On the other hand, research on the cultural transformation sparked by missions has brought more nuanced conclusions, pointing for instance towards increased discriminating behaviors towards non-Christians or towards those not conforming to Christian norms.

Keywords: Christian Missions, Development, History, Persistence

Christianity has been part of western imperialism ever since Father Juan Pérez joined Columbus' second expedition to the Americas. The Cross both followed and lead the globalization of western powers. Friars and

97

Jesuits were crucial actors in the Spanish conquest of Latin America, and numerous Protestant and Catholic societies settled in the British and French Empires since early nineteenth century (Bolton, 1917; Porter, 2008).

The missionary endeavor was much broader than spreading the gospel. Missionary work was normally described as an effort of "civilization," which roughly meant westernizing modes of living, with little regard for indigenous customs and traditions. A mission was supposed to be a place that offered more than church-centered religious services, which would be funded by European churches or local contributions. Basic literacy and numeracy skills would be taught, a school could likely be built, there might also be a dispensary, a hospital and sometimes a printing press. Looking in hindsight, missions engaged in activities that fall in the realm of what we would call today "international development"; today, Christian organizations are numerically and financially important actors in the non-government international development sector (Manji and O'Coill, 2002).

Since the late 2000s, Christian missions have been extensively researched in the fields of economic history and development economics. Jedwab *et al.* (2019) count more than 55 articles published over that period on the topic. Three related reasons can help us make sense of this surge in interest. First, missionaries invested in sectors that development economists care about, such as education and healthcare. They also were rather decentralized structures with a certain degree of independence from colonial authorities. They thus strongly resemble today's international development initiatives that are the focus of many evaluation efforts from development economists. Second, there is persistence in the provision of social assistance. In a recent study, Alpino and Hammersmark (2020) find that historical missionary locations in sub-Saharan Africa tend to receive today much more foreign aid, and that this is likely due to the persistence of political connections. In other words, missionary history is crucial to understand the geographical distribution of international aid today. Third, missions also left behind statistical records tracing where they located and the type of activities they engaged in. These three elements combined made missions appealing to two booming strands of literature: impact evaluation studies, interested in quantifying rigorously the causal effect of international development programs on local outcomes, and persistence studies, interested in identifying the long-term roots of development inequalities across nations.

In this chapter, we review the main findings of the literature on the long-term development impact of Christian missions and discuss both what they teach us about long-run development and their limitations.

1. Evaluating the Long-run Effect of Missionary Work

Missionary expansion sparked global cultural change. In America, and to a certain extent in the Pacific islands as well, the large-scale conversion of indigenous population and the subsequent eradication of many traditional religions and customs is proof of this. In Africa, there is evidence that Christianity, the most common religion on the continent today, spread from historical missionary sites (Nunn, 2010).

Despite the scale of this worldwide conversion movement, reducing the impact of missions to their religious legacy would still be an underestimation of their impact. Missionaries engaged in many other activities, especially education, medicine and printing. In this section, we review recent findings regarding the long-lasting effects of missions in education and health, the most common non-religious activities they engaged in.

Missions initially located in geographically favored areas, places where missionaries could reach a large number of people that were also less exposed to tropical diseases, especially malaria (Johnson, 1967; Jedwab *et al.*, 2019). Therefore, the main challenge faced when studying the long-run impact of missions on development is to isolate their effect from other geographical confounders of long-run development. The studies presented in this section employ different strategies to circumvent the issue and evaluate the legacy of different missionary activities on development.

1.1 *Missions and education*

Since reading the Bible is a central tenet of Protestant faith, conversion to Protestantism spread basic literacy everywhere it reached. Literacy indeed followed the sixteenth-century Reformation in Europe (Becker and Woessmann, 2009), and the same consequence naturally occurred around missions. Moreover, both Catholic and Protestant missions had further reasons to invest in education, beyond basic reading skills. Before European states started expanding schooling in the late nineteenth century, education was mostly provided by the Church. Religious groups that specialized in education, in particular Jesuits, continued their line of work in missions. Schooling was viewed as an effective institution for the goal of "saving the heathen" since the establishment of successful Jesuit and Franciscan missions in Latin America, particularly in Paraguay (Etherington, 2008).

Gallego and Woodberry (2010) show macro-level evidence that in Africa, provinces with more missions have higher literacy and schooling outcomes today. They also show that both Catholic and Protestant missions fostered education more when facing competition from each other. Missionary education attracted converts, so missionaries invested on schools when competing for the same souls. Using micro-level evidence, Wietzke (2014) documents large geographic inequalities in school provision in Madagascar today, that the author links to the location of missionary schooling during the colonial era. In Africa, especially in former British colonies, it is impossible to downplay the role of missions on the provision of schooling. Frankema (2012) demonstrates that the largest share of school provision in British African colonies until the 1950s was the work of African-convert missionaries. The *Africanization* of missions enlarged missionary ranks, in turn permitting large-scale expansion of missionary education (see also Meier zu Selhausen (2019)).

The African missionary movement expanded at a time of profound social and economic changes resulting from colonialism and rapid urbanization. It is thus difficult to fully assess the economic consequences of the human capital accumulation they ignited. Looking at Anglican marriage registers in Uganda from 1895 to 2011, Meier zu Selhausen et al. (2018) observe upward social mobility among men, especially into white collar jobs, even among the most modest families in their sample. They conclude that missionary education, required for these white collar jobs, allowed Christian men to climb up the social ladder and benefit from jobs in the new urban colonial centers, especially inside colonial administrations, missions and medical centers. Their sample focuses on Anglican registers; it thus leaves behind people of all other faiths, especially Muslims and Catholics who represented a large share of the population. Missionary education, for instance, was not equally open to Muslim boys, which makes it impossible to conclude from their study that missionary education structured a meritocratic society. However, their observations do portray significant and relatively equally distributed long-run returns to schooling among Anglican men.

Assessing more precisely the long-terms returns to schooling of missionary education, Wantchekon *et al.* (2015) concentrate on the case of Benin. They conduct a longitudinal study of the first students in colonial Catholic schools, their direct descendants and extended families. They identify a list of individuals who attended these schools and tracked their descendants. To construct suitable comparison groups, they sample individuals whose ancestors lived close to the schools but did not enroll and look at comparable villages without schools. In their data, schooled individuals had significantly higher living standards and levels of symbolic capital (more likely to speak French, better connected to white individuals and scored higher in a social network scale). In the long-run, these effects both persist and diffuse. They persist because descendants of the educated are also more educated and have higher living standards and more symbolic capital. They diffuse because the descendants of the uneducated in villages within the reach of colonial schools also end up more educated, with higher living standards and more symbolic capital. The authors show both qualitative and quantitative evidence that these spillovers work through extended family networks and are driven by a change in aspirations.

The returns to missionary schooling may have even been longer than the two to three generations effects identified in the Benin study. Valencia-Caicedo (2019) focuses on the seventeenth century Guaraní missions in modern-day Argentina, Brazil and Paraguay. The author shows that former missionary presence is associated with much higher educational attainment today and on average 10 percent higher individual incomes. These effects are driven by Jesuit missions, rather than Franciscan, and by missions that did not have to be abandoned. Because Jesuits emphasized formal education more, the author concludes that missionary investment in human capital is a key force behind these centuries-long persistent effects. Waldinger (2017) finds that, in Mexico, Catholic missions also left a legacy of more education recognizable today. However, the author's research indicates that Mendicant missions, as opposed to Jesuit ones, were the most influential in spreading education in Mexico. Comparing the organization of Guaraní and Mexican Jesuit missions, the author points to differences in funding for frontier missions to explain the gap in Jesuit educational legacies.

Taking a broader perspective on human capital, Bai and Kung (2015) focus on the case of China, where missionary presence greatly expanded following the Opium War (1839–1842). They claim that missions greatly contributing to the diffusion of "useful" knowledge, such as medical knowledge, which in turn they associate with increases in urbanization. To rule out that their effect is driven by confounding variables, they instrument Protestant presence with the distance to the region where political elites offered to protect foreigners after the "Boxer Uprising" (circa 1900). Their instrumented effects on urbanization are positive and significant, ruling out the possibility of their effects being entirely driven by geographical confounders of initial missionary location.

Finally, a crucial nuance in the investigation of literacy in the aftermath of missionary expansion comes from McCleary (2015). Focusing on the case of Guatemala, the author notices that the Pentecostal churches, part of the broad US religious movement, expanded and successfully converted many Guatemalans since the late 1800s. However, literacy remained low. Unlike earlier European missionary movements, Pentecostal churches emphasized less conversion through reading the Bible. Instead, they relied more on innovative technologies such as recordings, projections or radio programs. Since these communication technologies were arguably more effective at spreading a message to a large audience than print technologies, they were more successful at converting people. However, no human capital accumulations followed the American missionary expansion in Guatemala. Importantly, this study provides historical context to the previously cited findings. Most of them indeed study either missionary movements operating before the large communication technology revolutions of the twentieth century or missions traditionally oriented towards education provision.

1.2 Gender gaps in education

How equally distributed were the human capital gains from missions? Nunn (2014) documents that in sub-Saharan Africa, Protestant missions significantly increased female education, closing the gender gap, whereas Catholic missionary education mostly benefited males. Using census data from different African countries, Baten *et al.* (2020) observe that Christian missionary education lowered the large gender education gaps sparked by missionary schools. A similar pattern is observed in India by Lankina and Getachew (2013) and Calvi *et al.* (2020), who identify large increases in female education around missions. Calvi *et al.* (2020) point to the important role of missions with higher female presence, whereas Lankina and Getachew (2013) highlight the role of religious competition.

Although more research is necessary to generalize this as a global phenomenon, there are likely other countries where missionaries pioneered female education. For instance, Lee (1995) claims that the educational establishments for girls in China were set up by British missionaries.

Overall, missionaries appeared to have expanded education opportunities for both men and women. Less well known is how possible it was for women to use the skills they acquired in the labor market. Focusing again on Anglican marriage records from Uganda, Meier zu Selhausen (2014) documents that this increase in education did not generally lead to higher participation in the colonial labor market except for mission jobs. More research is needed to quantify the effect of missionary education for women on labor market outcomes in the post-colonial period and outside sub-Saharan Africa.

1.3 *Missions and Health*

Matthew 10:8 (NSRV) reads "Cure the sick, raise the dead, cleanse the lepers,[a] cast out demons. You received without payment; give without payment." Helping the sick is a prerogative across Christian denominations as an expression of Christian compassion. The Bible is also filled with references to the healing power of God and of humans as a divine gift. It is therefore not a surprise that healthcare has been at the core of Christian religious work for centuries, and that missions were no exception.

In sub-Saharan Africa, the expansion of western medicine is tied to the history of missions (Vaughan, 1991). Missionaries built hospitals and dispensaries, many of which still persist today. Despite this well known intervention in the health sector, this aspect of missionary work has received less attention in quantitative research.

Cagé and Rueda (2020) compare missions that had a hospital or a dispensary with those that did not. They find that around historical missions with health facilities, there is still today more health infrastructure and better health outcomes, in particular lower HIV prevalence.

Importantly, missionary medical services appear to have benefited a diverse and large group of patients. Analyzing historical patient records in

Uganda's largest rural medical mission over a long period of time (1908–1970), Doyle *et al.* (2019) observe that patients from all religious denominations were treated; patients could come from as far as 100 km to receive medical advice. As it spans across almost 70 years, this case study also illustrates the persistence of medical missions as regional health centers. Despite the diversity in patients, their records also suggest evidence of biases in medical practice, as certain doctors were far more likely to diagnose sexually transmitted diseases for non-Christians. More research is needed to fully understand the legacies of unequal treatment in missionary healthcare.

Missionary healthcare was also influential outside sub-Saharan Africa. Calvi and Mantovanelli (2018) observe that in India, among localities where missions settled, people tend to be healthier in those where the missionaries built health facilities, according to anthropometric indicators (BMI and height). Contrary to Cagé and Rueda (2020), they find that persistence in infrastructure plays no part in explaining their results. They point instead to the formation of persistent "health human capital": around historical health facilities, people have hygienic habits, better prenatal practices and better awareness of diseases. Both Calvi and Mantovanelli (2018) and Cagé and Rueda (2020) rule out potential confounding factors, especially the selection of geographically favored regions for missionary location, by focusing on localities exposed to missions.

2. Taking a Broader Perspective: The Cultural Legacy

Missionaries transformed religious beliefs, family structures, human capital accumulation and access to healthcare. Section 1 focused on evaluating their impact within their *mission*, that is the aspects of human life they intended to transform: christianization, education and healthcare. However, given the scope of their actions, their sphere of influence spread beyond their initial intentions. In this section, we review work that has uncovered more indirect missionary legacies.

2.1 *Missions, print technologies and liberal democracy*

In addition to spreading education, Protestant missionaries actively contributed to the consolidation of the public sphere. Cagé and Rueda (2016) observe that in sub-Saharan Africa, the development of the publishing sector is inherently tied to Protestant missions. To print religious and educational materials, missionaries formalized and started printing in languages that previously mostly existed in oral form. They observe that among localities where missionaries settled, people in those where that invested in printing exhibit today more media consumption, more engagement with current affairs and more social capital. This effect appears to be specific to Protestants, who played a more important role than Catholics in language standardization and printing in vernacular. Woodberry (2012) goes further, claiming that conversionary Protestants were at the roots of liberal democracy all over the world because they increased education and were instrumental in the formation of a public sphere, which in turn hampered elite power capture and broadened political participation.

Pengl *et al.* (2020) interpret more cautiously the legacies of missionary print technologies on liberal democracy. In Africa, with the standardization and printing in vernacular, previously malleable identities were consolidated into more precisely defined ethnic boundaries, akin to "imagined communities" (Anderson, 1983). They find that ethnolinguistic groups with a history of missionary printing and publishing tend to have stronger ethnic than national identity, hinting towards a role of missions on African ethnic politics.

2.2 *Missions, gender norms and sexuality*

Taking a broader perspective in the investigation of the long-term influences of Christian missions requires a critical look at the cultural change missionaries started. If we focus only on outcomes within the sectors that missionaries set to change, such as education or health provision, it is possible to miss more insidious consequences of what was, after all, a movement of cultural imperialism.

As they converted people to Christianity, missionaries effectively transformed preexisting norms and values, shaping them to conform with the Christian doctrine. One crucial aspect of this transformation was the christianization of family values and sexual norms. A first illustration of this fact comes from Fenske (2015), who establishes that polygamy today is less common in parts of Africa exposed to Protestant or Catholic missions. This finding is corroborated by Kudo (2017) in the case of Malawi. These observations matter because the family is one of the most important institutions shaping people's beliefs, norms and hence decision making (Alesina, 2010). Understanding this cultural transformation therefore permits to uncover different and "unintended" ways in which missions affected individual well-being today.

Ananyev and Poyker (2020) notice that the widespread grassroot and institutionalized homophobia across sub-Saharan African countries may result from recent changes in beliefs, given that many indigenous groups were tolerant to homosexual relationships before colonization. Today, in Uganda, a person involved in a homosexual relationship can face up to seven years in prison. Homosexuality is illegal in 32 African countries (Amesty International). Trying to understand the roots of these norms, they find evidence that conversion to Christianity had a causal long-lasting role in instigating homophobia, even in regions where homosexuality was commonly accepted before colonization.

Historical research has also shed light on the complex interplay between the focus on westernizing and christianizing family structures and sexual behaviors, and the design of fair and efficient public health campaigns. In modern day Uganda, a syphilis outbreak in 1907, that we know today was largely overestimated, illustrates this complex interplay. The public health response, largely orchestrated by missionaries, especially missionary doctor Albert Cook, focused on restoring morality through "social purity" campaign (e.g., preaching the importance of marriage and Christian purity to protect against the disease) (Doyle, 2012). Large-scale, often forced, tests and treatment campaigns were also conducted, but there is evidence suggesting vast over-diagnosing, especially among non-Christians (Doyle *et al.* 2019).

A modern counterpart of this complex interplay can be observed when studying the role of religion and religious institutions in the fight against HIV. Today, faith-based organizations have played a central role in the fight against the disease in Africa because of their omnipresent role in education and health and their connections to foreign aid donors. Although this role is crucial and important, there is evidence that some faith-based institutions may find it challenging to propose comprehensive sex education curricula that engage with the topic of sexual protection and condom use and thus tend to focus on sexual abstinence instead (Duflo *et al.* 2015). Cagé and Rueda (2020) engage with this question tying it to missionary history. They identify conflicting effects. On the one hand, persistent health infrastructure built by missionaries helps reduce HIV prevalence. On the other hand, locations around missionary settlements tend to have on average much higher prevalence rates. This effect cannot be fully accounted by urbanization and "modernization." Furthermore, the effect is mostly driven by Christians, who tend to have riskier sexual behaviors: more sexual partners throughout their lifetime and lesser knowledge about condom use.

3. Concluding Remarks

This chapter aimed at providing a concise overview of the last 15 years of quantitative literature evaluating empirically the legacies of Christian missions on development. This review is not exhaustive, and each of the papers cited here will provide additional useful references. The works cited here tend to distinguish themselves by the novelty of the data they collected or the argument deployed.

A noticeable pattern from this literature is that beneficial effects on development are more commonly investigated and published than negative ones. It would be wrong, however, to jump to a conclusion equating Christian missions and development. Instead, this lack of balance may result from a publication bias. The works cited in this review tend to be quantitative and tend to rely on data collected by missionaries themselves or colonial powers, as opposed to external, potentially critical, sources. As a result, research attention has concentrated in what missionaries had an interest in measuring, especially education and health provision. It is structurally much more difficult to measure unintended effects because the data measuring those may simply not exist or the effects may be more complex to identify. Although progress has been made on that front, as I have tried to show it in this section, a comprehensive understanding of missionary legacies on development requires engaging with historical work that critically leverages more diverse sources and methods.

Acknowledgment

I would like to thank Felix Meier zu Selhausen and Robert Sauer for comments.

References

Alesina, A. (2010). "The Power of the Family," *Journal of Economic Growth*, 15, 93–125.

Alpino, M. and Hammersmark, E. M. (2020). "The Role of Historical Christian Missions in the Location of World Bank Aid in Africa," *The World Bank Economic Review*.

Ananyev, M. and Poyker, M. (2020). "Organized Religion and Origins of Norms: Evidence from Africa," *Mimeo*.

Anderson, B. R. O'G. (1983). *Imagined communities: reflections on the origin and spread of nationalism*, Verso London.

Bai, Y. and Kung, J. K.-S. (2015). "Diffusing Knowledge While Spreading God's Message: Protestantism and Economic Prosperity in China, 1840–1920," *Journal of the European Economic Association*, 13(4), 669–698.

Baten, J., de Haas, M., Kempter, E. and Meier zu Selhausen, F. (2020). "Educational Gender Inequality in sub-Saharan Africa: A Long-Term Perspective," *AEHN Working Paper* (54/2020).

Becker, S. O. and Woessmann, L. (2009). "Was Weber wrong? A human capital theory of protestant economic history," *Quarterly Journal of Economics*, 124(2), 531–596.

Bolton, H. E. (1917). "The Mission as a Frontier Institution in the Spanish-American Colonies," *The American Historical Review*, 23(1), 42–61.

Cagé, J. and Rueda, V. (2020). "Sex and the mission: the conflicting effects of early Christian missions on HIV in sub-Saharan Africa," *Journal of Demographic Economics*, 86(3), 213–257.

Cagé, J. and Rueda, V. (2016). "The long-term effects of the printing press in sub-Saharan Africa," *American Economic Journal: Applied Economics* 8(3), 69–99.

Calvi, R. and Mantovanelli, F. G. (2018). "Long-Term Effects of Access to Health Care: Medical Missions in Colonial India," *Journal of Development Economics*, 135(c), 285–303.

Calvi, R., Hoehn-Velasco, L. and Mantovanelli, F. G. (2020). "The Protestant Legacy: Missions, Gender and Human Capital in India," *Journal of Human Resources*. http://jhr.uwpress.org/content/early/2020/11/12/jhr.58.2.0919-10437R2.abstract.

Doyle, S. D. (2012). *Before HIV: sexuality, fertility and mortality in East Africa, 1900–1980*. Oxford: Oxford University Press.

Doyle, S., Meier zu Selhausen, F. and Weisdorf, J. (2019). "The Blessings of Medicine? Patient Characteristics and Health Outcomes in a Ugandan Mission Hospital, 1908–19701," *Social History of Medicine*, 33(3), 946–980.

Duflo, E., Dupas, P. and Kremer, M. (2015). "Education, HIV, and Early Fertility: Experimental Evidence from Kenya," *American Economic Review*, 105(9), 2757–2797. https://www.aeaweb.org/articles?id=10.1257/aer.20121607.

Etherington N. (2008). "Education and Medicine," in *Missions and Empire*, N. Etherington, (ed.). pp. 262–284. Oxford: Oxford University Press.

Fenske, J. (2015). "African polygamy: Past and present," *Journal of Development Economics*, 117, 58–73.

Frankema, E. H. P. (2012). "The origins of formal education in sub-Saharan Africa: Was British rule more benign?" *European Review of Economic History*, 16(4), 335–355.

Gallego, F. A. and Woodberry, R. (2010). "Christian missionaries and education in former African colonies: How competition mattered," *Journal of African Economies*, 19(3), 294–329.

Jedwab, R., Meier zu Selhausen, F. and Moradi, A. (2018). "The Economics of Missionary Expansion: Evidence from Africa and Implications for Development," *CSAE Working Paper*, University of Oxford.

Jedwab, R., Meier zu Selhausen, F. and Moradi, A. (2019). "The Economics of Missionary Expansion: Evidence from Africa and Implications for Development," *African Economic History Working Paper*. https://ora.ox.ac. uk/objects/uuid:416f064d-dce0-431d-8501-59740b60204f.

Johnson, H. B. (1967). "The Location of Christian Missions in Africa," *Geographical Review*, 57(2), 168–202.

Kudo, Y. (2017). "Missionary Influence on Marriage Practices: Evidence from the Livingstonia Mission in Malawi," *Journal of African Economies*, 26(3), 372–431.

Lankina, T. and Getachew, L. (2013). "Competitive Religious Entrepreneurs: Christian Missionaries and Female Education in Colonial and Post-Colonial India," *British Journal of Political Science*, 43(1), 103–131. http://www. jstor.org/stable/23526133.

Lee, W. Y. (1995). "Women's education in traditional and modern China," *Women's History Review* 4(3), 345–367.

Manji, F. and O'Coill, C. (2002). "The missionary position: NGOs and development in Africa," *International Affairs*, 78(3), 567–584. https://doi. org/10.1111/1468-2346.00267.

McCleary, R. (2015). *Oxford Handbook of Latin American Christianity*, Oxford Handbooks Online chapter Protestant.

Meier zu Selhausen, F. (2014). "Missionaries and female empowerment in colonial Uganda: New evidence from Protestant marriage registers, 1880–1945," *Economic History of Developing Regions*, 29(1), 74–112.

Meier zu Selhausen, F. (2019). *Missions, Education and Conversion in Colonial Africa*, pp. 25–59, Cham: Springer International Publishing.

Meier zu Selhausen, F., van Leeuwen, M. H. D. and Weisdorf, J. L. (2018). "Social mobility among Christian Africans: evidence from Anglican marriage registers in Uganda, 1895–2011," *The Economic History Review*, 71(4), 1291–1321.

Nunn, N. (2010). "Religious Conversion in Colonial Africa," *American Economic Review Papers and Proceedings*, 100(2), 147–152.

Nunn, N. (2014). *Gender and Missionary Influence in Colonial Africa*, pp. 489–512, New York: Cambridge University Press.

Pengl, Y., Roessler, P. and Rueda, V. (2020). "Cash Crops, Print Technologies and the Politicization of Ethnicity in Africa," *CEPR Discussion Papers Series* (DP15162).

Porter, A. (2008). "An Overview: 1700–1914," in *Missions and Empire*, N. Etherington, (ed.). Chapter 3, pp. 40–63, Oxford: Oxford University Press.

Valencia-Caicedo, F. (2019). "The Mission: Human Capital Transmission, Economic Persistence, and Culture in South America," *Quarterly Journal of Economics*, 134(1), 507–566.

Vaughan, M. (1991). *Curing Their Ills: Colonial Power and African Illness*, Stanford, CA: Stanford University Press.

Waldinger, M. (2017). "The long-run effects of missionary orders in Mexico," *Journal of Development Economics*, 127, 355–378.

Wantchekon, L, Klašnja, M. and Novta, N. (2015). "Education and Human Capital Externalities: Evidence from Colonial Benin," *The Quarterly Journal of Economics*, 130(2), 703–757.

Wietzke, F.-B. (2014). "Historical Origins of Uneven Service Supply in Sub-Saharan Africa. The Role of Non-State Providers," *The Journal of Development Studies*, 50(12), 1614–1630.

Woodberry, R. (2012). "The Missionary Roots of Liberal Democracy," *The American Political Science Review*, 106(2), 244–274.

© 2023 World Scientific Publishing Company
https://doi.org/10.1142/9789811273148_0004

Chapter 4

Politics, Religion and the Evolution
of the Welfare State

Maleke Fourati[*,‡], Gabriele Gratton[†,§], and Federico Masera[†,¶]

University of Geneva, Geneva, Switzerland
†*UNSW Business School, UNSW Sydney, Australia*
‡*maleke.fourati@unige.ch*
§*g.gratton@unsw.edu.au*
¶*f.masera@unsw.edu.au*

Abstract

Many religious organizations supply goods and services that substitute for the modern welfare state. We review a burgeoning literature on the popular support for these organizations. This literature review offers insights into (1) the conditions that are more favorable for the rise and success of religious parties aiming to gain power within democratic constitutions; (2) the causes of popular support for religious rebels aiming to overturn the constitutional order and substitute themselves for the state. These insights form the basis for emerging theories of the co-evolution of religiosity, religious organizations and state institutions — in particular, the development of a welfare state.

Keywords: Religious Parties, Religious Organizations, Charities, Religious Rebels, Welfare State, Political Islam

1. Introduction

Religious organizations have profound effects on the cultural and economic development of societies.[1] Religious organizations contribute to the definition of social norms, values and beliefs (McCleary and Barro, 2006) and offer a platform to coordinate collective action (Clark, 2004a; Iannaccone, 1992; Norenzayan, 2013). Understanding the role of religious organizations — how they operate and what underpins their success — is then likely to offer important insights into both the political and economic development of countries. In the past decade, a burgeoning literature aimed at addressing these questions has stemmed from a key observation: Religious organizations often provide substitutes for state welfare, redistributing resources through the provision of public goods, such as healthcare and education, or directly as alms. In this chapter, we review this literature. Our focus is on recent contributions that study the origin of popular support for religious organizations, how this may translate into political power and its long term effects on the development and state institutions that provide welfare to citizens.

The observation that religious organizations provide public goods and redistribution has long historical roots. Throughout the middle ages, the Catholic Church directly controlled significant portions of the economic production in Europe and mobilized even greater resources through the collection of donations. In modern times, Christian organizations throughout the Western world operate hospitals and schools, often with the explicit objective to help the poor.[2] In the Middle East, Islamic charities — a central economic institution of Islam — by limiting the scope of the state, may be among the causes of the slow pattern of economic development of the region (Kuran, 2004, 2012, 2013).

In the twenty-first century, two types of religious organizations have caught the attention of scholars and commentators. The first type, which we label *religious parties* aim to gain power through popular support in democracies and directly control policies within the state institutions, from the imposition of traditional law to the size and level of

---

[1] The idea of a causal link between religious beliefs and organizations and economic development dates back at least to Weber, 2013 [1905].

[2] Grim and Grim (2016) estimate that in the US, Christian healthcare, higher education and charities alone represent a US $300 billion per year business.

decentralization of the state. Examples are the parties in the Arab Spring countries that take inspiration from the experience of the Muslim Brotherhood in Egypt. The second type, which we label *religious rebels*, are organizations that offer themselves as alternatives to the order provided by state institutions. Perhaps the most well-known examples are the Taliban in Afghanistan and the Islamic State in Syria. While most religious organizations who seek political power may distribute among a continuum within these two extremes, this distinction is analytically convenient and is useful to group the literature we review in this chapter.

Our focus is on three main topics. In Section 2, we review a series of studies which emphasize the political offering of religious parties and study what generates their popular support. One key insight from this literature is that religious parties, promoting a view of society in which charities should provide for the welfare of the poor, rather than state institutions, attract the support of vast parts of the population that may benefit from such economic policies. This insight offers a perspective into which conditions are more favorable for the rise of religious parties, the short term consequences of their access to power and the long term effects of the presence of religious parties on the development of state institutions.

In Section 3, we focus on a distinct literature aimed at understanding popular support for religious rebels. Among the major insights from this literature is that religious rebels are most likely to gain popular support — and therefore political power — if the state is weak and especially if it fails to deliver the public goods it promises. As greater support for religious rebels further reduces state capacity, religious rebels may induce a vicious cycle on the state institutions and even cause their total collapse.

The literature we review in Sections 2 and 3 emphasizes the economic incentives that lead to support for religious parties and rebels. Obviously, religious organizations also promote values and norms that conform to the principle of their religion, and offer teachings and indoctrination into the religion. As a result, there exists a two-way relation between religious organizations and the religious culture of a country. In one direction, a more religious population is more likely to support religious parties and rebels; in the other direction, more successful religious organizations are more likely to shape beliefs among its supporters, thus affecting the religiosity of the population. In Section 4, we review the literature that studies the co-evolution of religiosity and religious organizations. Because more successful religious organizations may hinder the development of state institutions, and because more developed state institutions reduce popular support for religious parties and rebels, the co-evolution of religiosity and religious organizations also determines a co-evolution of religiosity and state institutions — in particular, the development of a welfare state.

The relationship we study between the success of religious organizations and the evolution of the state is driven by forces generated by the substitutability of the goods and services they provide. In the developing world, religious organizations compete for the production of almost all public goods, including education, health and social insurance, and the provision of dispute resolution mechanisms — in some countries, up to 90 percent of all disputes are judged by informal resolution mechanisms that are often religious (Wojkowska, 2007). Examples of the extensive reach of religious organizations have been described for several countries, including Tanzania (Jennings, 2014), Nigeria (Aremu, 2015), Congo (Leinweber, 2011), Egypt (Phillips, 2011), Lebanon (Flanigan and Abdel-Samad, 2009), Indonesia (Chen, 2010) and Syria (Caris and Reynolds, 2014). Auriol *et al.* (2020) and Auriol *et al.* (2021) provide experimental evidence that churches are popularly conceived as a source of insurance (either real or perceived) that can substitute the type of social insurance usually provided by the state. The substitutability of religious and state-provided services has been extensively documented and discussed also in developed countries, including the US (e.g., Hungerman, 2005; Gruber and Hungerman, 2007; Dehejia *et al.* 2007).

The reader will easily notice that the focus of this review is on a political supply-side view of religious organizations. In this view, religious organizations, motivated by both ideological and economic objectives, supply political platforms and welfare that generates popular support for the organizations. This supply-side view of religious parties is not novel and reflects the long-held view in political science, summarized by Brocker and Künkler (2013), that religious parties are "more influence-seekers and message-seekers than vote-seekers or office-seekers." Naturally, this view is at best partial: some degree of popular support for ideological and economic objectives is at the origin of the creation of many religious organizations. Particularly important in the context of the literature we review, religious beliefs may be driving individual preferences for redistribution. Religious individuals may prefer less redistribution because they place emphasis on hard work and individualism (Bénabou and Tirole, 2006), or because they may believe they are "insured" against bad outcomes (Scheve and Stasavage, 2006). In the Islamic world, scholars such as Davis and Robinson (2006) have highlighted how Muslim orthodoxy supports income redistribution based on both moral and theological grounds. In all these cases, religious beliefs may drive the initial demand for religious organizations as well as their political platform. In parallel, religious values, through their effect on individual attitudes towards production and markets, affect economic development in multiple ways: Barro and McCleary (2003) show how beliefs in hell and heaven have a positive association with growth, while church attendance has an opposite effect; Guiso, Sapienza, and Zingales (2003) find that, on average, religious beliefs are associated with economic attitudes that are conducive to higher per capita income and growth; finally, Bénabou *et al.* (2015) show that religiosity and innovation are significantly and negatively related. As religious beliefs affect economic development, they are also likely to indirectly affect popular demand for differing economic policies and the work of charitable organizations. For example, Fourati (2018) shows experimentally that triggering feelings of envy and grievances against social injustice causes Tunisian subjects to donate more to religious charities rather than to secular charities.[3]

2. Popular Support for Religious Parties

Religious organizations are likely to affect economic policy through lobbying and coordinating the political actions of their members and affiliates. The most direct way in which religious organizations may affect policy is through religious parties. In many democracies, parties have explicitly or implicitly claimed to be the expression of a religion. In the aftermath of World War II, Christian democracies dominated the political scene of many Western European countries. In the past decade, the role played by religious parties has received renewed attention, partly because of the rise of Islamist parties in the Arab Spring countries. These parties

---

[3]Campante and Chor (2012) argue that the protest movement of the Arab Spring was fueled by the mismatch between educational investments and economic opportunities; relative deprivation (and in particular frustrated aspirations) may have spurred the increase in religiosity in recent decades in Egypt (Binzel and Carvalho, 2017). Both these phenomena may be linked to the enduring success of the Muslim Brotherhood and a persistent demand for organizations that provide public goods outside of state institutions.

are directly controlled or inspired by Egypt's Muslim Brotherhood — a transnational Sunni Islamist organization. In seeking to explain support for religious parties and political Islam in particular, early studies pointed to either preferences (religiosity and anti-Western sentiments) (Garcia-Rivero and Kotzé, 2007; Jamal and Tessler, 2008; Robbins, 2009; Tessler, 2010) or the clientelism of charitable organizations associated with religious parties (Cammett and Luong, 2014; Flanigan, 2008; Ottaway and Hamzawy, 2007). These explanations suggest that support for traditional values and religious parties comes from poorer voters, as they are often both more religious and more likely to depend on charitable organizations (Huber and Stanig, 2011; Chen and Lind, 2015). Yet this prediction is not supported by electoral results. From Egypt to Morocco, scholars have been puzzled by the fact that electoral support for Islamic parties comes from wealthier districts (Elsayyad and Hanafy, 2014; Pellicer and Wegner, 2014).[4]

A newer line of research stems from the observation that religious parties, especially in the Muslim world, are the political arm of a religious charitable organization (Berman, 2009; Clark, 2004b; Levitt, 2008). Huber and Stanig (2011) put forward the view that because poor, religious voters have access to religious welfare through charities, they may prefer lower redistribution at the state level. If religious parties are an expression of such voters, then their platform is likely to be one of low state redistribution, therefore potentially attracting the vote of richer voters. This logic is reminiscent of the literature on electoral competition when voters differ both in their income and their ideological preferences (Lindbeck and Weibull, 1987).[5] In particular, Krasa and Polborn (2014) study spillovers from exogenously given ideological platforms into economic

---

[4]Elsayyad and Hanafy (2014) match data from the 2011–2012 Egyptian election results with the 2006 census. At constituency level, controlling for education, higher poverty level is associated with a lower vote share for Islamic parties (the Freedom and Justice party and Al-Nour party). Pellicer and Wegner (2014) rely on the Moroccan 2004 census and 2002 and 2007 electoral data. At the municipality level, there is a positive association between literacy rate and support for the Islamic party, the Justice and Development party (PJD). In the 2007 election (but not in 2002 election), the PJD was more successful in richer districts. Fourati *et al.* (2019) exploit the 2011 Tunisian election and the 2004 census. Support for the Islamic party, Ennahda, is greater in richer districts.

[5]Aragonès *et al.* (2015) and Dragu and Fan (2016) study how parties may strategically select which dimensions are most salient during a campaign.

platforms (see also Krasa and Polborn, 2012; Xefteris, 2017). In their model, a party's ideological position exogenously determines its comparative advantages in the provision of public goods at different tax levels. In the context we are discussing, this implies that a religious party affiliated to a charity organization is less organized for the delivery of public goods such as education and healthcare within state institutions. Instead, a secular party which does not have a charity affiliation has a relative advantage in the organization of public good provisions within state organizations. In equilibrium, the more (ideologically) conservative religious party runs on more economically conservative platforms. Therefore, according to this theory, religious parties may attract the vote of sufficiently religious rich voters. The result is driven by the assumption that religious and secular parties have access to different technologies and this generates a trade-off for voters: voting for a more conservative party also implies voting for lower redistribution. Importantly, the trade-off is generated by the parties' supply of platforms to voters with the same income but differing ideologies have bliss points at identical tax rates.

Fourati *et al.* (2019) propose a model in which religious and secular parties have access to the same technology but propose differing policies. In their model, the religious party *and* more religious voters derive utility from the production of religious goods by the charity (or directly from the charity's budget). Since the charity is funded by donations, both more religious voters and the religious party have a preference for lower taxes. This creates a trade-off between ideological and economic preferences which is absent in the model proposed by Krasa and Polborn (2014).

More precisely, Fourati *et al.* (2019) study a model of electoral competition between two parties: *secular* and *religious*. They model the religious party as the political branch of a religious charitable organization (Berman, 2009; Clark, 2004b; Levitt, 2008), reflecting the typical structure of religious charities and parties in the Islamic world. In practice, their assumptions about the functioning of the religious party and the charity are molded into stylized facts about the functioning of the Tunisian party *Ennahda*. In the model, both the state and the charity provide welfare to the poor, but they differ in their ability to redistribute across regions, in the way they can fund their operations, and in the composition of the goods they provide — only secular or a combination of secular and religious goods. First, the activities of religious charities are more local, and they are more limited in their ability to redistribute income and wealth at the national level. Second, religious charities rely on donations as opposed to the imposition of taxes. Third, religious charities also provide religious goods, such as teachings, prayers and the advice of a priest or an imam. Both the secular and religious parties cater to the median voter, but the religious party also cares about the charity's budget, for example because it cares about the production of religious goods. Fourati *et al.* (2019) also assume that, if elected, the religious party imposes lifestyle restrictions that disproportionately affect the richer voters.

Fourati *et al.* (2019) take a simple stylized view of how religiosity affects preferences in their model: more religious voters benefit more from the production of religious public good. Their stylized model offers powerful predictions about the distribution of political support for the religious party. In equilibrium, the religious party chooses lower state taxes, as taxes reduce disposable income that is otherwise available for donations to the charity. Poor voters prefer the secular party, as it offers greater redistribution. Meanwhile, the richest voters also vote for the secular party because they are more affected by the lifestyle restrictions. Between these two groups, an intermediate "middle class" supports the religious party. In addition, the secular party's policies generate more inter-regional redistribution, which is preferred by voters in the poorer districts. The religious party is thus supported by a greater share of the voters in the richer districts. Their model also offers a way to think about the interaction between religiosity, economics and politics. In particular, as the population becomes more religious, the "middle class" that prefers the religious party becomes broader, including more poor and more rich voters. But this does not necessarily lead to a victory of the religious party. On the contrary, as the electoral base of the religious party extends, the platform of the secular party become economically more similar to the one of the religious party. Therefore, if the cost of the restrictions imposed by the religious party are sufficiently large, more voters who were voting for the religious party for economic reasons may switch to the secular party.

Fourati *et al.* (2019) argue that the equilibrium platform of the religious party in their model is consistent with Ennahda's economic program, as reviewed by Achcar (2013), Feuer (2012) and Marks (2012). More importantly, they test their predictions about popular support for the religious party on individual-level data on voting in the 2011 Tunisian elections. They establish that individual and district-level economic conditions played a role consistent with their predictions and were a major driver of the outcome of the election. The effect of income on the probability of voting for Ennahda is positive for poorer voters but negative for the richest ones. Controlling for individual religiosity, a small increase in socioeconomic status for the poorest voters, such as the ownership of one additional domestic asset (e.g., a refrigerator), increases the probability of voting for the Islamic party Ennahda by more than 8 percentage points. Furthermore, living in a district richer than the median district increases the probability of voting for Ennahda by a further 16 percentage points. As a comparison, a voter who prays every single day is 19 percentage points more likely to vote for Ennahda than one who never prays. Fourati *et al.* (2019) test for alternative explanations for the systematic pattern between wealth and support for Islamic parties that they document. While they find that some of these explanations contribute to the distribution of the vote for Ennahda in our sample, Fourati *et al.* (2019) conclude that they appear to only barely affect the relationship between wealth and vote for Ennahda.

The empirical literature we discuss in this section focuses on within-country variations in the support of religious parties. This focus has the positive effect of somewhat attenuating some of the endogeneity issues with these studies. However, the same focus also raises concerns about the external validity of the results. Fourati *et al.* (2019) compare their findings from Tunisia to voting patterns in other free democratic elections across the Muslim world. They focus on two key elections in which a new religious party for the first time rises to a significant position of power, as in the case of Ennahda in Tunisia: the 2012 presidential election in Egypt and the 1995 legislative elections in Turkey. In this section, we also include the 2012 election in Libya, also a key and (mostly) free election with a well-defined Islamic party. Following Fourati *et al.* (2019), we use individual data from the World Values Survey (WVS). The WVS captures political preferences with a question about voting intentions "if there were a national election tomorrow." Unfortunately, WVS data cannot be used to directly test the predictions by Fourati *et al.* (2019) at the same level of detail for two reasons. First, WVS data provide different level of administrative aggregation across countries, which in most cases constrains the analysis to exploit solely individual-level variation; second, they rely on self-reported socioeconomic status instead of a direct measure of wealth. However, as shown in Figure 1, the general pattern by which religious parties are not supported by poor voters, but rather from a largely wealthy middle-class, appears to be confirmed across the four elections.

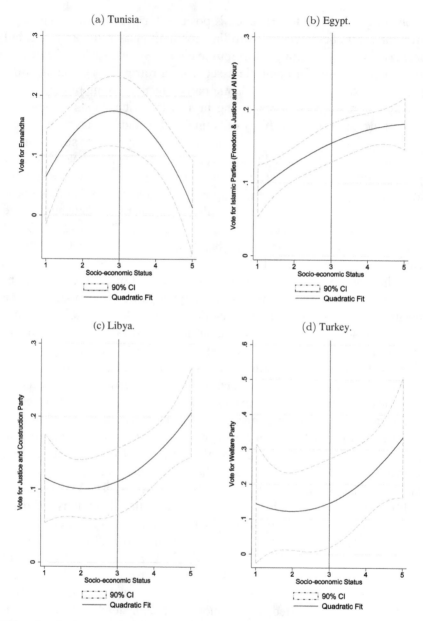

Figure 1:   Socioeconomic Status and Votes for Religious Parties

Note: Individual votes for Islamic parties as a function of socio-economic status using data from the WVS. (Tunisia: Ennahda, 2011; Egypt: Freedom and Justice Party and Al Nour, 2012; Libya: Justice and Construction Party, 2012; Turkey: Welfare Party, 1995.)

3. Popular Support for Religious Rebels

Section 2 discussed how religious organizations may affect the functioning of the state when they operate within the state institutions. Yet, religious organizations may affect policy and state institutions also through more violent actions. For example, religious organizations may try to intimidate legislators into adopting policies or they may establish a parallel state with the ultimate goal of replacing the formal state monopoly on the use of violence.

For such tactics to be effective, religious organizations need the support of the local population (Stewart, 2018). Popular support is necessary for three reasons. First, overthrowing the formal state requires the organization to recruit individuals willing to put their property and lives in danger. Second, violent actions, as well as maintaining an alternative to the formal state, need funding that normally comes from voluntary donations of citizens or the taxation of locals. Taxation is difficult to be maintained in the long-run without some level of support towards the religious organization. Third, religious organizations that wish to coordinate collective action need to collect information from the local population for planning effective actions against the formal state and at the same time, hide information from the formal state. Both processes are facilitated by local popular support.

Because religious organizations and the state provide similar public goods, one channel through which religious organizations can rally support is by convincing the local population that the state is a less able or efficient provider. When the formal state fails to provide the needed goods and services, the local population is more likely to support the religious organization. In this case, the local population may be willing to accept a certain level of violence if directed at the goal of hurting the formal state (Grynkewich, 2008; Atzili, 2010). This theory is in line with some recurrent features of successful competitors of the state. As reviewed by Felbab-Brown *et al.* (2017), goods and services provided by these organizations tend to resemble what a well-functioning state would do. Furthermore, these violent competitors of the state often thrive where and when the state is weaker, often filling the void left by the state.

Examples of religious organizations that follow these features are perhaps most visible in Muslim majority countries. In Lebanon, Hezbollah runs and maintains a large number of public service programs resembling those of most formal states (Flanigan and Abdel-Samad, 2009;

Grynkewich, 2008). Hezbollah is responsible for building and maintaining water delivery systems in areas of Beirut underserviced by the local official authorities. They also run a large number of medical clinics, dental clinics and hospitals providing healthcare to low-income families at close to no cost. The Hezbollah's educational unit provides a cheap alternative to the low-quality Lebanese public school system. Hezbollah also maintains what can be described as a welfare system offering financial assistance to poor families that have been affected by the war with Israel.[6]

Lebanon is not the only Muslim-majority country with religious rebels competing with the state. In the West Bank and Gaza, at least 10 percent of Palestinians use social services provided by Hamas (Szekely, 2015). As highlighted by Szekely (2015), the provision of these services by Hamas "serves as advertising for the kind of state the militant group will build if it takes power." This motivation appears to be shared by similar organizations in other Muslim-majority countries: in Somalia Al-Shabaab has seen success in places were the state is almost nonexistent (Menkhaus and Shapiro, 2010); the Islamic State in Syria and Iraq had the initial objective of overthrowing the failing local states and create an Islamic Caliphate (Hashim, 2014); in rural Afghanistan the failed formal state had been, over decades, practically substituted by a state run by local religious leaders (Barfield *et al.*, 2006).

Masera and Yousaf (2020) tests this theory by studying the competition between the Pakistani Taliban and the Pakistani state. The Taliban have a long history of providing for the local population when the state fails to do so effectively. The Taliban have for a long time provided security and a parallel court system that at its peak in 2006 was spread to all the Federally Administered Tribal Areas. Another common area of competition is the provision of educational services. The Taliban's *madrassahs* system reaches parts of the country under-provided or even untouched by the public school system.

Masera and Yousaf (2020) focus on a specific type of public good: natural disaster relief, including the provision of food and medicine immediately after a natural disaster and the subsequent reconstruction efforts. Studying natural disaster relief in Pakistan provides a unique opportunity to understand the effects of the competition between the

---

[6]For example, the Hezbollah Martyrs Foundation has delivered between US $300 and US $400 million in compensation to the victims of the conflict.

state and a rebel group. First, because once controlling for the underlying likelihood of a natural disaster the timing and place of natural disasters are random. Second, the ability to provide the needed relief by the Pakistani state has changed dramatically during the last 20 years. Before 2007, Pakistan was always receiving generous international aid donations especially due to the friendly relationship it had with the US. After the 2008 change in presidency both in Pakistan and US, the relationship between the two countries quickly deteriorated. This change in the international standing of Pakistan came with a decrease in the amount of aid received in case of a natural disaster.

Two important natural disasters happened around this period. The 2005 Kashmir Earthquake and the 2010 Pakistan Floods. In response to the 2005 natural disaster, Pakistan received substantial international aid. As a consequence, the Pakistani state was able to effectively provide relief, outperforming the Taliban. In comparison, international aid was small after the 2010 floods, leaving the Pakistani state unable to provide even the most basic of relief. The Taliban used this opportunity to show how effective they are compared to the Pakistani state and helped many of the communities affected by the floods.

The authors study how popular support for the Taliban differently changed after a natural disaster between places affected and unaffected by the natural disaster. In order to measure support for the Taliban, the authors use the electoral returns of the Muttahida Majlis-e-Amal party — an Islamist political alliance with a close relationship to the Pakistani Taliban and the only way for Pakistani citizens to express support for the Taliban when at the polls. After the 2005 disaster, the Pakistani state clearly outperformed the Taliban in the distribution of disaster relief. Consistent with the theory we discuss in this section, popular support for the Taliban sharply decreased after the natural disasters in the places affected by the disaster when compared with those unaffected. To the contrary, after the 2010 disaster the Taliban had a chance to show their superior ability to provide the much needed relief. In the next elections, the support for the Taliban substantially increased in the areas affected by the disaster when compared to areas of Pakistan left unaffected.

Overall, this shows how religious rebels can use the provision of goods and services to gain local popular support. This tactic is particularly effective in times and areas where the state is highly ineffective or non-existent.

4. The Co-evolution of Religiosity and the Welfare State

The arguments we reviewed in Sections 2 and 3 point to two potential effects of the competition between state and religious organizations on individual preferences and behavior. First, because the public goods produced by the two organizations are not identical and religious individuals prefer the ones produced by the organization (see Section 2 and references therein), religious individuals prefer a smaller role of the state. Second, as state capacity grows and state institutions become more efficient in the provision of public goods and services, individuals have less incentives to actively participate in and support the activities of the religious organization. In sum, these effects pertain to how religiosity affects political preferences and the development of the state welfare.

In this section, we explore how political competition and the evolution of the welfare state may be related to the development of individual religiosity. In particular, we highlight potential channels through which the competition between the state and religious organizations may shape religious participation and, in the long run, religiosity.

The evolution of the welfare state and religious participation in Western Europe suggests that there may be a long-term connection between the two. Figure 2 uses retrospective questions from the International Social Survey Programme to calculate the share of the population that participated in church activities at least once a week when young. The figure shows a remarkable decrease in church participation starting in the 1950s and 1960s, around the same time as the expansion of the modern welfare state.

To understand this phenomenon, we borrow from the literature on intergenerational cultural transmission (Bisin and Verdier, 2011). Within this theoretical framework, cultural norms are transmitted within the family, especially when parents find these norms advantageous. Thus, individual religiosity is likely to be an increasing function of the individual's parents' religiosity, especially when parents see religiosity and church participation as advantages for their children. On top of this force, Francis and Brown (1991) and Francis (1993) highlight the importance of childhood church participation and church attendance to the development of individual religiosity. Thus, individual religiosity is likely to be an increasing function of childhood church participation. The crucial connection we wish to highlight here is that church participation, and the social

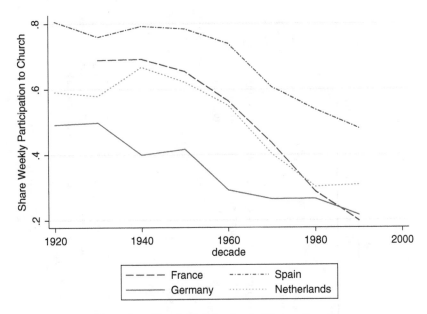

Figure 2:   Church Participation in Western Europe

advantages that may derive from it, are a decreasing function of the ability of the state to provide public goods. For example, in a society in which church participation may be the only way to receive primary education, parents may induce their children to participate in the church activities, therefore passing to them a social norm of religiosity. This incentive diminishes when public schooling becomes available

To empirically explore this connection, we use retrospective questions from the International Social Survey Programme regarding whether an individual was raised religiously or had parents that attended church when he was a child. We then study how these two forms of exposure to religiosity during childhood can predict church participation as an adult. Table 1 presents the results of this analysis. As expected, both being raised religious (Column 1) and attending church during childhood (Column 2) are positively correlated with adult church participation.

We then use information from Our World in Data to explore whether the percentage of GDP devoted to social expenditure by the formal state when an individual was a child affects the individual's adult church participation. According to the theory presented in the previous paragraphs, we should expect the size of social expenditure during childhood to have

Table 1:   Intergenerational Transmission of Religiosity

	(1) Part.	(2) Part.	(3) Part.	(4) Part.	(5) Part.	(6) Part.	(7) Part.	(8) Part.	(9) Part.	(10) Part.
Raised Religious	0.156***		0.137***		0.135***		0.147***		0.144***	
	(0.0118)		(0.0133)		(0.0129)		(0.0113)		(0.0107)	
Parents Attended Church		0.234***		0.221***		0.215***		0.214***		0.208***
		(0.0131)		(0.0125)		(0.0112)		(0.0122)		(0.0107)
Social Expenditure			−0.0663***	−0.0585***	−0.0583***	−0.0525***	−0.00986***	−0.0376***	−0.00321	−0.0343***
			(0.00644)	(0.00554)	(0.0115)	(0.0102)	(0.00368)	(0.00412)	(0.0103)	(0.00962)
Raised R. X Social Exp.							−0.0655***		−0.0663***	
							(0.00611)		(0.00662)	
Parents Att. X Social Exp.								−0.0587***		−0.0551***
								(0.00637)		(0.00674)
Observations	57141	56973	57141	56973	57141	56973	57141	56973	57141	56973
GDP	No	No	No	No	Yes	Yes	No	No	Yes	Yes
Decade Cohort FE	No	No	No	No	Yes	Yes	No	No	Yes	Yes

Notes: The table reports the estimated coefficients and clustered standard errors (in brackets). Clustering is performed at the country or region level depending on the availability of the information. The dependent variable in all specification is a dummy equal to 1 if the individual considers himself very religious or extremely religious. Countries included in the analysis are Australia, Austria, Belgium, Chile, Czech Republic, Denmark, Finland, France, Germany, Ireland, Israel, Italy, Japan, Latvia, Mexico, Netherlands, New Zealand, Norway, Poland, Portugal, Slovakia, Slovenia, South Korea, Spain, Sweden, Switzerland, Turkey and the United States. ***$p < .01$.

a negative effect on church participation today because parents are less likely to transmit religious values either at home or within the church community. This intuition is confirmed in Columns (3) and (4). Results are robust to controlling for the GDP of the country when the individual was a child as well as decade fixed effects.

Finally, we explore whether the correlation between the size of social expenditure as a child and church participation as an adult depends on the exposure to religious norms as a child. We expect particularly high levels of social expenditure as a child to negatively affect church participation as an adult for individuals coming from religious families. These results are confirmed in Columns (7) to (10) which show how intergenerational transmission of religious values is particularly weak when social spending is larger during childhood.

While Sections 2 and 3 provide theories for why religious individuals most likely prefer a small state, the results in Table 1 show that the size of the state influences the religiosity of future generations. Masera (2021) combines these two forces to study the dynamics between religiosity and the size of the state. The key variable driving these dynamics is the ability of the state to provide for the needs of the citizens. As the state become more able, voters will delegate more responsibilities to the state. This reduces the incentives to participate in religious organizations. Given the intergenerational transmission highlighted previously, this will lead to a weakening of the religious values of the next generation. Voters will therefore be even more willing to delegate responsibilities to the secular state, reinforcing the initial effects of the increase in the ability of the state. Masera (2021) shows that this can give rise to two possible long-run equilibria: One with a low share of religious individuals and in which an efficient state provides most or all public goods; and another with a large share of religious individuals and in which an inefficient state is relegated to the margins and religious organizations provide most public goods.

This section highlights that the intergenerational transmission of religious values is likely influenced by the size of the state. As a consequence, the competition between religious organizations and the state may have long-run effects on religious norms.

5. Conclusions and Directions for Future Research

We reviewed the literature drawing connections between the evolution of state welfare and religiosity. In particular, we highlighted three streams of literature: first, a literature that studies the popular support for religious organizations seeking to gain political influence within the democratic process — religious *parties*; second, a literature that studies the popular support for religious organizations seeking to gain political influence outside the state — religious *rebels*; third, a literature that connects the development of the welfare state to the decrease of popular support for religious organizations and church participation, eventually reducing individual religiosity through intergenerational cultural transmission.

Obviously, the distinction between religious parties and rebels is often arbitrary, as most organizations may exhibit characteristics of both models. Perhaps more importantly, most of these organizations are created with the same broad set of goals: promoting the production of religious public goods, realizing redistribution through charitable giving, and advocating and seeking to influence the political process promoting values that are important to the members of the organizations. Some of these organizations develop into political parties that contribute to the development of the state welfare in ways that the organization's members find more suitable to their religious values. This is by and large the development of Christian democracies throughout Western Europe in the post-WWII period. Some instead develop into rebel organizations who seek to substitute themselves for the state. What determines how religious organizations develop is an open question and one of great importance in the understanding of the co-evolution of state institutions and religiosity.

Political scientists and commentators alike are tempted to attribute the different patterns of developments of religious organizations to the deep values of the religion they represent. This viewpoint has spurred heated debates about the viability of an Islamic democracy akin to Europe's Christian democracies. While officially rejecting the label, both Turkish and Tunisian politicians have been put forward as representative of such an Islamic–democratic movement. Is there a sense in which democratic institutions in the Muslim world should be designed differently than in the West? Is there anything specific in Western European constitutions that led Christian organizations to be parties rather than rebels? The scope and limitations of such comparisons are of great importance if we are to better understand how democratic institutions should be designed to be robust to the formation of religious rebels around the world.

The literature we reviewed also makes the claim that state capacity and individual religiosity co-evolve. As religious organizations often promote values that are important for collective actions (anti-individualism, social responsibility, etc.), one may wonder whether state capacity may in time reduce if these values become less important for the individuals in the society.

References

Achcar, G. (2013). *The People Want: A Radical Exploration of the Arab Uprising.* Berkeley, CA: University of California Press.

Aragonès, E., Castanheira, M. and Giani, M. (2015). "Electoral competition through issue selection," *American Journal of Political Science,* 59(1), 71–90.

Aremu, F. A. (2015). "Faith-based universities in Nigeria and the consequences for citizenship," *Africa Today,* 62(1), 3–28.

Atzili, B. (2010). "State weakness and vacuum of power in Lebanon," *Studies in Conflict & Terrorism,* 33(8), 757–782.

Auriol, E., Lassebie, J., Panin, A., Raiber, E. and Seabright, P. (2020). "God insures those who pay? Formal insurance and religious offerings in Ghana," *Quarterly Journal of Economics,* 135(4), 1799–1848.

Auriol, E., Delissaint, D., Fourati, M., Miquel-Florensa, J. and Seabright, P. (2021). "Betting on the lord: Lotteries and religiosity in Haiti," *World Development,* 144, 105441.

Barfield, T., Nojumi, N. and Thier, J. A. (2006). *The Clash of Two Goods: State and Non-State Dispute Resolution in Afghanistan.* Washington, DC: United States Institute of Peace.

Barro, R. J. and McCleary, R. M. (2003). "Religion and economic growth across countries," *American Sociological Review,* 68(5), 760–781.

Bénabou, R., Ticchi, D. and Vindigni, A. (2015). "Religion and innovation," *American Economic Review P&P,* 105(5), 346–351.

Bénabou, R. and Tirole, J. (2006). "Belief in a just world and redistributive politics," *The Quarterly Journal of Economics,* 121(2), 699–746.

Berman, E. (2009). *Radical, Religious, and Violent: The New Economics of Terrorism.* Cambridge, MA: MIT Press.

Binzel, C. and Carvalho, J.-P. (2017). "Education, social mobility and religious movements: The Islamic revival in Egypt," *The Economic Journal,* 127(607), 2553–2580.

Bisin, A. and Verdier, T. (2011). "The economics of cultural transmission and socialization," in *Handbook of Social Economics,* Volume 1, pp. 339–416. San Diego, CA; Amsterdam, The Netherlands: Elsevier.

Brocker, M. and Künkler, M. (2013). "Religious parties: Revisiting the inclusion-moderation hypothesis — Introduction," *Party Politics,* 19(2), 171–186.

Cammett, M. and Luong, P. J. (2014). "Is there an Islamist political advantage?" *Annual Review of Political Science (Palo Alto, Calif.)*, 17, 187.

Campante, F. R. and Chor, D. (2012, May). "Why was the Arab world poised for revolution? Schooling, economic opportunities, and the Arab Spring," *Journal of Economic Perspectives*, 26(2), 167–188.

Caris, C. C. and Reynolds, S. (2014). "ISIS governance in Syria," *Middle East Security Report*, 22, 4–41.

Chen, D. L. (2010). "Club goods and group identity: Evidence from Islamic resurgence during the Indonesian financial crisis," *Journal of Political Economy*, 118(2), 300–354.

Chen, D. L. and Lind, J. T. (2015). "The Political Economy of Beliefs: Why fiscal and social conservatives/liberals come hand-in-hand," Technical report, NBER. http://nber.org/dlchen/papers/The_Political_Economy_of_Beliefs.pdf.

Clark, J. (2004a). "Social movement theory and patron-clientelism: Islamic social institutions and the middle class in Egypt, Jordan, and Yemen," *Comparative Political Studies*, 37(8), 941–968.

Clark, J. A. (2004b). *Islam, Charity, and Activism: Middle-Class Networks and Social Welfare in Egypt, Jordan, and Yemen*. Bloomington, IN: Indiana University Press.

Davis, N. J. and Robinson, R. V. (2006). "The egalitarian face of Islamic orthodoxy: Support for Islamic law and economic justice in seven Muslim-majority nations," *American Sociological Review*, 71(2), 167–190.

Dehejia, R., DeLeire, T. and Luttmer E. F. (2007). "Insuring consumption and happiness through religious organizations," *Journal of Public Economics*, 91(1–2), 259–279.

Dragu, T. and Fan, X. (2016). "An agenda-setting theory of electoral competition," *The Journal of Politics*, 78(4), 1170–1183.

Elsayyad, M. and Hanafy, S. (2014). "Voting Islamist or voting secular? An empirical analysis of voting outcomes in Egypt's 'Arab Spring'," *Public Choice*, 160(1–2), 109–130.

Felbab-Brown, V., Trinkunas, H. and Hamid, S. (2017). *Militants, Criminals, and Warlords: The Challenge of Local Governance in an Age of Disorder*. Washington, D.C.: Brookings Institution Press.

Feuer, S. J. (2012). "Islam and democracy in practice: Tunisia's Ennahda nine months," *Middle East Brief*, 66, 1–8.

Flanigan, S. T. (2008). "Nonprofit service provision by insurgent organizations: The cases of Hizballah and the Tamil Tigers," *Studies in Conflict & Terrorism*, 31(6), 499–519.

Flanigan, S. T. and Abdel-Samad, M. (2009). "Hezbollah's social jihad: Nonprofits as resistance organizations," *Middle East Policy*, 16(2), 122–137.

Fourati, M. (2018). "Envy and the Islamic revival: Experimental evidence from Tunisia," *Journal of Comparative Economics*, 46(4), 1194–1214.

Fourati, M., Gratton, G., and Grosjean, P. (2019). "Render unto Caesar: Taxes, charity, and political Islam," *European Economic Review*, 119, 114–146.

Francis, L. J. (1993). "Parental influence and adolescent religiosity: A study of church attendance and attitude toward Christianity among adolescents 11 to 12 and 15 to 16 years old," *The International Journal for the Psychology of Religion*, 3(4), 241–253.

Francis, L. J. and Brown, L. B. (1991). "The influence of home, church and school on prayer among sixteen-year-old adolescents in England," *Review of Religious Research*, 112–122.

Garcia-Rivero, C. and Kotzé, H. (2007). "Electoral support for Islamic parties in the Middle East and North Africa," *Party Politics*, 13(5), 611–636.

Grim, B. J. and Grim, M. E. (2016). "The socio-economic contribution of religion to American society: An empirical analysis," *Interdisciplinary Journal of Research on Religion*, 12, 3.

Gruber, J. and Hungerman, D. M. (2007). "Faith-based charity and crowd-out during the great depression," *Journal of Public Economics*, 91(5–6), 1043–1069.

Grynkewich, A. G. (2008). "Welfare as warfare: How violent non-state groups use social services to attack the state," *Studies in Conflict & Terrorism*, 31(4), 350–370.

Guiso, L., Sapienza, P. and Zingales, L. (2003). "People's opium? Religion and economic attitudes," *Journal of Monetary Economics*, 50(1), 225–282.

Hashim, A. S. (2014). "The Islamic State: From al-Qaeda affiliate to caliphate," *Middle East Policy*, 21(4), 69–83.

Huber, J. D. and Stanig, P. (2011). "Church-state separation and redistribution," *Journal of Public Economics*, 95(7), 828–836.

Hungerman, D. M. (2005). "Are church and state substitutes? Evidence from the 1996 welfare reform," *Journal of Public Economics*, 89(11–12), 2245–2267.

Iannaccone, L. R. (1992). "Sacrifice and stigma: Reducing free-riding in cults, communes, and other collectives," *Journal of Political Economy*, 100(2), 271–291.

Jamal, A. A. and Tessler, M. A. (2008). "Attitudes in the Arab world," *Journal of Democracy*, 19(1), 97–110.

Jennings, M. (2014). "Bridging the Local and the Global: Faith-Based Organizations as Non-state Providers in Tanzania," in *The Politics of Non-state Social Welfare*, pp. 119–136. Ithaca, NY: Cornell University Press.

Krasa, S. and Polborn, M. (2014). "Social ideology and taxes in a differentiated candidates framework," *American Economic Review*, 104(1), 308–22.

Krasa, S. and Polborn, M. K. (2012). "Political competition between differentiated candidates," *Games and Economic Behavior*, 76(1), 249–271.

Kuran, T. (2004, Summer). "Why the Middle East is economically underdeveloped: Historical mechanisms of institutional stagnation," *Journal of Economic Perspectives*, 18(3), 71–90.

Kuran, T. (2012). "The economic roots of political underdevelopment in the Middle East: A historical perspective," *Southern Economic Journal*, 78(4), 1086–1095.

Kuran, T. (2013). "The political consequences of Islam's economic legacy," *Philosophy and Social Criticism*, 39(4–5), 395–405.

Leinweber, A. E. (2011). *Faith Based Organizations and Public Goods in Africa: Islamic Associations in the Education Sector of the Democratic Republic of Congo*. Gainesville, FL: University of Florida.

Levitt, M. (2008). *Hamas: Politics, Charity, and Terrorism in the Service of Jihad*. New Haven, CA: Yale University Press.

Lindbeck, A. and Weibull, J. W. (1987). "Balanced-budget redistribution as the outcome of political competition," *Public Choice*, 52(3), 273–297.

Marks, M. (2012). "Speaking on the unspeakable: Blasphemy and the Tunisian constitution," *Carnegie Endowment For International Peace Sada Analysis*, 2012.

Masera, F. (2021). "State, religiosity and church participation," *Journal of Economic Behaviour & Organization*, 186, 269–287.

Masera, F. and Yousaf, H. (2020). "Filling the void: Evidence from two natural disasters on the determinants of Taliban support," Unpublished manuscript.

McCleary, R. M. and Barro, R. J. (2006). Religion and political economy in an international panel," *Journal for the Scientific Study of Religion*, 45(2), 149–175.

Menkhaus, K. and Shapiro, J. N. (2010). "Non-state actors and failed states: Lessons from al-Qa'ida's experiences in the horn of Africa," in *Ungoverned Spaces: Alternatives to State Authority in an Era of Softened Sovereignty*, pp. 77–94. Stanford, CA: Stanford University Press.

Norenzayan, A. (2013). *Big Gods: How Religion Transformed Cooperation and Conflict*. Princeton, NJ: Princeton University Press.

Ottaway, M. and Hamzawy, A. (2007). *Fighting on Two Fronts: Secular Parties in the Arab World*. Carnegie Endowment.

Pellicer, M. and Wegner, E. (2014). "Socio-economic voter profile and motives for Islamist support in Morocco," *Party Politics*, 20(1), 116–133.

Phillips, D. L. (2011). *From Bullets to Ballots: Violent Muslim Movements in Transition*, Volume 1. Transaction Publishers.

Robbins, M. D. (2009). "What accounts for popular support for Islamist parties in the Arab World? Evidence from the Arab barometer," *Harvard University Working Paper*. http://www.belfercenter.org/sites/default/files/legacy/files/Robbins-Support%20for%20Islamist%20Parties.pdf.

Scheve, K. and Stasavage, D. (2006). "Religion and preferences for social insurance," *Quarterly Journal of Political Science*, 1(3), 255–286.

Stewart, M. A. (2018). "Civil war as state-making: Strategic governance in civil war," *International Organization*, 72(1), 205–226.

Szekely, O. (2015). "Doing well by doing good: Understanding Hamas's social services as political advertising," *Studies in Conflict & Terrorism*, 38(4), 275–292.

Tessler, M. (2010). "Religion, religiosity and the place of Islam in political life: Insights from the Arab barometer surveys," *Middle East Law and Governance*, 2(2), 221–252.

Weber, M. (2013). *The Protestant Ethic and the Spirit of Capitalism*. London; New York, NY: Routledge.

Wojkowska, E. (2007). *Doing Justice: How informal justice systems can contribute*. Oslo, Norway: United Nations Development Program Oslo Governance Centre.

Xefteris, D. (2017). "Multidimensional electoral competition between differentiated candidates," *Games and Economic Behavior*, 105, 112–121.

Chapter 5

Ordinary People, Extraordinary Outcomes: The Occupational Status of American Jews Over the Twentieth Century[*]

Barry R. Chiswick

Department of Economics and Judaic Studies Program,
George Washington University, USA
brchis@gwu.edu

Abstract

This chapter focuses on the dramatic change over the course of the twentieth century in the economic status of Jews in the United States. Using data on the occupational attainment of men from census and survey sources from 1890 to 2000, it demonstrates both the rapid absolute and relative occupational advancement from lower-skilled jobs to professional employment. By 2000, 53 percent of Jewish men were in professional occupations, compared to only 20 percent of non-Jewish white men. Reasons for this impressive achievement are discussed.

---

[*]This chapter is a condensation of analyzes from various chapters in Barry R. Chiswick, (ed.) (2020). *Jews at Work: Their Economic Progress in the American Labor Market.* Berlin: Springer.

Keywords: Occupational Status, Jews, Census and Survey Data, Twentieth Century

1. Introduction

The twentieth century was one of the most extraordinary periods in Jewish history and has transformed both the Jewish people and world history. The two events in Jewish history that have received the most attention are, of course, the Holocaust and the establishment of the State of Israel. The first resulted in the death of one-third of the world's Jews and the destruction of Central and Eastern Europe as a religious and cultural center for world Jewry. The second was the fulfillment of a nearly 2,000 old yearning for the re-establishment of a sovereign Jewish state. Yet, there was a third development, not as momentous as the first two, that was in its own way quite extraordinary and that has shaped, and will continue to shape, Jewish history. This is the achievement of individual Jews in America, which when aggregated presents a picture of great achievement for the Jewish people, and for the world as a whole.

2. The Nobel Prize and Other Prizes

Every year in October the winners of the Nobel Prize in various fields — World Peace, Chemistry, Physics, Physiology or Medicine, and since 1969, Economics are announced. The winner of each prize is selected by a different committee, which recognizes a person's or number of persons' (or in the case of the World Peace Prize — a group's) fundamental contribution in their respective field. What is most striking is the preponderance of Jews among the winners. Some are known worldwide: Albert Einstein for Physics (1921), Elie Wiesel for World Peace (1986), Saul Bellow for Literature (1976), and Milton Friedman for Economics (1976) stand out among others with less name recognition (Table 1). They are all individuals with great accomplishments. Taken as a whole, within prize categories, the accomplishments of Jews are even more impressive. As shown in Table 1, as of 2020, of the worldwide winners of the six Nobel Prizes since their inception, the proportion of Jewish winners range from 8 percent for the World Peace Prize to 40 percent for Economics, while Jews currently constitute only 0.2 percent (i.e., two Jews for every 1,000 persons) of the world population. In literature, Jews have won 14 percent of

Table 1:   Jewish Nobel Prize Recipients as of 2020

Field (Number of Jews)	Examples	World Total (Percent)	U.S. Total* (Percent)
Chemistry (36)	Sidney Altman (1989)	19	29
Economics (34)	Milton Friedman (1976)	40	50
Literature (16)	Saul Bellow (1976)	14	38
World Peace (9)	Elie Wiesel (1986)	8	10
Physics (56)	Albert Einstein (1921)	26	39
Physiology or Medicine (57)	Rosalyn Yalow (1977)	26	38
Jewish population as percent of world and US population (2012)		0.2	2.0

Note: *Citizens of the United States at the time the Nobel Prize was awarded.
Source: www.jinfo.org/Nobel_Prizes.html (April 28, 2021).

the awards, and in the natural sciences, 19 percent in Chemistry, 26 percent in Physics, and 26 percent in Physiology or Medicine.[1]

Examining the Nobel Prize winners who were citizens of the United States at the time they received the award, the Jewish proportions as of 2020 are even higher (Table 1). While Jews now constitute about 2 percent of the US population (down from a peak of 3.5 percent in the late 1930s), Jews received 10 percent of the Peace Prizes and 50 percent (!!) of the Economics Prizes. Equally impressive are the 38 percent for Literature, 29 percent in Chemistry, 39 percent in Physics and 38 percent in Physiology or Medicine.

Jews have achieved substantial recognition in other areas as well. The Fields Medal in Mathematics is often referred to as the equivalent of a Nobel Prize, as there is no Nobel Prize in Mathematics. As of 2020, Jews have received 25 percent of the Fields Medals. Of the Pulitzer Prizes, Jews have received 14 percent of the prizes for fiction and 53 percent for non-fiction.

Clearly, individual Jews are overwhelmingly recognized among the giants in their fields by the Nobel, Fields and Pulitzer committees. These

---

[1] The sources for the data in this and the following paragraphs are: www.jinfo.org/Nobel_Prizes.html; www.jinfo.org/Fields_mathematics.html; www.jinfo.org/Pulitzer_fiction.html; www.jinfo.org/Pulitzer_non-fiction.html (April 28, 2021).

are individuals of truly extraordinary talent. The Jewish and non-Jewish prize winners constitute a very small group of individuals who have transformed science and literature or have been recognized for their efforts to promote peace. That Jews have done well in winning this recognition is an impressive tribute to both the individual winners and the Jewish people as a whole.

A community may have a small group of very high achievers, while the bulk of the community does not attain high levels of accomplishment. In more technical terms, there can be a highly skewed distribution of ability or talent, reflecting very high levels of achievement for a small proportion of a group, while the achievement for the bulk of the group is quite low. Is this the experience of American Jews?

3. American Jewish Occupational Attainment

The American Jewish population of today can trace most — and in many cases all — of its ancestors to the great wave of East European and Russian Jewish immigration to the United States in the years 1881–1920. Although a handful of their co-religionists won great prizes and awards, were the bulk of the Jewish immigrants and their descendants over the course of the twentieth century, ordinary people — just "plain folks" — compared to the rest of the US population, or were they in some way also top performers?

The question arises as to how best to measure their success. Achievement for the American population is best measured by labor market outcomes. Although economists, in particular, have a preference for measuring labor market success by earnings, data on earnings did not become generally available until after World War II, and it is not possible to identify Jews in most of these data. Occupational attainment is another measure of labor market outcomes. Occupations can be ranked with Professional/Managerial workers tending to have the highest earnings, educational attainment and greatest occupational prestige scores, followed by Clerical/Sales workers (white collar), then Service/Blue Collar workers (including production workers, operators of machines, and laborers), followed by agricultural workers. Various definitions of "who is a Jew" have been used to put together, from different Census and survey data sources collected over time, comparisons of the occupational attainment in the United States of Jewish men compared to white non-Jewish men (Chiswick, 2020).

Table 2:   Occupational Attainment, Males, 1890 (Percent)

	Jews*	Non-Jews	
Occupation	(D)	FB	NB
Professional/Managerial	7	9	9
Clerical/Sales	76	5	8
Service/Blue Collar	13	62	37
Agricultural	2	25	46
Not Reported	2	—	—
Total	100	100	100

Note: *Lived in United States in 1885. Mainly German Jews.

Notes to Tables 2–5: The data are for adult white males. Race is not separately identified for Jews, but approximately 99 percent of Jews are white. Jews identified by a direct (self-reported) Jewish identifier (D) or by Yiddish mother tongue of respondent or parents (Y). NB and FB identify native-born and foreign-born men. 2G identifies the native-born Yiddish mother tongue son of an immigrant. Data on non-Jews includes Jews in 1890, 1990, and 2000, and unidentified Jews in 1910 and 1940. Farm owners and managers were included in agriculture prior to 2000, and in managerial in 2000. Percentages may not add to 100 percent because of rounding. For details on the sources and the construction of occupational distributions see Chiswick (2020, Chapters 3, 6, and 7).

Table 2 compares data from a special survey of Jewish households conducted in 1890 by the US Census Office with data from the general 1890 Census. The survey of Jews was limited to those who were living in the United States in 1885, before the mass immigration from Eastern Europe and Russia. As a result, most of the Jews sampled were German Jews who immigrated from the 1840s through the 1860s, or their US-born children. About 76 percent of the adult male Jews were in clerical and sales jobs (ranging from merchants to back-pack peddlers), and only 15 percent in service, blue collar and agricultural jobs. In contrast, the 1890 general census shows 87 percent of the foreign-born and 83 percent of the native-born adult white men were in service/blue collar and agricultural employment.[2]

By 1910, the mass immigration of Eastern European and Russian Jews had dramatically changed the occupational structure of Jews (Table 3). Among the foreign-born Yiddish-speaking adult men, 60 percent were in service/blue-collar jobs — mainly as operatives (machine operators) in small scale manufacturing — and only 30 percent were in

---

[2]For more details, see Chiswick (2001) or Chiswick (2020), Chapter 3.

Table 3:   Occupational Attainment, Males, 1910 Census (Percent)

Occupation	Jews		Non-Jews	
	FB(Y)	2G(Y)	FB	NB
Professional/Managerial	10	16	6	10
Clerical/Sales	30	52	9	16
Service/Blue Collar	60	32	72	45
Agricultural	1	0	13	29
Total	100	100	100	100
Self Employed	38	16	22	36

clerical and service jobs. In contrast, among white non-Jewish immigrants, 72 percent were in service/blue-collar jobs (with a high proportion in larger factories), 13 percent in agriculture and only 9 percent in clerical/sales jobs. The second-generation Jews (native born but one or both parents foreign born), show a movement out of their parents' factory jobs (only 32 percent in service/blue-collar) toward clerical/sales jobs (52 percent). Among the native-born white men, most were in service/blue collar (45 percent) and agricultural (29 percent) jobs.

On the eve of World War II, in 1940, the proportion of American Jewish men in professional and managerial jobs had increased substantially to about 35 percent, while those in service and blue collar jobs shrank; it was only 27 percent among those born in the United States, (Table 4). While professional/managerial employment also grew among non-Jewish adult white men, to about 16 percent, they lagged far behind Jewish men.

By the end of the twentieth century, in 2000, over half of adult Jewish men were in professional/technical jobs (53 percent) and another 15 percent were in managerial jobs, in contrast to only 20 percent and 15 percent, respectively, for non-Jewish white men (Table 5). Another 32 percent of Jewish men were in clerical and sales jobs, with only 10 percent (primarily older workers) in service and blue collar employment, in contrast to 17 percent and 48 percent, respectively, among non-Jewish white men.

The data in Table 5 show a continuation of an interesting trend in the subcategories of Jewish professional work. In 1990, 47 percent of Jewish men were in the professional and technical occupations, and by 2020 it had grown to 53 percent. In both years, however, 12 percentage points

Table 4: Occupational Attainment, Males, 1940 Census (Percent)

Occupation	Jews		Non-Jews	
	FB(Y)	2G(Y)	FB	NB
Professional/Managerial	34	37	15	17
Clerical/Sales	17	35	7	14
Service/Blue Collar	47	27	69	50
Agricultural	0	0	8	20
Not Reported	1	1	0	0
Total	100	100	100	100
Self Employed	41	27	21	27

Table 5: Occupational Attainment, Males, 1990 and 2000 (Percent)*

Occupation	1990		2000	
	Jews (D)	Non-Jews	Jews (D)	Non-Jews
Professional/Technical	47	19	53	20
Medicine	5	1	5	1
Law	4	1	5	1
College and University Teaching	3	1	2	1
Other	35	16	41	17
Managerial	17	13	15	15
Clerical/Sales	22	17	22	17
Service/Blue Collar	14	47	10	48
Agriculture	0	4	0	1
Total	100	100	100	100
Self-Employed	27	14	23	14

Notes: *1990 and 2000 census and national Jewish population surveys.

were in medicine, law, and college and university teaching. Over the decade the proportion in other professional and technical occupations had increased from 35 to 41 percentage points. Thus, there had been a widening or broadening of the occupational categories among male Jewish professionals.

Jews had a high rate of self-employment early in the twentieth century (Table 3). In 1910, among foreign-born Jews, 38 percent were self-employed, primarily in retail trade (from peddlers to small merchants) and small-scale manufacturing. White non-Jews self-employment was on par with that of Jews, but was primarily in agriculture. By the eve of World War II self-employment remained very high among Jews, and even increased for the second generation (Table 4). The decline in self-employment among native-born white non-Jewish men from 36 percent in 1910 to 27 percent in 1940 was a result of a decline in the number of family-owned farms. By the end of the twentieth century, Jewish men still had a high rate of self-employment (23 percent) compared to non-Jewish men (14 percent) (Table 5). The industrial composition of Jewish self-employment, however, had changed in favor of professional self-employment at the expense of retail trade and owning small-scale manufacturing. The decline in self-employment among white non-Jewish men reflected the continued decline in the family farm.

Jewish men in the early twentieth century had very humble beginnings. Small-scale manufacturing and clerical and sales jobs were their primary employment, while non-Jewish men were primarily in large-scale manufacturing and farm employment. By the end of the twentieth century Jews had achieved sharp increases in their occupational attainment, both in absolute terms and in comparison to other white men. The most dramatic statistic is that by 2000, over half (53 percent) of adult Jewish men were in professional/technical occupations compared to only one in five (20 percent) white non-Jewish men. Thus, in one century the descendants of non-English speaking (primarily Yiddish speaking) Jewish immigrants from a backward part of Europe became high-level workers in professional/technical and managerial jobs (68 percent!). This extraordinary progress of the majority of the American Jewish community provides evidence that the high level of success was not confined to the small group of extraordinary winners of prestigious prizes but was widespread throughout the Jewish community.

4. Opportunities and Niches

To what might we attribute this widespread high level of success in the American Jewish community? These achievements were not set on a platter before American Jews. Jews in America did experience discrimination in access to higher education, particularly before World War II, sometimes direct, but often in the form of restrictive quotas and in the name of "geographic diversity." They also experienced discrimination in the labor market, finding limited opportunities in many major industries, including durable goods manufacturing, insurance, finance and banking, as well as in major law firms and hospitals. Added to this were "restrictive" practices in housing and social organizations that limited Jewish access to networks that were important in the business world.

Rather than viewing these anti-Semitic behaviors as insurmountable barriers to training, employment, housing and networks, Jews operated on two fronts. One was creating institutions (organizations such as the B'nai B'rith Anti-Defamation League) to use legal action and public education to combat anti-Semitism. The other, and in the long run perhaps the more important, was combating prejudice by building parallel non-discriminating institutions. Jewish law firms and banks, Jewish-sponsored hospitals and community organizations (including country clubs), and Jewish-sponsored and supported educational institutions served as avenues for mitigating discrimination. The success of these initiatives demonstrated the cost of their actions to those engaged in anti-Semitic behavior, thereby reducing discrimination.

Barriers to entry into business sectors resulted in Jewish energies being devoted to finding niches in the economy where Jews could flourish. This meant identifying and entering sectors where anti-Semitism was either non-existent or minimal. These opportunities were most prevalent in the creation of new industries (e.g., movies, radio, television) and in transforming previously existing industries (e.g., retail trade, from peddling to major department stores and the garment industries). These were also highly competitive sectors in which little capital was needed to start a business. Combined with searching for or creating niches were both a willingness to work hard and put in long hours, and a willingness to take financial and business risks. Many, perhaps most, of these businesses failed fairly quickly, but given their characteristics, re-entry was relatively easy, and many owners eventually met with success.

We think of these characteristics, particularly the entrepreneurial and decision-making skills and the willingness to take risks, as the hallmark of success for business owners. They are, however, also requirements for success as salaried professionals and independent professionals. Scientists, writers and other professionals who play it safe and stay on the well-trod path do not make the breakthroughs that result in broad recognition and prestigious awards.

Jewish entrepreneurial talent focused on innovation in the management, distribution (retailing) and marketing aspects of businesses, as in

the garment industry and in the twentieth-century entertainment industries. Curiously, it was less in the "tinkering" or invention aspects of
starting new businesses. The Jewish immigrants' entrepreneurial and
decision-making skills were passed on to their US-born children and made
valuable contributions to their children's success as they became independent professionals and moved into the corporate world and government as
salaried professionals. As the economy changed, the size of enterprises
increased and anti-Semitic practice declined in the corporate world, in colleges and universities, and in the professions. The American Jewish entrepreneurial spirit and skills remained but played out in a different arena.

5. Why the Jewish Success?

The question remains, why were Jews so successful in the twentieth century, especially in America and also in (pre-state and post-independence)
Israel and other countries of the diaspora?[3] Some have proposed that as
economic opportunities became available in the secular world, the Jewish
cultural/religious emphasis on learning and study was transferred to the
secular world. Perhaps the emphasis on the study and analysis of sacred
texts, as distinct from rote learning, sharpened Jewish decision-making
skills, which were able to express themselves in relatively free economic
and political systems, such as the United States (Friedman, 1985).
Others have suggested that the answer may be selectivity over the past
2,000 years based on who left Judaism and who remained in the fold
(Botticini and Eckstein, 2012). The high cost of passing on a Jewish
education may have resulted in a sustaining Jewish population that was
well-suited for learning and for talent in independence and decision
making. Or, perhaps centuries of anti-Semitism shaped Jewish sensitivity
toward economic opportunities and gave them the ability to recognize and
respond rapidly to these opportunities (niches) in the modern world.
Perhaps the answer rests, in part, in all of the above.

Yet, one conclusion stands out: in spite of the anti-Semitism that did
exist, America offered Jews an environment in which they could develop
their talents and seek out opportunities for their talents to flourish. In the

---

[3] For studies of the economic success in other diaspora countries see, for example, Elazar
and Medding (1983).

exercise of their talents in a free country, both America and its Jewish population prospered.

References

Botticini, M. and Eckstein, Z. (2020). *The Chosen Few: How Education Shaped Jewish History, 70-1492*. Princeton: Princeton University Press.

Chiswick, B. R. (2001). "The Billings Report and the Occupational Attainment of American Jewry, 1890," *Shofar: An Interdisciplinary Journal of Jewish Studies*, 19(2), 53–75.

Chiswick, B. R. (ed.) (2020). *Jews at Work: Their Economic Progress in the American Labor Market*. Berlin: Springer.

Elazar, D. J. and Medding, P. (1983). *Jewish Communities in Frontier Societies: Argentina, Australia and South Africa*. New York: Holmes and Meier.

Friedman, M. (1985). "Capitalism and the Jews," in *Morality of the Market: Religious and Economic Perspectives*, Chapter 8, W. Block, G. Brennan, and K. Elzinga (eds.), pp. 401–418. Vancouver, BC: Fraser Institute.

Chapter 6

Competition versus Monopoly in the Religious Marketplace: Judaism in the United States and Israel[*]

Carmel U. Chiswick

George Washington University, USA
cchis@gwu.edu

Abstract

Economic analysis is used to compare different paradigms for under-standing the marketplace for religions and religious ideas. The "Sacred Canopy" paradigm deems it necessary for social stability to grant monopoly power to an official State religion. The "New Paradigm" views separation of Church and State, leading to competition in the religious marketplace, as guarantor of freedom of conscience. Judaism in the United States illustrates the outcome in a competitive religious

---

[*]This chapter benefits from feedback obtained at the Conference on Religion and Economic Liberty: A Match Made in Heaven? (Jerusalem, Israel, May 20–24, 2012, sponsored by the Jerusalem Institute for Market Studies (JIMS) in honor of the 100th anniversary of the birth of Milton Friedman), and at the 16th World Congress of Jewish Studies (Jerusalem, Israel, July 28–August 1, 2013). A modified version was published as Studies of Jews in Society I (2018). "The Jewish State and State Judaism: An Economic Perspective" in *Jewish Population and Identity*, S. Della Pergola and U. Rebhun (eds.), pp. 143–150. Berlin: Springer.

environment. Judaism in Israel illustrates the outcome in a monopoly experiencing potential competition, possibly leading to an oligopoly structure.

Keywords: Religion, Religious Marketplace, New Paradigm, Monopoly, Competition, Judaism

1. Introduction

The Constitution of the United States of America was the late eighteenth century's Great Experiment on two fronts. It gave the common people freedom to elect their own rulers, a condition that was widely supposed to result in political anarchy. It also separated the powers of Church and State, a condition that was widely supposed to result in moral anarchy and degeneration. As we know from hindsight, neither of these suppositions came to pass, and both of these freedoms are treasured as fundamental to the American national identity. The Constitution also secured free inter-state trade and the interstate movement of free people, thus supporting the competitive markets that are a prerequisite for true political freedom. This chapter looks anew at the relationships between economic, political and religious freedom from the perspective of recent literature on the Economics of Religion.

2. The Religious Marketplace

Religious groups compete with each other for followers. This is explicit in a country with religious pluralism, but even in countries with an official religious establishment there are always non-believers as well as dissenters and dissenting religions. (Surely no one understands this better than the Jews, a group of people who have followed their own religion in many different countries — and time periods — with an official religion other than Judaism.) Sociology views competition as waged in a "marketplace of ideas," the implicit "price" of an idea being related to its compatibility with a person's non-religious ideas and emotional preferences. Economics looks at religion as a "self-produced consumer good," the price of which is related to the resources — time and money — required for religious observance. As with any such good, the quantity demanded is negatively related to its full price — the money price plus the value of time spent consuming it — and positively related to income.

Establishing an "official" State religion is analogous to granting a monopoly to a business enterprise. Monopoly is justified by a desire to control the market, often in the belief that competition is inefficient and wasteful of resources. Similarly, governments establish an official religion in the belief that it will bind citizens into a single society and buttress their loyalty to the nation. We economists know, however, that a competitive industry actually uses resources more efficiently than a monopoly, produces more output, and charges consumers a lower price. Similarly, we observe that the citizens of religiously pluralistic countries, characterized by free entry and exit of religious groups and even religions, are if anything even more religious than people in countries with an official State religion. A religious monopolist, like an industrial monopolist, relies on the protective power of the State to prevent entry by new firms offering their product for a lower price or higher quality. In extreme cases other religions are outlawed, perhaps even punishable by death, but in any case dissenters are subject to rules established by the official Church. (*Note:* Church is used here in its generic sense to mean the institutional structure of the relevant religion.)

In recent decades, a substantial literature in the Sociology of Religion has expanded on this theme, drawing many implications from the analogy of a religious marketplace. This literature speaks of a new paradigm for understanding religious behavior. The old paradigm, often referred to as the "Sacred Canopy," presumes that the common man would sink into moral anarchy without a leadership instructing him in correct religious belief and when necessary even compelling correct behavior. The so-called "New Paradigm" presumes that religion is a matter of conscience and that the common man is just as capable as anyone else of behaving morally, regardless of his religious choices.

3. The Sacred Canopy

In awarding monopoly power to a religious group, the State typically undertakes no responsibility for religion other than enforcing that monopoly. That is done by a bureaucracy headed by a CEO — a Pope, a Chief Rabbi, or some other Head of Church. The Head of Church delegates tasks to appointed functionaries, some of whom are clergy and some laymen. The central bureaucracy appoints and supervises regional and local representatives by establishing local churches (or church-equivalents) and sending clergy to staff them. The church bureaucracy also provides para-religious services such as caring for the sick and the needy, educating children, or publishing reading matter deemed appropriate for the faithful. The Head of Church, like any good CEO, is the public face of the religious group and its spokesperson when dealing with public officials. He is the ultimate lobbyist for religious interests, and he is also the object of government pressure in cases of conflict between the Church and State.

By establishing a religious monopoly, State and Church enter into a symbiotic relationship. The State can use its legal powers to enforce religious law in general, and the religious monopoly in particular, and the Church can use its moral power to promote social stability in general and the government's legitimacy in particular. The Church undertakes to provide social services to the population, and the State agrees to provide it with revenues, sometimes by giving it (and enforcing) the power to tithe but more often by allocating to the Church some of the government's tax revenues.

Much as local rebellions or warlords threaten the legitimacy and power of the State, competition from other religions or dissenting churches threaten the legitimacy and power of an established Church. The Sacred Canopy is a sort of bargain between the two powers: the State awards and enforces the monopoly power of the Church, the Church supports the State and provides social stability among its people. Like any monopoly, however, an established Church is a "price-setter" in the religious marketplace, reducing the quantity and quality of its product so as to maximize the excess of revenues over costs. Adam Smith made this point eloquently:

> The teachers of [religion] ..., in the same manner as other teachers, may either depend altogether for their subsistence upon the voluntary contributions of their hearers; or they may derive it from some other fund to which the law of their country may entitle them .... Their exertion, their zeal and industry, are likely to be much greater in the former situation than the latter .... The clergy of an established and well-endowed religion frequently become men of learning and elegance ... but they are apt gradually to lose the qualities, both good and bad, which gave them authority and influence with the inferior ranks of people .... Such a clergy ... have no other resource than to call upon the magistrate to persecute, destroy, or drive out, their adversaries, as disturbers of the public peace. (Smith, 1776)

In effect, a Church supported by government revenues enjoys a rent analogous to monopoly profit, as it "gradually" reduces the quality of service delivered to the public even as average revenue (received from taxpayers) rises above average cost.

4. Religious Pluralism

A competitive marketplace requires free entry and exit of firms. Whether an entrepreneur enters an existing industry or tries to sell a new product, the new startup succeeds or fails depending on whether customers can be found to buy its output at a price that covers costs. In a competitive religious marketplace, anyone can start a new congregation or even a new religion, but whether the new church succeeds or fails depends on its ability to attract followers. Religions compete with each other for adherents, and congregations compete with each other for members. This competition provides consumers with a variety of options, and consumers typically sort themselves into religious groups according to their spiritual and social preferences.

Competition in the religious marketplace results in a "congregationalist" market structure where each congregation is independently founded and funded by voluntary contributions from its members. Laymen manage the congregation, including the hiring — and firing — of clergy. Clergy compete with each other for congregations, and congregations compete with each other for clergy. Just as a competitive industry operates without the direction of an industry-wide CEO, congregationalism operates without a Head of Church. Congregations within the same religious group often form an "umbrella" organization — that is, an organization whose members are congregations rather than individuals — to serve common interests and to present a single face to the outside world. Congregationalism also gives rise to para-religious organizations, non-church institutions for social welfare and other activities associated with a specific religion but not actually religious and not efficiently served by each congregation separately. In a competitive religious market the functions served by a State religion are fulfilled by the combined activities of churches (or church-equivalents), their umbrella organizations, and the para-religious organizations affiliated with that religion.

Judaism in the United States is congregationalist because of the American separation of the Church and State. Jewish consumers of religion face a wide variety of options, ranging from the ultra-orthodox to the almost secular, and can select a synagogue that best meets their religious preferences. Synagogues are funded by membership fees and donations and managed by laymen, typically a president, treasurer, and board of directors elected by the congregation. The lay leadership hires the clergy — usually a rabbi and a cantor — in a labor market where they compete with other synagogues and where clergy compete with each other for synagogue positions.

Although some synagogues prefer to remain unaffiliated, most join together in one of the synagogue "movements," the major ones being Reform, Conservative, Orthodox and Reconstructionist. Each of these synagogue movements has its own umbrella organization: the Union for Reform Judaism (formerly Union of American Hebrew Congregations), the United Synagogue of Conservative Judaism (formerly United Synagogues of America), the Union of Orthodox Jewish Congregations of America (known as OU, the Orthodox Union) and the Jewish Reconstructionist Movement (formerly Jewish Reconstructionist Federation). The umbrella organizations serve religious functions beyond the scope of individual synagogues, such as the training of clergy and curriculum development for synagogue-based religious classes.

The American Jewish community also supports a wide variety of para-religious organizations unaffiliated with any particular synagogue or synagogue movement. These include organizations serving the welfare of individuals (e.g., hospitals, orphanages, food banks), of the Jewish community as a whole (e.g., Bnai Brith, Anti-Defamation League, Hillel Foundation), and of world Jewry (e.g., a wide variety of Zionist organizations). The para-religious organizations in each community typically join together in a Jewish Federation, and these affiliate in turn with their national umbrella organization, the United Jewish Communities (UJC). The community supports the non-religious activities of the Jewish para-religious organizations through a joint fund-raising campaign conducted annually by the local Federation.

5. Oligopoly and Potential Competition

Judaism in Israel is structured very differently than Judaism in the United States. Israel's government has a Ministry of Religious Services that grants monopoly "licenses" to representatives of several religious groups. Jewish affairs are the responsibility of an official Board of Rabbis presided over by two Chief Rabbis (alternating each year), aided by local

Religious Councils funded jointly by municipalities and the Ministry of Religious Services. The Chief Rabbis and their Board approve the appointment of municipal rabbis, and the Ministry has a development budget which sometimes contributes to the establishment of new synagogues. The local Religious Councils, which usually follow the religious directives of the rabbinate and administrative guidelines set by the Ministry, have exclusive legal power to register Jewish marriages, but the Chief Rabbis and their Board decide which rabbis may perform those marriages. Local councils manage the ritual baths within their municipal boundaries, but the central Board of Rabbis manages a Rabbinical Court with exclusive power for Jewish conversions and a dozen other Rabbinical Courts with absolute authority over Jewish divorces. The central religious authority also oversees a network of kosher supervisors, determines who may be buried in a Jewish cemetery, and responds to queries on religious matters from Jews around the world.

For historical, political and religious reasons, Israel wants to remain a Jewish State rather than follow the American model of religious pluralism. Yet the recent growth of dissenting Jewish groups, whether indigenous to the Israeli Jewish population or Israeli branches of the American synagogue movements, is evidence that the religious establishment monopoly is not meeting the diverse needs of the lay population. When it has difficulty competing with dissenters in the marketplace of ideas, the establishment expects the government to enforce its monopoly over religious affairs. As Adam Smith observed, this is the inevitable result of a monopoly following its own best interest.

In Israel's religious politics, "pluralism" does not refer to the disestablishment of the State religion but rather the licensing of different Jewish groups to create a sort of oligopoly, or "monopolistic competition," in the market for religious Judaism. Israeli branches of the American synagogue movements have been working for recognition as legitimate forms of Judaism whose clergy have legal rights comparable to those of the religious establishment. The greater the government subsidy involved in this protected market, the greater the incentive to acquire official status. From the monopolist's point of view, the more effective the emerging competition, the greater the incentive to block dissenters. As of this writing, monopolist and dissenting groups alike allocate considerable resources to politics. Although Israel's religious establishment has the lion's share of resources and a large voting bloc at the polls, dissenting groups have had some success in Israel's courts and have the sympathy of a growing share of the population.

The outcome of Israel's political "religious war" may be an oligopoly in which multiple religious groups are recognized as authentic Judaism. Alternatively, a "potential competition" structure may emerge in the Jewish religious marketplace. Potential competition leads a monopoly to voluntarily keep its own "profits" low enough to discourage new firms from entering the market. (In business, this is most likely to happen in industries where start-up costs are high but not prohibitive.) The idea is that if the religious establishment does not want to lose its monopoly power, it may undermine alternatives (dissenting groups) by better serving the religious needs of the population. The only incentive for this, however, is a credible threat from dissenting groups for pressure to be recognized and from the State to accede to their pressure.

6. Judaism and Religious Freedom

The idea of the Sacred Canopy is ancient, in Judaism as in virtually every other major religion. Torah itself establishes a priesthood, headed by the High Priest, ruling over religious affairs independently of the Head of State. Yet the Torah also supports the idea that ordinary people are capable of religious freedom without intermediation from that very priesthood. The passage most quoted to this effect is from Moses' final message to the Jewish people shortly before his death, in which he describes Torah as follows:

> For this commandment which I command thee this day is not too hard for thee, neither is it far off. It is not in heaven that you should say "Who shall go up for us to heaven and bring it unto us and make us hear it, that we may do it?" Neither is it beyond the sea that you should say "Who shall go over the sea for us and bring it unto us, and make us hear it, that we may do it?" But the word is very close to you, in your mouth, and in your heart, that you may do it. (Deuteronomy 30: 11–14)[1]

This summation toward the end of the Torah expresses a faith in the religious sensibility and integrity of the common man. It is this same fundamental principle that inspired the separation of Church and State in the

---

[1] See: Tanakh, a new translation of the Holy Scriptures according to the traditional Hebrew text. Jewish Publication Society 1985.

United States' Constitution and gives us the "New Paradigm" for under-standing behavior in the religious marketplace.

References

Chiswick, C. U. (2010). "Economics and Religion," in *21st Century Economics: A Reference Handbook*, R.C. Free (ed.), Chapter 76, Vol. 1. London: Sage Publications.

Chiswick, C. U. (2014). *Judaism in Transition: How Economic Choices Shape Religious Tradition.* Stanford: Stanford University Press.

Iannaccone, L. R. (1991). "The consequences of religious market regulation: Adam Smith and the economics of religion," *Rationality and Society*, 3, 156–177.

Smith, A. (1776). *The Wealth of Nations.* New York: Modern Library Edition (1937).

Warner, R. S. (1993). "Work in progress toward a new paradigm for the sociological study of religion in the United States," *American Journal of Sociology*, 98(5), 1044–1093.

Chapter 7

Ultra-Religious Women in the Labor Market: Integration and Empowerment by Responding to Work Motives

Yael Goldfarb[*,‡] and Shoshana Neuman[†,§]

*Department of Organizational Psychology, University of Haifa,
Israel Vocational, Rehabilitation and Training Center — Gal College,
The Loewenstein Institute, Israel
†Department of Economics, Bar-Ilan University, Israel
Faculty of Economics, Ashkelon Academic college,
Israel, IZA, Bonn
‡yaelg@galcollege.org.il
§shoshana.neuman@biu.ac.il

Abstract

The Israeli ultra-religious (Haredi) population is estimated at about 12% of the Jewish Israeli population, and is expected to more than double within two decades. The norm in a typical ultra-religious household is that the husband is fully devoted to the study of Torah, while his wife provides financial support for the family. The typical occupation of *Haredi* women is teaching at schools of *Haredi* girls — usually in part-time, low-pay jobs. This type of occupation matches their culture and is adjusted to their values, but has unfavorable consequences in terms of labor market integration, poverty, and economic status.

We suggest a rather novel policy (borrowed from the field of Career Psychology) that could lead to more successful integration of *Haredi* women into the labor market, coupled with elevated job satisfaction and empowerment: The design of tailor-made training programs that respond to work motives; coupled with a working environment that caters to special needs; and complemented with counseling and monitoring.

The suggested strategy is illustrated and investigated using a case study of Israeli ultra-religious young women. The motives behind their occupational choices are explored, based on data collected by a field experiment. Three types of motives behind occupational choice are discussed: (i) a "calling" motive; (ii) intrinsic/internal motives — the interest in work, as a means for self-fulfillment, and self-expression; and (iii) extrinsic/external motives that are related to receiving something apart from the work itself, such as a reward (income) or societal benefits. Based on the empirical findings, policy implications are suggested.

Keywords: Ultra-Orthodox (*Haredi*) Women, Low-Employability Populations, Economic Empowerment, Occupation, Work Motives, Job satisfaction, Israel

1. Introduction and Motivation

The Israeli ultra-Orthodox (*Haredi*)[1] population is estimated at about 12 percent of the Jewish Israeli population, and due to a higher-than-average fertility rate it is expected to become more than double within two decades (Ben-Moshe, 2012). A very recent study (Malach and Cahaner,

---

[1] The definition and classification of ultra-Orthodox (*Haredi*) Jews is somewhat problematic, as CBS Labor Force Surveys do not classify individuals by their level of religiosity. Ultra-Orthodox Jews are usually defined using the question on "last institution of study." Male respondents, who report that *yeshiva* (an institution for the advanced study of Jewish religious texts) is their last place of study, are labeled as ultra-Orthodox. A similar approach is used also for the classification of ultra-Orthodox women. In some of the CBS Annual Social Surveys (2002, 2008, 2009, 2013) there is a direct question on religiosity ("how would you define your level of religiosity?"). The 2009 Social Survey was devoted to "Religiosity and Family" and includes questions on various aspects of religion and religiosity.

2019) offers the projection of the doubling of the share of the *Haredi* population every 16 years (if current growth rates are maintained).[2]

The Jewish *Haredi*/non-*Haredi* religious sub-groups are highly segregated: Data from the CBS 2009 Social Survey (Module: Religiosity and Family) indicate that about 95 percent of *Haredi* individuals marry within the *Haredi* population. Residential segregation and separate educational systems further exacerbate segregation, separation and stratification.

The norm in a typical ultra-Orthodox (*Haredi*) household is that the husband is fully devoted to the study of Torah (and of other religious scriptures), while his wife provides financial support for the family. Girls are educated from early childhood that working in order to free the husband to study Torah is the female core role in life. A primary concern of the ultra-Orthodox education system is to persistently stress that a girl's education is meant to serve the family rather than personal needs or wishes for self-fulfillment (Friedman, 1988; Almog and Perry-Hazan, 2011). The drive to take on this extra job of working (in addition to all other female responsibilities, in particular household duties and care for the large family) stems from the profound conviction that by taking on the role of a sole working parent, allowing the husband to devote himself to the study of Torah, they get a share in his spiritual reward: a feeling of protection and bliss, and an equal share in the after-life reward.

Over the years, most women in the *Haredi* society worked in the education sector, as teachers in preschools, elementary schools and high-schools (*seminars*) of *Haredi* girls (for more detail, see Section 2).

The lower and disadvantaged participation of *Haredi* women in the labor market is the result of: education that is less suitable for the labor market; high birth rates — more than double compared to birth rates within the general Jewish population[3]; and various sociological/religious/cultural barriers (Berman, 2000).

Indeed, efforts of increasing labor opportunities have been targeted at *Haredi* population groups and made this unique group a focus of interest and public policy (Neuman, 2014). A central policy tool was the development of alternative educational opportunities for the female *seminar* (high school) students in addition to the existing teachers' tracks. It started in

---

[2]Historical data show that within three and a half decades (1980–2015), the share of the *Haredi* population increased from 4 percent to about 12 percent (Kasir [Kaliner], 2019).

[3]In 2012, the Total fertility Rate (TFR) was about 7 for *Haredi* women, compared to 3.1 for the general Israeli population (Weinreb *et al.*, 2018).

2004, when several government agencies supported a private initiative, and established a curriculum for a "Practical Engineering — PE" track in *Haredi* seminars (see Section 2, for more information on the PE track). However, the main motivation was to increase labor force participation rates (LFPRs) and to decrease poverty of *Haredi* households, rather than the empowerment of women and the increase of job satisfaction. The designers of these new training tracks did not consider work motives of *Haredi* women — accounting for those motives could further improve the design and implementation, and have the value added of more job satisfaction and female empowerment.

The efforts to improve the socioeconomic status of the *Haredi* population were supplemented by research on various features and perspectives of the *Haredi* society: Gottliev (2007) addressed the causes for poverty in the community, and offered long-term procedures for its reduction. He emphasized the need for an increase in LFPRs of the women, in order to compensate for the low participation of men and to decrease poverty rates; Lupu (2003) reviewed new fields of vocational training and of academic studies in the *Haredi* society, and marked 1996 as a year of significant change in the positive attitude to acquiring a professional education; Dahan (2004) conducted a qualitative evaluation analysis of an experimental program at the Hebrew University to train orthodox women as social workers. The findings pointed out special innovative strategies for training *Haredi* women students such as an extra role of cultural mediator, staffed by a Rabbi who is also a trained therapist. It also showed the shift in attitudes, from skepticism to a positive evaluation of the outcomes of this new program.

The relatively restricted economic literature on the integration of female *Haredi* women in the Israeli labor market is still missing a career-development perspective, which relates also to aspects of motives/preferences, job satisfaction and economic empowerment. This chapter focuses precisely on this important career aspect. One of the questions that this chapter sets out to explore is whether the only motive behind the occupational choice of a *Haredi* woman is indeed to facilitate the husband's preferred time allocation. Is the ultra-religious woman indeed different from other "regular" women who are driven by motives of self-fulfillment, economic empowerment, self-esteem, and more? An understanding of motives behind occupational choice of *Haredi* women, will also facilitate the design of tailor-made training programs that will respond to motives/preferences. The structured training; coupled with a working environment that caters to special needs/restrictions; and complemented with counseling and monitoring is expected to lead to increased work performance and productivity, and to job satisfaction and economic empowerment.

The motives and preferences behind the occupational choices of *Haredi* women were explored based on data collected by a field experiment[4] conducted in 2010–2011. Interviews with ultra-Orthodox high-school graduates were used in order to fill out a comprehensive questionnaire, related to study and work. A sample of high schools (*seminars*), which had both the newly designed Practical-Engineering (PE) track (see Section 2 for details on the PE occupation), as well as the conservative Teachers' track, was first chosen. Graduates of each of these two tracks, who began their first year of study between 2005 and 2008, were then randomly sampled in each *seminar*. The final sample was composed of 512 women. About 278 were graduates of the Practical-Engineering Track, and 234 women were graduates of the Teachers' Track, who studied in the same seminars at the same time.

The statistical analysis is expected to lead to policy implications: The design of training and employment that fit work motives and work limitations of this special group, and consequently lead to job satisfaction and economic empowerment, as well as an increase in labor force participation, and a decrease in poverty rates.

This channel could be generalized and used for other conservative/religious female populations as well. An in-depth exploration of incentives (and limitations) of other groups (e.g., Israeli Arab women; Muslim religious women; traditional women in Asia) could lead to the adjustment of training, and of labor-market institutions and regulations, to cater better to their work motives and needs, and thus raise employment levels, productivity and satisfaction.

The chapter is structured as follows: Section 2 describes the setting of the ultra-Orthodox (*Haredi*) Israeli sub-population and some relevant literature; Section 3 discusses the potential motives behind occupational

---

[4] Interestingly, it appears that the three winners of the 2019 Nobel Prize in Economics (Michael Kremer, Abhijit Banerjee, and Esther Dufllo; announced by the Swedish Academy on October 15, 2019), used a similar approach to fight poverty in low-income countries: They used field experiments that expose the motives that shape the behavior of the poor. By responding to these motives (in the fields of health, education employment) behavior can be changed, and the well-being of the poor cab be elevated.

choice, followed by an empirical case study of *Haredi* women in Section 4, and a discussion of the findings in the Section 5; Section 6 offers policy evaluations and implications.

2. The Ultra-Orthodox (*Haredi*) Population in Israel

The ultra-Orthodox (*Haredi*) group is a distinct group within the Israeli population, with a special set of norms, culture and life style. Even on the background of the stratified Israeli population, it stands out as a very exclusive group.

Unique cultural and religious characteristics of the *Haredi* ultra-religious group, based on Jewish rabbinic tradition, support the existence of two separate distinctive sets of religious obligations for the two genders: While *Haredi* men are expected to be fully dedicated to the study of religious texts, women are exempt from this duty and distanced from it (Ross, 2004). Accordingly, the *Haredi* community is a "community of (male) scholars," in which the majority of *Haredi* men spend most of their day studying in religious institutions (*yeshiva* for single men, or *kollel* for married men), achieving fulfillment on a personal-religious level (Friedman, 1988), while the wives are the ones who work in order to provide financial means for the family. The standard route for a young *Haredi* girl is to complete an elementary school, and then move on to study in *Haredi* high-schools and higher education institutes (*seminars*). The *seminars* combine classes of general education (strictly adjusted to the religious norms and life-style) and classes of professional education (mainly the profession of teachers) (Lupu, 2003). As the *Haredi* population in Israel grew (about 12 percent of the total Jewish population, up from about four percent in 1980; Kasir (Kaliner), 2019), it became clear that a stable source of financial means to provide for the family is essential, and that *Haredi* families can no longer depend exclusively on donations, community support and government welfare transfers (e.g., child allowances; some stipends for *Kolel* students). Thus, women (who are not obligated to study Torah) were encouraged to join the labor market.

Indeed, the employment rate of *Haredi* women increased quite dramatically — considering the working age (25–64), it increased from 49.5 percent in 2004, to 75.9 percent in 2018. It is however still lower than the employment rate of non-*Haredi* Jewish women (83 percent in 2018). Moreover, about one-third of *Haredi* women work part time, compared to less than 20 percent of non-*Haredi* women. This is also reflected in the average number of weekly hours of work — 28.6 hours per week among *Haredi* women, compared to 35.9 hours within non-*Haredi* female workers (Kasir (Kaliner), 2019). The absence of labor-market skills and secular/general education, combined with religious/cultural restrictions that prevent *Haredi* women from working in secular work places, are the main obstacles for employment of this group (Berman, 2000).

The employment rate among *Haredi* men (who willingly favor the study of Torah over employment) is much lower compared to women, and dramatically lower compared to the non-*Haredi* population (at the same working age of 25–64) — in 2018 it was 50.7 percent, versus 75.9 percent for *Haredi* women, and 87.6 percent for non-Haredi men (Kasir (Kaliner), 2019). Moreover, the employment rate of *Haredi* men decreased over the last three decades (Regev, 2013; Fuchs and Weiss, 2018).[5]

As noted previously, over the years, most women in the *Haredi* society worked in the education sector. For instance, in 2011, more than 60 percent of working *Haredi* women (in the prime working age of 35–54), were employed in the education sector (Regev, 2013). This type of occupation matched their needs, both from an ideological perspective (the mother/woman being an agent of education and culture) and a practical one (working within the community is adjusted to their values and way of life, and is also convenient for raising their own children). Disparities between the growth-rates of *Haredi* female teachers and pupils, led to over-supply of teachers (Regev, 2013). Consequently, many women were unemployed or could find only a part-time job. As a result, in 2019 the share of *Haredi* women employed in the education sector dropped to 43.8 percent. The proportion of *Haredi* women employed in the education

---

[5] A potential explanation for the decrease in employment rates of *Haredi* men is the decrease in their educational attainments. The population of *Haredi* men is the only group in Israel (and maybe in the industrialized world) where the (secular/general) educational attainments were decreasing with time, rather than increasing: In 2010, about 47.4 percent of *Haredi* men had only 0–8 years of formal education (up from 31.3 percent in 2002). The parallel figure for the age group of 20–24 is even higher — 68 percent — another indication for the significant decrease over time in educational attainments; only 11.7 percent had 9–12 years of education (down from 25.6 percent in 2002). The share of individuals with academic education was 7.5 percent within the age group of 25–44, compared to 15 percent within the age group of 45–64 — an additional signal of the decline in educational attainments. *Haredi* women are more educated than men and the majority of them have at least 12 years of schooling (Regev, 2013).

sector is still much higher compared the respective proportion of 19 per-cent within the non-*Haredi* Jewish female population (Kasir (Kaliner), 2019).

This process also led to an urgent need to create alternatives and new training channels to direct the excessive supply to other employment branches. The pressing need for new jobs and non-traditional occupations is also an opportunity to re-direct *Haredi* women into occupations and careers that will better cater to their work motives, and will thus lead to more job satisfaction and economic empowerment.

Policy makers (e.g., The Ministry of Industry, Trade and Employment) started already the design of tailor-made jobs for the *Haredi* female popu-lation. However, their main motivation was to increase LFPRs and to decrease poverty of *Haredi* households (Neuman, 2014).[6] We propose that this experimental policy should be used to also increase job satisfaction and economic empowerment of *Haredi* women. The first step for the achievement of job satisfaction and empowerment is to explore work/career motives of *Haredi* women, and accordingly design training and jobs that will respond to those motives. Our study sets out to investigate these work motives. The adjustment of the workplace to the special needs and restrictions of the group under discussion (e.g., working in groups, minimal contact with male workers and access to a strictly "kosher" kitchen) is another crucial component, and the whole process should be complemented by counseling and monitoring procedures.

The efforts to develop alternative educational/training opportunities for the female *seminar* (religious high-school) students started in the early 2000s, with the establishment (in 2004) of a curriculum for a "Practical Engineering" (PE) track in addition to the existing conservative "Teachers" track (Goldfarb, 2011). "Practical Engineering" is a professional degree granted by technical colleges in Israel, upon completion of a curriculum that combines theoretical syllabi with practical training. The PE study track constitutes an intermediate level of training between engineers and technicians, and is approved by the National Institute of Technological Training of the Ministry of the Economy (Horowitz and Sagi, 2013). The PE track offered to *seminar* female students was based on collaboration

---

[6]Poverty rates are very high among the *Haredi* group. In 2017, 48.6 percent of *Haredi* households were below the poverty line. The parallel figure for non-*Haredi* Jews was 8.3 percent (Kasir [Kaliner], 2019).

between several government agencies and also with potential employers who were willing to create a work environment customized to the religious/cultural needs of *Haredi* female workers. Employers agreed to comply with these restrictions due to a shortage in "practical engineers" in the Israeli labor market. Some were also motivated by ideological aspects and by the national urgent need to absorb *Haredi* workers into the labor market. Four sub-fields of study were offered: computer software, computer graphics, architecture and industrial management. The classes of these new fields are inside the *seminars*, integrating religious studies with professional courses. The studies are approved and monitored by Rabbis and educational principals, who are also searching for employment opportunities after graduation, which fit the *Haredi* religious needs and lifestyle. Evaluation projects assessed various employee/employer aspects of the new vocational tracks, pointing to a successful and satisfactory application of these innovative programs (Goldfarb, 2011 and 2014). However, the designers of these new training tracks did not consider work motives of *Haredi* women — accounting for those motives could further improve the design and implementation of new training schemes, and have the value added of more job satisfaction and female empowerment.

The economic literature offers various policies for the increase of LFPRs of low-employability female populations: schooling and training oriented at labor-market skills; better home-to-work transportation; equal-pay strategies; cheaper and better day-care facilities; and more family-friendly work environments. These policies could be relevant also for *Haredi* women. Work motives and job satisfaction are however marginalized in the economic literature. The Organizational Psychological literature on occupational choice and career development can be used to further enrich the economic models.

3. Motives behind Occupational Choice

The Organizational Psychological literature documents several types of motives that drive occupational choice: (i) the perception of "calling"; (ii) intrinsic motives; and (iii) extrinsic motives. We assume that the motives behind the occupational choice of *Haredi* women will also group into these three principal factors — calling, intrinsic motivation and extrinsic motivation.

These types of motivation, followed by hypotheses related to their relevance for *Haredi* women, are discussed below.

3.1 *The perception of "calling" and its role in occupational choice of Haredi women*

One of the work motives that is discussed in the literature is a response to some kind of "calling." (Hunter *et al.*, 2010; Hagmaier and Abele, 2012; Wrziesniewski, 2012; Duffy and Dik, 2013). Dik and Duffy (2009) document three main components of the concept of "calling" in the work domain: the feeling of being summoned by an external force (a superpower, god, society, a legacy, etc.); the association of work with a sense of purpose in life, meaning that through work the individual can express her/his ideals and morals; and a pro-social orientation being carried out through work, by using the career to help others or do good. The need to explore the construct of "calling" in diverse populations has been emphasized (Duffy and Dick, 2013), in order to substantiate its relevance within different cultures and societies. While a growing amount of research in recent years has focused on the concept of "calling" (e.g., Dik *et al.*, 2008; Elangoven *et al.*, 2010; Hunter *et al.*, 2010), empirical studies are fairly scarce (Duffy and Dik, 2013).

In this study we explore the relevance of "calling" behind occupational choice within the ultra-Orthodox (*Haredi*) group of Israeli women. It is plausible that the construct of "calling" is dominant in a religious ultra-Orthodox society. In fact, the word "calling" was originally used in a religious context (Wrzesniewski *et al.*, 1997). All three components documented by Dik and Duffy (2009) seem to be present: fulfilling god's will is a basic component that affects all spheres of life, including the work domain of females; workers express through work their role and purpose of working — to enable the spouse to stay away from work and study Torah; and work is driven by a pro-social motive of contribution to family and society. While the "calling" factor is expected to be a significant driving force behind the occupational choice of the two groups (PEs and Ts), given the special role of teachers in shaping the personality of their students and their pro-social role, it is reasonable that the "calling" motive will be more pronounced within the group of Teachers.

This leads to our first hypothesis:

Hypothesis 1: *The "calling" motive is significantly more dominant for Teachers than for PEs.*

3.2 *Intrinsic versus extrinsic work motivation in the Haredi population*

While it is plausible that *Haredi* women follow some kind of religious/ social "calling," there are most probably also other motives that drive their occupational behavior.

Work motives can be clustered into two categories: (i) intrinsic motivations — that are related to engagement in work primarily for its own sake, because the work itself is satisfying (Amabile *et al.*, 1994; Gagne and Deci, 2005) and/or gives the individual the opportunity to express personal interests, in particular, an aspiration for self-fulfillment and self-definition in the world of work (Super, 1970; Blustein, 2006); and (ii) extrinsic motivations — that are related to receiving something apart from the work itself, such as a reward or recognition from others.

What is the dominant type of motivation that is driving the work of *Haredi* women? Is it "intrinsic" or "extrinsic?" As noted earlier, women in the *Haredi* community are encouraged to work in order to support their family, while work *per se* does not carry any value (Caplan, 2007). Moreover, the term "career" is mentioned almost exclusively in a negative context (Neriya-Ben Shahar, 2015). It therefore follows that the motivation can be seen as primarily extrinsic, being embedded in the spiritual and family spheres of life, and only weakly correlated with work roles. If intrinsic motives are also at work, they are expected to be more meaningful for the PE students. This could also stem from a selection bias: The young women who chose to study PE represent a group of pioneers who chose an innovative and uncommon path. Making the uncommon choice could suggest that they were looking for self-fulfillment and felt a need to express themselves in the work arena (an intrinsic motive). Shea-van Fossen and Vredenburgh (2014) found a positive relationship between a proactive personality and career orientation, a connection that supports the assumption that young women who chose the uncommon PE track will express higher intrinsic motives. On the other hand, girls who preferred the teachers' track, follow the conservative path, probably because they do not have the drive for change and for a more fulfilling career.

We therefore arrive at our second and third hypotheses:

Hypothesis 2: *Extrinsic motives behind occupational choice will be significantly more dominant than intrinsic motives for students of both tracks: PEs and teachers.*

Hypothesis 3: *Intrinsic motives behind occupational choice will play a more significant role within the group of PEs than within the teachers' group.*

3.3 *Job satisfaction*

Optimally, a worker should be satisfied with his job. A cross-examination of work motives *vis-á-vis* job satisfaction could shed light on the interrelationship between these two angles of work. In particular: Is job satisfaction affected by the intensity of work motives? Are workers with higher scores on the work motives, also report more job satisfaction? Naturally, the intrinsic motives are expected to exhibit a stronger correlation with job satisfaction. While job satisfaction is important for its own sake, it could also lead to side effects of better performance and intensified productivity.

We therefore arrive at our fourth hypothesis:

Hypothesis 4: *The scores of intrinsic motives will be positively correlated with scores of job satisfaction, in particular among PEs who are believed to have higher valuations of intrinsic motives.*

4. Field Study of Work Motives and Job Satisfaction among *Haredi* Women

4.1 *Participants and the questionnaire*

The study presented in this chapter is based on data collected by a field study conducted in 2010–2011, which used telephone interviews with high-school (*seminar*) graduates to fill out a comprehensive questionnaire, related to study and work. A sample of high schools (*seminars*), that had both the PE track and the Teachers' track, was first chosen. Graduates of each of these two tracks, who began their first year of study between 2005 and 2008, were then randomly sampled in each *seminar*. The final sample was composed of 512 women. A total of 278 are graduates of the PE Track, and 234 women are graduates of the Teachers' Track, who studied in the same *seminars* at the same time.

Subjects were first asked to share the socioeconomic background details about: average monthly income for the last three months of work, marital status, number of children, number of siblings, education and work status of parents, level of income in their family of origin.

The core section of the questionnaire listed 13 potential motives that may influence vocational choice. Subjects were asked to rate each of these 13 items, on a scale of 1–5, according to the degree in which it influenced their vocational choice (1 — the item did not influence the decision at all, and 5 — the item strongly influenced the decision).

Nine items were taken from Pieser's questionnaire (Pieser, 1984): interesting training for the profession; interesting job/profession; challenge in work; expression of abilities; income; job stability; favorable job conditions; social status; in line with expectations of the family and/or society. These nine motives can be divided into intrinsic (the first four) and extrinsic motives (that can be sub-divided into: job conditions and societal effects).

The next item in the questionnaire relates to the distinctive structure of the *Haredi* society, in which the wife works in order to provide for her family, so that the husband can devote himself to the study of Torah and religious texts: "a desire to enable my husband to study Torah."

The last three items are closely related to the feeling of "calling." As a standard scale for assessing "calling" has not yet been developed during the time of the survey, items were phrased based on Dik and Duffy's (2009) conceptualization: "a desire to fulfill god's will"; "a sense of destiny and purpose in life"; and "a desire to contribute to society." The first of these three items refers to the feeling of being summoned by an external force, the second relates to the sense of purpose in life, and the third to pro-social behavior (these three factors are labeled by Dik and Duffy, 2009, as components of the "calling" motive).

The questionnaire includes also questions related to work satisfaction.

4.2. Results

4.2.1 Socio-economic background of respondents

The background information provided by the respondents indicates that: The age range of the respondents is 21–25 (average age is 22.6). Over 60 percent have more than 6 siblings (the percentage of 6-and-over siblings is significantly larger within the group of Teachers). The parental occupational data indicate that male full engagement in studying Torah is not new and is not restricted to young males — more than half (51.1 percent) of the *fathers* of the sampled graduates are not employed and are fully engaged in the study of Torah at an institution for religious studies. Only about one-third (36.4 percent) of fathers are full-time employees, and the rest are part-time employees or self-employed. The socioeconomic background within the family of origin seems to be somewhat more favorable in the families of PE graduates: a higher percentage of employed mothers and higher family income.

4.2.2 Descriptive statistics — Scores and rankings of the 13 work motives

For a first approximation of the importance of the 13 potential motives, averages of the responses have been calculated. Table 1 presents the averages (along with their rankings) for the whole sample and also separately for PEs and teachers (Ts). Figure 1 adds a graphical presentation of the average grades.

Starting from the whole sample: Not surprisingly, the motive that ranks first relates to the desire to enable the husband to dedicate himself to the study of Torah (average of 4.34, in a range of 1–5). This motive (which in the factor analysis presented later on, is found linked to the concept of "calling") is the most dominant motive. Quite unexpected are the high rankings of two intrinsic motives that rank second and third, not very far from the first motive. They are: "interesting training" (average of 4.11) and "interesting job/profession" (average of 3.93). These two come before the (expectedly) significant "calling" motive to "fulfill god's will." The two motives that rank last, with an average of less than three are: "family/society expectations" (2.52); and "social status" (2.49). Considering the whole sample, earned income does not play a pivotal role and has a middle rank (ranks eighth, with an average of 3.49).

A decomposition of the sample by track of training is presented in columns (3) and (4). Average grades for the 13 motives and their ranks within the sub-samples are presented separately for PEs and for Teachers (columns (3) and (4)), along with the significance level of the difference (last column). As is evident from columns (3) and (4), the averages and rankings vary by field of training.

In general, Teachers tend to "tone-down" the grades given to work motives, indicating that motives might play a diminished role behind

Table 1:   Average Scores and Ranks (in Parentheses) for the 13 Work Motives

(1) Description of Motive	(2) Whole Sample	(3) PEs	(4) Teachers (Ts)	Sig. of Difference between PE and T
Allow husband study	4.34 (1)	4.52 (1)	4.15 (1)	***
Interesting training	4.11 (2)	4.20 (3)	3.95 (3)	**
Interesting profession	3.93 (3)	3.87 (5)	3.94 (4)	not sig.
Fulfill god's will	3.68 (4)	3.36 (8)	3.98 (2)	***
Challenge in work	3.68 (5)	3.94 (4)	3.37 (8)	***
Expression of abilities	3.65 (6)	3.51 (6)	3.74 (7)	not sig.
Sense of destiny	3.53 (7)	3.24 (9)	3.86 (5)	***
Income	3.49 (8)	4.23 (2)	2.62 (10)	***
Contribute to society	3.26 (9)	2.78 (11)	3.82 (6)	***
Favorable job conditions	3.16 (10)	3.16 (10)	3.11 (9)	not sig.
Job stability	3.01 (11)	3.49 (7)	2.50 (13)	***
Family/society expect.	2.52 (12)	2.44 (12)	2.57 (12)	not sig.
Social status	2.49 (13)	2.33 (13)	2.62 (11)	**

Notes: The range of answers is 1–5 (1 — "not important at all"; 5 — "highly important"); the sample sizes are somewhat different for the different items, due to missing values; *** denotes significance at the 1 percent significance level, ** — at the 5 percent level.

their occupational choice, maybe because teaching is the conservative "default" occupation for *Haredi* women.

The same core motive of: "freeing the husband from labor to allow him to study Torah," ranks first in the two groups. Within the sub-sample of Teachers it is the only item that averages above 4 (4.15). This element is the most powerful drive behind labor force participation of all *Haredi* women in our sample. The other three components of the "calling" motive are ranked significantly higher by the Teachers (ranked 2nd, 5th and 6th for Teachers, compared to 8th, 9th and 11th for PEs), indicating a more significant role for the "calling" motive among Teachers.

The most pronounced difference relates to the importance of income, which ranks 2nd for PEs and only 10th for Teachers. This indicates that the (higher) wages received by PEs, compared to Teachers, play a pivotal role behind the choice of the PE track.

In parallel to what was found within the whole sample — intrinsic motives (e.g., "interesting training" and "interesting profession") play an important role also within each of the two sub-samples.

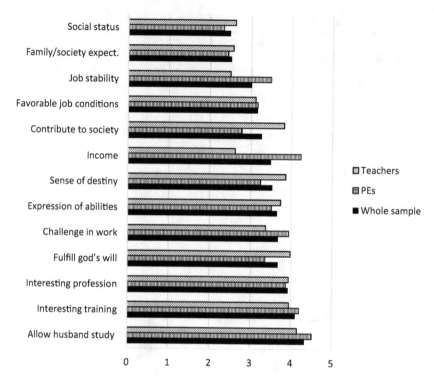

Figure 1:   Average Grades of the 13 Work Motives (Each Motive Ranges between 1 and 5)

The differences (by track) in average grades are significant at the 1 percent level for seven of the motives. For two items they are significant at the 5 percent level, and differences are insignificant (at a significance level of 5 percent or less) for the rest four motives.

To conclude: descriptive measures lend a first approximation for the dominance of the "calling" motive behind occupational performance of both PEs and Teachers. However, it seems to be more pronounced within the Teachers group. A less expected finding is that intrinsic motives play an important role in the two groups of female workers.

4.2.3   Factor analysis for the identification and scoring of the principal factors driving occupational choice

In an attempt to classify the various motives and identify more sharply the three types of motives ("intrinsic," "extrinsic" and "calling"), a Varimax

Table 2: Factor Analysis of the 13 Work Motives: Clusters and Factor Loadings

(1) Item Description	(2) Factor 1: Intrinsic Motives	(3) Factor 2: Calling Motives	(4) Factor 3: Extrinsic Motives: Job Conditions	(5) Factor 4: Extrinsic Motives: Societal Effects
Interesting training	0.71	—	—	—
Interesting profession	0.70	—	—	—
Challenge in work	0.60	—	—	—
Expression of abilities	0.59	—	—	—
Fulfill god's will	—	0.74	—	—
Contribute to society	—	0.66	—	—
Sense of destiny	—	0.61	—	—
Allow husband study	—	0.51	—	—
Income	—	—	0.67	—
Job stability	—	—	0.71	—
Favorable job conditions	—	—	—	—
Family/social expectations	—	—	—	0.67
Social status	—	—	—	0.56
Average score of factor	3.84 (0.94)	3.70 (1.1)	3.25 (1.2)	2.50 (1.2)
Explained variance (percent)	15.01	13.61	10.17	7.91
Reliability level (α)	0.78	0.75	0.61	0.58

Notes: The sample size used for the Factor Analysis is 450 women who graded all 13 incentives; Factor loadings < 0.5 are suppressed; Standard deviations of scores — in parentheses.

Rotation Factor Analysis was conducted. Table 2 presents the Factor Analysis results for the whole sample.

Four principal factors involved in vocational choice are identified. The four factors are closely related to the types of motives defined in our study: An "intrinsic" factor, a "calling" factor and an "extrinsic" factor which is sub-divided into: extrinsic motives that relate to work conditions, and social extrinsic motives. Interestingly, the four motives that are believed to relate to a "calling" concept (following the conceptualization of Dik and Duffy, 2009), are indeed components of the same factor (column (3)). The intrinsic factor, which includes four motivational components, ranks first in terms of all relevant parameters: average score, explained variance and reliability level (score = 3.84; explained variance = 15.01 percent; α = 0.78), even above the "calling" factor that ranks 2nd (score = 3.70; explained variance of 13.61 percent; α = 0.75). Interestingly, the four motives that are believed to relate to a "calling" concept (following the conceptualization of Dik and Duffy, 2009), are indeed components of the same factor ("calling" Factor 2). Though the motive of "freeing the husband to study Torah" (that is one of the components of the composite "calling" factor) ranked first in the list of the 13 individual motives (Table 1 and Figure 1), when composite factors are derived — the "intrinsic" factor precedes the "calling" factor. This means that the three remaining "calling" components are less dominant (compared to "intrinsic" components). The two extrinsic sub-factors (job conditions; effect on society), each with two components — rank third, and fourth (respective average scores of 3.25 and 2.50; respective explained variances 10.17 percent and 7.91 percent; α = 0.61 and 0.58, respectively).

While Table 1 already provided some preliminary suggestions of the role of the "calling" and intrinsic/extrinsic motives within each sub-sample, a sharper and more accurate distinction (by track of study) can be provided by employing the decomposition into principal factors presented in Table 2, in order to calculate and compare the average grades of the composite set of intrinsic/calling/extrinsic motives, within the separate sub-samples of PEs and Teachers.

As is evident from Table 3, average scores of the "calling" factor are significantly higher within the Teachers' group, while averages of the "intrinsic" factor are significantly larger for the PEs group.

Table 3:　Average Factor Scores (SD in Parentheses), for the Whole Sample and by Type of Training, and t-Tests for Differences between Scores of PEs and Ts

Group/Factor	Intrinsic	Calling	Extrinsic (Job Conditions)	Extrinsic (Societal Effects)
PEs	3.92 (0.84)	3.48 (0.99)	3.83 (0.83)	2.41 (1.14)
Teachers	3.75 (1.05)	3.97 (1.13)	2.56 (1.11)	2.61 (1.19)
t-statistic for differences between PEs and Teachers	2.04	5.25	14.43	1.88
p-value	0.04	0.000	0.000	0.06

4.2.4 *Job satisfaction*

A related important aspect for female economic empowerment and well-being is *job satisfaction*. In particular, we want to look into the correlation between the type of motives behind occupational choice and job satisfaction. An interesting question is whether intensified "intrinsic" and "calling" motives (which are the core motives behind occupational choice) also lead to more work satisfaction, i.e., if women who exhibit higher scores of these two significant principal work motivational factors also report higher work satisfaction. Regression analysis is employed in order to answer this question. The dependent variable is general work satisfaction (a scale of 1–5). The independent variables include the respondents' scores of the "intrinsic" factor and "calling" factor. In order to arrive at net effects of the work motives, socioeconomic background variables were controlled for. They include dummy variables for: work in the field of training (=1, if employed in an occupation that is different from the one trained for); number of siblings (=1, if >6); income in the family of origin (=1, if higher than average); and mother's education (=1, if mother's years of schooling >12).

Regressions were run for PE and T graduates separately. The regression model of Teachers turned out to be insignificant (R-Squared = 0.042, $p = 0.232$), indicating that teachers' work satisfaction is not affected by work motives and/or by socioeconomic background variables.

The regression results for the PE graduates are presented in Table 4.

Table 4: Determinants of Work Satisfaction (1–5), OLS regression, Sample of PE Graduates

Variables	Coefficients (t-statistics)
Does not work as PE	−0.377 (−3.689)***
Has more than 6 siblings	0.275 (2.845)***
Income of family of origin — higher than average	0.217 (2.093)**
Mother has more than 12 years of schooling	0.365 (2.068)**
Intrinsic motive (average of intrinsic components)	0.213 (2.969)***
Calling motive (average of calling components)	0.099 (1.975)*
Sample Size	129
R-squared	0.374

Notes: *significant at 0.10; **significant at 0.05; ***significant at 0.01.

Socioeconomic variables play a significant role in job satisfaction of PE graduates: women who originate from a wealthier than average family, have an educated mother and have more than six siblings express more work satisfaction. Obviously, those who are not employed as PEs (although they were trained as PEs), report less work satisfaction. Turning to our core motive variables: being affected by "calling" work motives affects job satisfaction only marginally. However, more pronounced "intrinsic" motives of the respondent, lead to increased job satisfaction (in the practical-engineering profession that highly values intrinsic motives): an increase of one unit in the composite intrinsic motive (on a scale of 1–5) leads to an average increase of 0.213 units in job satisfaction (scale of 1–5).

4.2.5 Hypotheses testing (summary)

Based on the Factor Analysis results (presented in Tables 2 and 3), and on the "job satisfaction equation" (presented in Table 4), Hypotheses 1–4 can be tested and concluded.

Hypothesis 1: *The "calling" factor is significantly more dominant among Teachers than among PEs.*
As is indicated in Table 3, the "calling" composite factor is indeed significantly higher within the group of Teachers (composite values of 3.97 and 3.48, for Teachers and PEs, respectively). The difference is significant at the 0.01 significance level ($t = 5.25$, $p = 0.00$).

In order to test **Hypothesis 2**, that *expects extrinsic motives to be more dominant than intrinsic motives (for the whole sample)*, two t-tests for paired-samples were conducted, comparing intrinsic motives (clustered by factor analysis) with each of the extrinsic motivation sub-factors: "job conditions" and "effect on society" (based on the results of Table 2). Results show a significant difference between the scores of the intrinsic factor and the extrinsic factor related to "job conditions," $t = 10.23$, $p < 0.01$, but in the opposite direction: Contrary to the hypothesis, the score of the intrinsic motivation factor ($M = 3.84$, $SD = 0.94$) is significantly higher than the score of the factor of extrinsic motives relating to job conditions ($M = 3.25$, $SD = 1.16$). Results also show a significant difference between the respective scores of the factors of intrinsic motives and extrinsic motives related to "effects on society," $t = 22.45$, $p < 0.01$.

Here too, the opposite direction is evidenced: the score of the intrinsic motives' factor ($M = 3.84$, $SD = 0.94$) is significantly higher than the parallel score of the factor composed of extrinsic motives related to effect on society ($M = 2.5$, $SD = 1.16$). Hypothesis 2 is therefore rejected, and our findings propose a more dominant "intrinsic motivation."

Hypothesis 3: *Intrinsic motives behind occupational choice play a more significant role within the group of PEs than within the Teachers' group.*
Our data support this Hypothesis, the composite "intrinsic" motive is larger among PEs (respective figures of 3.92 and 3.75). The difference is significant at the 0.04 significance level ($t = 2.04$, $p = 0.04 < 0.05$).

The findings reported in Table 4 lend support to **Hypothesis 4:** *The scores of the composite intrinsic motives will be positively correlated with scores of job satisfaction, in particular among PEs who have higher valuations of intrinsic motives* (significance level < 0.01, for the "intrinsic motives" variable in the "job satisfaction equation" for PEs).

5. Discussion

The current research set out to shed light on motives that lead *Haredi* young women in choosing their work path, and on the effects of job motives on job satisfaction. On the background of the very special nature of the community of *Haredi* individuals, who rate the goal of the study of Torah (by the males) high above any other life objective, it is not surprising that the motive that is ranked highest (among the 13 work motives presented to the respondents, by both groups of women) is the "desire to enable the husband to study Torah" (by taking on employment responsibilities and providing for the financial needs of the family; Ringel, 2007).

This motive, along with "a desire to fulfill god's will," "a feeling of purpose" and "a desire to contribute to society" (three items phrased in line with the conceptualization of the "calling" motive by Dik and Duffy, 2009) are linked to the sense of "calling" and compose a significant principal factor (albeit the "calling" principal factor ranked second in the set of four principal factors, revealed by the Principal Factor Analysis, after the "intrinsic" that ranked first). This finding supports the theory, that in certain religious/spiritual cultures, the intensity of religious/spiritual commitment can result in "calling" being a widespread norm (Dik and Duffy, 2009) that affects also the work arena. While in the general society married women sometimes facilitate their spouse's career by taking on the role of wife and mother, in the case of the *Haredi* society women also take the role of providers and see the male as their representative in spiritual practice.

It is also not surprising that the sense of "calling" is more dominant within the Teachers' sub-sample. The *Haredi* community assigns special ideological importance to the profession of teaching, which entails the mission of educating the next generation and in particular, passing on the value of studying Torah (Caplan, 2007). The special role of the female teachers is mirrored by the higher rated item of "a desire to contribute to society" (ranked 6th by Teachers and 11th by PEs). In the case of Teachers, "society" overlaps with the students they teach and coach. The results demonstrate that the sense of "calling" is indeed part of the wide set of motives in both groups, but is significantly more pronounced in the group of teachers.

Much less expected is the finding that intrinsic motives play a significant role is shaping *Haredi* women's occupational choices, even above the role of "calling" motives. Religious/spiritual leaders of the *Haredi* society preach that work (in particular in a profession other than teaching) does not have any value of its own. It is a necessity that cannot be avoided, in order to facilitate the study of Torah by the husband (Caplan, 2007). This is however not what our respondents are telling us. They seem to highly value intrinsic motives, like self-fulfillment and an interesting job.[7] It appears that what is aired publicly is not what is valued personally — intrinsic motives compose the most important principal factor, and *Haredi* employees do express personal interests in the world of labor. The important role of intrinsic motives is more pronounced within the sub-sample of PE's.

6. Policy Implications and Evaluations

(1) The study presented in this chapter seems to be the first analytical study that looks into occupational choices of individuals within the distinct *Haredi* community, using the same methodological/statistical tools used by career economists and psychologists to study more

---

[7]It is important to note that the two do not necessarily contradict. The values of providing for your family and having a meaningful job, can coexist.

"common" societies/groups. Apparently, this application proves successful and leads to the unraveling of both expected ("calling") and
much less expected ("intrinsic") motives. "Intrinsic" motives (e.g.,
interesting training, interesting job and other personal interests in the
world of labor) are found to be the main principal factor of work
motives. The findings of the important role of "intrinsic" motives in
attracting *Haredi* women, and the role that intrinsic motives play
towards job satisfaction, and consequently also toward empowerment
of *Haredi* women, suggest that new vocational programs which cater
to their (intrinsic) work motives should be designed and offered. First
steps in this direction have already been taken (starting in the early
2000s), offering new/unconventional tracks of: accountancy, practical
engineering, social work, interior design, computer science, economics (and more), which were designed specifically for this sector.
However, if the design of new tracks will also consider more closely
work motives of *Haredi* women — the new tracks will better accommodate the women's needs, and consequently result in more job
satisfaction and female empowerment.

(2) When dealing with populations with low employability there is
important role for career counseling and monitoring. Preliminary
steps in this direction have already been taken, and career guidance
services for *Haredi* women were developed and offered (Goldfarb,
2014). Based on accumulated experience — these services could be
extended and improved.

(3) While the new training tracks, already offered to *Haredi* women (such
as the Practical Engineering track), were not based on a systematic
study of work motivations, they do respond to motives that seem to
be desirable by the women (e.g., intrinsic motives). More awareness
and responsiveness to work motivation of *Haredi* women could lead
to the careful design (or revision) of tracks that will cater more closely
to work motivation, leading to more job satisfaction and enhanced
well-being and female empowerment.

(4) There is already some preliminary evidence that could indicate the
success (in terms of employment rates) of occupational policies that
cater to work motives (even if not through a systematic process of
examination of work motives). The employment rate of *Haredi*
women increased dramatically within one decade and accelerated
in recent years: Relating to the working ages of 25–64, it was
50.5 percent in 2005, climbed up to 65.1 percent in 2010, to 68

percent in 2013, and further accelerated to 74.9 percent at the end of the third quarter of 2015 — a spectacular rise of 48 percent during the decade of 2005–2015. Even more dramatic is the rise of more than 10 percent in the two last years — 2013 to 2015 (Ministry of Industry, Trade and Employment, various publications and press releases). More recent data (collected for the Finance Committee of the Israeli Parliament, by the Knesset's Center for Research and Information) show some minor additional improvement in the employment rates of working age *Haredi* women — to 75.9 percent in 2018 (Eizencot, 2018).[8] Obviously, it is not possible to isolate the effect of the revision in occupational policy on the rise in employment. However, we believe that it is safe to say, that at least part of the change is due to the changes in policy noted above. Moreover, a fine-tuning of training schemes, based on work motives, is believed to further increase employment rates, and more importantly — increase job satisfaction and women's empowerment.

(5) These new job opportunities were believed to also lead to an increase in wages. While *Haredi* women are entering the labor force in large numbers, and pave their way into new sectors of employment (such as high-tech sectors), their wages are significantly lower compared to wages of non-*Haredi* Jewish women: Figures for 2019 show that the average monthly salary (for women at the ages of 25–64) are 7,197 shekel for *Haredi* women, compared to 10,082 shekel for the general female working force — a gap of 40 percent. A major part of the salary differential can be explained by differences in working hours (weekly average of 28.6 hours for *Haredi* women, compared to 35.9 for non-*Haredi* Jewish women). Indeed — if figures of hourly wages are compared, the difference shrinks to 7 percent — respective hourly wages of 57.6 and 61.9 (Kasir [Kaliner], 2019).[9] The positive news are that wage differentials are decreasing constantly (Eizencot, 2018). The closing of the wage gap is most probably also due to the new

---

[8]The recent figures are way above the target set by the Israeli government — an employment rate of 63 percent in 2020 (Eizencot, 2018).
[9]Two other potential reasons for the wage disparities are: (1) inferior human capital of *Haredi* women (compared to the general population) — as most *Haredi* women studied and were trained at the religious *seminars,* and not in the better-quality academic institutes; and (2) employment restrictions, e.g., working places for women only.

training/employment schemes that cater to work motives and to employment restrictions.

(6) We focus in this study on women, who are the main providers in the *Haredi* community.[10] Efforts are recently made to also try and attract more *Haredi* men to the labor market, by offering them new training tracks and work opportunities. Unlike women who study also general studies in high-schools (and are exempt from the study of Torah), men study only Torah at the *yeshiva*. Occupational tracks can therefore not be part of their curricula at the *yeshiva* and new venues need to be established. Unraveling motives for male occupational choice is therefore crucial and needs to be examined in order to develop and implement successful training tracks. Career counseling seems to be even more crucial for men, who have no background of general studies and who are obliged to switch from total commitment for the study of Torah, to commitment to the job and labor market. Counselors who belong to the *Haredi* community have an obvious counseling advantage.

(7) Higher employment rates of *Haredi* women and men are also believed to have favorable implications on social tensions between the *Haredi* and non-*Haredi* populations. The tension stems from the fact the *Haredi* population contributes very little to taxes, and gets an unproportional share of welfare and transfer payments. A study by Regev (2014) that is analyzing data of the 2011 Survey of Household Expenditures, indicates that the respective average monthly compulsory payments[11] of non-*Haredi* versus *Haredi* households are: 1,721 versus 226 shekel — for direct taxes (660 percent more); 619 versus 171 shekel for National Insurance Institute fees (3.5 times more); 616 versus 308 shekel for the health insurance tax (double) (Regev, 2014, Figure 11, p. 40). On the other hand, a *Haredi* household receives on average benefits and transfer payments of 3,256 shekel, compared to 1,964 received by a non-*Haredi* household (Regev, 2014, Figure 5, p. 28). Obviously an increased attachment of the *Haredi* population to

---

[10]As noted above, in 2018, the employment rate of *Haredi* men (at the working age of 25–64), was 50.7 percent, compared to an employment rate of 75.9 percent of *Haredi* women, and an employment rate of 87.6 percent for non-*Haredi* Jewish men (Kasir [Kaliner], 2019).

[11]Household monthly compulsory payments in Israel are comprised: income tax, National Insurance Institute (NII) payments, and healthcare insurance tax.

the labor force will change dramatically this uneven balance and will also lower significantly the government's budget deficit.

(8) A similar approach of responding to work motives and to work restrictions can be used for other "non-common" population groups: either other religious/traditional female groups (e.g., Muslim Israeli-Arabs, Muslim females in Europe, traditional/religious women in Asia and Africa[12]), or other groups with low attachment to the labor force (e.g., disabled individuals, the elderly, recent immigrants). The study of motives behind occupational choice is essential in order to design occupational tracks that will satisfy the motives, preferences and limitations of potential workers who currently have limited labor-force attachment.

(9) Increased participation in the labor force of populations that are currently only marginally attached to the labor market could also lead to positive macro outcomes, in terms of: increased economic growth; reduced poverty within the low-employability populations; and a lower burden on welfare budgets. Furthermore: the design of occupations that cater to intrinsic motives (and consequently lead to more job satisfaction), coupled with the documented positive relationship between job satisfaction and performance/productivity could further add to economic growth.

References

Almog, S. and Perry-Hazan, L. (2011). "The Ability to Claim and the Opportunity to Imagine: Rights Consciousness and the Education of Ultra-Orthodox Girls," *Journal of Law and Education*, 40(2), 273–303.

Amabile, T. M., Hill, K. G., Hennessey, B. A. and Tighe, E. M. (1994). "The Work Preference Inventory: Assessing Intrinsic and Extrinsic Motivational Orientations," *Journal of Personality and Social Psychology*, 66(5), 950–967.

Ben-Moshe, E. (2012). *Changes in the Structure and Composition of the Israeli Population in the Coming Twenty Years, by Cultural/Religious Segment, and Its Implications for the Labor Force.* Jerusalem: Ministry of

---

[12] Traditional/religious women in Africa and Asia also face employment restrictions and low labor force participation rates. There is an urgent need for government intervention in order to overcome restrictions (e.g., credit restrictions), empower women, and increase their employability (Hanmer and Dahan, 2015; The World Bank, 2018; Sioson and Chul, 2019; Taghizadeh-Hesary *et al.*, 2019).

Industry, Trade and Employment: Administration of Planning, Research and Economics (in Hebrew).

Berman, E. (2000). "Sect, Subsidy, and Sacrifice: An Economist's View of Ultra-Orthodox Jews," *The Quarterly Journal of Economics*, 115(5), 905–953.

Blustein, D. L. (2006). *The Psychology of Working: A New Perspective for Career Development, Counseling, and Public Policy*. New Jersey: Lawrence Elbaum Associates Inc.

Caplan, K. (2007). *Internal Popular Discourse in Israeli Haredi Society*. Jerusalem: The Zalman Shazar Center for Jewish History (in Hebrew).

Dahan, N. (2004). *Inter-Cultural Encounter: An Experimental Training Program for Social Workers, for Haredi Women*. Ph.D. Thesis. Jerusalem: Hebrew University, School of Social Work and Social Welfare (in Hebrew).

Dik, B. J. and Duffy, R. D. (2009). "Calling and Vocation at Work: Definitions and Prospects for Research and Practice," *The Counseling Psychologist*, 37, 424–450.

Dik, B. J., Sargent, A. M. and Steger, M. F. (2008). "Career Development Striving: Assessing Goals and Motivation in Career Decision Making and Planning," *Journal of Career Development*, 35, 23–41.

Duffy, R. D. and Dik, B. J. (2013). "Research on Calling: What Have we Learnt so Far and Where are we Going?" *Journal of Vocational Behavior*, 83, 428–436.

Eizencot, M. (2018). "Employment of the *Haredi* Sector: Government National Targets and Data for Recent Years," *Center for Research and Information, The Israeli Knesset*. Report prepared for the Finance Committee of the Knesset.

Elangoven, A. R., Pinder, C. C. and McLean, M. (2010). "Calling and Organizational Behavior," *Journal of Vocational Behavior*, 76, 428–440.

Friedman, M. (1988). *The Haredi Women*. Jerusalem: The Jerusalem Institute for Israel Studies.

Fuchs, H. and Weiss, A. (1918). "Israel's Labor Market: An Overview," in *State of the Nation Report, 2018*, Weiss A., (ed.), pp. 85–104. Jerusalem: The Taub Center for Social Policy Studies in Israel.

Gagne, M. and Deci, E. L. (2005). "Self-Determination Theory and Work Motivation," *Journal of Organizational Behavior*, 26, 331–362.

Goldfarb, Y. (2011). *Alternative Training Modes in Girls' Schools of the Haredi Population: The "Chen" Program*. The Ministry of Industry, Trade and Employment: Administration of Planning, Research and Economics (in Hebrew).

Goldfarb, Y. (2014). *Evaluation of the "Chen" Program: Vocational Counseling in Seminars for Haredi Women*. The Ministry of Industry, Trade and Employment: Administration of Planning, Research and Economics (in Hebrew).

Gottliev, D. (2007). *Poverty and Labor Market Behavior in the Ultra-Orthodox Population in Israel.* Jerusalem: Van Leer Jerusalem Institute (in Hebrew).

Hagmaier, T. and Abele, A. E. (2012). "The Multi-Dimensionality of Calling: Conceptualization, Measurement and a Bicultural Perspective," *Journal of Vocational Behavior,* 81, 39–51.

Hanmer, N. and Dahan, M. (2015). "Identification for Development: Its Potential for Empowering Women and Girls," The World Bank: Voices.

Horowitz, N. and Sagi, K. (2013). *Practical Engineering Policy in Israel, in the Context of the New Labor Market.* The Ministry of Industry, Trade and Employment: Administration of Planning, Research and Economics (in Hebrew).

Hunter, I., Dik, B. J. and Banning, J. H. (2010). "College Students' Perceptions of Calling in Work and Life: A Qualitative Analysis," *Journal of Vocational Behavior,* 76, 178–186.

Israel, Central Bureau of Statistics (CBS) (2002). *Social Survey, Module: Pensions and Retirement Savings.*

Israel, Central Bureau of Statistics (CBS) (2008). *Social Survey, Module: Social Mobility.*

Israel, Central Bureau of Statistics (CBS) (2009). *Social Survey, Module: Religiosity and Family in Israel.*

Israel, Central Bureau of Statistics (CBS) (2013). *Social Survey, Module: Welfare.*

Israel, Ministry of Industry, Trade and Employment (various press releases).

Kasir (Kaliner), N. (2019). *Haredi Employment.* Jerusalem: The Haredi Institute for Public Affairs.

Lupu, J. (2003). *A Shift in Haredi Society: Vocational Training and Academic Studies.* Jerusalem: The Floersheimer Institute for Policy Studies (in Hebrew).

Malach, G. and Cahaner, L. (2019). *2019 Statistical Report on the Ultra-Orthodox Society in Israel.* The Israel Democracy Institute.

Neriya-Ben Shahar, R. (2015). "To Be the Wife of a Torah Scholar," *Journal of Haredi Society Research,* 2, 192–169 (in Hebrew).

Neuman, S. (2014). *Job Quality in Segmented Labour Markets: The Israeli Case.* International Labor Office (ILO) Project on: "Country Case Studies on Labour Market Segmentation," ILO Discussion Paper No. 55.

Pieser, C. (1984). *The Relationship between Information and Interests in the Same Vocational Fields: Its Nature and Relevance to Vocational Choice and Success.* Haifa: University of Haifa, Department of Psychology, Ph.D. Thesis (in Hebrew).

Regev, E. (2013). "Education and Employment in the *Haredi* Sector," in *A Report on the State of the Nation: Society, Economy and Policy,* D. Ben-David, (ed.), pp. 119–162. Jerusalem: The Taub Center for Social Studies in Israel.

Regev, E. (2014). "Making Ends Meet — Household Income, Expenditures and Savings in Israel," in *Report on the State of the Nation: Society, Economy and Policy*, D. Ben-David, (ed.), pp. 19–90. Jerusalem: The Taub Center for Social Studies in Israel.

Ringel, S. (2007). "Identity and Gender Roles of Orthodox Jewish Women: Implications for Social Work Practice," *Smith Studies in Social Work*, 77(2/3), 25–44.

Ross, T. (2004). *Expanding the Palace of Torah: Orthodoxy and Feminism*. Waltham, MA: Brandeis University Press.

Sioson, E. P. and Chul, K. (2019). "Closing the Gender Gap in Financial Inclusion through Fintech," Asian Development Bank Institute, DP No. 2019-3.

Shea-van Fossen, R. J. and Vredenburgh, D. J. (2014). "Exploring Differences in Work's Meaning: An Investigation of Individual Attributes Associated with Work Orientations," *Journal of Behavioral and Applied Management*, 15(2), 101–120.

Super, D. E. (1970). *Work Values Manual*. Boston: Houghton Mifflin.

Taghizadeh-Hesary, F., Yoshino, N. and Fakuda, L. (2019). "Gender and Corporate Success: An Empirical Analysis of Gender-Based Corporate Performance on a Sample of Asian Small and Medium-Sized Enterprises," Asian Bank Institute Working Paper Series, WP No. 937.

The World Bank (2018). *Global Gender Gap and Economic Participation and Opportunity*.

Weinreb, A., Chernichovsky, D. and Brill, A. (2018). "Israel's Exceptional Fertility," in *State of the Nation Report*, A. Weiss, (ed.), pp. 271–312. Jerusalem: The Taub Center for Social Policy Studies in Israel.

Wrzesniewski, A., McCauley, C., Rozin, P. and Schwartz, B. (1997). "Jobs, Careers, and Callings: People's Relations to their Work," *Journal of Research in Personality*, 31, 21–33.

Wrziesniewski, A. (2012), "Callings," in *Oxford Handbook of Positive Organizational Scholarship*, K. Cameron and G. Spreitzer (eds.), pp. 45–54. New York: Oxford University Press.

Chapter 8

Religion and Volunteering

John Wilson

Duke University, Durham, NC, USA
john.wilson@duke.edu

Abstract

Volunteering is a form of prosocial behavior that involves a freely chosen decision to commit a sustained amount of time and effort to helping another person, group or cause, typically through an organization. Religion is a powerful and consistent predictor of volunteer activities in many countries however it is measured (e.g., church attendance) and whether or not the volunteer work is narrowly religious or broadly secular. Religion also helps explain variations in volunteering by country, race or ethnicity, gender and age. Recent research has uncovered reasons for the positive effect of religion, most prominently the role of social networks.

Keywords: Volunteer, Church Attendance, Affiliation, Congregations, Salience, Networks

1. Introduction

This chapter is about the relation between religion and a particular kind of work — volunteering. To understand the place of voluntary work in modern economies it is necessary to recognize that what constitutes work as opposed to something else, such as leisure, is not whether it is paid but whether it provides a service to others or produces goods for the consumption of others. Volunteering is unpaid work formally performed in the public sphere, where formal means organized. It is different from not only paid work but also from household or family work, informal public work such as unpaid caring for an elderly neighbor, and informal economic activity, such as babysitting for a co-worker (Taylor, 2004).

In an article written just over three and a half decades ago Smith (1983) observed that researchers had almost entirely overlooked the possibility that "voluntary action" and religiosity might be associated. Evidently, things had not improved much 10 years later when Cnaan *et al.* (1993) remarked how little research had addressed the connection between volunteering and religious beliefs or participation in religious institutions. But research on volunteering in general has taken "a giant leap recently" (Nieburr *et al.*, 2018: 1234) and dozens of articles have been published on the relation between religion and volunteering (see Polson, 2018), not to mention many studies that have included a measure of religion as a "control" in research exploring other determinants of volunteering (Musick and Wilson, 2008; Nieburr *et al.*, 2018). It is now largely accepted that religion rivals education as a "powerful correlate of most forms of civic engagement" (Putnam, 2000: 67).

As more research has accumulated on the association between religiosity and volunteering, new insights have emerged. Religiosity has a positive effect not only on volunteering on behalf of the church and its members but also "service-oriented volunteering" in the wider community (Wuthnow, 2004: 106) or broadly speaking on secular volunteering (Storm, 2015b). As interest in the religiosity-volunteering connection has grown, more careful attention has been paid to each of the various dimensions of religion and how they might connect in their own way to volunteering. Cultural or motivational dimensions of religion such as beliefs, values and salience are compared with structural dimensions such as affiliation, worship service attendance, religious group activity and religious social networks. And as the effects of the various religion dimensions are explored, attention turns to how these effects are moderated by religious affiliation, denomination, and the nature of the volunteer work.

The relation between religion and volunteering is, at first glance, simple: the more religious people are, the more likely they are to volunteer. All the dominant religions preach the virtue of caring for others.

Helping the needy and seeking justice are "essential tenets of most religions" (Cnaan *et al.*, 2016: 475). For example, Christians are told that it is more blessed to give than receive. Religious people certainly see themselves as being prosocial and are seen as such by others (Saroglou *et al.*, 2005: 342). More religious people tend to be empathetic, charitable, forgiving, cooperative, and helpful (Schumann, 2020). Closer inspection, however, reveals the extreme complexity of the relation. This is because both phenomena are multi-dimensional: religion has many different sides to it and volunteer work can take many forms. And both phenomena are shaped by their social environment: the role of religion varies from one community or country to another; the meaning of and the role played by volunteering varies for similar reasons. This means the relation between them will also vary by social circumstances.

What follows is a description and assessment of research into the religion-volunteering link over the past three decades. (For a review of earlier work see Jackson *et al.* (1995).) Its scope is confined to economic, psychological and sociological studies, most of them using survey data of some kind. Attention will be limited to formal volunteer work; i.e., help provided to others that takes place in the context of an organization. Informal volunteering — helping others on a personal basis — will not be considered. Although a broad definition of volunteering includes what is referred to as "social activism" much of the work in that area is excluded due to limited space, as is the research on religion and political participation, some of which includes volunteer work. Thus, the fact that religion played a very important role in the civil rights movement in the United States and several other countries is not considered here. It is also important to bear in mind that mere membership or "participation" in voluntary associations is not itself volunteering.

The survey is arranged by level of analysis. First, studies that rely on individual-level or micro-level data are described. Here the information pertains to the individual. Since religion can be roughly divided into beliefs and practices, at this level the focus is not only on a person's "subjective dispositions," such as beliefs, values, norms and attitudes but it also includes the importance of religion in one's life (salience), strength of religious identity (the importance of the religious role in relation to other roles), a person's religious practices, such as worship service attendance, level of participation in congregational or parish activities, and more private, spiritual observances such as prayer and meditation.

At the micro level volunteer work is measured by intensity (e.g., hours per week or month) or frequency (e.g., how many times a year), the domain in which the work is located (e.g., school, health, politics, neighborhood safety), the kinds of tasks performed (e.g., tutoring, fundraising), and the degree to which a person identifies with the volunteer role. The last is important to consider because volunteering can become not merely a leisure pastime but a way to define one's self, especially if volunteer work provides an opportunity to express core values. In this respect, religion would not necessarily increase the likelihood of volunteering but influence the meaning and significance of the work. It might transform volunteering into a vocation, or a calling (Gronlund, 2012).

At the meso level attention turns to the influence on volunteering of the immediate religious context. Are those with many religious people among their friends more likely to volunteer? How does the social organization of the religious congregation or parish affect the probability of volunteering among members of that organization? How does the relation between different congregations in a community affect the volunteer rate in that community? The "dependent variable" in this case is, strictly speaking, the rate of volunteering in a particular entity (congregation, social network) but a hybrid form of meso-analysis uses the individual as the dependent variable. How is an individual's volunteer behavior affected by the religiosity of the individual's social context?

At the macro level the focus is broader. Units of analysis might be neighborhoods, counties, cities, geographical regions or countries. Do more secular countries have lower volunteer rates? Do volunteer rates decline as countries become more secular? Does the role of religion in promoting volunteer work expand or contract with the rise of the welfare state? Here, again, the pure form of macro-analysis uses the rate of volunteering in the entity as the dependent variable. Does the rate of religiosity in a country affect the rate of volunteering in that country? But a hybrid form would ask whether an individual who moves to a more religious country is more likely to volunteer (i.e., the dependent variable is at the individual level).

The survey ends by describing how the relation between religion and volunteering is *moderated* by factors other than context. The precise influence of religion on volunteering is partly determined by the individual characteristics of those involved. This is due to the multidimensional character of both phenomena. Thus, different actors will espouse different religions depending on their social status and this will alter its influence on volunteer work. Similarly, the meaning and significance of volunteer work is partly dependent on the actors involved: some are drawn to volunteer work that provides help to individuals on a face-to-face basis; others are drawn to volunteer work that is closer to a form of social activism. Thus, older adults might "use" their religion to motivate a very different form of volunteering than younger adults. Age is thereby conditioning the influence of religion on volunteering. The same is likely to be true of gender, social class, race/ethnicity, immigrant status, marital and parent status as well as many other social statuses.

2. What is Volunteering?

Volunteering is a form of prosocial behavior that involves a freely chosen decision to commit a sustained amount of time and effort to helping another person, group or cause, typically through a non-profit organization or an institution such as a school or hospital (Stukas *et al.*, 2014).

Volunteer work can assume many forms and take place in many domains. Not all surveys differentiate types of volunteering, which is an obstacle to measuring the effect of religion on volunteering because religious volunteering is very popular, especially in the United States, where, according to one breakdown, 42.3 percent did not volunteer, 23.4 percent volunteered for the community but not through their church, 22.1 percent volunteered both through their church and not through their church, and 12 percent volunteered for the community only through their church (Mencken and Fitz, 2013). Consonant with this finding religiousness (measured by a latent factor consisting of church attendance, religious identity ("are you a religious person?"), reading sacred texts, and prayer) was not correlated at all with volunteering in the community although it was positively related to community volunteering organized by the church (Tsang *et al.*, 2015). It is therefore quite important to know what people are actually doing when they volunteer.

In some cases, religiousness actually inhibits secular volunteering such as working on behalf of a political campaign or a trade union. This is shown in a survey covering many different European countries, where attending religious services and religious salience positively affected volunteering for both religious and secular organizations but belonging to a religious organization (a different dimension of religion) was a deterrent to secular volunteering (Storm, 2015b). Similarly, in the United States, religious salience, traditional beliefs and private practices positively affected volunteering for religious causes sponsored by the church but negatively affected volunteering for non-religious causes (Monsma, 2007). This division of volunteer labor between religious and secular is moderated by denomination. Liberal Protestants in the US encourage community engagement, Evangelicals discourage it (by absorbing members' time in religious volunteering such as helping organize worship services), while the Roman Catholic Church does not encourage community engagement by members in the belief that it is largely the responsibility of the church itself (Uslaner, 2002: 240).

And yet it would be unwise to presume that religious and secular volunteering are always at odds with one another, that time spent on one detracts from time spent on the other. In the US and Canada more than 80 percent of people who volunteer for religious causes also give their time to secular groups (Uslaner, 2002: 245). Indeed, it is often difficult to distinguish between religious and secular volunteering. Volunteering in the community, such as serving meals at a soup kitchen or homeless shelter, providing emergency assistance to impoverished people, organizing blood drives and health screenings, ministering to prison inmates, advocating for community needs, sponsoring support groups, while they might be considered secular, can be regarded as forms of mission work, as a way to practice one's religion (McClure, 2017).

3. What is Religiosity?

As with volunteering, religiosity is a complex phenomenon. It has long been recognized that "measuring religiosity with only one index is obviously misleading" (Wilson, 1978: 441). In addition to the more public and social aspects of being religious, such as attending worship services, engaging in collective rituals, and participating in activities organized by the congregation, there are more private aspects, such as praying at home and watching religious programs on television, or simply being "spiritual" and practicing religious enhancement techniques such as meditation. In addition to these private practices, religiosity is also a personal and social identity, helping determine who one socializes with, how one educates one's children, who one votes for and so on. Also included in the more private aspects of religion are the uses of religious ideas and practices to cope with the stresses of everyday life and to inform decision-making.

Finally, and independent of both public and private aspects of religion, there is the "belief dimension": the values, beliefs and norms taught by whatever religious tradition the individual commits to.

4. Why Does Religion Affect Volunteering?

Broadly speaking, there are two types of reasons why religiosity encourages volunteering: they can be referred to as conviction and community (Wuthnow, 1991). Conviction means that religion motivates volunteering by shaping people's opinions about what is right and wrong, generating concern for other people's well-being, fostering trust in fellow citizens, and deepening feelings of responsibility for others. Religion has the potential to change the way people think about themselves and their relationship to others. It is quite plausible that people who think of themselves as religious and who believe that religion is important to them in their everyday life will internalize a duty to help others if this is what their preachers teach them. For example, being "spiritual" or having a "spiritual experiences" is often described as a feeling of "oneness" with others. This is just as likely to create a feeling of duty to help others as is regularly attending church. In the case of private religion there is little interactional connection to volunteerism: the subjective aspects of religion, such as identification, and the personal practices of religion, such as meditation, imply no specific patterns of interaction or connection but can nevertheless motivate charitable activities.

Community means that religion motivates people to volunteer by creating an interactional context in which people are made aware of opportunities to give help and are likely to be asked, even pressed, to do so. Community also signifies that religiosity has an organizational infrastructure (e.g., congregation) with maintenance needs that must be met, if only partially, by volunteer labor. Sociologists place much emphasis on the flow of information and influence through the social ties that arises out of the social life of the church. For example, obligations are part of this information flow: prosocial norms taught by the church are more likely to be respected by those who are in weekly contact with fellow believers who can monitor their behavior. But the community mechanism is structural: volunteering is the result of people meeting people or being recruited because they participate in a group, perhaps to work on behalf of the group.

With this in mind it is possible to see that public and private religion operate in different ways, through different mechanisms. Public religion works mainly through social connections; private religion works mainly through changing the way people think about themselves and the world around them. Of course, there is overlap between these two forms of religiosity and few people will practice one in the absence of the other, but testing for the effects of one while controlling for the other throws more light on exactly how religiosity works its effect on volunteering.

5. Research at the Micro Level

At this level the unit of analysis is typically the individual. What separates volunteers from non-volunteers as far as individual characteristics are concerned and is religiosity one of these characteristics?

5.1 *Affiliation and denomination*

It is logical to begin by asking whether the religion to which a person belongs shapes volunteer behavior. Belonging is typically thought of in terms of "affiliation" and "denomination." *Affiliation* is a term used to describe the broad religious tradition to which a person belongs, such as Jew, Protestant Christian, Catholic Christian, Hindu or Muslim. *Denomination* is a term used to describe the particular religious organization to which a person might belong such as Methodist, Lutheran, Southern Baptist, Episcopalian, Church of England or Reformed Jewish. Differences in the rate of volunteering across these broad divisions have been uncovered in a number of studies.

Within the Christian tradition, Catholics volunteer less than Protestants (Beyerlein and Hipp, 2006; Driskell *et al.*, 2008; Hoge and Yang, 1994; Kirchmaier *et al.*, 2018; Musick and Wilson, 2008: 90; Taniguchi and Thomas, 2011; Wuthnow, 1991: 322; Yen and Zampelli, 2014: 66). Volunteer work in the community has special affinities with the mainline Protestant traditions. In the United States especially, it is large component of what it means to be religious (Lichterman, 2005: 246). Evidence on volunteering by members of smaller denominations is scarce because they do not show up in large numbers in social surveys. Jews in the United States, especially those belonging to the more liberal Reform denomination, have a strong tradition of service to the wider community, while ethnic Jews "lacking denominational identification are much less active in general community voluntary associations" (Lazerwitz and Harrison, 1979: 662). A survey of "emerging adult" Mormons found that they volunteer more frequently than their Christian peers, in large part because they place heavy emphasis on eternal family unity and volunteer work geared to the needs of the Mormon religious community. Highly religious Mormons are especially likely to volunteer for the benefit of family and church (Johnson *et al.*, 2016). Reliable data on whether these affiliation differences are also found in areas such as Latin America or in African countries, to the extent religion is organized in the same way, are not available.

5.2 *Religious or secular volunteering*

The effect of affiliation or denomination cannot be accurately gauged without separating religious from secular volunteering. Within Protestantism, Evangelicals volunteer for secular causes at a lower rate than Moderate or Liberal Protestants (e.g., United Church of Christ, Unitarian, Presbyterian, and Episcopalian). Actually, the US Evangelicals volunteer at a higher rate than other Christians or non-Christians but most, if not all, of the labor time they donate is devoted to church-related tasks (Schwadel, 2005). Their volunteer work is aimed at saving souls rather than community development (Wilson and Janoski, 1995). Kim and Wilcox (2013) argue that the religiosity of conservative denominations does not directly discourage secular involvement: rather, the strong "familism" of such denominations creates an insularity that shuts off outreach to the wider community. (For a contrasting finding on US Pentecostals where they are no less likely than members of other denominations to volunteer for secular causes, see Dougherty *et al.*, 2011.)

If US Evangelicals do engage in volunteer work in the community they are more likely than other Protestants to use religious language (e.g., "mission") to describe what they are doing (Lichterman, 2005). They are less likely to volunteer for social change organizations than individuals with no religious beliefs (Guo *et al.*, 2013). Thus, Evangelical Protestants devote the majority of their volunteer time to their church and mission work, Liberal Protestants devote most of their volunteer time to secular causes, and Mainline and Black Protestants and Catholics distribute their volunteer time evenly.

Although these findings are derived from the US survey data Evangelicals elsewhere exhibit the same patterns. They cultivate social connections and social networks among their own kind, whereas mainline Protestant churches forge connections beyond their own communities. They foster strong in-group ties at the cost of secular civic participation, because Evangelical churches expect more commitment from their members, offer more activities in addition to Sunday worship, and emphasize their distinctiveness from the secular world (Vermeer and Scheepers, 2019). Furthermore, these small group activities also strengthen friendship bonds within the congregation, limiting the propensity of evangelicals to engage in secular and non-church activities. This stands in contrast to other Protestants where congregations are more likely to mobilize volunteers for secular organizations in addition to their promotion of religious volunteer work (Ammerman, 2002: 154).

5.3 Affiliation moderates the effect of other religious dimensions on volunteering

In the sections that follow many examples will be given of affiliation or denomination moderating (changing) the effect of another religious dimension on volunteering. For example, frequency of church attendance has no effect on volunteer work among Mormons for whom religious beliefs and values are more influential (Johnson *et al.*, 2013). Religious salience is more important for Black Protestants and Evangelical Protestants in predicting secular volunteering than for Catholics. Social network effects also vary by affiliation. For example, level of involvement in congregation activities (beyond attending religious services) has substantially stronger effects on secular volunteering for Black Protestant, mainline Protestant and Catholic congregations than for Evangelical Protestant congregations. This suggests that religious traditions act as proxies for congregational features that affect member participation in civic activities connecting to and serving the wider community (Johnston, 2013).

While religious affiliation and denomination are obvious markers of religiosity, their distinctive contribution to volunteer work is uncertain. It is probably true that those who report *some* affiliation are more active volunteers than those who report none (Monsma, 2007). But the extent of the influence of affiliation, *independent of other religious dimensions*, is open to question. People typically decide to volunteer for a congregation after being asked to do so by congregational friends and fellow members. Volunteering by church goers depends on the social networks their congregation creates rather than their denominational affiliation or their liberal or conservative theology. Thus, both liberals and conservatives in the religious world volunteer to the same extent but interpret their volunteer activity in different ways. Liberals consider their volunteering as a civic duty and as helping others around them, while conservatives consider their volunteering as a spiritual act expressing their religious beliefs. Finally, while some contend that, once other religiosity measures are controlled, affiliation or denomination by themselves have little influence on volunteering, it is probably more accurate to conclude that they moderate the effect of other religious measures and that much depends on whether the volunteer work is religious or secular (Campbell and Yonish, 2003).

5.4 *Attendance at worship services*

Almost all studies of religion and volunteering include a measure of frequency of church attendance. In fact, it could be argued that how often you go to church is a more important predictor of whether you volunteer than the denominational affiliation of the church you attend (Campbell and Yonish, 2003: 98). Bennett (2015: 90) adds strength to this argument in an analysis of survey data from 113 countries showing that inhabitants with a religious affiliation are much more likely to volunteer than those without one and that affiliation differences in average frequency of church attendance helps explain much of this difference.

In a meta-analysis of four longitudinal studies published between 2010 and 2015 each showed a positive effect of church attendance on volunteering (Nieburr *et al.*, 2018). In a more recent longitudinal analysis, those who attended religious services more often at baseline increased their volunteer hours at a faster rate over the life course than those who attended religious services infrequently. In other words, the rate of change in religious attendance was positively associated with the rate of change in volunteering. (Kim and Yang, 2017). In an interesting refinement, Petrovic *et al.* (2021) separated the decision to volunteer from the number of hours volunteered. They find that, among those who volunteer, frequency of church attendance has a positive effect on the amount of time spent volunteering. Musick and Wilson (2008) delve into deeper detail to report that frequency of church attendance has an effect on the odds of performing particular volunteer tasks in the church, such as assisting the clergy and teaching. It could be, of course, that undertaking volunteer work is encouraging more regular and frequent church attendance.

5.5 *Reasons why church attendance affects volunteering*

The reasons why church attendance might influence volunteering can be grouped under two broad headings. The first is cultural. Attending worship services frequently and regularly serves as a formal venue for the transmission of the virtues of benevolence and charity toward others. Messages about helping others are often embedded in sermons, group prayers, and hymns. The second is structural. Attending church on a regular basis increases the chances of being asked by fellow church members to do volunteer work (Musick *et al.*, 2000). Frequent church attendance not only increases the chances of being asked but also the chances of agreeing to volunteer if asked (Musick and Wilson, 2008).

5.6 *Comparison of church attendance with other religious dimensions*

Frequency of church attendance is a stock item in general social surveys. But it is only one dimension of religion. (Others will be described in detail below.) One important issue is whether church attendance continues to have a positive effect when other dimensions of religion are taken into account. Here the evidence is mixed. For Musick and Wilson (2008: 284) church attendance does not have a positive effect on volunteering, net of other religious activities such as choir practice, outreach programs or prayer meetings, and particularly net of how often the individual participates in church groups. An analysis of congregational influence on "participation in bridging organizations" concluded that "the majority of mechanisms through which congregations mobilize bridging civic engagement are encompassed in congregation activities other than religious services" (Beyerlein and Hipp, 2006: 114). And yet in one recent Dutch study using four measures of religion to simultaneously predict hours of volunteering *per* week (church membership, service attendance, private prayer, belief in God and belief in theological concepts, e.g., existence of Heaven) all were independently and positively related to volunteer hours per week (Kirchmaier *et al.*, 2018). A survey conducted in Finland found a similar pattern, although churchgoing remained the best predictor of volunteering even when an item on frequency of prayer and a question on the importance of God were included (Yeung, 2004).

5.7 *Type of volunteering: Religious or secular*

What kind of volunteer work is most affected by church attendance? Reports vary as to whether or not church attendance's influence is limited to volunteer work in connection with the church itself. In some cases, church attendance has a stronger effect on religious than secular volunteering and in some cases there is no effect on secular volunteering at all. Clearly, it is wise for researchers to specify the type of volunteer work. Those that do yield mixed results. An effect of church attendance on both religious and secular volunteering is reported by Wuthnow (2004). In some cases attendance is more strongly associated with religious than secular volunteering (Bekkers and Schuyt, 2008; Mersianova and Schneider, 2018; Musick and Wilson, 2008: 279) or not related to secular volunteering at all (Jackson *et al.*, 1995; Paik and Navarre-Jackson, 2011). Church attendance even has a negative effect on secular volunteering in some instances (Lam, 2002; Park and Smith, 2000) especially where controls for other religious dimensions are used. A more detailed breakdown of volunteering activities in connection with the church is used in a survey of Indiana residents in the US. Church attendance was positively related to volunteer work that consisted of providing religious services, providing direct services to members of the community and maintenance of buildings and grounds. It was not related to fundraising, managing or communications (Kronbjerg and Never, 2004). On the other hand, Yeung (2018) found that frequent church attendance predicted 10 types of volunteer work, including health, educational support, recreational activities, youth development and political campaigns. "Private" religiosity, such as prayer, was not related. Within the secular domain the most powerful effects of religion were found in the humanitarian domain, followed by the cultural and work-related, with the least being in the domain of the political (Yeung, 2017). (It should be noted these findings are drawn from a limited sample.)

5.8 *Moderation of church attendance effect*

Some of the mixed results described previously might be due to the fact that attendance's effect is moderated by other factors. As already noted, the significance of church attendance depends to some degree on denomination (Wilson and Janoski, 1995). Another moderator is age. Thus, among young liberal Protestants, the most significant difference in volunteering is between casual church goers (i.e., once or twice a month) and those who never attend. By the time these same respondents reach middle age, the relation has become more linear and the volunteer difference between frequent church attendance and never attending church is more pronounced. The volunteer rate among Moderate Protestants, on the other hand, is unaffected by frequency of church attendance at any age, while young adult Catholics who attended church weekly are more likely than infrequent attenders to volunteer, the difference becoming more evident as they reach middle age. In short, simply measuring frequency of church attendance without considering how its effect might be moderated by other religious dimensions (and by age) is not the most accurate way of determining its effect on volunteering.

5.9 *Indirect effects of church attendance*

Given religion's many dimensions it is possible that frequency of church attendance has an effect on volunteering "through" one of these other dimensions. This is a mediation effect. Thus, Jackson *et al.* (1995) were unable to detect any effect of church attendance on secular volunteering once the respondents' level of activity in "church groups" was included in the analysis. This suggests that church attendance was having an indirect effect on volunteering, through church groups. Going to worship services increased the chances of participating in a church group during the week which in turn increased the chances of volunteering (Musick and Wilson, 2008: 284). A Dutch study confirms this pattern: church attendance was not directly related to secular volunteering but did have some influence on it through religious volunteering (de Hart and Dekker, 2013).

5.10 *Global relevance of service attendance*

Judging by multi-country surveys and studies conducted within a single country, the positive association between worship service attendance and volunteering seems to be universal. A positive effect is found in the US (Musick and Wilson, 2008), Australia (Bellamy and Leonard, 2015; Petrovic *et al.*, 2021), Canada (Sinha, 2015), Denmark (Henriksen *et al.*, 2008), Germany (Heineck, 2017), the Netherlands (Bekkers and Schuyt,

2008; Van Tienen *et al.*, 2011), the United Kingdom (Storm, 2015a) and the Russian Federation (Mersianova and Schneider, 2018). Multi-country surveys using data sets such as the European Social Survey and World Gallup Poll largely confirm this pattern (Bennett, 2015; Glanville *et al.*, 2016). Further confirmation comes from another multi-country analysis in which "public religiosity" (measured by church attendance) was an important factor in predicting volunteering. The effect of attendance changed only very slightly when measures of "private religiosity" (religious salience and prayer) were included (Paxton *et al.*, 2014). Problematically, different types of volunteering are rarely distinguished in these multi-country studies. One that focused on volunteering to help the needy found that in 10 countries the association with frequency of church attendance was positive (although varying in strength) but in seven countries (India, Kyrgyzstan, Mexico, Philippines, Spain, Uganda and Macedonia) there was no significant association (Luria *et al.*, 2017). (This study included several controls for cultural differences between countries (e.g., "individualism/collectivism") that might help explain the inconsistent effect of church attendance.)

In conclusion, frequency of church attendance is often the simplest question to ask in social surveys but its value as an accurate measure of religion's effect on volunteering is debatable. It is closely tied to other dimensions of religion, such as participation in church-related organizations (Monsma, 2007). People who participate in church social activities of any kind tend to also volunteer and *vice versa*. No doubt the motivations driving attendance, participation in church groups and volunteering overlap, motivations that include the gratification of spending time with fellow church members and doing meaningful tasks in their company. Volunteering is such a close "cousin" to worship attendance that it is questionable whether they should be separated for observation (Hoge *et al.*, 1998).

5.11 *Salience*

If religion is only marginally relevant in a person's life it will not have much influence on thinking or behavior. A measure of how important religion is to a person is typically referred to as "salience" (Hoge and De Zulueta, 1985). The relation between religious salience and volunteering has been examined in many different contexts, with varying results. In the Netherlands, salience was positively associated with religious but not secular volunteering (Bekkers and Schuyt, 2008). Another study found that salience was a predictor of volunteering until church attendance was added to the model (Van Tienen *et al.*, 2012). A cross-sectional analysis covering 15 European countries found that, even with church attendance taken into account, religious salience had a positive effect on both secular and religious volunteering (Paxton *et al.*, 2014). In addition, stronger feelings of religious salience enhanced the positive effect of church attendance and *vice versa*. When Becker and Dhingra (2001) surveyed members of four US Protestant congregations about their volunteer work salience had a positive effect when all members were counted but no effect among regular church goers. Volunteering by church goers depended more on their social integration into the congregation.

Longitudinal data on the connection between salience and volunteering throw a somewhat different light on the association. Johnston (2013) found that the effect of religious salience disappeared once church attendance was included in the analysis. Perhaps attendance was acting as a mediator of the effect of salience: if people think religion is important in their lives they will attend church frequently and this in turn will increase their chances of volunteering. When the analysis was confined just to volunteers, religious salience increased the number of hours volunteered. In a growth curve analysis of the same US data religious salience (controlling for church attendance) had no effect on either the intercept or slope of general volunteering (Kim and Yang, 2017). Based on these two sophisticated studies (albeit of the same data) it seems improbable that salience has an independent effect on volunteering when other religious dimensions are included in the analysis. (For example, Choi (2003) finds that religious salience has a positive effect on volunteering among older Americans but does not control for church attendance.)

5.12 *Different types of volunteering*

Perhaps salience is more closely connected to certain kinds of volunteer work. A more detailed breakdown of volunteer activities is used by Gil-Lacruz *et al.* (2016) in an analysis of youth volunteering in Europe. Volunteer activities are divided into "social conscience," "professional," "leisure" and "social justice" types. Salience was measured by religion being "an important aspect of life." It was positively related only to social justice volunteering. (No measure of church attendance was included in the study.) In a multi-level analysis of the same data but including respondents in all age groups salience was measured at the national level: that is, the mean response in the country to a question asking if religion was an important part of the respondent's life. No significant effect of national-level salience on volunteering in any of the volunteer categories was found (Gil-Lacruz *et al.*, 2017).

5.13 *Spirituality*

Many people consider themselves to be religious but not in the formal sense of memberships, affiliations, attendance at worship services, participation in groups and so on. They identify as "spiritual but not religious." This is an aspect of religiosity that Wuthnow (2004: 104) calls "spiritual practice": various religious activities that can saturate a person's daily life, such as daily prayer, studying scriptures, meditation and "otherwise expending efforts to grow in one's spiritual life." Spirituality refers to the feeling that a person is connected to a larger world outside themselves, which could be expressed by the term "god" but would also include various forms of non-personal transcendence. Spirituality is much more individualistic than traditional forms of religion (although they are not exclusive). It does not entail participation in group-centered rituals such as worship service nor does it necessarily involve social activities. Because not all "religious" people feel the need to belong to or participate in organized religion, the question arises as to whether these people are, like their more orthodox counterparts, more likely to volunteer. One reason that daily spiritual experiences may cause individuals to help others is that they encourage empathy. If a person feels a spiritual connection or oneness with other people, that person is more likely to be emotionally affected by the suffering of others and motivated to help them.

Scientists have invented a number of scales to measure spirituality. In fact, most of the people who have daily spiritual experiences are also religious in other ways. For example, one daily spiritual experiences scale consists of five descriptions of subjective states, and respondents are asked how often they experience these states on a scale of one ("never") to four ("often"). These states are "A feeling of deep inner peace or harmony," "A feeling of being deeply moved by the beauty of life," "A feeling of strong connection to all of life," "A sense of deep appreciation" and "A profound sense of caring for others." A survey in which this scale is used does not separately measure religious volunteering but there is an "other" volunteer category and, the location being the United States, it is plausible that religious volunteers comprise a large proportion of those indicating they volunteered for this category. A high score on the spiritual experiences scale was associated with more "religious" volunteering but the scale was not related to secular volunteering (Einolf, 2013). In experiments with undergraduate students Saroglou *et al.* (2005) found that spirituality was more closely related to prosocial behavior than more "public" aspects of religion. This probably is a reflection of the age of the subjects. A study disaggregating various forms of being non-religious found that people who described themselves as "spiritual but not religious" were more likely than religious people to volunteer for (or participate in) hobby and interest groups but less likely to contribute to religious groups while those who responded "nothing in particular" were less likely to volunteer/ participate overall, in large part because they did not attend church (Frost and Edgell, 2018). In the Netherlands, "new spirituals" (having an interest in spiritual matters but outside a church group) volunteer at a lower rate than either church-going liberals or fundamentalists but at a higher rate than the "religiously not interested" (de Hart and Dekker, 2013). Another Dutch study found that volunteering did increase with but only for those who attended religious services (Van Tienen *et al.*, 2012). And the fact that a study of older Americans (64–67) found that religiosity as measured by spirituality was unconnected to volunteering (Okun *et al.*, 2015) suggests caution in making general statements about the influence of spirituality, especially if measures of other religious dimensions are available.

5.14 *Identity*

Even religious people (e.g., regular church goers) vary in how deeply embedded their religious identity is in their sense of self. Is religion a vital part of who they are or is it merely a leisure time pursuit? Where does their religious identity rank in relation to other identities they might have, such as a mother, a worker, an activist? In an analysis of interview data with a largely Christian sample, subjects who engaged in volunteering were more likely to report that their religious beliefs were very important to their sense of identity (Einolf, 2011b). Older US adults with a strong religious identification were more likely to be repeat volunteers: specifically, to volunteer across two different surveys conducted 10 years apart (Choi and Chou, 2010). A meta-analysis of four longitudinal studies published between 2010 and 2015 found that religious identification had a "small positive association" with volunteering (Nieburr *et al.*, 2018).

Very few surveys included detailed questions on religious role identity and much remains to be learned on this topic.

5.15 *Values*

Religiosity could be important for volunteering because it changes what is valued. Regardless of their religious affiliation, age or gender, religious people attribute more importance to the value of benevolence and the moral principles of care and justice than the non-religious (Saroglou, 2013). However, whether values affect volunteering net of other religious dimensions is far from clear as is the issue of exactly how values combine with these other dimensions. For example, it might be expected that people who attend church frequently will know more about the values of the church and feel more motivated to act upon them. But one study found that church attendance did not seem to make much difference to people's support of altruistic values. Virtually all regular attenders (97 percent) agreed that giving time to help others is at least fairly important to them but so too did 92 percent of irregular attenders. Making the world a better place was endorsed by 97 percent of regular attenders and 94 percent of irregular attenders. Helping people in need was valued by 90 percent of both groups (Wuthnow, 2004: 123). Values and attendance seemed to be operating independently. On the other hand, volunteers were more common among church members who had heard sermons on social issues and caring for the poor. Once hearing the sermons was taken into account the effect of church attendance became insignificant, suggesting that attendance might well be a proxy measure of the effect of culture or "conviction" on volunteering (Wuthnow, 2004).

5.16 *Beliefs*

People who connect their religious beliefs specifically to helping others are more likely to volunteer (Einolf, 2011b). That is, explicit beliefs are more persuasive than general beliefs. Lessons learned through the religious language of sermons, texts and conversations with other believers could increase motivation for both religious and secular volunteering (Wuthnow, 1991). Many religious ideas are culturally transferred through widespread charitable narratives such as "loving one's neighbor" and the "golden rule" so that they are no longer regarded as particularly religious.

Thus, individuals with higher levels of religious beliefs may find common ground with people in non-religious volunteering organizations interested in voluntary activism and giving back.

An important part of major theistic religions is the image of God they teach. Believers with an image of God as understanding and forgiving are less likely to have negative attitudes toward the needy and more likely to reach out to help them. They are more compassionate toward and forgiving of those in need. Those who believe in an angry and judgmental God on the other hand are disinclined to help those in the wider community. A random sample of American adults were asked to indicate their agreement or disagreement with the statement that God is "angered by human sins" and "angered by my sins." A judgmental image of God reduced the odds of volunteering for the community outside the church. Respondents would rather not volunteer at all than perform volunteer work unrelated to their place of worship. The image of God thus seemed to steer people's altruism toward the in-group and away from out-group members in the wider community (Mencken and Fitz, 2013).

Religious belief on its own does not always connect to volunteering because other dimensions of religion with which it is associated have a more powerful effect. A study of 15 European countries throws more light on its precise role. A factor analysis of four questionnaire items was used to measure religious beliefs: belief in God, belief in the afterlife, belief in Heaven, and belief in Hell. This latent factor was negatively related to the level of volunteering when attendance, salience and prayer were included in the model. But, interestingly, when interacted with attendance the effect of beliefs became positive. This suggests that strong theological beliefs, in the absence of participation in the religious community, deter volunteering and is consistent with the idea that such beliefs foster an otherworldly focus (Paxton *et al.*, 2014).

Religious belief can also be treated as a mediator, connecting another religious dimension to volunteering. According to a 2014 US survey, 69 percent of "highly religious" Christian respondents (defined by frequency of prayer and church attendance) believed that helping the poor and needy was an "essential" component of the Christian identity compared to 43 percent of the not highly religious. Among the highly religious it was rated as more important than attending services, helping in the congregation and reading the Bible (Pew Research Center, 2016). The highly religious were also more likely to have volunteered in the past week. Once again, it is difficult to disentangle the various dimensions of religion: Do people with firm beliefs go to church more often or does frequent church attendance strengthen their belief?

5.17 *Norms*

A social norm is something that is usual, typical, standard or expected. Norms play an important role in guiding people to volunteer especially in a group setting where rule breaking can be observed and sanctioned (Simpson and Willer, 2015). From a rational choice point of view, norms help solve the free-rider problem. Why should anyone, regardless of their capabilities or even their interests, volunteer to provide services to a group or community while others sit back and enjoy those services? The normative answer to this question is that people volunteer because they believe it is their duty to do so and because they expect others to feel the same way. They fear the sanctions imposed if they do not follow the rule and value the social approval and good reputation that comes if they do follow it. And if they have internalized the norm, they feel guilty if they violate it and "feel good" if they respect it.

One investigation of the role of religion in fostering norms to encourage volunteering looked at longitudinal data in the US to determine the influence of having been raised in a religious home on the sense of obligation to help others (a norm) and subsequent volunteering. Does religion affect volunteering by teaching obligations? "Public" religiosity was measured by church attendance and participation in church group meetings. "Private" religiosity consisted of items such as salience. Respondents were asked how important religion was in their home when they were growing up. They were asked about their volunteer work and they also responded to questions asking about their sense of altruistic and civic obligation to help others. The results of the study showed that parental religion had no *direct* effect on respondents' volunteer work as adults. What is more, children reared in religious homes felt no more obliged to help others or serve their community than the children of parents for whom religion was unimportant. It would not be correct, however, to conclude that parental religion exerted no influence over either the off-spring's sense of obligation or volunteering because the parents had "passed on" their religiosity to their children who, as a result, felt more obliged to volunteer and, in most cases, did so (Son and Wilson, 2012).

Religion can therefore influence volunteering by teaching that it is one's duty to help others to whom one has an obligation. To demonstrate this a comparison was made between the influence of three reasons for helping the needy on two types of volunteer work, one targeting the wider community and the other directed at fellow church members. The reasons were: make you feel good, civic responsibility and religious duty. The religious duty or obligation had no effect on the volunteer work directed at the wider community but was positively related to volunteer work to benefit fellow church members (Beyerlein and Vaisey, 2013). (Notably, church attendance, which was controlled for in the analysis, had a positive effect on both types of volunteering.) The conclusion is that the norm or obligation to help others taught by congregations extends mainly to the in-group of believers.

Once again, more light can be thrown on the role of this religious dimension — norms — by considering interactions with other measures of religion. A survey asked older (60+) Australians how much importance they attributed to doing volunteer work, using a scale containing items such as: "It is my responsibility to take some real measures to help others in need." Not surprisingly, agreement with such items was positively related to having performed volunteer work in the previous 12 months but of more significance is the fact that this norm entirely accounted for the positive effect of church attendance frequency (Jongenelis *et al.*, 2020).

5.18 *Motives*

Motives are the reasons people give as to why they feel impelled to act. Although motives for volunteering can be secular (e.g., justice) or instrumental (e.g., making friends) religion is perhaps the most fertile and effective source of reasons to volunteer. People learn stories from their religion about caring for others (e.g., The Good Samaritan) and incorporate them into their own personal narratives. A fellow church member who asks an acquaintance to do volunteer work typically issues not only an invitation to help but also a religiously informed reason why the invitation should be accepted and ought not to be refused. Volunteers can then use this reason to explain to others and to themselves why it makes sense to engage in the activity (Wuthnow, 2004: 129). This is especially true if they belong to a religious community, such as a congregation, where others share their sense of morality and goodness, and where opportunities to discuss volunteer activities and receive encouragement in support of them are provided on a routine basis (Wuthnow, 2004: 132). This moralistic understanding of why volunteer work is worth doing is less readily available in most secular organizations.

Although volunteer motivation has been thoroughly researched, information on the precise role religion plays in determining reasons for volunteering is somewhat scarce. Using data from 18 European countries, Hustinx *et al.* (2015) show that both church attendance and importance of God in one's life are positively related to altruistic motivations for volunteering (e.g., identifying with people who are suffering) while they weaken the importance attached to self-interested motivations (e.g., volunteering to make new friends). Among older Americans, religiosity (measured by service attendance and spirituality) was linked to "value-expressive" motives for volunteering (e.g., "I feel compassion toward people in need"). These motives helped account for the positive connection between attendance and volunteering. Religious people were more likely to volunteer *because* they were differently motivated (Okun *et al.*, 2015).

In truth, most people have mixed motives for their behavior and the same helping activity can be inspired by both religious and secular reasons. Religion can thus be used to bolster other motivations, such as concern over the fate of the environment. In addition, different dimensions of religion can furnish their own motivation to volunteer. Some religious people will be motivated by teachings while others are motivated by a concern to be part of the religious community or by missionary activities (Gronlund, 2011).

5.19 *Mechanisms*

Before leaving the micro level of analysis, where the focus is on individual characteristics, it is necessary to recognize that the effect of religion on volunteering might be indirect. This pattern has already been observed in the case of norms or obligations: religion affects volunteering because it affects norms, not necessarily in a direct manner. Indirect effects can also be found when the focus turns to some of the ways religion can influence our conception of ourselves and our relations to others.

5.20 *Mattering*

Mattering means a feeling of being noticed by others, a belief that one is important to others, and that others rely on one for help. People who volunteer have a stronger sense of "mattering" in the world. They believe that what they do has some significance beyond themselves. Concern for others is a value promoted by all of the major world religions: thus, frequent church going can foster feelings of mattering just as prayers can foster a feeling of identification and empathy with those in distress, providing a springboard to volunteer work (Schieman *et al.*, 2010). There are other, similar, concepts that need to be explored for their mediation potential, including sense of control and self-esteem, both of which could be cultivated by religion and both of which could be associated with volunteering.

5.21 *Generativity*

Generativity is a state of mind in which people think of themselves as having certain qualities that predispose them to engage in prosocial activities, such as volunteer work. Part of the explanation of why religiosity encourages volunteering might lie in the fact that religious people tend to be more generative and people who are generative are more likely to volunteer. This was demonstrated in a two-wave panel study of US data using a four indicator latent factor measure of religiosity and a standard measure of generativity. Parents who were "sociable" had children who were more generative and these children were, when they became adults, more likely to volunteer (Son and Wilson, 2011).

5.22 *Trust*

Generalized trust, the belief that most people share your fundamental moral values, even if they have different religions or ideologies, may be essential to the more demanding forms of civic engagement, such as volunteering (Uslaner, 2002: 241). From this standpoint, volunteering is not motivated by people's expectations of reciprocity nor is it a matter of paying society back for good deeds that others have done for them. Instead, people who trust others see the world as a beneficent place and believe that they have an obligation to make it better. In particular, trusters feel a moral obligation to help people less fortunate than themselves.

The research on religion, trust and volunteering has not yielded consistent results. Welch *et al.* (2007) find that trust in strangers is unaffected by either frequency of church attendance or activity in religious organizations. Rather, affiliation seems to make the most difference with Liberal Protestants being more trusting. Interestingly, Liberal Protestants might be more trusting *because* they encourage engagement with the wider community. In Canada, much the same pattern is found, with mainline Protestants the most trusting, Catholics less trusting and Pentecostals least trusting of all (Dilmaghani, 2016). As far as generalized trust and volunteering is concerned it does appear that trusting people are more likely to become volunteers (Bekkers, 2012) but the pattern varies by country (Taniguchi, 2013). In Nordic countries, generalized trust does seem to help explain the positive effect of church attendance on volunteering (Grizzle and Yusuf, 2015). The role of trust as a mediator between religion and volunteering is therefore unclear at present.

6. Research at the Meso Level

6.1 *Social networks*

One reason why people are drawn into volunteer work is that their religion supplies them with a network of friends and acquaintances who tell them about volunteer activities and set an example by volunteering themselves. A person is therefore more "at risk" of volunteering if he or she participates in the social activities of the church, such as Bible study groups, choir practice and youth sports teams as well as by making new friends at church social events. Indeed, it is possible that friendships are the principal mechanism through which religion promotes volunteering. Densely religious social networks are those in which a large proportion of network members are religious with whom there is likely to be frequent talk about religion, and shared membership in ancillary organizations. The religious density of networks increases peer pressure to do good works because friends who are religious are more likely to be volunteering themselves and more likely to bring up moral issues in conversations. Religious networks also buttress norms of altruism and reciprocity (Merino, 2013). (For an overview of social network research on religion, see Everton, 2015.)

The contribution of religious networking to volunteering has been widely documented (Bekker and Dhingra, 2001; Campbell and Yonish, 2003: 95; Musick and Wilson, 2008; Paik and Navarre-Jackson, 2011; Taniguchi, 2012). By participating in the social life of the congregation people multiply their chances of volunteering, both religious and secular, and their religious volunteer work can be a springboard to volunteer work in the wider community (McClure, 2017; Wuthnow, 2004: 114). Unfortunately, it is difficult for social networks to be accurately measured through social surveys and sometimes religious networking is proxied by memberships in religious organizations. These are also positively related to volunteering (Wang *et al.*, 2017).

Church goers who are more socially embedded in their congregation, or who draw a larger proportion of their friends from their congregation (Whitehead and Stroope, 2012: 274), are more likely to provide social support to other members, to be civically engaged, and to be involved in community organizations not connected to their congregation (McClure, 2015, 2017; Schwadel, 2012). Congregations also play some role in directing volunteer work: they form a context in which members can be more active in the community through volunteering (Becker and Dhingra, 2001). Krause (2015) finds that, among older people, receiving spiritual support at church has a substantial impact on performing volunteer work connected to the church. Those who routinely confide in fellow church members are more likely to volunteer for congregational activities. The reverse is also possible: volunteering within a congregation provides more opportunities to develop deeper and closer friendships with other members. The influence of networks is so pervasive that non-religious individuals who do not regularly participate in religious congregations but have religiously observant friends are more likely to volunteer (Lim and McGregor, 2012).

6.2 Networks and religious versus secular volunteering

It is logical to assume that religious networking has its main effect on religious volunteering but the evidence is mixed. In a survey of members of two evangelical Protestant churches in the US the number of in-church friendships was positively associated with both religious and secular volunteering while the number of non-church friendships was unrelated to volunteering (Schwadel *et al.*, 2016). But another study found that dense congregational friendship networks increased the likelihood of religious but not secular volunteering. Rather than propelling individuals out into other community agencies and non-profit organizations, dense congregational networks increased the likelihood that someone would volunteer for a feeding program, youth services program or community service project through their own congregation (Polson, 2018).

6.3 *Social networks and other religious dimensions*

Individuals who participate frequently in the social activities of their church and have many close friends in their congregation are also likely to attend church frequently and consider religion as an important part of their lives. This raises the question of whether networks have an independent effect on volunteering. For the most part their contribution has been confirmed. Participation in congregational activities (excluding worship services) has a positive effect on the probabilities and mean levels of volunteering in general both without a control for church attendance (Wang *et al.*, 2017) and with a control (Yen and Zampelli, 2014: 65). According to a US study, a person who participated in congregational activities was 33 percent more likely to volunteer and volunteered 10 more times a year than someone who never participated in such activities, an effect which outweighed that of church attendance. According to the same survey religious affiliation, religious belief, and religious salience were ineffective *unless* the person was involved in organized religious activities (Wuthnow, 1991: 156). One plausible reason for this relationship is that congregants who engage with and participate in church-sponsored groups tend to have larger and more heterogeneous social ties outside the congregation and this in turn increases their chances of being asked to do secular volunteer work (Merino, 2019).

6.4 *Social networks help explain differences in volunteering associated with other religious dimensions*

There are at least two ways networks can help explain the influence of other religious dimensions. First, differences in networks can help explain denominational differences in volunteering. The social networks of theologically conservative churches are typically denser with fellow members than those of theologically liberal ones. Members of the former are more likely to say that more than half of the people they associate with are from their congregation than are members of theologically liberal ones. Similarly, a far higher percentage of members of conservative churches have close friends in their congregation than members of liberal churches (Stark and Bainbridge, 1985). Vermeer and Scheepers (2019) attribute high rates of religious volunteering among Dutch Evangelicals to the same cause: Evangelicals are more likely to volunteer for a religious organization because they are more likely to have close friends who worship in the same congregation. The social networks of Evangelicals tend to be composed of other Evangelicals because they have strong feelings of connection with their own community and their own faith. This "religious particularism" is negatively associated with volunteering for secular organizations and positively associated with volunteering for one's church (de Hart and Dekker, 2013).

Second, networks can help explain the effect of church attendance (Lewis *et al.*, 2013; Musick and Wilson 2008; Putnam and Campbell, 2010). A longitudinal study followed American adults over a 15-year period. Respondents who attended religious services more often than others at Time 1 as well as those who increased religious attendance between Times 1 and 4 were more likely to increase their volunteer hours during the 15-year period as a result of their more frequent participation in meetings or programs of groups, clubs or organizations that they belonged to between Times 1 and 4 (Kim and Yang, 2017). Although this study did not single out religious groups it does suggest that organizational memberships or activities help explain why church attendance increases volunteering. Among a sub-sample of frequent church-attenders the effect of church attendance on secular volunteering was channeled through participation in group activities such as Bible study and choir practice (Park and Smith, 2000).

6.5 *Problems with determining causal order*

Almost all of the research on social networks and volunteering assumes that the first is the cause of the second but it is possible that religious individuals agree to volunteer in order to increase social ties within their group. Their strengthened religious networks are the result of their volunteer work. The possibility of reciprocal effects has not been investigated. There is also the problem of determining the relation of each dimension of religion and volunteering, both religious and secular. A study in the United Kingdom, using four religious measures (affiliation, attendance, frequency of prayer and salience) found that affiliation did not predict volunteering with the other dimensions controlled and any effect attendance and salience might have had disappeared once membership in religious organizations was introduced into the analysis. It is difficult to sort out the causal pathway indicated by these findings but here the problem is the causal relation *between dimensions* (Storm, 2015a). Volunteers are more likely to attend church frequently and attach more importance to religion because they are members of a religious organization and this in turn increases the chances of volunteering, giving causal priority to organizational membership, a form of social network theory.

7. Congregations

A study of the role of congregations in mobilizing volunteers is an important part of the meso-level analysis. Religious institutions are organizational phenomena: they comprise congregations, temples, parishes, voluntary associations and the like. What influence does this level of religion have on individual behavior? Which congregational features, if any, determine the odds of members of those congregations volunteering? If the same individual moved from one congregation to another would that individual become more likely or less likely to volunteer?

Congregations "match people to tasks; provide support and guidance of a kind which each volunteer finds acceptable; recognize the contribution of volunteers; ensure that continuity of activities is maintained as volunteers come and go; keep good working relationships between paid staff and volunteers; and strike a balance between meeting the aspirations of volunteers and meeting the organizational needs of the congregation" (Harris, 1996). In the US about 90 percent of congregations use time during worship services to provide information about opportunities to volunteer (Glazier, 2020: 2). But some congregations mobilize volunteers better than others and it is important to know why.

7.1 *Congregational size*

Members of large congregations are more likely to volunteer than members of small congregations, probably because larger congregations have more individual and collective resources and they sponsor more programs (Glazier, 2020; Wuthnow, 2004: 113). McClure (2015) adds a qualification to this argument. Social embeddedness (having close friends in the congregation) is positive related to "involvement in community organizations" but this relation is stronger for members of larger congregations. The likelihood of involvement in (secular) community organizations is strongest among members of smaller or average-sized congregations and among those who are more socially embedded in their congregations. Members of larger congregations who have low levels of social embeddedness in them are the least likely to be volunteering for community organizations.

7.2 Congregational homogeneity

Religious congregations, like many voluntary associations, tend to be homogeneous in terms of social class and race and ethnicity. What is the effect on volunteering of this characteristic? Does extreme diversity discourage joint efforts? Information on the social composition of congregations is scarce but one US study was able to determine the socio-economic heterogeneity of 434 congregations. When age and income homogeneity in the congregation increased worshipers became less active in the church but more active outside it. Apparently, mixing with people of the same age and social class means mixing with people who have similar interests which led to volunteer work outside the church (Nisanci, 2017).

7.3 Congregations as infrastructure in the community

The density of congregations in the community should help explain why some communities (e.g., neighborhoods, cities) have more volunteers than others. Shortage of reliable or complete data on congregations at the community level makes it difficult to determine this with any certainty. Two studies, one at the level of states in the US (Rotolo and Wilson, 2012) and the other at the level of cities in the US (Rotolo and Wilson, 2014), found that the more congregations there are in a state/city the more volunteers there are in the state/city controlling for individual differences in the inhabitants. (It should be noted that no controls for individual religiosity were available and the effect was confined to religious volunteering.) Another study, of Lutherans in the US found that "free loading" is more common when a particular denomination has a larger "market share" in the community whereas being one of the smaller congregations in a community decreases free loading (Brewer et al., 2006).

7.4 Congregational effects vary by denomination

Each religious tradition has its own theology as to the organization and operation of its administrative units. In some cases, congregations go to great lengths to get their members to volunteer. Becker and Dhingra (2001) witnessed a Protestant congregation that responded to the difficulties of recruiting and retaining lay volunteers by setting up rotas for members for a wide range of tasks, including Sunday school teaching and being the verger. More broadly, they found that Catholic parishes and Moderate Protestant congregations were equally likely to foster volunteer activities intended to maintain the congregation (committee members, Sunday School or religious education teacher) and activities that reach out beyond the congregation's own four walls (e.g., food pantry, rescue mission, pro-life counseling center). Liberal Protestant congregations set up volunteer activities devoted mainly to congregational maintenance while Evangelical Protestant congregations had twice as many congregational-maintenance activities as they had outreach activities. Ecclesiology determined organization which in turn determined volunteer demands.

Some denominations are more democratic in their local structures than others. Vertical and hierarchical organizations, such as the Catholic Church, are less likely to foster voluntary work than horizontal and voluntary organizations such as those of Evangelical Protestantism. In vertical organizations, subordinates can shirk, bosses can exploit, and norms of reciprocity and trust never develop. In horizontal organizations, social networks are denser as people interact as equals. Horizontal organizations, such as many Protestant churches, allow many members to obtain important civic skills (e.g., letter writing and meeting organization) because a wide range of members is involved in decision making. Vertical organizations, such as the Catholic Church, limit this skill development to a select few. Also, belonging to a strict congregation (one with significant behavioral and moral restrictions) deters members from volunteering in the wider community rather than for their own congregation. While the experience of tension between the congregation and the wider world does not reduce volunteering overall (in fact, it might encourage volunteering for the organization), identification with a strict religious congregation discourages non-congregational community volunteering. Possibly, strict congregations view volunteering through congregational service programs as a way to reinforce distinctions between themselves and society thus helping maintain social boundaries between members and non-members (Polson, 2018).

8. Geographical Areas

The most expansive types of macro-level analysis use geographical areas such as counties, cities, regions and countries as the unit of analysis. For example, does the rate of church attendance in a country affect the level of volunteering in that country? To answer this question it is important to control for individual-level differences in religiosity (and other individual characteristics) to ensure that any variation is indeed the result of country-level factors and not of differences between individuals living in a different countries. For example, does the *rate* of education in an area have an independent effect on volunteering in that area? Since education is known to be related to volunteering at the individual level this might simply be due to the fact that the area has more highly educated people living in it. The question is whether living in an area surrounded by highly educated people affects volunteering regardless of one's own education. Answering this question demands the use of multi-level models. In the case of religion, they can determine whether people feel the effect of a country's religiosity (e.g., average church attendance frequency) regardless of their own religiosity. There are other methods. One is to organize the data hierarchically with individuals nested within countries, using information at the individual level to determine volunteering. A fixed-effects random intercept model that avoids confounding country-level with individual-level effects can then be estimated.

8.1 *Religion helps explain country variations in the rate of volunteering*

This overview will focus on country-level variations because that is where most of the research has been directed, partly because data on smaller geographical areas are not publicly available (usually to respect the anonymity of survey respondents). The first and most obvious question is whether religiosity explains between-country variations in volunteer rates. Parboteeah *et al.* (2004), using World Values Survey data and controlling for religious salience at the individual level, find that religiosity (the percentage of people in the country attending religious services) is positively related to the rate of volunteering in the country. However, an analysis of Gallup World Poll data from 156 countries finds that national level of devoutness has a *curvilinear* relationship with the rate of volunteering, where volunteering is more common in relatively secular and devout countries (Lim and MacGregor, 2012). Damien (2019), analyzing European data, finds that average church attendance has a *negative* effect on volunteering. A negative effect of church attendance on volunteering is also found in other reports from Europe (de Hart and Dekker, 2013; Prouteau and Sardinha, 2013; Storm, 2015b).

One explanation for the negative association in European countries is that their non-profit sectors have evolved mainly through secular organizations whereas in countries such as the United States religious organizations have played a more prominent role in welfare provision (Musick and Wilson, 2008: 358).

These multi-level studies of contextual effects of level of religiosity on the level of volunteering are cross-sectional. Damian (2019) analyzes changes over time in the relation between country-level religiosity and volunteering using four waves of the European Values Survey. Cross-sectionally, average church attendance in a country had a negative effect on the rate of volunteering; however, a change over time in average church attendance was not associated with a change in the rate of volunteering, suggesting that the results of the cross-sectional studies might be biased by unmeasured covariates at the national level.

8.2 Religious composition and country level differences in volunteering

Religion helps explain country-level differences in volunteering by means of differences in affiliation. It is well established that Protestants have the highest volunteer rate. In a study of 44 European countries the average volunteer rate in the country was positively related to proportion of Protestants in the country (Hart and Dekker, 2013). Thus, a country, such as the United States, will have a higher volunteer rate than, for example, Italy, because a higher proportion of its religious inhabitants are Protestants. Religion can also help explain country-level differences by inciting competition between people to provide services to church members and the general population. This means that more religiously pluralistic societies should have higher volunteer rates than homogeneous religious cultures. This, too, would explain why the volunteer rate is higher in the US than in Italy, although it is probably truer of volunteering in connection with the church (Musick and Wilson, 2008). And yet the study of the influence of religious composition on volunteering is highly complex. For example, in the Netherlands Protestants volunteer for religious organizations at a higher rate than members of other denominations, but in a neighboring and quite similar country, Denmark, they do less religious volunteering than others (de Hart and Dekker, 2013). The precise contribution of religious denomination to volunteering should not be assumed to be the same in every country.

8.3 Country-level change in religion and changes in the rate of volunteering

An important macro-level issue with respect to religion and volunteering is secularization. Is a decline in the level of religiosity in a country followed by a decline in the rate of volunteering? Van Ingen and Dekker (2010) propose that as the religious proportion of the population drops the effect of religion on volunteering at the individual level will strengthen. In a secularizing society fewer religious people are available to be recruited for religious volunteer work. In addition, the shrinking religious community may become more cohesive and homogeneous as a result of secularization, which increases the pressure to respond positively to volunteering requests. In short, the effect of church attendance on volunteering should strengthen, which is what they find in their analysis of Dutch data, although they do not distinguish between religious and secular volunteering.

A largely unexplored issue is whether changes in the nature of religion in a society is followed by a change in the nature of volunteer work in the society. For example, change can take the form of the de-institutionalization of religion in which religious practices become more individualized, less communal and less effective as an infrastructure for volunteering. If it does not change the overall rate of volunteering does it change the characteristics of volunteering so that it, too, becomes more individualized (Gronlund, 2012)?

8.4 Country-level differences in the distribution of volunteer work across domains

Americans volunteer more for religious organizations than any other type (Campbell and Yonish, 2003: 90). For example, while 39.4 percent of US volunteers work for a religious organization in the UK only 6 percent do so (Storm, 2015a). This can be explained by a vibrant third sector beyond government and business in the US which has relied on congregations, parachurch agencies, faith-based non-profits, and informal giving for support throughout its history. Religious actors and institutions supply the preponderance of volunteer hours, develop community leaders, and often serve as central gathering spaces for polling places, neighborhood associations, Boy Scouts or Alcoholic Anonymous meetings. Faith remains the motivating factor for the volunteering and civic engagement of many Americans, and their diverse religious institutions often serve as the avenue through which they demonstrate their motivation and engagement (King, 2019). In other countries religious volunteering takes second or third place to other domains of volunteer activity such as sports and recreation. As noted earlier, the effect of church attendance on religious volunteering is stronger than its effect on secular volunteering but this too varies by country: the religious "spillover" effect on secular volunteering is much stronger in the US than in Europe (Norris, 2013).

8.5 *The religious composition of the country*

The contextual effect of religion is typically measured using an indicator of overall religiosity in the country, for example, average frequency of church attendance. But some scholars believe it is not the overall rate of practice that is important but the religious composition of the country. Bennett (2015) finds that the level of religious diversity of a society increases the likelihood of volunteering, although the Gallup World Poll used does not distinguish between the religious and secular types. And it is worth mentioning here that in a study where *counties* in the US were the unit of analysis, Borgonovi (2008) found religious pluralism to be a powerful predictor of between-county differences in individuals' propensity to volunteer for religious purposes. The probability that an individual would volunteer for non-religious organizations was not, however, associated with how pluralistic the religious environment was.

8.6 *The contextual effect of level of religiosity moderated by other factors*

As is the case at the micro level, the influence of religion on volunteering at the macro level could be conditioned or moderated by some other factor. Thus, Guo *et al.* (2020) find no overall relation between the national level of religiosity and rates of volunteering in the World Values Survey data. But they do find a positive connection in low GDP *per capita* countries. Only in poorer countries does national religiosity predict national-level volunteering. It is likely that in affluent countries there are others factor that function more efficiently than religion in encouraging volunteering.

Moderation effects in WVS data are also found by Luria *et al.* (2017), whose main focus is on the role of values in explaining country-level differences in volunteering but who also examine the extent to which these values interact with religion to set volunteer rates. Values are measured by: (1) a *traditional-secular values index* such as importance of God, national pride, respect for authority, obedience and marriage, disapproval of abortion; (2) and *a survival values-self-expression values index* measuring priority of security over liberty, non-acceptance of homosexuality, abstinence from political action, distrust in outsiders, and a weak sense of happiness. First, they find a stronger relationship between religious attendance and general volunteering in secular-rational cultures than in traditional cultures. In traditional cultures, people tend to participate in general volunteering regardless of the level of religious attendance. However, in secular-rational cultures individuals with frequent religious attendance engage in more general volunteering than non- or low attenders. Second, there is a stronger relationship between religious attendance and volunteering to help the needy in cultures with high self-expression values. Third, in cultures with high survival values, individuals tend to volunteer regardless of their religious attendance, while in high self-expression cultures individuals volunteer if they attend religious services. The general conclusion of this enterprising study is that countries are distinguished by their value systems and these systems moderate the way religion relates to volunteering. Overall, it is highly likely that the macro-level relation between religion and volunteering is conditioned not only by the country's religious culture (e.g., is it mainly Protestant) but also by other economic, social and cultural phenomena.

8.7 The individual-level effects of religiosity is moderated by the religiosity of the country

Another important question about country differences in volunteering is whether the religiosity of the country makes any difference to the role of individual religion in explaining individual volunteering. This means an interaction between micro- and macro-levels. One argument hypothesizes a spillover effect whereby the non-religious are more likely to volunteer in countries that are highly religious, as measured by church attendance rates, because they are more likely to have religious people in their social networks, in comparison to non-religious people in more secular countries. As a result the volunteer "gap" between religious and non-religious residents is narrower. Ruiter and De Graaf (2006), using World Values Survey data, found that the difference between individual religious and non-religious volunteering is indeed narrower in devout countries. Storm (2015b) finds that, in Europe, religious service attendance has a stronger influence on volunteering in less religious countries or, alternatively, that when it comes to volunteering, the religiosity of a country matters less for religiously observant individuals. The same logic can be applied to the problem of whether the religious composition of a country influences individual effects. Thus, Musick and Wilson (2008: 367) find that the positive effect of church attendance on volunteering is stronger in mainly Protestant countries.

8.8 *The relation where religion does not conform to the Western model*

Most macro-level studies focus on Western societies. It is unclear whether societies where religion and volunteering assume completely different forms from those found in the West show the same pattern. For example, in Japan only about 10 percent of the population has a religious affiliation, mostly Buddhist or Shinto, but more than half regularly worship at temples and shrines. By treating this practice as "attendance" and adding a salience question ("Do you think that religious mind is important?") it is possible to see if religion helps characterize the third of the population who volunteer. As it turns out, both "religious mind" and religious attendance increase the odds of volunteering and their effect is more powerful than education (Mitani, 2014). Another Japanese survey study (Taniguchi, 2010) omitted a question on church attendance as being unsuitable but did ask respondents if they would describe themselves as a religious "follower" (e.g., "devoted," "not very"). Devoted followers volunteered more hours.

9. Religion and Volunteering over the Life Course

Life course analysis means looking at the way behavior changes as one moves through the stages of life. The life course begins in childhood and adolescence. At this stage the major influence parental or cross-generational.

9.1 *Cross-generational effects*

Parents who are religious are more likely to have children who are religious. Parents who are volunteers are more likely to have children who volunteer. An interesting question is how much of children's volunteering is due to (1) their parents' religion (2) their own religion "inherited" from their parents and (3) their parents' volunteer work.

There is little doubt that adolescents whose parents are church members value volunteering more (Wuthnow, 1995) but what about actual practices? A US longitudinal study found that parental religion had no direct effect on their off-spring's volunteer work in middle-age. Offspring reared in religious homes felt no more obliged to help others or serve their community than the off-spring of parents for whom religion was unimportant. This did not necessarily mean that parental religiosity was inconsequential. One possibility is that the ongoing religiosity of the middle aged offspring had "absorbed" all the effect of parental religion. It is because they are now religious that they feel more obliged to help, and they are more religious now because their parents were religious when they were growing up (Son and Wilson, 2012). Three Dutch studies confirm the existence of cross-generational effects of religion. One survey found that adult respondents were more likely to be currently volunteering if, when they were 15, their parents were church members (Kirchmaier et al., 2018). Another discerned more precisely that children of parents who volunteered for the church were more likely to become volunteers for the church themselves because they adopted the religious involvement of their parents, not because parental volunteering had an additional modeling effect. In the case of a child's secular volunteering, however, controlling for parental religiosity did not mediate the effect of parental volunteering, suggesting that role modeling was more important than religion in the case of secular volunteer work (Bekkers, 2007). Vermeer and Scheepers (2011) found that the religious socialization provided by parents in the Netherlands fostered volunteer work among their adult children even in the secular sphere.

Another longitudinal study divided respondents into four groups: "exclusively activists" who attended a meeting or event for a political, environmental or community group while not doing any unpaid volunteer work; "exclusive volunteers" who did unpaid volunteer work but did not attend a meeting or event for a political, environmental or community group; "mixed motivational activist and volunteer non-activist" who reported both; and "non-civic minded," those who did neither. Parental religious devotion was a robust predictor of the off-spring's exclusive activism as opposed to the non-civic minded group: offspring with religiously devout parents were 1.94 times more likely to be exclusive activists than non-civic minded. A greater degree of parental fundamentalism also reduced the likelihood of exclusive voluntarism (Caputo, 2009). Parental religion therefore seemed to be steering children into particular kinds of volunteer work.

9.2 *Adolescence*

It is not realistic to measure volunteer work earlier than adolescence by which time some sense of free will engagement can be assumed. Religious organizations are adept at functioning much like a family, drawing multiple family members into congregational activities and introducing teenagers to the idea of helping strangers through the church. About 30 percent of all teenagers in the US volunteer through a religious organization (Wuthnow, 1995: 123). Those with a strong religious faith are more likely to volunteer, especially if they get personal satisfaction from their involvement in their church (i.e., their parents do not force them to attend), although fewer than half mention spiritual concerns as an important motivation for their volunteer work (Wuthnow, 1995: 85).

The general picture, in the United States at least, is that religiosity begins positively inducing volunteer work early in the life cycle (Martyn *et al.*, 2019; Youniss *et al.*, 1999). Religious beliefs and practices acquired in adolescence can also have long-term effects, as shown by a longitudinal analysis of Canadian data in which religious involvement as a youth helped explain adult levels of volunteering. The effect of youth religious involvement did not decline with age as respondents became further removed from their youth religious experiences (Perks and Haan, 2011). Data from the United States, however, suggest that adolescent religion had a positive effect on later adult volunteering only in the case of work performed on behalf of the church (Campbell and Yonish, 2003: 99).

Ascertaining the effect of early religion and volunteering on subsequent volunteering can be a difficult task and requires longitudinal data. One study followed US respondents across surveys conducted in 1965, 1973 and 1982. In the case of liberal Protestants none of the 1965 religious and volunteering measures predicted either 1973 or 1982 volunteering. The relation between volunteering in 1973 and 1982 was very strong for liberal Protestants but the seeds were not planted by early religious activity in 1965. The picture was different in the third wave, by which time the liberal Protestants had reached middle age, for now the relation between religiosity in 1982 and volunteering in 1982 was positive, indicating that religion had helped boost volunteering over its 1973 level.

On the other hand, Moderate and Conservative Protestants' volunteering in 1982 was unaffected by either the religious activism of their parents or their own earlier religiosity in 1973 and subsequent religiosity did nothing to either increase or decrease volunteer levels between ages 26 and 35. Catholics resembled the liberal Protestants. Catholics active in their church between 1973 and 1982 were likely to increase their volunteering over their 1973 levels (Janoski and Wilson, 1995). (In this study, no distinction is made between different types of volunteering.) Clearly life course analysis of the relation between religion and volunteering needs to take into account not only life stage but also affiliation.

9.3 *Life-course events: Getting married and having children*

Social relations change as the life course unfolds and new relations mean a change in the role of religion in volunteering. One of the most important of these changes is forming a stable partnership or getting married. At this point partners and spouses begin to play a potential role in volunteering. Does the decision whether or not to volunteer have anything to do with the religion of one's spouse? And is one partner in a marriage more likely to volunteer if both partners are of the same religion? After all, couples in which spouses share the same religion reap joint benefits from their investment in congregations such as the services congregations provide to children, like pre-school or sports teams, which benefit both parents although not necessarily equally. Research on the way family relations might moderate the role of religion is scarce. One of the few published studies found that, while the religiosity of one spouse increases the odds of that spouse volunteering it does not influence the volunteering of the other spouse (Kim and Dew, 2016).

Religions have definite beliefs about what a marriage should be and how each spouse should behave toward the other. Is there any evidence that these beliefs influence volunteering? One enterprising study examined the effect of "marital sanctification" on volunteering. Sanctification occurs when an individual perceives an aspect of life as having special spiritual or divine character and significance. Couples who endow marriage with transcendent significance tend to put more effort into protecting their marriage by engaging in relational maintenance behaviors and they are more likely to have high levels of marital satisfaction. Apparently, marital sanctification enhances the influence of one spouse's behavior and attitudes on the other. Thus, the wife's feelings of marital sanctification is positively associated with not only her own but also her husband's volunteering. The sanctity of marriage motivates couples to engage in volunteering as a way of enacting their view of marriage (Kim and Dew, 2016).

Some marriages end in divorce. How does this affect the volunteering of the couples involved? This might well depend upon the gender of the spouse. For men, divorce means a decline in religious volunteering, attributable to a decline in frequency of church attendance, but an increase in secular volunteering. Women's volunteering also declines after divorce but this is due to financial strain rather than religion (Kim and Yang, 2018).

9.4 The "third age" and retirement

As people enter the third age of life many of them make the transition out of the labor force and into retirement. Much research has been devoted to examining the volunteer behavior of older adults. Space limitations prohibit a comprehensive survey but it is true that people attend church more frequently as they grow older, in the United States at least, and they are more likely to volunteer, perhaps as a result (Cornwell *et al.*, 2008). Older adults are also more likely to volunteer for religious organizations than younger adults (Musick and Wilson, 2008). However, a recent review of the research on the topic of older adults volunteering (41 publications) concludes that "religiosity was not a significant predictor of older adults' volunteerism" (Lu *et al.*, 2020). A more cautious conclusion would be that there is no strong evidence that the mobilizing role of religion is moderated by age.

10. Race and Ethnicity

Race and ethnicity are major status markers in modern societies and racial and ethnic communities each have their own distinctive religious beliefs, practices and volunteer habits. Race and ethnicity moderate the effect of religion on volunteering, especially if race/ethnicity coincide with immigrant status to further identify and marginalize groups of people. Religion sometimes operates to ease problems with assimilation for recent immigrants by fostering engagement in the new community. Immigrants who volunteer through their religion may increase their stock of human capital and broaden their social networks, which in turn improves their chances

in the labor market and aids their civic, social and political integration into
the host society.

10.1 *Racial and ethnic moderation of the effect of religion on volunteering*

Racial and ethnic groups tend to have their own distinctive religious
cultures and practices even when they adopt or inherit the religious affiliations of the majority of the population. This raises the question of
whether religion plays the same role in fostering volunteer work regardless of race or ethnicity. Some research suggests that religion plays the
same role. Thus a study of Asian Americans in the US found that adherents of the two main Christian religions (Catholic and Protestant) had
higher civic participation levels than those belonging to non-Christian
religious traditions, as is the case of the general population (Ecklund and
Park, 2007). Church attendance has the same positive effect on volunteering among Hispanics in the US as it does on non-Hispanics (Wang and
Graddy, 2008).

Ethno-religious minorities, such as Muslims in Western countries,
might be expected to gravitate toward organizations within their own cultural, ethnic or religious communities as their preferred site of volunteering. While it is true that some members of such minorities self-isolate in
this manner it is also true that Muslims have about the same rate of
volunteering as adherents of other religions in countries such as the US
and Australia. And the tendency of religion to encourage not only religious but also secular volunteering is also found in Muslim populations
(Peucker, 2020).

Other research suggests that, because racial/ethnic groups often
import their own patterns of religious affiliation and because churches in
the host country vary in how welcoming they are to recent immigrant
groups they will gravitate toward communities in the country with which
they feel most comfortable to do their volunteer work. For example, in the
US Korean Americans are drawn to Evangelical denominations and they
disproportionately use volunteer work for support of the church itself or
as missionary work on behalf of other Korean Americans in the community. Their attraction to Evangelicalism means they see assimilation as, in
part, the obligation to participate in church-sponsored community services
(Ecklund, 2005).

The prominent role of the church in the African-American community in the US is well documented. Although there is debate concerning the political impact of Black churches (some seeing them as conservative influences) there can be little doubt that Black churches are more active in their communities than White churches (Cavendish, 2000). An interesting comparison of predominantly White and predominantly Black Catholic parishes found that the latter were much more likely to provide social services and engage in actions for social change than the former (Cavendish, 2000).

A direct comparison between White and African-American volunteering in the US reveals an interesting difference in the effect of church attendance. Compared to Whites, African Americans report more frequent prayer, service attendance and Bible study, a stronger commitment to religious beliefs, more orthodox theological views and stronger feelings of being "close to God." For all kinds of volunteering except the entirely secular Black volunteering is more influenced by church attendance than is White volunteering, a reflection of the more prominent role of the church in the African-American community. When it comes to volunteering for secular activities, Black church attendance has a negative effect. Does this mean that African-Americans focus entirely on their religious or religiously-inspired needs? Blacks are indeed more likely than Whites to volunteer for church-related activities but they are also more likely to volunteer for community-action groups, work-related organizations and political groups, although they are less likely than Whites to volunteer in other areas, such as those related to youth, education, the environment, and the arts. There is little to suggest that Black volunteering is entirely focused on the church (Musick *et al.*, 2000).

In the Netherlands, gaps between immigrants and natives in the propensity to participate in secular and religious volunteering are not entirely due directly to race or ethnicity but indirectly through variations in individual resources (labor market position, education and income), religiosity and solicitation (the likelihood of being asked to volunteer). Natives are more likely to participate in secular volunteering, which is explained by their superior social resources, while immigrants are more likely to participate in religious volunteering, which is explained by immigrants having higher levels of religiosity (Carabain and Bekkers, 2011). In Denmark, the effect of being a non-Western immigrant on the propensity to participate in secular volunteering is negative, partly due to having fewer resources (e.g., education) and fewer social networks, but there is no effect of immigrant status in the case of religious volunteering (Qvist, 2018).

11. Gender

Gender differences in the propensity to volunteer have been examined by many scholars. The pattern tends to vary from one country to another: in the United States women tend to volunteer more than men but the opposite is true in European societies. It is likely that this difference can be explained, in part, by religiosity. Women tend to be more religious than men and insofar as religiosity is linked to volunteering this might help explain the gender difference. This is exactly what a US study found: US women were slightly more likely to volunteer than men mainly because they attend church more frequently (Musick and Wilson, 2008: 181). In addition, women in the US are more likely to volunteer for religious organizations than men. In Germany, where religious volunteer organizations are less common, women are no more likely to volunteer for them than men (Dittrich and Mey, 2015).

11.1 *Gender moderates the effect of religion*

Gender can also moderate religion's effect on volunteering. Generally speaking, there is a gendered division of labor in the volunteer world, with women consigned to more "domestic" activities (Rotolo and Wilson, 2007). This gender bias might affect the relation between religion and volunteering. A European study showed that religious salience had a negative effect on volunteering (for professional and educational organizations) in the case of women but no effect in the case of men (Gil-Lacruz *et al.*, 2019). A US study, on the other hand found no gender difference in the effect of church attendance on volunteering — although the outcome variable did not distinguish between types of volunteer work (Einolf, 2011a). But research on African-American women shows that religious organizations serve as a primary catalyst for their volunteer engagement (Gutierrez and Mattis, 2014) suggesting gender moderation within this racial group. "Religious work" in general, including volunteer work on behalf of the congregation, tends to be gendered as are other forms of work, with women in the church performing the more private, domestic work, such as preparing the alter for service, while men are more likely to perform more public roles such as reading from the Bible (Heyer-Gray, 2000).

12. Conclusion

Much has been achieved in understanding the complex relation between religion and volunteering but much work remains to be done and the existing research can be criticized on a number of grounds.

First, most of the survey data are gathered from advanced industrial societies in the West, with the exception of surveys (e.g., World Values Survey) that gather information from many different countries but are limited in the amount of detail they can gather on either activity. In addition, both religion and volunteering vary widely, in form and culture, from one society to another. In the predominantly Protestant, Catholic, Orthodox, Jewish and Muslim countries religion is institutionalized on an organizational basis where, to varying degrees, adherents are expected to help the religious organization thrive and to engage in missions on the behalf of the organization that often take the form of volunteer work. In those same countries, for the most part, volunteer work is institutionalized on an organizational basis: people volunteer through and on behalf of organizations. Most of these countries also have a vibrant civil society in which religious and volunteering organizations can operate and receive support, often from the state. This is not the case in many other countries. Even in these countries welfare regimes condition the influence religion can have on volunteering. Too much focus on countries with social safety nets and collectivist philosophies paints a misleading picture of how religion and volunteering are related.

A good example of the difficulties posed is China. The sociology of religion on which nearly all of the studies described in this review draw and which informs the design of surveys is biased toward the "membership" model of religion. In China, this preoccupation with the institutional aspects of religion rather than religious practices as such is not very useful, in addition to which there is limited political tolerance of social surveys, particularly those culling information on the private sphere. Chinese religion is much more oriented to practice, interaction with spirits, be they God, gods, ancestors, ghosts or evil spirits (Hu, 2014). It is the influence, if any, of these practices on volunteer work that should be the focus of research. In China, also, the state plays a large role in determining the content and form of religious charitable organizations. The organizations must collaborate with the state on all fronts of their philanthropic activities in exchange for political protection (Weller *et al.*, 2020). Thus, while there has been an increase in volunteering for organized philanthropy in China and while to some extent this increase has been inspired and motivated by Confucian, Daoist and Buddhist teachings, the exact influence of religion on volunteering is politically determined. China is also a country where, to the extent that volunteer work exists at all, it is mainly organized by the state (Xu, 2014). Even the dominant Confucian religion teaches that the government should be the primary welfare provider. The room for much of an impact of religion on volunteering is therefore very limited. The same limitation is observable in the mainly Buddhist and Shinto Japan where formal or organized volunteerism has only recently emerged, few people openly express and practice their religiosity, and where adhering to a specific religious group is uncommon. Even members of faith-based volunteer groups (with a few exceptions) fail to discuss their work in religious terms. Their volunteer identity is mainly secular. They rarely use religious language when describing their volunteer work, nor do they refer to religious doctrines to express their volunteering (Cavaliere, 2015).

Another example of the bias created by the focus on advanced industrial societies comes from Sub-Saharan Africa where religiosity rates are quite high, with the possible exception of South Africa. In these more traditional societies gender differences are wide and women are excluded from political volunteering. They are instead steered toward more "feminine" types of volunteer work such as caring for the sick and elderly. Religion plays a role here, particularly in the form of religious socializing, because women who mix socially with fellow believers are more likely to become political volunteers, partially overcoming social barriers to their entry into politics, but gender relations nevertheless shape the influence of religion more than it does in more industrialized countries (Greif *et al.*, 2011).

Second, the failure to include and control for different dimensions of religion has been noted on a number of occasions. For example, Evangelicals volunteer predominantly for their own congregations because they are more scrupulous in attending worship services than members of other denominations. Careful consideration should be given to the possibility that there are interactions between dimensions as shown by the fact that the effect of church attendance is moderated by religious affiliation. The examination of interactions should be standard practice.

Third, there is wide variation in the meaning and measurement of volunteering. This is not only because of different definitions of what constitutes volunteer work. Detailed information on volunteer tasks combined with detailed information on religion is rarely available. An older small sample study that distinguished 10 different types of volunteer work (e.g., help with communication) found that church attendance was related only to providing religious services and providing direct services to the needy (Gronbjerg and Never, 2004). Too many studies in this areas fail to make the crucial distinction between volunteering for religious and secular causes. And yet there are problems associated with this distinction. In the case of religious congregations, since they are both member-benefit and public-benefit organizations, it is often impossible or appropriate to pinpoint whether the beneficiaries of a particular activity are inside or outside of the congregation (Harris, 1996).

Fourth, studies rarely draw a distinction between volunteer status (a binary variable) and volunteer hours (a continuous variable) when the latter is the preferred measure even though problems with recall or inflation might be present. It is quite possible that religiosity is firm enough to prompt *some* volunteering but has little additional effect on how intense is the person's commitment to volunteer work.

Fifth, although most studies are careful to control for possible confounders the possibility remains that the association between religiosity and volunteering is spurious, the result of their both being related to a third factor such as having a prosocial personality. For example, a statement that there are religious affiliation differences in volunteering must take into consideration that educational differences between denominations are the real cause. Longitudinal data with fixed effects models to examine within-person changes in both religiosity and volunteering are the most desirable method of dealing with unmeasured heterogeneity.

Sixth, causality issues are often noted but rarely resolved. In the case of most survey-based studies, especially those relying on cross-sectional data, the possibility cannot be ruled out that people intent on volunteering join a church in order to do so or they see a church as a way to put into practice what they want to achieve through their volunteer work (Cnaan *et al.*, 2016). The teachings of the church are not necessarily the main reason people join and become active in a congregation, rather they are attracted by its social activities and communal life, including its volunteer programs. A noteworthy study looked at the effect of church attendance on participation in local government meetings — a voluntary act.

Once "selection effects" were taken into account (i.e., prior levels of volunteering) church attendance bore no relation to volunteering. (McKenzie, 2001).

Causality concerns also call into question the act of separating religion (the stimulus and volunteering the response) when for many people they are both parts of the same identity. Such people do not compartmentalize their lives into religious ideas and actions and helping strangers because they see them as an integrated whole. In this more holistic concept, volunteering is just one manifestation of religious identity. Helping is part of what it means to be religious (Einolf, 2011b). Volunteering is a religious act, particularly if it takes place within the church itself. This raises the possibility that they are actually the "same thing."

Seventh, there is little dispute that religious networks play some role in motivating volunteers. Social networks, rather than beliefs, dominate as the mechanism leading to volunteering and it is the social networks formed within congregations that make congregation members more likely to volunteer (Becker and Dhingra, 2001). But data on religious networks are scarce. Most studies rely on survey questions that serve as proxies for social networks, which seldom capture the social context in which religious beliefs and practices are embedded.

Finally, survey research on the topic probably suffers from desirability bias since both religiosity and volunteering are regarded favorably in the societies typically surveyed: church attendance frequency is over-reported and the habit of over-reporting one's generosity might be especially common among religious people, who are weekly exhorted to "love your neighbor."

References

Ammerman, N. (2002). "Connecting Mainline Churches with Public Life," in *The Quiet Hand of God: Faith-Based Activism and the Public Role of Mainline Protestantism*, R. Wuthnow, (ed.), pp. 129–158. Berkeley, CA: University of California Press.

Becker, P. and Dhingra, P. (2001). "Religious Involvement and Volunteering: Implications for Civil Society," *Sociology of Religion*, 62(3), 315–335.

Bekkers, R. (2007). "Intergenerational Transmission of Volunteering," *Acta Sociologica*, 50, 99–114.

Bekkers, R. (2010). "Who Gives What and When? A Scenario Study of Intentions to Give Time and Money," *Social Science Research*, 39, 369–381.

Bekkers, R. (2012). "Trust and Volunteering: Selection or Causation? Evidence from a 4 Year Panel Study," *Political Behavior*, 34, 225–247.

Bekkers, R. and Schuyt, T. (2008). "And Who is Your Neighbor? Explaining Denominational Differences in Charitable Giving and Volunteering in the Netherlands," *Review of Religious Research*, 50(1), 74–96.

Bellamy, J. and Leonard, R. (2015). "Volunteering among Church Attendees in Australia," in *Religion and Volunteering*, L. Hustinx, J. von Essen, J. Haers and S. Mels (eds.), pp. 121–143. Switzerland: Springer International Publishing.

Bennett, M. (2015). "Religiosity and Formal Volunteering in Global Perspective," in *Religion and Volunteering*, L. Hustinx, J. von Essen, J. Haers and S. Mels (eds.), pp. 77–96. Switzerland: Springer International Publishing.

Beyerlein, K. and Hipp, J. (2006). "From Pews to Participation: The Effect of Congregational Activity on Bridging Civic Engagement," *Social Problems*, 53(1), 97–117.

Beyerlein, K. and Vaisey, S. (2013). "Individualism Revisited: Moral World Views and Civic Engagement," *Poetics*, 41, 384–406.

Borgonovi, F. (2008). "Divided We Stand, United We Fall: Religious Pluralism, Giving, and Volunteering," *American Sociological Review*, 73, 105–128.

Brewer, S., Jozefowicz, J. and Stonebraker, R. (2006). "Religious Free Riders: The Impact of Market Share," *Journal for the Scientific Study of Religion*, 45(3), 389–396.

Campbell, D. and Yonish, S. (2003). "Religion and Volunteering in America," in *Religion as Social Capital: Producing the Common Good*, C. Smidt, (ed.), pp. 87–106. Waco, TX: Baylor University Press.

Caputo, R. (2009). "Religious Capital and Intergenerational Transmission of Volunteering as Correlates of Civic Engagement," *Nonprofit and Voluntary Sector Quarterly*, 38(6), 983–1002.

Carabain, C. and Bekkers, R. (2011). "Religious and Secular Volunteering: A Comparison between Immigrants and Non-immigrants in the Netherlands," *Voluntary Sector Review*, 2(1), 23–41.

Cavaliere, P. (2015). *Promising Practices: Women Volunteers in Contemporary Japanese Religious Civil Society*. Leiden: Brill.

Cavendish, J. (2000). "Church-Based Community Activism: A Comparison of Black and White Catholic Congregations," *Journal for the Scientific Study of Religion*, 39, 371–384.

Choi, L. (2003). "Factors Affecting Volunteerism among Older Adults," *Journal of Applied Gerontology*, 22(2), 179–196.

Choi, N. and Chou, R. (2010). "Time and Money Volunteering among Older Adults: The Relationship between Past and Current Volunteering and Correlates of Change and Stability," *Ageing and Society*, 30, 59–581.

Choi, N. and DiNitto, D. (2012). "Predictors of Time Volunteering, Religious Giving, and Secular Giving," *Journal of Sociology and Social Welfare*, 34(2), 93–129.

Cnaan, R., Kasternakis, A. and Wineberg, R. (1993). "Religious People, Religious Congregations and Volunteerism in Human Services: Is There a Link?" *Nonprofit and Voluntary Sector Quarterly*, 22(1), 33–51.

Cnaan, R., Zrinscak, S., Gronlund, H., Smith, D., Hu, M., Knoti, M., Knorre, B., Kumar, P. and Pessi, A. (2016). "Volunteering in Religious Congregations and Faith-Based Associations," in *The Palgrave Handbook of Volunteering, Civic Participation, and Nonprofit Associations*, D. Smith, R. Stebbins and J. Grotz (eds.), pp. 472–494. New York, NY: Palgrave Macmillan.

Cornwell, B., Laumann, E. and Schumm, L. (2008). "The Social Connectedness of Older Adults," *American Sociological Review*, 73, 185–203.

Damian, E. (2019). "Formal Volunteering in Europe: Evidence Across Nations and Time," *Cross-Cultural Research*, 53(4), 385–409.

Dawson, C., Baker, P. and Dowell, D. (2019). "Getting into the Giving Habit: The Dynamics of Volunteering in the UK," *Voluntas*, 30(5), 1006–1021.

de Hart, J. and Dekker, P. (2013). "Religion, Spirituality and Civic Participation," in *Religion and Civil Society in Europe*, J. de Hart, P. Dekker and L. Halman (eds.), pp. 169–188. Dordrecht: Springer.

Dilmaghani, M. (2017). "Religiosity and Social Trust: Evidence from Canada," *Review of Social Economy*, 75(1), 49–75.

Dittrich, M. and Mey, B. (2015). "Gender Differences in Volunteer Activities: Evidence from German Survey Data," *Economics Bulletin*, 35(1), 349–360.

Diop, A., Johnston, T., Trung Le, K. and Li, Y. (2018). "Donating Time or Money? The Effects of Religiosity and Social Capital on Civic Engagement in Qatar," *Social Indicators Research*, 138, 297–315.

Dougherty, K., De Jong, F., Garofano, R., Jamire, J. and Park, N. (2011). "Bonding and Bridging Activities of U.S. Pentecostals," *Sociological Spectrum*, 31, 316–341.

Driskell, R., Lyon, L. and Embry, E. (2008). "Civic Engagement and Religious Activities: Examining the Influence of Religious Tradition and Participation," *Sociological Spectrum*, 28, 578–601.

Ecklund, E. (2005). "Models of Civic Responsibility: Korean Americans in Congregations with Different Ethnic Compositions," *Journal for the Scientific Study of Religion*, 44(1), 15–28.

Ecklund, E. and Park, J. (2007). "Religious Diversity and Community Volunteerism among Asian Americans," *Journal for the Scientific Study of Religion*, 46(2), 233–244.

Einolf, C. (2011a). "Gender Differences in the Correlates of Volunteering and Charitable Giving," *Nonprofit and Voluntary Sector Quarterly*, 40(6), 1092–1112.

Einolf, C. (2011b). "The Link Between Religion and Helping Others: The Roles of Values, Ideas, and Language," *Sociology of Religion*, 72(4), 435–455.

Einolf, C. (2013). "Daily Spiritual Experiences and Prosocial Behavior," *Social Indicators Research*, 110, 71–87.

Everton, S. (2015). "Networks and Religion: Ties that Bind, Loose, Build Up and Tear," *Journal of Social Structure*, 16, 1–34.

Frost, J. and Edgell, P. (2018). "Rescuing Nones from the Reference Category: Civic Engagement among the Nonreligious in America," *Nonprofit and Voluntary Sector Quarterly*, 47(2), 417–438.

Gil-Lacruz, A., Marcuello-Servos, C. and Saz-Gil, M. (2016). "Youth Volunteering in Countries in the European Union," *Nonprofit and Voluntary Sector Quarterly*, 45(5), 971–991.

Gil-Lacruz, A., Marcuello-Servos, C. and Saz-Gil, M. (2017). "Individual and Social Factors in Volunteering Participation Rates in Europe," *Cross-Cultural Research*, 51(5), 464–490.

Gil-Lacruz, A., Marcuello-Servos, C. and Saz-Gil, M. (2019). "Gender Differences in European Volunteer Rates," *Journal of Gender Studies* 28(2), 127–144.

Glanville, J., Paxton, P. and Wang, Y. (2016). "Social Capital and Generosity: A Multi-Level Analysis," *Nonprofit and Voluntary Sector Quarterly*, 45(3), 526–547.

Glazier, R. (2020). "The Differential Impact of Religion on Political Activity and Community Engagement," *Review of Religious Research*, 62, 1–26.

Greif, M., Adamczyk, A. and Felson, J. (2011). "Religion and Volunteering in Four Sub-Saharan African Countries," *Interdisciplinary Journal of Research on Religion*, 7(11), 1–15.

Grizzle, C. and Yusuf, J. (2015). "Trusting, Happy, Religious, and Giving: Explaining Volunteering in the Context of Nordic Exceptionalism," *Journal of Civil Society*, 11(4), 384–401.

Gronbjerg, K. and Never, B. (2004). "The Role of Religious Networks and Other Factors in Types of Volunteer Work," *Nonprofit Management and Leadership*, 14(3), 263–298.

Gronlund, H. (2011). "Identity and Volunteering Intertwined: Reflections on the Values of Young Adults," *Voluntas*, 22(4), 852–874.

Gronlund, H. (2012). "Religiousness and Volunteering: Searching for Connections in Late Modernity," *Nordic Journal of Religion and Society*, 25(1), 47–66.

Gutierrez, I. and Mattis, J. (2014). "Factors Predicting Volunteer Engagement among Urban-Residing African American Women," *Journal of Black Studies*, 45(7), 599–619.

Guo, Q., Lui, Z. and Tian, Q. (2020). "Religiosity and Prosocial Behavior at the National Level," *Psychology of Religion and Spirituality*, 12(1), 55–65.

Guo, Ch., Webb, N., Abzug, R. and Peck, L. (2013). "Religious Affiliation, Religious Attendance, and Participation in Social Change Organizations," *Nonprofit and Voluntary Sector Quarterly*, 42(1), 34–58.

Harris, M. (1996). "'An Inner Group of Willing People': Volunteering in a Religious Context," *Social Policy & Administration*, 30(1), 54–68.

Heineck, G. (2017). "Love Thy Neighbor — Religion and Prosociality," *International Journal of Social Economics*, 44(7), 869–883.

Henriksen, L., Koch-Nielsen, I. and Rosdahl, D. (2008). "Formal and Informal Volunteering in the Nordic Context: The Case of Denmark," *Journal of Civil Society*, 4(3), 193–209.

Heyer-Gray, Z. (2000). "Gender and Religious Work," *Sociology of Religion*, 61(4), 467–471.

Hoge, D. and Yang, F. (1994). "Determinants of Religious Giving in American Denominations," *Review of Religious Research*, 36(2), 123–148.

Hoge, D. and De Zulueta, E. (1985). "Salience as a Condition for Various Social Consequences of Religious Commitment," *Journal for the Scientific Study of Religion*, 24(1), 21–38.

Hoge, D., Zech, C., McNamara, P. and Donahue, M. (1998). "The Value of Volunteers as a Resource for Congregations," *Journal for the Scientific Study of Religion*, 37(3), 470–480.

Hu, A. (2014). "Gifts of Money and Gifts of Time: Folk Religion and Civic Involvement in a Chinese Society," *Review of Religious Research*, 56, 313–335.

Hustinx, L., van Rossem, R., Handy, F. and Cnaan, R. (2015). "A Cross-National Examination of the Motivation to Volunteer," in *Religion and Volunteering*, L. Hustinx, J. von Essen, J. Haers and S. Mels (eds.), pp. 97–120. Switzerland: Springer International Publishing.

Jackson, E., Bachmeier, M., Wood, J. and Craft, E. (1995). "Volunteering and Charitable Giving: Do Religious and Associational Ties Promote Helping Behavior?" *Nonprofit and Voluntary Sector Quarterly*, 24(1), 59–78.

Johnson, K., Okun, M. and Cohen, A. (2013). "Intrinsic Religiosity and Volunteering during Emerging Adulthood: A Comparison of Mormons with Catholics and Non-Catholic Christians," *Journal for the Scientific Study of Religion*, 52(4), 842–851.

Johnson, K., Cohen, A. and Okun, M. (2016). "God is Watching You ... But Also Watching Over You: The Influence of Benevolent God Representations on Secular Volunteerism among Christians," *Psychology of Religion and Spirituality*, 8(4), 363–374.

Johnston, J. (2013). "Religion and Volunteering over the Life Course," *Journal for the Scientific Study of Religion*, 52(4), 733–752.

Jongenelis, M., Dana, L., Warburton, J., Jackson, B., Newton, R., Talati, Z. and Pettigrew, S. (2020). "Factors Associated with Formal Volunteering Among Retirees," *European Journal of Ageing*, 17, 229–239.

Kim, Y. and Dew, J. (2016). "Marital Investment and Community Involvement: A Test of Coser's Greedy Marriage Thesis," *Sociological Perspectives*, 59(45), 743–759.

Kim, Y. and Dew, J. (2019). "Religion and Volunteering in Marital Relationships," *Review of Religious Research*, 61(4), 323–340.

Kim, Y. and Jang, S. (2017). "Religious Service Attendance and Volunteering: A Growth Curve Analysis," *Nonprofit and Voluntary Sector Quarterly*, 46(2), 395–418.

Kim, Y. and Jang, S. (2018). "Explaining Gender Differences in Changes in Volunteering after Divorce," *The Sociological Quarterly*, 60(1), 138–167.

Kim, Y. and Bradford Wilcox, W. (2013). "Bonding Alone: Familism, Religion, and Secular Civic Participation," *Social Science Research*, 42, 31–45.

King, D. (2019). "Religion, Charity and Philanthropy in America," *Oxford Research Encyclopedia, Religion in America*, J. Corrigan, (ed.), Oxford: Oxford University Press.

Kirchmaier, I., Prufer, J. and Trautmann, S. (2018). "Religion, Moral Attitudes and Economic Behavior," *Journal of Economic Behavior and Organization*, 148, 282–300.

Krause, N. (2015). "Assessing the Religious Roots of Volunteer Work in Middle and Late Life," *Research on Aging*, 37(5), 39–463.

Lam, P. (2002). "As the Flocks Gather: How Religion Affects Voluntary Association Participation," *Journal for the Scientific Study of Religion*, 41(3), 405–422.

Lazerwitz, B. and Harrison, M. (1979). "American Jewish Denominations," *American Sociological Review*, 44, 656–666.

Lewis, V., MacGregor, C. and Putnam, R. (2013). "Religion, Networks, and Neighborliness: The Impact of Religious Social Networks on Civic Engagement," *Social Science Research*, 42, 331–346.

Lichterman, P. (2005). *Elusive Togetherness: Church Groups Trying to Bridge America's Divisions*. Princeton, NJ: Princeton University Press.

Lim, C. and MacGregor, C. (2012). "Religion and Volunteering in Context: Disentangling the Contextual Effects of Religion on Voluntary Behavior," *American Sociological Review*, 77(5), 747–779.

Lu, P., Xu, C. and Shelley, M. (2020). "A State of the Art Review of the Socio-Ecological Correlates of Volunteerism among Older Adults," *Ageing and Society*, 41, 1833–1857.

Luria, G., Cnaan, R. and Boehm, A. (2017). "Religious Attendance and Volunteering: Testing National Culture as a Boundary Condition," *Journal for the Scientific Study of Religion*, 56(3), 577–599.

Martyn, B. and Dimitra, P. (2019). "Social and Demographic Factors Linked to Youth Civic and Political Engagement," in *Youth Civic and Political Engagement*, M. Barett and P. Dimitra (eds.), pp. 45–75. London: Routledge.

McClure, J. (2015). "The Cost of Being Lost in the Crowd: How Congregational Size and Social Networks Shape Attenders' Involvement in Community Organizations," *Review of Religious Research*, 57, 269–286.

McClure, J. (2017). "'Go and Do Likewise': Investigating Whether Involvement in Congregationally Sponsored Community Service Activities Predicts Prosocial Behavior," *Review of Religious Research*, 59(3), 341–366.

McKenzie, B. (2001). "Self-Selection, Church Attendance, and Local Civic Participation," *Journal for the Scientific Study of Religion*, 40(3), 479–488.

Mencken, F. and Fitz, B. (2013). "Image of God and Community Volunteering among Religious Adherents in the United States," *Review of Religious Research*, 55(3), 491–508.

Merino, S. (2013). "Religious Social Networks and Volunteering: Examining Recruitment via Close Ties," *Review of Religious Research*, 55, 509–527.

Merino, S. (2019). "Religious Involvement and Bridging Social Ties: The Role of Congregational Participation," *Socio-Historical Examination of Religion and Ministry*, 1(2), 291–308.

Mersianova, I. and Schneider, F. (2018). "Russian Faith Matters: Religiosity and Civil Society in the Russian Federation," *Sociology of Religion*, 79(4), 495–519.

Mitani, H. (2014). "Influences of Resources and Subjective Dispositions on Formal and Informal Volunteering," *Voluntas*, 25, 1022–1040.

Monsma, S. (2007). "Religion and Philanthropic Giving and Volunteering," *Interdisciplinary Journal of Research on Religion*, 3, 1–28.

Musick, M. and Wilson, J. (2008). *Volunteers: A Social Profile*. Bloomington, Indiana: Indiana University Press.

Musick, M., Wilson, J. and Bynum, Jr. W. (2000). "Race and Formal Volunteering: The Differential Effects of Class and Religion," *Social Forces*, 78(4), 1539–1570.

Nieburr, J., van Lente, L., Liefbroer, A., Steverink, N. and Smidt, N. (2018). "Determinants of Participation in Voluntary Work: A Systematic Review and Meta-Analysis of Longitudinal Cohort Studies," *BMC Public Health*, 18, 1213–1243.

Nisanci, Z. (2017). "Close Social Ties, Socioeconomic Diversity and Social Capital in US Congregations," *Review of Religious Research*, 59, 419–439.

Norenzayan, A. and A. Sharif (2008). "The Origin and Evolution of Religious Prosociality," *Science*, 322, 58–62.

Norris, P. (2013). "Does Praying Together Mean Staying Together? Religion and Civic Engagement in Europe and the United States," in *Religion and Civil Society in Europe*, J. de Hart, P. Dekker and L. Halman (eds.), pp. 285–305. Dordrecht: Springer Publishing.

Okun, M., O'Rourke, H., Keller, B., Johnson, K. and Enders, C. (2015). "Value-Expressive Motivation and Volunteering by Older Adults: Relationships with Religiosity and Spirituality," *Journals of Gerontology: Psychological Sciences*, 70(6), 860–870.

Paik, A. and Navarre-Jackson, L. (2011). "Social Networks, Recruitment, and Volunteering: Are Social Capital Effects Conditional on Recruitment?" *Nonprofit and Voluntary Sector Quarterly*, 40, 476–496.

Parboteeah, K., Cullen, J. and Lim, L. (2004). "Formal Volunteering: A Cross-National Test," *Journal of World Business*, 39, 431–441.

Park, J. and Smith, C. (2000). "'To Whom Much Has Been Given ...' Religious Capital and Community Voluntarism among Churchgoing Protestants," *Journal for the Scientific Study of Religion*, 39(3), 272–286.

Paxton, P., Reith, N. and Glanville, J. (2014). "Volunteering and the Dimensions of Religiosity: Cross-National Analysis," *Review of Religious Research*, 56, 597–625.

Perks, T. and Haan, M. (2011). "Youth Religious Involvement and Adult Community Participation: Do Levels of Youth Religious Involvement Matter?" *Nonprofit and Voluntary Sector Quarterly*, 40(1), 107–129.

Petrovic, K, Chapman, C. and Schofield, T. (2021). "Religiosity and Volunteering over Time: Religious Service Attendance is Associated with the Likelihood of Volunteering, and Religious Importance with the Time Spent Volunteering," *Psychology of Religion and Spirituality*, 13(2), 136–146.

Peucker, M. (2020). "Muslim Community Volunteering: The Civic-Religious 'Culture of Benevolence' and its Sociopolitical Implications," *Journal of Ethnic and Migration Studies*, 46(11), 2367–2386.

Pew Research Center (April 12, 2016). *Religion in Everyday Life*. Washington, DC: Pew Research Center.

Polson, E. (2018). "An Examination of the Relationship between Characteristics of Sect-Like Religiosity and Community Volunteering among U.S. Churchgoers," *Review of Religious Research*, 60, 247–274.

Prouteau, L. and Sardinha, B. (2015). "Volunteering and Country-Level Religiosity: Evidence from the European Union," *Voluntas*, 26, 242–266.

Putnam, R. (2000). *Bowling Alone: The Collapse and Revival of American Community*. New York: Simon and Schuster.

Putnam, R. and Campbell, D. (2010). *American Grace: How Religion Divides and Unites Us*. New York: Simon and Schuster.

Qvist, H. (2018). "Secular and Religious Volunteering among Immigrants and Natives in Denmark," *Acta Sociologica*, 61(2), 202–218.

Rotolo, T. and Wilson, J. (2007). "Sex-Segregation in Volunteer Work," *The Sociological Quarterly*, 48, 559–585.

Rotolo, T. and Wilson, J. (2012). "State-Level Differences in Volunteering in the United States," *Nonprofit and Voluntary Sector Quarterly*, 41(3), 452–473.

Rotolo, T. and Wilson, J. (2014). "Social Heterogeneity and Volunteering in U.S. Cities," *Sociological Forum*, 29(2), 429–452.

Ruiter, S. and De Graaf, N. (2006). "National Context, Religiosity and Volunteering: Results from 53 Countries," *American Sociological Review*, 71(2), 191–210.

Sampson, B. and Willer, R. (2015). "Beyond Altruism: Sociological Foundations of Cooperation and Prosocial Behavior," *Annual Review of Sociology*, 41, 43–63.

Saroglou, V. (2013). "Religion, Spirituality and Altruism," in *APA Handbook of Psychology, Religion and Spirituality*, K. I. Pargement, J. Exline and J. Jones (eds.), pp. 439–457. Washington, D.C.: American Psychological Association.

Saroglou, V., Pichon, I., Trompette, L., Verschueren, M. and Dernelle, R. (2005). "Prosocial Behavior and Religion: New Evidence Based on Projective Measures and Peer Ratings," *Journal for the Scientific Study of Religion*, 44(3), 323–348.

Schumann, K. (2020). "A Force For Good: When and Why Religion Predicts Prosocial Behavior," *Journal of Moral Theology*, 9(1), 34–50.

Schwadel, P. (2005). "Individual, Congregational, and Denominational Effects on Church Members' Civic Participation," *Journal for the Scientific Study of Religion*, 44(2), 159–171.

Schwadel, P. (2012). "Social Class and Finding a Congregation: How Attendees are Introduced to Their Congregations," *Review of Religious Research*, 54, 543–554.

Schwadel, P., Cheadle, J., Malone, S. and Stout, M. (2016). "Social Networks and Civic Participation in Two Evangelical Protestant Churches," *Review of Religious Research*, 58, 305–317.

Schieman, S., Bierman, A. and Ellison, C. (2012). "Religious Involvement, Beliefs about God, and the Sense of Mattering among Older Adults," *Journal for the Scientific Study of Religion*, 49(3), 517–535.

Sinha, M. (2015). *Volunteering in Canada*. Ottawa: Statistics Canada.

Smith, D. (1983). "Churches are Generally Ignored in Contemporary Voluntary Action Research: Causes and Consequences," *Review of Religious Research*, 24(4), 295–303.

Smith, D. (1994). "Determinants of Voluntary Association Participation and Volunteering: A Literature Review," *Nonprofit and Voluntary Sector Quarterly*, 23(3), 243–263.

Son, J. and Wilson, J. (2011). "Generativity and Volunteering," *Sociological Forum*, 26(3), 644–667.

Son, J. and Wilson, J. (2012). "Using Normative Theory to Explain the Effect of Religion and Education on Volunteering," *Sociological Perspectives*, 55(3), 473–499.

Stark, R. and Bainbridge, W. (1985). *The Future of Religion*. Berkeley, CA: University of California Press.

Storm, I. (2015a). "Civic Engagement in Britain: The Role of Religion and Inclusive Values," *European Sociological Review*, 31(1), 14–29.

Storm, I. (2015b). "Religion, Inclusive Individualism, and Volunteering in Europe," *Journal of Contemporary Religion*, 30(2), 213–229.

Stukas, A., Snyder, M. and Gil Clary, E. (2014). "Volunteerism and Community Involvement: Antecedents, Experiences, and Consequences for the Person and the Situation," in *The Oxford Handbook of Prosocial Behavior*, D. A. Schroeder and W. Graziano (eds.). New York: Oxford University Press. Published online.

Taniguchi, H. (2010). "Who Are Volunteers in Japan?" *Nonprofit and Voluntary Sector Quarterly*, 39(1), 161–179.

Taniguchi, H. (2012). "The Determinants of Formal and Informal Volunteering: Evidence from the American Time Use Survey," *Voluntas*, 23(4), 920–939.

Taniguchi, H. (2013). "The Influence of Generalized Trust on Volunteering in Japan," *Nonprofit and Voluntary Sector Quarterly*, 42(1), 127–147.

Taniguchi, H. and Thomas, L. (2011). "The Influences of Religious Attitudes on Volunteering," *Voluntas*, 22, 335–355.

Taylor, R. (2004). "Extending Conceptual Boundaries: Work, Voluntary Work and Employment," *Work, Employment & Society*, 18(1), 29–49.

Tsang, J., Rowatt, W. and Sharif, A. (2015). "Religion and Prosociality," in *The Oxford Handbook of Prosocial Behavior*, D. Schroeder and W. Graziano (eds.). New York: Oxford University Press. Published online.

Uslaner, E. (2002). "Religion and Civic Engagement in Canada and the United States," *Journal for the Scientific Study of Religion*, 41(2), 239–254.

Van Ingen, E. and Dekker, P. (2011). "Changes in the Determinants of Volunteering: Participation and Time Investment between 1975 and 2005 in the Netherlands," *Nonprofit and Voluntary Sector Quarterly*, 40(4), 682–702.

Van Tienen, M., Scheepers, P., Reitsma, J. and Schiilderman, H. (2011). "The Role of Religiosity for Formal and Informal Volunteering in the Netherlands," *Voluntas*, 22, 365–389.

Vermeer, P. and Scheepers, P. (2011). "Religious Socialization and Non-Religious Volunteering: A Dutch Panel Study," *Voluntas*, 23, 940–958.

Vermeer, P. and Scheepers, P. (2019). "Bonding or Bridging? Volunteering among the Members of Six Thriving Evangelical Congregations in the Netherlands," *Voluntas*, 30, 962–975.

Wang, L. and Graddy, E. (2008). "Social Capital, Volunteering, and Charitable Giving," *Voluntas*, 19(1), 23–42.

Wang, L., Mook, L. and Handy, F. (2017). "An Empirical Examination of Formal and Informal Volunteering in Canada," *Voluntas*, 28(1), 139–161.

Welch, M., Sikkink, D. and Loveland, M. (2007). "The Radius of Trust: Religion, Social Embeddedness and Trust in Strangers," *Social Forces*, 86(1), 23–46.

Weller, R., Huang, C. and Wu, K. (2020). "Philanthropy and the Religious Life of Goodness in China," in *Handbook of Religion in China*, S. Feuchtwang, (ed.), pp. 54–74. Cheltenham, UK: Edward Elgar Publishing.

Whitehead, A. and Stroope, S. (2015). "Small Groups, Contexts, and Civic Engagement," *Social Science Research*, 52, 659–660.

Wilson, J. (1978). *Religion in American Society*: Englewood Cliffs, N.J.: Prentice Hall.

Wilson, J. and Janoski, T. (1995). "The Contribution of Religion to Volunteer Work," *Sociology of Religion*, 56(2), 137–152.

Wilson, J. and Musick, M. (1999). "Attachment to Volunteering," *Sociological Forum*, 14(2), 243–272.

Wolfer, T., Myers, D., Polson, E. and Bevis, B. (2017). "Baby Boomers as Congregational Volunteers in Community Ministry," *Religions*, 8(4), 66–84.

Wuthnow, R. (1991). *Acts of Compassion: Caring for Others and Helping Ourselves*. Princeton, NJ: Princeton University Press.

Wuthnow, R. (1995). *Learning to Care: Elementary Kindness in an Age of Indifference*. New York, NY: Oxford University Press.

Wuthnow, R. (2004). *Saving America? Faith-Based Services and the Future of Civil Society*. Princeton, NJ: Princeton University Press.

Xu, Y. (2014). "Volunteer Participation and the Development of Civil Society in China: A Case Study of Jinan," *Nonprofit Policy Forum*, 5(1), 139–168.

Yen, S. and Zampelli, E. (2014). "What Drives Charitable Donations of Time and Money? The Roles of Political Ideology, Religiosity, and Involvement," *Journal of Behavioral and Experimental Economics*, 50, 58–67.

Yen, S. and Zampelli, E. (2017). "Charitable Contributions of Time and Money: A Multivariate Sample Selection Approach," *Eastern Economic Journal*, 43, 43–63.

Yeung, A. (2004). "An Intricate Triangle — Religiosity, Volunteering, and Social Capital: The European Perspective, the Case of Finland," *Nonprofit and Voluntary Sector Quarterly*, 33(3), 401–422.

Yeung, J. (2017). "Religious Involvement and Participation in Volunteering: Types, Domains and Aggregate," *Voluntas*, 28, 110–138.

Yeung, J. (2018). "Are Religious People Really More Helpful? Public and Private Religiosity and Volunteering Participation," *Nonprofit and Voluntary Sector Quarterly*, 47(6), 1178–1200.

Youniss, J., McClellan, J. and Yates, M. (1999). "Religion, Community Service, and Identity in American Youth," *Journal of Adolescence*, 22, 243–253.

Chapter 9

Judaism, Liberalism and the Market

Jonathan Jacobs

John Jay College/City University of New York, USA
jajacobs4884@gmail.com

Abstract

The three main claims of the discussion are that (i) values and perspectives integral to Judaism are especially congenial to liberal democracy as a political order and had a role in early modern theorizing about the liberal state, (ii) they are also congenial to the market as a basic economic arrangement on account of how Judaism regards the dignity, accountability and independence of the individual, and (iii) while there is no guarantee that the market will benefit everyone it is defensible on the basis of how it constructively interacts with the pluralistic civil society that a liberal order makes possible. Judaism's core notions of voluntariness and concern for others can contribute to a morally endorsable form of market activity.

Keywords: Civil Society, Equality, Liberalism, Luck, Rule of Law

1. Introduction

In the present discussion I argue that (i) there are aspects of Judaism that are especially well suited to a broadly liberal democracy. And (ii) there are aspects of Judaism and Jewish history favorable to endorsement of the market as the fundamental form of economic activity. I also present some reasons why Jews might be skeptical of the notion of public reason as an important feature of liberal democracy. This issue is included because the notion of public reason is widely endorsed by theorists of liberalism and democracy and there are reasons to think that Jews (and others to whom religion is important) are much better served by societies that encourage habits of toleration rather than adherence to criteria of public reason. This is a more promising, plausible element of a liberal and democratic political culture. Of course, many Jews are non-religious. Despite that, the points concerning the political order, the market and public reason still stand, largely on account of how Jews often regard their religion as shaping moral, political and social values even when they are not religiously observant.

At the outset we should note that there are many different Jewish traditions and perspectives and some are very different from the ones highlighted in this discussion. Moreover, there are indeed many people whose illiberal commitments and whose hostility to an open, diverse civil society are grounded in and fueled by religion. Also, there are forms of Jewish community life (especially among various *Haredi* groups) that are largely indifferent to the wider political culture as long as those communities can lead Jewish lives in accord with their commitments. Even with various qualifications it is important to see how the nexus of the liberal political order, civil society and the market is supported by significant currents of Jewish thought and aspects of Jews' historical experience.

2. Jewish Roots and Resonances in the Liberal Political Order

Jewish responses to emancipation in Europe, from the Enlightenment to more recent times, were very diverse. In addition, the reception on the part of the host societies was quite diverse and uneven. Also, European nations exhibited a broad range of political forms in Europe and in the Western hemisphere. The political culture of the Habsburg monarchy was quite different from, say, that of the Netherlands or the UK. Nonetheless, there were important respects in which Jews were prepared for life in increasingly liberal democratic states and fuller participation in market economies despite the fact that Judaism had not developed a tradition of political theorizing. Jews had been in exile and under the political authority of non-Jews since the fall of the Second Temple. There was no independent Jewish state about which to theorize. Despite that, Jews had extensive experience with forms of basically democratic self-rule regarding many aspects of community life and courts. They also had experience as a minority group needing to protect its interests without antagonizing the powers that claimed sovereign authority over Jewish communities. The *kehillot* might not have been fully democratic but many Jews had more experience in various aspects of community self-governance than non-Jews in the wider society.

The ruling political authority was sometimes tolerant, and at other times exercised its coercive power in very damaging ways. Jews almost everywhere experienced numerous exclusions and prohibitions if not expulsion, mass murder or forced conversion. Still, as Ruth Wisse has argued, "unable to rely on coercive power, Jews had been forced to compete at a severe disadvantage. Like athletes that train with weights, Jews were more than ready for the competition once their handicaps were lifted" (Wisse, 2007: 91). In those places where civil society was genuinely open to Jews many were eager to participate and they often met with success, but in many places a popular notion that "Jews were unworthy of the legal and social position conferred upon them" became derisive, explicit and powerful (Wisse, 2007: 87).[1] Even as various official impediments were lifted there was a great deal of popular anti-Semitism in the press, politics, literature and other contexts.

Nonetheless, core values of Judaism are well suited to a broadly liberal democratic political order, especially in regard to basic matters of moral anthropology. The Bible does not present an explicit theory of free will but there is a pronounced role for the individual agent's voluntariness and choice in regard to responding to the authority and wisdom of the law. The Bible is an important source of what we might call "the unavoidability of accountability." According to Judaism, we each have agency and accountability but we are not ourselves the ultimate authority with respect to what is good. We can respond to that authority through reason, through virtues informed by an aspiration to understand. Individual agency and responsibility are fundamental, though we are not ourselves the creators of the good. We are not the ultimate authors of the good but we can strive to realize it by living lives of holiness. These biblical notions had an important

---

[1] "Quoting sociologist Jacob Katz."

role in shaping liberal democratic notions of persons as "free and equal" even when there was no acknowledgment of their Judaic roots.

That we are created in the image of God underwrites the moral regard due to each human being. It is what makes possible relations with others on the basis of a recognition of the distinctive value of a person and on the basis of requirements fashioned by wisdom and benevolence.[2] It is what underwrites our conceptions of ourselves as having worth and dignity, whatever our station in life and whatever our circumstances. Worth and dignity do not depend upon fortune. That human beings possess intellect and will is the basis of respect for, and concern for, all human beings. It is also the basis for the inestimable value of each person as an individual, for the "separateness of persons" as distinct individuals.[3]

Notions such as the rule of law, limitations on the powers of political leaders, the importance of courts and judges for adjudicating disputes, even the social contract as having roots in the notion of covenant; sources of these features of liberal democracy are all plausibly findable in Judaism. In fact, Jewish texts had influenced some especially important thinkers whose works contributed to the theorizing about the early modern liberal state. During a brief but very consequential period of early modern political thought numerous Christian Hebraists, especially among the English and Dutch, regarded the Hebrew Bible as a source of crucially important political ideas. Many of the early modern Christian Hebraists regarded the Noahide Laws, with their textual basis in Genesis 9, as a model of natural law, and the rabbinic tradition has long regarded the Noahide Laws as applying universally to all human beings (the children

---

[2] Many Jewish thinkers argued that each of the (613) commandments has some rational justification, even if it is not evident. We are not to regard any of God's commandments as arbitrary, rather than reflecting divine wisdom and benevolence. Even commandments concerning ritual matters have a rationale and the commandments as a whole constitute a discipline of holiness, and the more committed we are to fulfilling them, the better we will understand the reasons for them. Maimonides, for example, was explicit in presenting this sort of view. Saadia and others held similar views. In such views the practices are interpreted as encouraging and sustaining various virtues, and not simply doing what one is command.

[3] Rawls used the notion of the "separateness of persons" as part of his critique of utilitarianism in *A Theory of Justice*. Rawls argued that one of the defects of utilitarianism is that it fails to adequately recognize the separateness of persons. The failure is in the way that utilitarianism focuses on the good overall brought about by an action or a policy, without morally distinguishing the impact on individuals.

of Noah), not only the Jewish people. Figures such as Milton, Harrington, Selden, Cunaeus, Grotius and others had key roles in shaping early modern liberal and republican thought, and often referred and deferred to the Hebrew Bible as a source of political wisdom. The period of intense attention to the Hebrew Bible was brief but it had lasting impact in the way it shaped ideas of the republic, of limited political powers, and of governance by law.[4]

Jews are enjoined in the Bible to love the stranger as oneself (Lev. 19: 33–34), to provide one law for the stranger and the Israelite alike (Exod. 12–49), and to provide the stranger with food, clothing, and agricultural charity (Lev. 23: 22; Deut. 24: 19) (Stone, 2006: 17). Moral notions such as these shaped some of the early modern thinking about universal rights and obligations to all persons. Also, we read: "justice, justice you shall pursue" (Deut. 16: 18) as a central theme. There is a scholarly debate over whether Jewish thought includes natural law theorizing, at least implicitly if not explicitly. Numerous Christian thinkers interpreted the Noahide laws as an early form of natural law. While there is almost no presence of explicit natural law theorizing in Judaism until fairly recently, it is not difficult to see why scholars might think that Jewish thought at least overlaps with natural law theorizing on some important points.[5] Whether or not we regard Jewish thought as including natural law it is clear that there are significant points of contact between Judaism and the natural law tradition.

Tanakh (the Jewish Bible) is a source of ideas and ideals that have been incorporated into modern secular liberal political thought. Care for other human beings is an oft-repeated thematic refrain in the Pentateuch.

---

[4]For scholarship on Political Hebraism, see Oz-Salzberger, F. (2002). "The Jewish Roots of Western Freedom," *Azure*, 13(5762), 88–132; Manuel, F. (2002). *The Broken Staff: Judaism through Christian Eyes*. Cambridge, Mass.: Harvard University Press; Jacobs, J. (2006). "Return to the Sources: Political Hebraism and the Making of Modern Politics," *Hebraic Political Studies*, 1(3), 328–342.

[5]In recent decades scholars such as Lenn Goodman, Tamar Rudavsky and David Novak have argued that Judaism can and should be interpreted as including elements of natural law. In several places I have argued against that view while acknowledging there are reasons one might claim to find natural law in Judaism. See my "Natural Law and Judaism," in *Research Handbook on Natural Law Theory*, J. Crowe and C. Lee (eds.), pp. 130–147. Cheltenham: Edward Elgar Publisher, 2019, and "The Reasons of the Commandments: Rational Tradition Without Natural Law," in *Reason, Religion and Natural Law: Plato to Spinoza*, J. A. Jacobs, (ed.), pp. 106–132. Oxford: Oxford University Press, 2012.

The Prophets, too, urge it emphatically and repeatedly. Concern for one's fellow human beings is the centerpiece of concern for the created order. Contributing constructively to that order, contributing on the basis of reason and commitment to the good, is the basic form of human participation in the created order. Even that one shall rebuke one's neighbor is part of that contribution because proper rebuke is a reminder and is guidance, setting the wrongdoer on the right path. It is not simply punitive, and rebuke should never shame or humiliate the offender. It is a constructive, morally educative form of concern for the other.

The exhortation to care for the needy and the destitute is important not only as calling for compassion but for how those virtues can help others become self-supporting. In turn, that is significant for how it supports one's dignity. There is dignity in work, and there is dignity in providing for one's self and one's family. That is a vital element of the human contribution to the created order. The more dependent a person is, the more constraints there are on that individual's voluntariness and self-determination. The more independent a person is, the more occasions and opportunities there are to exercise agency and to be acknowledged by others *as an agent*. That can be important to one's sense of dignity and capabilities.

The sixteenth and seventeenth-century Hebraists were not generally interested in fuller relations with the Jewish communities but at least they had considerable respect for elements of Jewish thought and its textual bases. The Enlightenment was less kind to Judaism; the view of it as primitive and anachronistic, and as theologically and morally superseded by Christianity had considerable currency, often on the basis of almost complete ignorance of Jewish religion and texts.[6] Far from being the

---

[6]Richard I. Cohen writes of the many debates and controversies regarding the "ownership" of the Hebrew Bible, "In fact, controversy about the Bible, a struggle over authority and interpretation, raged from the eighteenth through the early twentieth centuries in Western and Central Europe .... [763]" "A significant challenge to the position of the Jews came not only from the cultural and political forces that opposed their integration and emancipation but also from scrutiny of the Talmud and the Bible. [763]" "Although influential thinkers still celebrated the biblical teachings, others challenged the very legitimacy of the book upon which Judaism had built its basic premise and created its link to the past. [764]" Treating the Hebrew Bible as relatively primitive religion was a way to deny Jews the authority of the book on which much of their very identity rested. Cohen, R. I. (2002). "Urban Visibility a Biblical Visions: Jewish Culture in Western and Central Europe in the

desiccated anachronism many Enlightenment thinkers took it to be there are important respects in which core values of Jewish religion support modern moral and political values and ideals.[7] The notion of the individual as meriting respect and as never to be treated merely as a means has deep roots in the biblical anthropology of human beings as created in God's image. As noted previously, that political rule is to be the rule of law, and its legitimacy is grounded in the justice of law and not the will of the ruler, has biblical roots. The notion that it is wrong to degrade or humiliate another, that it is wrong to oppress others or to abandon the weak and the destitute, all have biblical roots.

For the central argument of this chapter it is helpful to distinguish the political form, liberal democracy, from the civil society it helps make possible. The latter is an open, dynamic civil society including all manner of contexts and modes of human activity and interaction.[8] In authoritarian and repressive states there is very limited civil society because there are very limited opportunities for voluntary action, interaction, association and expression. The exercise of agency on the part of individuals is highly policed and constrained. Civil society in liberal democracies comprises very numerous contexts, settings and modes of activity. Economic life (work, commerce, financial transactions and so forth) aspects of

---

Modern Age," in *The Cultures of the Jews*, David Biale, (ed.), pp. 731–789, New York: Schocken Books.

[7]Like many other critics, Kant appeared to be unaware of the crucial role in Judaism for understanding the reasons for the commandments and of the way in which a great deal of Jewish law concerns ethical life. He held that the Jewish faith lacked any genuine moral element and was a collection of "mere statutory laws upon which was established a political organization; for whatever moral additions were then or later appended to it in no way whatever belonged to Judaism as such. Judaism is really not a religion at all but merely a union of a number of people who, since they belonged to a particular stock, formed themselves into a commonwealth under purely political laws, and not into a church; nay, it was intended to be merely an earthly state so that, were it possibly to be dismembered through adverse circumstances, there would still remain to it (as part of its very essence) the political faith in its eventual reestablishment (with the advent of the Messiah)." This is just ignorant caricature. Kant, I. (1960). *Religion Within the Limits of Reason Alone*, T. Greene and H. Hudson, (trans.) p. 116. New York: Harper and Row.

[8]I provide a fuller discussion of the relation between the liberal political order and civil society — and the ways they can be mutually reinforcing (or weakening) in *The Liberal State and Criminal Sanction: Seeking Justice and Civility*. New York: Oxford University Press, 2020. See especially Chapter 1.

education, cultural activity and leisure pursuits, the arts, religious life and other aspects of people's lives take on a large number of forms on account of a broad diversity of interests, commitments and perspectives. There is genuine scope for value-pluralism in the respect that the ways people lead their lives reflect diverse and irreducible conceptions of value, of worth and significance. The principles and values shaping political institutions and the rule of law enable persons to exercise extensive freedoms, and that exercise can shape a complex, dynamic civil society.

Myriad forms of transaction and interaction in an open civil society require that persons be typically trustworthy and also trusting. So much of what we do in civil society depends on the good will and good faith of others — in many cases, complete strangers — and we would be severely handicapped by not being able to trust people. In many contexts it is appropriate to check someone's background or *bona fides*, and to make sure that the person is an authorized agent or is in fact certified to be offering the good or service offered, and so forth. However, for a vast amount of what we do that is just not necessary and the occasions when we are cheated or have been taken advantage of are the exceptions. Granted, they can be disastrous, but for most people, most of the time, they are not large in number and they are not disastrous.

Regarding and treating individuals as free and equal are basic principles of a liberal democracy but it is also important that people should acquire the habits and attitudes through which they can exercise voluntariness and accountability. Those have to be learned; they are not just part of the natural maturation of a human being. This is a key reason that the political order is so important. The liberal order helps sustain the kinds of conditions — the rules, institutions, practices and perspectives — through which those habits and attitudes can be developed and exercised. An open, dynamic civil society provides numerous contexts in which people can acquire the attitudes and habits through which they develop effective deliberative capacities. This is how a great many persons acquire much of their moral education. It might be that religious upbringing involves teaching a young person many specific moral requirements but one acquires a more fully informed and discriminating moral understanding in the actual contexts of decision and action.

Jewish responses to emancipation and their views of assimilation took many different forms, much depending on the receptivity of the wider society and the ability of Jews to participate in civil society. There have been many different forms of Jewish life and Jews have adapted to a large number of different political and social cultures. In recent decades, and especially in liberal democracies many Jews have left behind much of traditional Jewish family and community life, and Jews have developed sense of Jewish identity in numerous forms. Among emigrants many wanted to participate in American (or other) civic culture and distance themselves from much of what they regarded as a more insular, more tradition-bound, and socially limiting form of life in "the old country."

Large numbers of Jews, and this was perhaps especially true of many immigrants to the US, felt a Jewish identity strongly but not in a way that comprehensively shaped their lives and activities. Thinking of oneself as Jewish, but without studying Talmud, without a kosher diet, without regular observance and without attention to God throughout all departments of one's life — that became possible on a scale that was unprecedented.

At the same time, because religious identity was very important to many Jews, even if religious worship and the knowledge of sacred texts were not, the neutrality of the state toward religion in the US was a way of preserving Jewish cultural identity, in contrast to Jewish children growing up thinking that "normal" people are Christian. Many Jews in contemporary American society have a strong sense of Jewish identity, though they do not practice the religion. Still, it is important to them to be able to participate in civil society as Jews. As Hillel Fradkin has noted, "Perhaps most Jews today, including many who are not very observant, see a strong link between democracy and traditional Jewish teachings. They regard this link so seriously that they believe it may inform their own political actions and justify their own understanding of what democracy requires."[9] Jews have long had reason to fear populist — even unofficial — oppression of Jewish culture and identity. The separation of religion and state appealed to many Jews as a way to keep whatever faith happened to be the majority from an increasing role in education and politics. (Of course, the situation in Israel, a Jewish state in which Judaism is the majority religion, is unique.)

Historically, there have been important Judaic contributions to the political culture of liberal democracy at least through indirect influence providing conceptual resources for elaborating liberal-democratic ideas and values. Also, in several countries where Jews could be citizens and

---

[9]Fradkin, H. (2004). "Judaism and Political Life," *Journal of Democracy*, 15(3), 122–136.

where their emancipation was genuine many were eager to participate in the open, dynamic civil society and have been consistent supporters of liberal democratic values and institutions.

3. Civil Society, Judaism and the Market

Civil society is a mode of social and economic life in which a diversity of values is pursued and there is openness to changing patterns of interaction, shifting interests, and patterns of association. There is extensive scope for individual and group purposefulness but there is no overall "plan." Civil society, especially when the market is the basic form of economic activity, is a complex of spheres in which there is a combination of extensive rule-governedness along with contingency. As an economic arrangement, the market multiplies contexts and occasions for agency. As a result, participation in the market can habituate and educate persons in prudence and accountability. This is not because the market makes each person the master of his or her own fate. It is true that the market makes demands upon deliberation, planning and taking care with risk, with one's resources, and with looking after one's interests. At the same time, it is shot through with contingency and unpredictability. Part of the education in prudence provided by the market is education in coming to grips with one's lack of complete control over circumstances and over the future. That, too, is important to the maturation of accountability. It is also a kind of self-understanding that Judaism recognizes. We are voluntary, accountable agents in regard to the actions we perform and the moral quality of our exercise of self-determination. But we do not control the way of the world and we need to realize that we live our lives at an intersection of desert and luck (in the sense of fortune, the many ways that reality is not shaped by our desires and intentions).

Participation in the market can help educate people in the kind of humility appropriate to that realization. We should always strive to be just and to do what is right but nature does not guarantee that benefits and burdens are distributed in accord with deserts. That should not be interpreted as a failure of the market but it is instructive in important ways. A reasonable, realistic awareness of the imperfect justice of the natural and social worlds, and of the extent to which it is reasonable to seek to rectify those imperfections, can help guard against large-scale, illiberal projects that substitute command and policy for the spontaneity and contingency of market activity. The values mentioned earlier, values such as caring for the destitute, respecting persons' dignity, and being steadily committed to seeing that justice is done are not somehow made secondary to the market; they remain fundamental and imperative. We will comment further on this point below.

In the modern world many Jews found that, when impediments were removed, they could prosper, finding the challenges and opportunities of market competition congenial in numerous respects. It is true that in several countries Jews were involved in Socialist movements and some supported Communism, mainly out of hope of political and social reform elevating them from second-class or worse political and social standing. But where conditions were less repressive and reactionary many Jews generally were content to lead their working lives in market economies and they were able to develop the sorts of abilities, habits and skills enabling them to succeed in market economies. Where the political order supported a vibrant civil society Jews were often able to compete successfully in many different activities from literature and the sciences, to commerce and banking, entertainment, academic scholarship, real estate and other areas including even politics if the jurisdiction was not stubbornly anti-Semitic.

Values integral to Judaism — and often inculcated whether or not a person was also raised to be observant — have helped Jews as market participants. We mentioned the importance Judaism places on the independence of persons, their effective ability to lead lives of self-determination through looking after themselves. That is one of the chief reasons imprudent indulgence, recklessness and profligacy are condemned. Of course, there are circumstances in which a person cannot avoid being dependent. Significant misfortune could put any of us in that condition. As aforementioned, it is human dignity and not just welfare that is stake in conditions of poverty. Our ability to work and the efforts we make are the basis of the human contribution to the created order. The more dependent a person is, the more constraints there are on that individual's voluntariness and self-determination. Dependence, even when it does not involve humiliation or condescension, puts limits on the exercise of agency in ways that can be demoralizing and limit one's participation in civil society.

In addition, independence makes it possible for a person to be generous to others, to serve the community and to enjoy meaningful leisure. The market is a crucial element of civil society because of its openness to initiative, creativity and opportunity. Also, participation in it can enable a person to acquire prudence and grow accustomed to accountability. The case for the market is not that the market generally rewards persons in accord with desert; it does not do that in any sort of regular way. (*Nothing* does that, or at least nothing in the natural world. If there is ultimate justice, through which persons are rewarded in proportion to virtue, it is not something human beings have the understanding and power to actualize.) As noted previously, participation in the market helps people become accustomed to the intersection of luck and desert that is an unavoidable aspect of human agency. There are significant respects in which Judaism involves values and commitments congenial to that nexus.

Edward Shils wrote, "The hallmark of a civil society is the autonomy of private associations and institutions, as well as that of private business firms" (Shils, 1997: 330). Furthermore, he noted that, "The pluralism of civil society is two-fold. Its pluralism comprises the partially autonomous spheres of economy, religion, culture, intellectual activity, political activity, etc., *vis-à-vis* each other .... The pluralism of civil society also comprises within each sphere a multiplicity of many partially autonomous corporations and institutions" (Shils, 1997: 330). He mentions business firms, churches and sects, universities, independent newspapers, periodicals, broadcasting corporations, political parties, and philanthropic and civic associations (Shils, 1997: 330).

The values necessary for civil society find some of their strongest cultural anchors in biblical religion, even if their idiom in secular society fails to refer to that anchor. Again, Shils' view is apt:

> Our appreciation of the value of the individual human being and of the value of his self-expression and self-protection is fundamentally an appreciation of the sacredness of his existence. That we call this appreciation self-evident is itself a product of a long tradition. The system of freedom — with its self-restraint of the powerful, its acknowledgment of the worth of other persons, its reluctance to submit to authority, and, above all, its aspiration to rational self-determination — can flourish only if it is permeated with a largely unreflective acceptance of these rules of the game of the free society. (Shils, 1997: 110)

The market, as a basic economic arrangement, is significant in ways that extend well beyond matters of production, distribution and efficiency. The ways in which it extends beyond them have significant implications for the moral psychology of individuals and society. The modes of voluntariness permitted and encouraged by the market shape attitudes and dispositions with effects not confined to the economic context. Market participation can be an education of voluntariness and can encourage trust and trustworthiness and educate moral imagination in some ways. To be sure, it can also shape a social world in which there is envy, anxious competition and formal and informal contests for political and social influence. But that is hardly unique to the market.

In *Innovative Tradition: Jewish Culture in the Polish-Lithuanian Commonwealth*, Moshe Rosman writes of the Jews of Poland in the early modern era:

> At a time in Europe when competition was a dirty word and merchants were expected to respect each others' divinely apportioned market share, Jews engaged in competitive, capitalistic commercial tactics. Jewish merchants traveled to distant suppliers at source, rather than purchase from middlemen. Jews organized syndicates to buy in volume and sometimes even cornered the market in certain commodities. They exploited Jewish solidarity to gain commercial credit, avoided and evaded paying staple duties that towns had the right to impose on all doing business within their confines, lowered profit margins, and advertised and promoted their products. (Rosman, 2002: 523–524)

In different countries Jews encountered very different circumstances and responded in different ways. However, what Rosman describes is one example — of numerous situations — in which Jews managed to develop market-suited dispositions even if those were not valued generally.

There are plenty of critics of the market and of the ways that market-based economies result in various forms of alienation between persons, commodification of many things, and dispositions of self-interest and greed. In at least some respects it is true that, where there are significant elements of a market economy, "market relations tend to expand into areas of human life which had previously been outside the scope of the market" (Buchanan, 1988: 101). "'Market relations' here refers not only to the physical activities of exchange, but also to the legal institutions, and even ways of thinking which are characteristic of the market" (Buchanan, 1988: 101). Elaborating this point, Peter Singer argues that, "if we allow market relations to dominate most or all spheres of human activity, we may no longer be motivationally capable of certain forms of altruism" (Singer, 1972).[10] Allen Buchanan notes that while there is considerable

---

[10] Peter Singer, quoted on p. 102 of Buchanan (1988).

debate over "the scope and validity of the generalization that the market drives out altruism, there is a great deal of plausibility to the more guarded claim that human life would be greatly impoverished if all interpersonal relationships were market relationships" (Buchanan, 1988: 102–103).

However, many of the objections to the market are overstated and distorting in some of the same ways as objections to the liberal political order. With regard to both, many critics argue that they encourage atomistic individualism and socially corrosive self-interest. With regard to the liberal political form the objection often fails to acknowledge that the liberal order is especially supportive of the kind of open, dynamic civil society in which individuals can strive to realize all kinds of values and can interact, cooperate, and collaborate with others in all manner of ways. Also, a key element of early modern liberal theory was that arbitrariness should be eliminated from the rule of law. Liberalism highlighted the equal application of the rule of law even to those in positions of considerable power. The liberal form of the rule of law and the associated fundamental political institutions are congenial to a rich texture of human relations and pursuits. That does not guarantee that people will not become selfish or morally callous but the liberal order does not ignore or disdain the society's welfare. Rather, one of the merits of the liberal order is the breadth of contexts and avenues for people to strive to realize personal and social welfare. Significant inequalities can develop, but that is not an inevitable feature of the market. When it is genuinely a free market without corrupting rent-seeking participants and all sorts of political interference there is no necessary tendency toward inequalities that also involve significant poverty. In any case, poverty is the more significant issue.

There can be many inequalities that are not morally objectionable. In fact, inequalities will begin to be visible very swiftly if there are meritocratic bases for various rewards given the extent to which people's interests, motivations, and abilities differ. Policies of equalization are not likely to be very effective at eliminating inequalities based on meritocratic considerations. Moreover, I suggest that people generally will support meritocratic rewards even while recognizing that those do not reflect morally "pure" or unproblematic desert.

If people are destitute or prevented from improving their lot in life, that is more troubling than inequality as such. An egalitarian democracy of dignity is more difficult to maintain when some people are very impoverished. Even in that case, it is not primarily equality of wealth (or even, minimizing inequalities) that is needed to help support dignity; it is being able to participate effectively in civil society. That does not require equal wealth or income. Many supporters of liberal democracy might have considerable apprehension regarding egalitarianism of wealth or income largely because of the extent of interference in the voluntariness of civil society that would be required on an ongoing, pervasive basis. Interference as well as poverty can diminish the scope of civil society.

Also, there is no reason that a deficit of concern for the society's welfare will be an inevitable consequence of a liberal, market-oriented order. For one thing, extensive economic freedom, along with the rule of law and the protection of private property has a good prospect of resulting in higher rather than lower standard of living, and the society overall will be able to afford goods and services that contribute to social welfare. The extreme inequalities we see between, say, corporate heads and workers in the US are not what *of course* happens in a market economy. It is what happens when dubious rules of corporate governance and arcane and inequitable tax laws enable small numbers of people to acquire massive holdings or to be compensated on an astronomical scale despite the disproportion between those holdings or compensation on one hand, and their actual contribution on the other. In addition, in a market economy that is generally fair there is reason to expect philanthropic dispositions on the part of many people supporting education, the arts and the sciences. Many people who have done well or been especially fortunate are quite willing to "give back to society" or help others who might need support, and so forth. Why would it be better for support for such things to always be political decisions, and the support always come from the public treasury?

We have acknowledged that the market does not distribute on the basis of deserts. First, there will some plausible meritocratic bases for many types of outcome. Second, a market-based economy need not be one in which the fate of everyone and everything is entirely the result of the workings of the market, all as hostages to fortune. There would likely be numerous significant roles for the state regarding various crucial services, a social safety net, and other aspects of social welfare even while production and distribution are mainly left to the market. How would people develop habits of prudence, accountability and strive for the realization of the values that matter most to them if the full range of people's interests is addressed by the state? Imprudence and financial illiteracy cause a good deal of avoidable harm and it is plausible to suspect that improvements in education (various types of improvement in various areas of education) could do some real good, perhaps in ways that diminish (at least somewhat) the scale of dependence on the public treasury. A politics of competitive entitlement is certainly not a long-term guarantor of social welfare. The changes alluded to here are matters of policy that are to be decided and executed by the state. It has that important role. I am not advocating a "night watchman" state. But the policies should encourage the habits and dispositions people need in order to be independent.

We should not assume that the liberal state is unconcerned with social welfare. Nicola Lacey remarks on:

> the falseness of the dilemma set up by traditional liberalism between personal autonomy and social good: because of the relationship between autonomy and a certain range and quality of possible lives, and because the value of the exercise of autonomy depends to some extent on the background social environment, any straightforward opposition between personal autonomy and welfare or social good can be seen to misrepresent the moral situation. (Lacey, 1988: 179)

However, I do not see why such a dilemma is an inevitable upshot of traditional liberalism. To a large extent, its concern was to provide protections for individuals' rights and liberties, to limit arbitrary state power, explicate the specific powers of political institutions, and enforce a rule of law recognized as legitimate by those to whom it applied. There had also been concerns about state-granted monopolies and the grounds on which monarchs and princes went to war. It is true that burgeoning commercial interests were often on the side of the advocates of the liberal state but limiting the state so that individuals can trade, sell, enter into contractual agreements, and can rely on predictable, promulgated rules of governance need not result in morally callous egoists concerned only with the accumulation of wealth, and largely indifferent to social welfare.

Still, Buchanan was correct to observe that many areas of human life would be spoiled by being fully assimilated to market relationships and nothing more. A friendship thus assimilated would simply cease to be genuine friendship. Many relations in which there might be some role for the market — in some settings, perhaps between students and teachers, or between patients and physicians, or between authors and their agents, or between suppliers and retailers — could also be damaged by becoming *nothing but* market relationships. But that is not a reason to *exclude* the market from them. Singer is simply mistaken if he holds that market relationships make altruism impossible unless what he means by market relations dominating "most or all spheres of human activity" tautologically implies that those spheres have become *nothing but* market relationships. But is there reason to think that people would allow market relations to "dominate most or all spheres of human activity?" The market's tendency to expand in more areas is not an irresistible force and the moral issue is not the evil of the market but the evil of greed, callousness, cruelty, dishonesty, and other vices. All of those vices have been found fully capable of flourishing in non-market economic arrangements and illiberal states. The latter seem to almost invariably be governed by thuggish kleptocracies, wherein those in power arrange economic affairs to mainly aggrandize themselves and their friends. Are the stewards of command economies and central planning notable for single-minded concern for social welfare and the good of various groups such as the elderly, those in especially dangerous occupations, the very young and the physically or mentally handicapped?

We should keep in mind, as well, that the market works best on the basis of relations shaped by trust, honest representation, transparency of accountability, when the "rules of the game" are known and are fair, and when people have information. Those features remind us that the market need not be understood in narrowly amoral terms. These points comport with what I said above about the sorts of dispositions and perspectives encouraged by Judaism, and especially with Judaism's view of the importance of charity; namely, that it should enable persons to become *independent*. In addition, many of the commandments and a great deal of Talmud address issues concerning the ways persons interact with each other, what constitutes fairness, and how justice and compassion are both needed throughout the full range of human affairs. Justice and compassion are crucial in relations between individuals and in the context of the community overall. Judaism has deeply rooted bases for a view of persons as self-determining and responsible, while having responsibilities to and for the community. This is not to say that Judaism unambiguously supports the market economy. Nevertheless, Judaism does emphasize values and a view of human beings including numerous considerations consistent with an economy in which the market is the basic arrangement.

4. Judaism and Public Reason

What is the relevance of the debate over public reason to the main issues of the present discussion? Supposing that, for many people, some of their basic valuative commitments are religiously grounded, should those considerations be politically "sanitized" so that they are fully explicable independent of religious grounding? If they are not, should they be excluded from public debate? Exponents of a criterion of public reason argue that only by respecting such a standard can political ideas and reasons be equally intelligible to all persons, and thereby respect persons as free and equal. There is reason to regard this claim with skepticism.

While the appeal of such a view might seem apparent there are some respects in which the matter is more complicated, and a criterion of public reason could have illiberal implications. In explicating public reason Rawls wrote: "As reasonable and rational, and knowing that they affirm a diversity of reasonable religious and philosophical doctrines, [people] (they) should be ready to explain the basis of their actions to one another in terms each could reasonably expect that others might endorse as consistent with their freedom and equality" (Rawls, 1993: 218). Another defender of public reason, Habermas, wrote, "The truth contents of religious contributions can enter into the institutionalized practice of deliberation and decision-making only when the necessary translation already occurs in the pre-parliamentary domain, i.e., in the political public sphere itself" (Habermas, 2006: 10).

With regard to some values and principles there are ways of making a case for them without appeal to elements of a religious tradition but many people who endorse them do so on religious grounds, and that grounding might be integral to their commitment. That does not make them unreasonable and it is not clear why they should be encouraged (or required) to accept those values and principles without their religious commitments. Instead of excluding various considerations because of how they are religiously grounded, and striving for an overlapping consensus without the involvement of any comprehensive views, we might be better served by encouraging habits of civility and toleration. Committed Catholics and Mormons (just to pick two faith traditions; many others would do as well) might regard each other's faith commitments as dubious in the extreme and perhaps even as involving a kind of delusion or blindness to the truth. They might — if they are also committed to liberal democratic values and principles — recognize the right of each other to participate in the political process without suspending the faith commitments that underwrite many of their values. They need to work out a mode of mutual toleration and agreement on a sufficient number of fundamental matters so the political process is not utterly stymied or incapable of producing any constructive results (and open hostility is avoided). Working on that, rather than on articulating an overlapping consensus in a way that suspends or eliminates religious beliefs, might be the most instructive and practically efficacious approach. People can share concerns and aims without also sharing in detail the considerations that underwrite the concerns and aims. That is part of the appeal and the strength of liberalism.

Despite the fact that a great many recent theorists of liberalism seem to regard religion as a sort of peculiar hobby but one that can be safely privatized, historically, much of the impetus for the liberal order arose from the need to accommodate religious pluralism in a way that minimized conflict. Granted, at the time, "pluralism" basically meant "any of a modest number of Christian denominations." (An early and even classical liberalism was not yet firmly liberal *democracy*. The democratic dimension was added incrementally over several generations.) However, it is worth noting that one of the key motivations for a liberal order was the search for a political form in which people were free to practice their religion without coercive interference by the state. This is still very important to many people and it should not be assumed that skepticism regarding public reason is part of a strategy of bringing religion into politics. I am not endorsing a political order that is a free-for-all, wide-open contest to see who can make their religion predominant. It is not as though that is the only alternative to public reason. The main point is a moral-psychological point; that actual practices through which compromise and toleration are learned and achieved will better support social diversity and value pluralism than a criterion for what can be included in political discourse. In any event, the latter probably could not function anyway without the former.

In the contemporary world many Jews who are not observant and do not study Jewish texts nonetheless strongly identify as Jews, and many do so in a way that is connected with their moral commitments. They think of Judaism as the source of many of their basic values and for many of them commitment to those values came through upbringing framed in a particular religious tradition, even if without regular worship and extensive ritual. While not striving to fulfill the commandments, overall they take moral matters to be critically important and might find it difficult to detach certain commitments from the traditions, images, historical narratives and valuative examples through which they were first introduced. People can strive to be good even if they do not strive to be holy through comprehensive fulfillment of the commandments. There can be a strong sense of religiously anchored identity and value commitment even without religious practice. For many non-religious Jews, leading a morally sound life is understood as *what the religion requires*, and they regard that as significant even though they are not otherwise responsive to the religion's requirements.

The issue is not that they want to be able to bring their Judaism directly into political debate and decision but that they object to having their Jewish value-identity separated from public political discourse. How does it do violence to, or impose erroneous limits on, the freedom and equality of others if some citizens regard a religious grounding as crucial to their commitment to certain values even if those values are significant in the political and social context? Why must the content of their valuative commitments be detached from their grounding if there is no insistence that others accept that grounding as equally indispensable to them? That need not introduce centrifugal forces into politics and the social world; it might help enlarge mutual understanding and provide a richer conception of the values in question. That cannot be counted on; but neither should it be counted out.

Liberal democracies address the issue of religion and politics in a variety of ways. Some of those liberal democracies have state churches though there are not religious requirements or qualifications of a sort that systematically disqualifies or excludes various groups from political participation or imposes limits on their rights in ways meant to target them in particular. Maybe the monarch of England must be a Church of England communicant but that is just one position, and a largely figurehead position. Different states have developed different approaches to religious pluralism (and ethnic diversity). In some states there have been (or there are) some very frictional controversies concerning religion; France is a notable example. I am not arguing that the version of neutrality in the US is a model for other states. Differences in political culture can matter quite a lot. However, I do believe that the neutrality of the US approach reflects some wisdom about human beings and politics lacking in a public reason approach. The latter could be a basis for significant illiberal potential.

What is the basis for confidence that all reasonable persons will converge on a common standard of public reason? Consider that there continues to be debate over (i) whether there is Natural Law, and (ii) what Natural Law comprises if there *is* Natural Law; (iii) what distributive justice requires and, (iv) the primary aims and justification of criminal sanction and issues such as preventive detention.

Rawls had written:

> A citizen engages in public reason, then, when he or she deliberates within a framework of what he or she sincerely regards as the most reasonable political conceptions of justice, a conception that expresses political values that others, as free and equal citizens might also reasonably be expected reasonably to endorse. (Rawls, 1993: 450)

In discussing public reason Nicholas Wolterstorff has argued that if we suppose that someone has followed the overall method Rawls advocates:

> ... no matter what those resultant principles of justice may be, the reasonable thing for her to expect is *not* that all reasonable people who use their common human reason will agree with her results, but that *not all* reasonable people will agree. It would be utterly *unreasonable* for her to expect anything else than disagreement. (Wolterstorff, 1997: 174)

Many Jews might agree that, of course one should offer the best reasons one can, and make an effort to make them intelligible to others. However, they would also maintain that seeing issues in certain ways through participation in a tradition relevant to one's identity can be part of the basis for one's reasons. The tradition can be an important avenue of access to that understanding and an important source of the motivation of commitment. To disqualify that avenue of access is to regard the tradition as not meriting political respect.

What is more needed in a diverse, pluralistic liberal democracy — agreement on a criterion of public reason, or sturdy but modifiable habits of mutual respect and toleration? One of the reasons Jews have been strongly supportive of the Constitutional arrangement in the US is that its neutrality, in contrast to an endorsement of public reason, does not disturb the diverse sources that underwrite the valuative commitments crucial to liberal democracy, even if they are anchored in religion. Neutrality does not require participants to suspend or otherwise disengage from values and commitments that might be basic to how people understand themselves and others, and even how they understand what justice requires. A standard or criterion of public reason can require people to reconstruct the way they articulate their values, to make them presentable. This requirement might be felt as a form of disqualification of one's commitments.

I concur with Wolterstorff's judgment that, "[r]arely do we succeed in reaching consensus even among reasonable people of all these different stripes; but we try. Then, finally, we vote. Are we, in voting under these circumstances, all violating somebody's freedom and equality?" (Wolterstorff, 1997: 174). The dialectic of many political debates will be frictional; that is a near certainty. To require working out specific criteria for what can be brought to the debates might seem a way of ensuring common terms of reasonable agreement but it could require many persons to suspend some of what they take to be fundamental, or require them to re-describe some of their commitments, perhaps in ways that are not fully accurate, so that those can be brought into public discussion. That could result in subtle forms of hypocrisy, not mainly to deceive others but to make one's view presentable to them (Goodman, 2014: 5). For Jews, it would mean that participation in public politics would require disavowal of the identity that is for many, the source of their commitment to democracy. Why should being respected as a member of a political community require considering oneself independent of specific life-guiding commitments that support one's fundamental values? Of course, what those values *are* matters; not just *any* commitments can be countenanced as acceptable. Many people hold values that are rationally defensible though many persons hold them on different bases, often including sacred texts and religious traditions.

5. Conclusion

Biblical moral anthropology includes the notion of the community being governed by the rule of law along with the notion of the individual having significant standing. Each individual possesses reason and will, and each is an accountable agent with a relationship to God through the exercise of his own thought, choices and actions. The idea that there is a fundamental choice to be made between commitment to the law and anarchic voluntarism is a significant biblical theme. Law, justice, concern for others, the worth of all persons; these are all elements of Judaism's legacy and even when Jews became largely secularized and involved in the wider society they have often maintained a sense of Jewish identity and awareness of values they regard as especially important to Judaism.

I have not argued that religion, or Judaism in particular, implies only one political form — liberalism — and also that *only* the market can be justified as an economic arrangement. That would be quite implausible. Important currents of Jewish thought and Jewish life have included — and do include — other views. Certainly, actual historical circumstances have made a very great difference to what Jews in one place or another, at one time or another could or would support. In those parts of the world where liberal democracy or at least some form of constitutional democracy has become the settled form of political order Jews have generally been able to participate in politics and society in a considerable diversity of ways.

In some of those ways Judaism has been crucial to persons' sense of moral identity even if they are not practicing the religion except as it informs moral life. (That is not an insignificant matter but the contrast with a life of Jewish religious practices and study is worth noting.) The relation between religious legacy, identity, perspective, and moral commitment, and political values can take many different forms. It is a mistake to think that religion and politics must be kept separate from each other and religiously serious persons should do their utmost to separate out distinctively religious commitments when engaging public politics. There is no question that dogma and religious narrow-mindedness have the potential to corrupt public debate and complicate it in needless and unhelpful ways. So do many other views and commitments. How are decisions to be made regarding what counts as an inappropriate element of a comprehensive view, religious or otherwise? Do all of them introduce irrelevant or inappropriate considerations? Would people (correctly) regard public reason as potentially disvaluing what the liberal state is meant to protect?

Judaism as a source of values has helped to shape liberal democracy and Jews have benefited a great deal from the opportunity to live in liberal democracies. Where there has been a good deal of market freedom that has been a huge relief from the economic disabilities so often imposed on Jews and it has created scope for the broad exercise of voluntary activity, association and exchange in civil society. It would be regrettable, and a tragic irony if liberalism were to develop in a way that — in the name of reason — excluded from political discourse some of the commitments and perspectives that have shaped and motivated liberalism, possibly along with other commitments integral to people's conceptions of themselves. Of course, liberalism cannot permit just anything, no matter how morally and politically suspect. Many views are not allowable in a liberal state. But it should have room for diverse grounds of some of the very values to which a liberal rule of law is committed.

References

Buchanan, A. (1988). *Ethics, Efficiency, and the Market*, Totowa, NJ: Rowman & Littlefield Publishers, Inc.

Goodman, L. E. (2014). *Religious Pluralism and Values in the Public Sphere*, New York: Cambridge University Press.

Habermas, J. (2006). "Religion in the Public Sphere," *European Journal of Philosophy*, 14(1), 1–25.

Lacey, N. (1988). *State Punishment*, Padstow, Cornwall: Routledge.

Rawls, J. (1993). *Political Liberalism*, New York: Columbia University Press.

Rosman, M. (2002). "Innovative Tradition: Jewish Culture in the Polish-Lithuanian Commonwealth," in *Cultures of the Jews*, D. Biale, (ed.), pp. 519–570. New York: Schocken Books.

Shils, E. (1997). The *Virtue of Civility*, S. Grosby (ed.). Indianapolis: Liberty Fund.

Singer, P. (1972). "Altruism and Commerce: A Defense of Titmuss against Arrow," *Philosophy & Public Affairs*, 2(3), 312–317.

Stone, S. L. (2006). "Judaism and Civil Society," in *Law, Politics, and Morality in Judaism*, M. Walzer (ed.). Princeton: Princeton University Press.

Wisse, R. R. (2007). *Jews and Power*, New York: Schocken Books.

Wolterstorff, N. (1997). "Why We Should Reject What Liberalism Tells Us about Speaking and Acting in Public for Religious Reasons," in *Religion and Contemporary Liberalism*, P. J. Weithman, (ed.), pp. 162–181. Notre Dame, IN: University of Notre Dame Press.

Chapter 10

"Economic Doctrine" in the Church of England since the Reformation

A. M. C. Waterman

St John's College, Winnipeg, Canada
Anthony.Waterman@umanitoba.ca

Abstract

Until the mid-twentieth century, the Church of England maintained its
age-old function of teaching and monitoring economic rights and duties.
And after 1815 an ideological alliance of Christian theology and political economy promoted private property rights and the market economy.
Victorian radical critics attacked this alliance, and many bishops and
theologians became socialists. "Christian Socialism" remained the preferred economic doctrine for Anglo-Catholics until the mid-twentieth
century. In 1942, Archbishop William Temple provided the classic statement of Anglican economic doctrine: a realistic "Christian Socialism"
that recognized the achievements of capitalism and the validity of self-
interest as an incentive.

Keywords: Economic Thought, Church of England, Social Doctrine,
Socialism, Theology, History

1. The Novelty of "Christian Social Teaching"

That any Christian Church should have an "economic doctrine" is a new idea, first appearing in the encyclical *Rerum Novarum* of Pope Leo XIII (1892).

When the Roman Empire became Christian in the fourth century, "Church" and "State" were one and the same, and the Emperor was Head. After the division of the Empire in the fifth century this relationship persisted in the Eastern half until the fall of Constantinople to the Turks (1453), and has been continued in the Eastern Orthodox churches, including those of Ukraine and Russia. After the Western Empire fell to the barbarians in the fifth century, the bits and pieces soon became Christian, recognizing the Bishop of Rome as spiritual head while becoming incipiently sovereign states.

In each of these, all members of society were Christian subjects of the same monarch: whose duty, often specified in the Coronation oath, was to govern his people in accordance with Christian teaching. There was not, nor could there have been, any conception of "the Church" delivering "economic doctrine" to "the State." Every individual was a member of each, and all were more or less instructed in the duties of a Christian in such matters as respect for property rights, stewardship of one's own property, charity to the poor, and the mutual obligations of buyers and sellers, employers and employees, lenders and borrowers, landlords and tenants. The economic maintenance of the Church itself was a duty of the sovereign.

With continual modification with respect to specific institutions and practices, and with regional variation, this understanding of economic affairs in a Christian society persisted in Europe until the Reformation. And although the Reformation destroyed the unity of Western Christendom, and in Protestant countries created a distinction between "the State" and a now contested headship of "the Church," it did not destroy Christianity. Until the end of the eighteenth century, each European nation was what Clark (1985) has described as a "confessional state" — in which the national church, whether Romanist or Protestant, continued to monitor the economic activities of its members. The existence of dissenting sects in many Protestant countries provided theological excuses for those who resisted the dominant economic ethic; but for the most part the effect on national culture was slight.

This state of affairs was destroyed by the French Revolution, which was a frontal attack on Christianity and the ancient culture of Christian

Europe. Though a Bourbon Restoration after 1815 brought back monarchy and nobility to France, the Revolution had inflicted irreparable harm upon the Roman Catholic Church, which was never again to be the "established church" of the West (Waterman, 2016). The deliberate secularization of French political life became permanent, and was widely followed in those European nations which had been much affected by French ideas and practices. By 1829, 86 percent of all diocesan bishops in the world — wide Roman Church — chiefly in Europe — were appointed by the State (Duffy, 2006: 297). After 1815 therefore, the papacy became as politically detached from Roman Catholic, as it had been from Protestant, countries. And it was deeply conscious of this. With the sole exception of *Singulari Quidem* (1856), papal encyclicals from *Mirari Vos* (1832) to *Quanta Cura* (1864) denounced "the philosophy of this age" supposed to have inspired the French Revolution (Waterman, 2016). By the pontificate of Leo XIII "Church" and "State" were perceived in Rome as radically distinct; the former having a duty to instruct the latter in the political implications of the Christian religion. And in *Rerum Novarum* (1891) — which was itself a belated response to the French Revolution — Leo addressed social and specifically economic issues for the first time. "We approach the subject with confidence," Leo asserted, "for no practical solution of this question will be found apart from the intervention of religion and of the Church" (1891: para 16). Thus was born the conception of "Catholic (or Papal, or Christian) Social Doctrine."

Britain was the only West European nation to have been completely insulated from the political and intellectual consequences of the French Revolution. Protected by the Channel and the Royal Navy from Napoleonic incursions, and by the Whig rhetoric of Edmund Burke (1790) from the meretricious glamour of Jacobin ideas, England and Scotland (though not Ireland) underwent no major social or political change from 1789 to 1815.

The Church of England was almost completely unaffected by the events in France — though one of its clerics composed the most radical and damaging refutation of Jacobin ideas ever written (Malthus, 1798). Thus it became the only national Church in Western Europe to preserve unbroken continuity with its past. And that past went back at least to the Norman Conquest.

For though it had separated from the Papacy after the excommunication of Elizabeth I in 1570, as much continuity as possible had been preserved with the pre-Reformation church in liturgy, order and governance.

That continuity was challenged by a powerful and subversive Puritan faction, which hijacked the Church and imposed Calvinist doctrine and order during the Great Rebellion (1642–1659). But it was deliberately resumed at "the Restoration" of Crown, Church and Parliament in 1660–1662. The final and definitive recension of *The Book of Common Prayer* (BCP, 1662) provided the doctrinal framework within which the Church of England continued its age-old duty of monitoring the economic rights and duties of its members.

2. Before the French Revolution

The traditional instruction in, and monitoring of, the economic rights and duties of Christians was codified by the Church of England at the Reformation.

In preparation for Confirmation all children were taught a *Catechism* (1549) which included social and economic duty.

> *Question*: What is thy dutie towards thy neighboure?
>
> *Answere*: My duetie towards my neighbour is to loue hym as myself ....
> To submitte myself to all my teachers, spirituall pastours, and maisters.
> To ordre myself lowlye and reuerentelye to al my betters ... To bee
> true and iust in al my dealing .... To kepe my hands from picking and
> stealing ... Not to couet nor desire other mennes goodes. But learne and
> laboure truly to geate my owne liuing, and to doe my duety in that state
> of life: unto which it shal please God to cal me.

The intellectual tradition within which such duties were taught in every parish church was part of the training of the clergy.

By the eighteenth century, according to R. H. Tawney (1947: 147) "The social teaching of the Church had ceased to count, because the Church itself had ceased to think." Tawney was mistaken in supposing that the Church of England had ever delivered "social teaching" in the sense of *Rerum Novarum*. And he was quite wrong to assert that there was no significant social *thinking* in the eighteenth-century Church.

In an important sense, Anglican social thinking had begun in the seventeenth century with *Leviathan* (Hobbes, [1651] 1957), a powerful defence of the power and authority of the sovereign in a Christian society, based on the assumption of generally scarce resources and the consequent competition for these among humans. John Locke ([1689/90] 1967) differed fundamentally from Hobbes in proposing a normative theory of human society dependent upon the quasi-religious conception of "natural rights" associated with the medieval Christian tradition of "natural law," which humans can know by "reason." Men are "naturally" free and equal, can agree on social order, and Hobbesian absolute monarchy is unnecessary. The obvious incompatibility between Hobbes's positive account of society and Locke's normative account is the background to Anglican social thinking in the eighteenth century. Much of this took place in Cambridge, and was associated with incipient economic thought — itself an attempt to explore the implications for modern society of Hobbes's assumption of resource scarcity.

Yet Locke, though an Oxford man, was important in Whiggish Cambridge where his most influential disciple was Edmund Law (1703–1787), Master of Peterhouse and later Bishop of Carlisle. Law attracted the friendship of several of the brightest of his younger colleagues in the university, including William Paley (1743–1805); and in striking contrast with Hobbes, believed that the human race is gradually and continuously progressing in religion at the same rate at which it progresses in all other knowledge. In the second half of the eighteenth century however, Paley and some of his contemporaries slightly modified this optimistic view of the human condition by explicit recognition, in their teaching of undergraduates, of what we should now call "economic" factors (Waterman, 2017a).

All undergraduates were obliged to attend lectures in their own colleges and were allowed to do so in other colleges as well. An important part of the curriculum for future bishops, magistrates, legislators, "spirituall pastours," and "maisters" in a Christian society was social ethics. For the way in which the Church of England monitored the economic life of its members was through the teaching and influence of its educated elite, especially but not exclusively the clergy, all of whom were trained at one of the two universities.

Paley was typical in delivering a course in the 1760s on "Principles of Moral and Political Philosophy," which eventually became his most famous book (Paley, 1785); and in which — Book VI, Chap. XI "Of Population and Provision" — what was later to be known as "political economy" was explicit for the first time (Waterman, 1996, 2017). For though "social thinking" must be normative, there can be no obligation to perform that which is unfeasible. Therefore, knowledge of the real world in which ethical decisions must be made is essential. Though Paley's incipient political economy took no account of resource scarcity, it analyzed for the first time the conception of optimization — which does imply the opportunity cost of foregone possibilities, and therefore the fact of scarcity in a more general sense (Waterman, 1996: 680, 681, 685).

Paley's lectures included treatment of the ethics of certain economic topics including contracts of sale and productive services, and most importantly, property. The right to property in land does not depend, as Locke had argued, upon anything done by its owner, but simply upon positive law (Paley, 1785: 101). The ethical criteria are utilitarian: for that tradition of ethics was born in Cambridge — 50 years before Jeremy Bentham (1789) — with John Gay's "Dissertation concerning the Fundamental Principle of Virtue or Morality," published as a preface to the English translation by Paley's patron Edmund Law (1739) of William King's *De Origine Mali* (1702). Hence, for Paley and his Cambridge contemporaries, "Virtue is the doing good to mankind, in obedience to the will of God, and for the sake of everlasting happiness" (Paley, 1785: 35).

An exact contemporary, neighbor, fellow-Yorkshireman and probably friend of Paley, John Hey (1734–1815), fellow and tutor at Sidney Sussex College from 1758 to 1779, and in 1780 first Norrisian Professor of Divinity, also gave a series of lectures on "Morality" in the 1770s for his college pupils which attracted the voluntary attendance of undergraduates from other colleges including William Pitt, then (1773–1776) at Pembroke College. Hey's Norrisian (1796) lectures in Divinity had been a great success; but the enormous prestige of Paley's *Principles* forestalled the possibility of publishing his own "Lectures in Morality," which may now be read in manuscript in his college library (Hey, 1815). These were utterly unlike Paley's, not only in style but also in content. And indeed they more closely resembled the kind of Christian social thinking mourned by Tawney as forgotten. A brief excerpt illustrates the style.

Lecture 37 "Of permutatory contracts: and first of the general laws by which all such contracts ought to be regulated."

It is generally said, that in all permutatory contracts there must be an equality of value in the rights alienated by the contracting parties; but this does not seem satisfactory; if two oxen were exactly of the same value, that is, if it was quite indifferent to me which I had, it were trifling to change them. The value of anything is, in strictness, relative not absolute; tho' some standard may be found convenient for the purpose of distinctness; but certainly what is more valuable to one is less valuable to another; and indeed upon this depends the whole good of permutatory contracts: therefore it does not appear how equality of value of two things in an exchange can be computed absolutely. (Hey, 1815, Vol. III [MS 12]: p. 1273).

Like Paley however, Hey employed what we should now call "economic analysis," including an incipient theory of market price. Hey suggests that the best way "to conceive the value of anything according to men's general wants" would be "to suppose all men bidding for it at an universal auction." In developing this idea Hey's exposition seems to be a possible source of the first-ever formal demand function, specified by Malthus (1800).

In one very important respect Paley and Hey were at one. The normative social theory of each was utilitarian in the original, Cambridge, sense. There seems little reason to suppose that their treatment of social ethics was not typical in Cambridge.

There was no attention to social ethics in Oxford during the eighteenth century, where the undergraduate curriculum, such as it was, was based on Latin literature (Sutherland and Mitchell, 1986: 477–481).

3. Effects of the French Revolution

Though Britain was spared the drastic political and social upheaval of the French Revolution, both Anglicans and Dissenters were compelled to make up their minds about the new possibilities it created and the ideas on which it appeared to be based.

The first leading Anglican thinker to react to the French Revolution was William Wilberforce (1759–1853), Cambridge-educated, "evangelical" layman, Member of Parliament, social reformer and campaigner against slavery. His "Practical View" of current Anglican religion contrasted with "Real Christianity" (Wilberforce, 1797) supplied the impetus for a wide-ranging series of social reforms, from the abolition of slavery to the welfare of chimney sweeps, and remained influential throughout the nineteenth century. Wilberforce was a member of the "Clapham Sect" which included the pioneer in monetary theory, Henry Thornton (1760–1815), and other experienced bankers and merchants, most of whom were allied with Wilberforce in his campaigns. But the evils to be remedied seemed too obvious to require much in the way of social theory, and not until later did evangelicalism (or evangelicals) play any significant part in the "social thinking" of the Church of England.

However, for the first time since the Glorious Revolution what we should now call "ideological" questions demanded answers; and some of these questions seemed amenable to the new science of Political Economy. But Britain was still a "confessional state": satisfactory answers had therefore to be theologically acceptable to the authorities of the Established Church. Over the next four or five decades, an influential group of Anglican clerics — two of whom eventually became Archbishops — worked out an ideological alliance of Political Economy and Christian Theology (Waterman, 1983a) which provided the conceptual framework of social thinking in the Church of England for the first half of the nineteenth century.

The events of 1789 had attracted little attention in England at first. Only Edmund Burke (1790) saw clearly their implications: the revolution in Paris, which was quite unlike the Glorious Revolution of 1690, would lead inevitably to bloodshed, tyranny and war. Burke's predictions were fully substantiated over the next two years, and an anti-Jacobin ideology began to be constructed as a theoretical defence of the *status quo*. Many in England however, especially among Protestant Dissenters, remained faithful to the ideal of human perfectibility through institutional reform. The most influential of these was William Godwin (1756–1836), whose *Political Justice* (1793, 1796, 1798) recaptured the intellectual high ground for revolution and was widely popular (Waterman, 1991: 22–24).

Godwin's work might have died a natural death after Britain joined the coalition of European powers in 1792 and began a 23-year war against France and its Revolution. But by 1797 support for subversive ideas appeared to be reviving in Britain — at least to the *Anti-Jacobin Review* founded by George Canning in that year. The Fleet mutinied at Spithead and the Nore; the French landed in Pembrokeshire; Grey's campaign for Parliamentary reform was defeated. Godwin's second edition had greatly strengthened his argument for "equal liberty and justice for all." And an important part of his argument was his attack on "the established administration of property." It was this that became the principle target of the most radical and influential attack on revolutionary ideas ever mounted in Britain. Its anonymous author was then an obscure clergyman. The subsequent development of his argument by himself and others created a fundamental and long-lasting mutation in the social thinking of the Church of England (Waterman, 1991).

Robert Malthus (1766–1834) was a Fellow and sometime Exhibitioner of Jesus College Cambridge, and Ninth Wrangler of his year. William Paley, though by now Archdeacon of Carlyle, was still a powerful influence in Cambridge. *Moral and Political Philosophy* was published in Malthus's freshman year, and immediately adopted by the university as a textbook. In 1798, Malthus was Curate of a small parish near his parents' estate and in frequent conversation with his father, Daniel (1730–1800), who — though a Churchman — favored liberal political ideas, was a friend of Rousseau and Hume, and sympathetic to Godwin's notions. The *Essay on Population* (1798) which grew out of these conversations considered "the Future Improvement of Society," and contained "Remarks on the Speculations of Mr Godwin, M. Condorcet, and Other Writers." At the center of its demolition of Godwin in Chapter X was a revival of Hobbes's insight into resource scarcity, which had been deliberately ignored by Locke and his disciples.

Malthus performed a Hume-type "mental experiment." Let us imagine Godwin's "beautiful system of equality realized in its utmost purity." As all economic thinkers of the eighteenth century had realized, population would then grow exponentially (e.g., Smith [1776] 1976: I, viii, 39, 23). Food production would also grow, but "at best" only arithmetically because land is limited. Hence per capita income must fall. Long before it reaches the "subsistence" (zero population growth) level, falling real income reawakens "the mighty law of self-preservation." Theft and falsehood undermine the mutual trust on which "benevolence" depends. "Self-love resumes his wonted empire and lords it triumphant over the world." And as Hobbes ([1651] 1957: 82) had explained, human institutions — government, property rights, laws — must then exist: to contain the human propensity "to invade and destroy one another." The "inevitable laws of nature" thus create "a society, constructed on a plan not essentially different from that which prevails in every known State at present" (Malthus, 1798: 207). Godwin's plan of "equal liberty and justice for all" is self-reversing. The economic and social *status quo* is a position of stable equilibrium (Waterman, 1991: 27–50).

Though the central argument of the first *Essay* was generally accepted as decisive, there was much criticism of detail. In particular, the last two chapters, in which Malthus attempted to supply a theodicy of scarcity, were regarded by all as confused or heterodox or both (Waterman, 1983b).

Abandoning anonymity, Malthus (1803) wrote a second *Essay* which dropped the amateurish theology and marshaled demographic evidence for the "principle of population." Over the next 23 years he produced four more recensions of the *Essay*, and a *Summary View* in 1830.

Because of the high political importance of Malthus's case against revolution, it was essential that the Anglican Establishment be assured that its argument was consistent with Christian orthodoxy. Over the next four decades therefore, a series of influential authors, beginning with Paley (1802), corrected Malthus's defective theology, developed the wider social implications of his analysis, and (with Malthus himself) refined the political economy on which it was based — and answered the objection that the new science of political economy was "hostile to religion." The most important of these was John Bird Sumner (1780–1862) whose seminal work inaugurated what became known as "Christian Political Economy" (Waterman: 1991).

Sumner's *Treatise on the Records of the Creation* (1816), which Malthus (1817: Vol. 3, 423) acknowledged as a "masterly development (sic) and completion of his views," was decisive. "Inequalities of Ranks and Fortunes," Sumner argued, is the condition best suited to human development and the exercise of virtue. It is proof of the Divine wisdom that this order of things is "universally established, by the operation of a single principle": the "principle of population" (Waterman, 1991: 160–170). In the immediate aftermath of the French Revolution and the French Wars which were one of its consequences, "economic doctrine" in the Church of England — though a product of "liberal" political economy, and notwithstanding the seemingly radical nature of Wilberforce's reformism — was predictably conservative, not to say reactionary.

This was no mere political success. Sumner's work received the applause of all, including the tiny fraternity of political economists. David Ricardo thought *Records* "a clever book" and regretted that Sumner was abandoning economics for theology (Waterman, 1991: 157). In part, the reason for its success was its theological moderation. Sumner was a King's Scholar, and like Wilberforce a Simeonite evangelical; but with a broad and comprehensive view of the Church, and with intellectual roots in the Cambridge tradition of Paley and Hey. As with them, the natural theology of Newton's *Principia* was central. He treated Hume with great respect, and explicitly recognized the authority of Paley's natural theology. His intellectual achievement was to remove from the icy realm of theodicy the seeming evil produced by the "principle of population," and transplant it to the genial soil of Paley's teleology (Waterman, 1991: 164–165). It was not a "natural evil" to be excused and explained, as even Malthus had supposed, but an example of "the Wisdom and Goodness of God."

Though Paley had rejected the optimism of Locke, he ignored the pessimism of Hobbes. Resource scarcity has no place in his social theory. But it was precisely in the thin slice of time between the last of his Cambridge lectures in 1775 and Malthus's *Essay* (1798) that *Wealth of Nations* (1776) appeared; and the new science of "Political Economy" was transplanted from France where it was born (Faccarello, 1999) to Britain. Malthus himself was one of the first students of *Wealth of Nations*, which he first encountered at Warrington Academy while in his teens (Waterman, 2006); and by 1805 was the foremost English authority on Adam Smith. His friendship with Ricardo a few years later led eventually to their foundation of the Political Economy Club in 1821 (Waterman, 2008). Political Economy, later to mutate into "Economics," had become a permanent — if unwelcome — addition to British intellectual life.

In 1816 Sumner was an obscure usher at Eton. The success and importance of his *Treatise* was immediately followed by a series of valuable preferments, and eventually consecration to the episcopate (Chester) in 1828. In 1848, he became Archbishop of Canterbury.

It was Sumner's achievement to co-opt the new science into the main stream of Anglican social thinking. Serious thinking by Christians about social order henceforth must take account of resource scarcity. Hobbes was right. Locke was wrong.

For nearly a century, Anglican social thought had been a purely Cambridge enterprise. From the beginning of the nineteenth century, however, there had been a revival of intellectual life in Oxford centered on Oriel College, led successively by two distinguished Provosts: John Eveleigh and Edward Copleston (1776–1849; Provost, 1814–1828; Bishop of Llandaff, 1827–1849). Copleston played an active part in public affairs, was a friend and frequent visitor of Lord Grenville at Dropmore, and consulted by other leading political figures on government policy. He had studied Adam Smith and Malthus, followed the proceedings of the Bullion Committee of 1810; and the publication of his two *Letters to Peel* (1819a, b) on the causal nexus between protection, currency reform and the Poor Law in relation to the work of Malthus and Sumner "raised Christian Political Economy to a new level of analytical sophistication" (Waterman, 1991: 179).

Copleston's most distinguished pupil at Oriel, Richard Whately (1787–1863; Archbishop of Dublin, 1831–1863) became a Fellow of that college, and in 1831 was elected the second Drummond Professor of Political Economy — succeeding his former pupil Nassau Senior. Though not a seminal thinker like Malthus or a brilliant analyst like Copleston, he had a clear grasp of the importance of Malthus and Sumner in the construction of CPE, and of the new science on which it was based. And it seemed to him that "before too long, political economists, of some sort or other, must govern the world" (Waterman, 1991: 206). It was essential, therefore, to incorporate the science into Christian social thought; and in backward-looking Oxford to begin by dispelling the fear that it was "hostile to religion." But his *Introductory Lectures in Political Economy* (1831) were all he was able to deliver before his abrupt and entirely unexpected elevation as an Archbishop prevented his writing more about the subject himself.

Whately was first and foremost a logician and philosopher, and his most important contribution to Economics (and Christian Political Economy) was epistemological: to establish the difference between "secular knowledge" (of Nature) and "sacred knowledge" (of God). The former is based on theory and is subject to empirical test. The latter comes by faith, by means of which we can see God's self-revelation in "Scripture." This crucial distinction became of high importance four decades later, when Darwinian evolution appeared to many to falsify the Creation myths in *Genesis*. Whately's demarcation permitted Anglican theologians to welcome Natural Science rather than denying it: as some Protestant Christians did (and still do). But in one respect Whately was untypical of Christian Political Economy. Unlike the Cambridge authors (save Paley) and Copleston, resource scarcity plays no part in his thinking. For him, Political Economy is not "Economics" but "Catallactics" — a conception revived and adopted in the twentieth century by Hayek and by James Buchanan and his associates (Marciano, 2011).

By the 1830s, CPE had become the main stream of Anglican social thinking, generally accepted in the two universities and represented in the House of Lords by two highly regarded prelates, J. B. Sumner and Whately.

An eminent Scottish cleric, Thomas Chalmers (1780–1847), was closely associated with, and a contributor to, CPE (Waterman, 1991: Chap. 6). His numerous publications on Political Economy in relation to Christian theology were influential upon social thinking in the Church of Scotland.

4. The Victorian Period

Though Queen Victoria had reigned for 11 years when Sumner became Archbishop of Canterbury, and 25 when he died, he and Whately — though still eminent and authoritative — were products (and creators) of the Regency culture. But new voices were now raised in the national conversation on Christian social thinking, some of which were highly critical of the Christian Political Economy.

The most radical of these, literary Romantics such as the Lake Poets, rejected political economy altogether (Waterman, 2003). Some rejected the Malthusian conception of the human condition. Others rejected the "classical" assumptions of CPE: the equilibrium outcomes of free and competitive markets may not always be preferable to deliberate allocation of scarce resources by the State. Those like Marx and Engels and their followers, who rejected Christianity and all religion as ideological deception, had no interest at all in Christian social thinking. Underlying all this was a profound transformation of English society and culture, and the place of the Church in that culture, wrought by industrialization, population growth and urbanization.

What Donald Winch (1996: 418) has called "the schism, or fault line, separating economists from the self-appointed spokesmen for human beings" was inaugurated in Robert Southey's ([1804] 1994) maledictory review of Malthus's second *Essay* (1803). S. T. Coleridge, who had hated Malthus since his undergraduate days, took the lead in the Lake Poets' attack on Political Economy, which was perfectly captured in Wordsworth's (1950: 354–355) sonnet on King's College chapel:

Tax not the royal Saint with vain expense,
With ill-matched aims the Architect who planned —
Albeit labouring for a scanty band
Of white-robed Scholars only — this immense
And glorious Work of fine intelligence!
Give all thou canst; high Heaven rejects the lore
Of nicely calculated less or more:
So deemed the man who fashioned for the sense
These lofty pillars ...

The lore "Of nicely calculated less or more" was an affront to warm imaginations excited by the rediscovery of mediæval art, architecture,

Christian culture and social order in the first half of the nineteenth century. The Romantic hatred of economistic thinking was powerfully amplified by Carlyle, Ruskin, Dickens, Kingsley and many another canonical author; and has remained a permanent feature of British intellectual life (Waterman, 2003).

The Romantic critique was eventually co-opted by Marxist socialists, for example, "The Victorian *bourgeoisie* had constructed from bits of Adam Smith and Ricardo, Bentham and Malthus a cast-iron theoretical system" with which "to justify and perpetuate exploitation" (Thompson, 1976: 8–9). But as early as 1848, the very different "Christian Socialists" associated with F. D. Maurice, Charles Kingsley and Thomas Hughes inaugurated a tradition of Anglican Christian Socialism which long remained influential (Norman, 1976). Despite the growing technical elaboration in this period of what became known as "Neoclassical Economics" (Waterman, 2019/2020: 331–336), a considerable body of educated opinion in the Church of England entertained far less confidence in the efficacy of free and competitive markets than the proponents of CPE. By the 1890s this mutation of social thinking in the Church of England had led to the creation in Oxford of the Christian Social Union inspired by the principles of Maurice and his associates (Jones, 1968).

CPE had emerged in the final decades of Peter Laslett's *World We Have Lost* (1965): in which the entire population save that of London and Bristol lived in rural communities and small towns; in which everyone knew his neighbors; and in which the all-powerful trio of Squire, Parson and Schoolmaster performed the traditional pastoral function of monitoring the economic rights and duties of parishioners. Despite Methodism and Dissent, the Church of England was still to a great extent the national religion, as it had been since the Reformation.

But in the first half of the nineteenth century, innovation in textiles, coal mining and iron production created a strong demand for labor that relocated under-employed and starving farm-hands into the new factory towns huddled around the Dark Satanic Mills. They lived in tenements near the factories, there were few if any parish churches to attend, and those who wished to remain faithful depended on Methodist or other non-Anglican missions. Cut off from the immemorial culture of their rural ancestors, they quit the Church. And in general, urbanization in England, which increased from 15 percent in 1750 to 85 percent in 1900, produced the same result. By 1851 the Religious Census revealed that of 10.4 million possible worshippers, only 4.6 million attended a Sunday morning service; and only 2.5 million of these were Anglican (http://www.brin.ac.uk/religious-census-1851-online/).

But traditional Anglican culture, romanticized in the Barsetshire novels, persisted in rural areas having few close contacts with great cities. The age-old instruction in, and monitoring of, the economic rights and duties of Christians continued in each parish school under the watchful eyes of Squire, Parson and Schoolmaster, or at any rate of the second of these. But we never see what actually goes on in Josiah Crawley's school at Hogglestock or that of Mark Robarts at Framley.

In many parts of the South and West of England the ancient rural culture was still alive, if not well, into the early twentieth century, and was acutely observed by Flora Thompson from the viewpoint of one of the village children. In "Lark Rise" the Parson visits the school every day for "Scripture," and to teach the older children their Christian duties: in particular "To ordre myself lowlye and reuerentelye to al my betters." His Sunday sermons to the villagers emphasize that theme:

> Another favourite subject was the supreme rightness of the social order as it then existed. God, in His infinite wisdom, had appointed a place for every man, woman and child on this earth and it was their bounden duty to remain contentedly in their niches. A gentleman might seem to some of his listeners to have a pleasant, easy life, compare to theirs at field labour; but he had his duties and responsibilities, which would be far beyond their capabilities. He had to pay taxes, sit on the Bench of Magistrates, oversee his estate, and keep up his position by entertaining. Could they do these things? No, of course they could not; and he did not suppose that a gentleman could cut as straight a furrow or mow or thatch a rick as expertly as they could. (Thompson 1945: Chap XIV)

Now it is obvious that this is a perversion of the original Anglican doctrine, according to which the catechumen learns indeed to respect authority, but also "to doe my duety in that state of life: unto which it shal please God to cal me." The Rector of "Lark Rise" implicitly changes "shal" to "hath" and "please" to "pleased," and no one seems to notice.

But this is only a straw in the wind and may not be typical at that date. By Queen Victoria's Diamond Jubilee a new Vicar of "Candleford" had drastically changed the relations between the gentry at the vicarage and even the humblest parishioners. His excellent and extremely popular sermons "made you feel two inches taller" (Thompson, 1945: Chap. XXXIX). Even in "Candleford," The World We Have Lost was finally lost forever.

5. The Twentieth Century

By the end of Victoria's reign the Church of England was no longer the national religion (Inglis, 1963). "Social thinking" persisted however — and indeed flourished — among some of the educated élite in the twentieth century, but in an increasingly new and inhospitable world. For after "the greatest of all divisions in the history of the West — that which divides the present from, say, the age of Jane Austen and Scott" (Lewis, 1969: 7) there could eventually be no "national religion" whatsoever. And not only England but the whole of Western Christendom has been "unchristened." Though belief may survive in individuals, it no longer shapes our culture (Lewis, 1969: 4–5, 9–10). As others, including Flora Thompson, have perceived, this is a consequence of a fundamental change in productive technique: an economic and cultural shift that Marx and Engels would have expected.

> Between Jane Austen and us, but not between her and Shakespeare, Chaucer, Alfred ... comes the birth of the machines .... This is on a level with the change from stone to bronze, or from a pastoral to an agricultural economy. It alters Man's place in nature. (Lewis, 1969: 10)

Yet the profound social mutation that C. S. Lewis correctly identified in his Inaugural Lecture at Cambridge in 1954 was hardly apparent to most in England, whether Christian or not, until after the First World War; and only obvious to all after the American and European cultural revolution of the late 1960s. For most English, whether rural or urban, life carried on pretty much as usual until 1914; despite the great and permanent effects of the War resumed in many places until 1939. In the countryside at any rate, there were still many parishes in which the ancient tradition of instruction in, and monitoring of, the economic rights and duties of Christians persisted until the Second World War. Only in the 1950s did it finally disappear: as mechanization on the farms reduced the demand for labor, and villagers were replaced by industrial workers relocated from nearby towns.

Meanwhile the "social thinking" of its élite continued the consensus that emerged in Oxford in the Christian Social Union, founded in 1889 by the Professor of Divinity, Canon Henry Scott Holland together with Charles Gore and J. R. Illingworth to propagate and develop the social doctrine of the then Archbishop of Canterbury, Edward Benson (1889). The Archbishop had written: "there is much in 'socialism' as we now understand it, which honestly searches for some beneficial remedy — much of which is purely religious and Christian."

The characteristic feature of that consensus was the kind of "Christian Socialism" first proposed in the 1840s by F. D. Maurice, Charles Kingsley and Thomas Hughes. Its starting point was a complete rejection of Christian Political Economy and the case for reconciling capitalism and the market economy with Christian ethics. Unlike Romantic Political Economy however, it did not abjure all economic thinking. For though orthodox economics at that time was strictly neoclassical, and devoted to exploring the optimum allocation of scarce resources by free markets, its analytical technique did provide the conceptual framework for a rational socialism (Waterman 2019/2020); and even the less rigorously specified Christian Socialism avoided the seeming anti-intellectualism of the Romantics. What "Socialism" seems to have meant to Anglican intellectuals at this time was the assignment to government rather than the market of some important economic functions such as utilities and transport; and comprehensive and coherent policies to improve the welfare of the poor through education, health and income support.

There was a high correlation, in the years between 1889 and 1914, between commitment to this kind of socialism and the "Anglo-Catholic" movement in the late Victorian Church. As William Temple (1908: 199), a leading figure in that movement had put it, "The alternative stands before us, Socialism or Heresy." The Anglo-Catholic Christian Socialist movement had its origins of in the work of Scott Holland and Stewart Headlam, each of whom had been followers of F. D. Maurice. Headlam was priest of a working-class parish in Bethnal Green where he founded the Guild of St Mathew, later succeeded by the Church Socialist League in 1906 which was a response to the founding of the British Labour Party in that year (http://anglicanhistory.org/academic/hopkins1982/01.pdf).

Anglo-Catholic missions to industrial working-class parishes, conducted by Oxford-educated sons of the upper classes and assisted in vacation time by undergraduates such as Temple, were a hallmark of this manifestation of Anglican social thinking.

Anglo-Catholic Christian Socialism remained influential in the Church of England until the 1950s, strongly abetted by the "Christendom Group" led and funded by Maurice Reckitt (1888–1980); and which included such well-known social thinkers as T.S. Eliot, Alec Vidler, and V. A. Demant (mbreckitttrust.org/index.php/articles/49-twenty-years-of-the-christendom-trust). The recent Archbishop of Canterbury (2003–2012), Rowan Williams, is or was an Anglo-Catholic Christian Socialist who has been an outspoken critic of nuclear "deterrents," the "market state," "consumerism," tax avoidance, economic inequality both domestic and international, and environmental degradation.

His successor however, Justin Welby, is an Evangelical and a former business executive, neither of which would predispose him to Anglo-Catholic Christian Socialism. Yet his position on the social and economic problems facing Britain appears to differ little, if at all, from that of Williams. "Our economic model is broken ... the gains from growth are being diverted into profits rather than wages ... We are failing those who will grow up in a world where the gap between the richest and the poorest parts of the country is significant and destabilising" (*Guardian*, 5 September 2017).

The background to these archiepiscopal observations on economic and social affairs was provided 70 years before by William Temple, who had repented him of his useful dogmatism; and though still a friend and colleague of his Rugby school-fellow and friend R. H. Tawney, a lifelong socialist, and a member of the Labour Party for some years, no longer believed that we must choose between Socialism and heresy. As Bishop of Manchester (1921–1929) he became acquainted with industrial culture and the realities of the capitalist economy, and mediated between coal-miners and their employers. He became Archbishop of York (1929–1942) at the moment that the world economy collapsed into the longest and deepest depression in history, only ending in the greatest war of the twentieth century. And in 1942 he was nominated to the primatial see of Canterbury by Winston Churchill, who disapproved of his socialist principles but who recognized his superlative abilities (Robbins, 1993: 223).

It was in that year that he produced *Christianity and Social Order* (Temple, 1942), the nearest to a definitive statement of Anglican social doctrine that has ever been written, and lastingly influential. As Edward Heath, Conservative Prime Minister (1965–1970) wrote for its republication in 1976,

The impact of William Temple on my generation was immense ... (He) was foremost among the leaders of the nation, temporal or spiritual, in posing challenging, radical questions about the nature of our society and its economic basis ... his book brings home to every one of us the continuing importance, not so much as having cut-and-dried schemes for every eventuality as of being able to rely on a body of principle by which our plans and our actions can be both motivated and judged (Temple, 1976, pp. 1, 2).

An Oxford economist of the 1960s judged that it was "one of the foundation piers of the Welfare State" (Munby, 1960: 157).

Though short (114 pages) and popular in style, Temple had taken much trouble with its composition, and had asked Lord Keynes to read the page proofs. For by the late 1930s Temple was beginning to discover at least as much in common with advanced Liberals like Keynes and Sir William Beveridge (1879–1963) as with doctrinaire, upper-class Christian socialists in the Labour Party. Keynes and Beveridge, eminent economists whose opinions and advice were studied with close attention and respect by government, were the principle architects of the post-war macro-economic and social policies implemented by the Labour government (1945–1951) of Clement Atlee.

Keynes was reassuring. Of course the Church has the right to "interfere" in public policy, which is "essentially a branch of ethics ... I should have supposed that it was a very recent heresy indeed to cut these matters out of its province." Keynes reminded Temple of the important contributions to political economy made by clerics such as Swift, Fleetwood, Berkeley, Paley and Malthus; and he pointed out that "Archbishop Sumner's early work was on economics" (Temple, 1976: 9); not realizing, perhaps, that this work was fundamentally opposed in its political implications to everything Temple stood for.

The first chapter asked "What Right has the Church to Interfere?" in public policy, to which Keynes responded. The second asked, "How Should the Church Interfere?" the answer to which is through the actions of individual Christian people like Wilberforce; never by committing itself corporately to "a programme of detailed action" (p. 41); though Christian groups and organizations can engage in politics. And "the Church" may and sometimes *intervene* — as in industrial disputes. Chapter 3 asked, "Has the Church Claimed to Intervene Before?" and is a brief but substantial treatment of Christian doctrines of property, usury, the just price and enclosures.

Chapter 4 considers "primary" Christian Social Principles: announced by the Church but to be implemented by "Christian citizens acting in their civic capacity," who must "re-shape the existing order in closer conformity to the principles" (p. 58). However, because of Original Sin, "Self-interest is always exercising its disturbing influence." Therefore, "The art of government in fact is the art of so ordering life that self-interest prompts what justice demands" (p. 65). Forty-nine years later Pope John-Paul II, almost certainly in ignorance of Temple's book, amplified exactly this point in *Centesimus Annus* (John-Paul, 1991: para 25), which affirmed the market economy for the first time in papal history (Waterman, 2017b: 393–394). Together with the recognition that

> Whether or not our existing form of Capitalism in Great Britain offends against "Natural Law," it has certainly given to the great mass of the people a higher standard of life … than any previous system, (p. 81).

this realistic understanding of the human material with which "the Church" must work in baptizing Social Order is a measure of how far Temple had come from his youthful dogmatism.

Chapter 5 deals with "derivative" principles; 6 is a critique of "Natural Law" theorizing; and 7 concludes with "The Task Before Us," followed by a superbly balanced and judicious Appendix outlining "A Suggested Programme" — which must not be regarded as "the political programme which Christians ought to support" for there can be no such programme (p. 114).

Though Christian "Economic Doctrine" in the Church of England will doubtless persist among Anglicans unless or until their religion becomes extinct, it can never in the foreseeable future be a matter of national importance as it was in Temple's day. For as C. S. Lewis correctly perceived, not only England but the whole of Western Christendom has been "un-christened." Though belief may survive in individuals, it no longer shapes our culture. William Temple was the last — and perhaps the greatest — Archbishop of Canterbury since the Reformation to be recognized by almost all as *ex officio* spiritual head of the nation.

References

BCP (1662). *The Book of Common Prayer and Administration of the Sacraments and Other Rites and Ceremonies of the Church according to the Use of the Church of England together with the Psalter or Psalms of David Pointed as They Are to be Sung or Said in Churches and the Form and Manner of*

Making, Ordaining and Consecrating of Bishops, Priests, and Deacons. London: HM Printer.

Benson, E. F. (1889). *Christ and His Times.* London: Macmillan.

Bentham, J. (1789). *An Introduction to the Principles of Morals and Legislation.* London: Payne.

Burke, E. (1790). *Reflections on the Revolution in France and on the Proceedings of Certain Societies in London Relative to that Event. In a Letter Intended to Have Been Sent to a Gentleman in Paris.* London: Dodsley.

Catechism (1549). "A Catechisme, That Is To Say, An Instruction To Be Learned Of Eury Childe, Before He Be Brought To Be Confirmed Of The Bushop," in *The Booke of Common Prayer and Administracion of the Sacramentes, and Other Rites and Ceremonies of the Churches after the Use of the Churche of England.* Londini in Officina: Edouardi Whitchurche.

Clark, J. C. D. (1985). *English Society, 1688–1832: Ideology, Social Structure and Political Practice during the Ancien Régime.* Cambridge: Cambridge University Press.

Copleston, E. (1819a). *A Letter to the Right Hon. Robert Peel ... on the Pernicious Effects of a Variable Standard of Value, especially as it regards the Condition of the Lower Orders and the Poor Laws.* Oxford: Murray.

Copleston, E. (1819b). *A Second Letter to the Right Hon. Robert Peel ... on the Causes of the Increase in Pauperism, and on the Poor Laws.* Oxford: Murray.

Duffy, E. (2006). *Saints and Sinners. A History of the Popes.* Newhaven CT and London: Yale University Press.

Faccarello, G. (1999). *The Foundations of Laissez-faire: The Economics of Pierre de Boisguilbert.* London: Routledge.

Hey, J. (1796). *Lectures in Divinity delivered in the University of Cambridge by John Hey DD as Norrisian Professor.* Cambridge: Cambridge University Press.

Hey, J. (1815). "Lectures in Morality," in Nine bound vols., mss 10–18, in Muniment Room, Sydney Sussex College, Cambridge. Undated, deposited by his heirs, 1815.

Hobbes, T. ([1651] 1957). *Leviathan, or the Matter, Forme and Power of a Commonwealth Ecclesiasticall and Civil,* M. Oakshott, (ed.). Oxford: Blackwell.

Inglis, K. S. (1963). *Churches and the Working Classes in Victorian England.* London: Routledge and Kegan Paul.

Jones, P. d'Alroy (1968). *Christian Socialist Revival, 1877–1914: Religion, Class and Social Conscience in Late-Victorian England.* Princeton NJ: Princeton University Press.

King, W. (1702). *De Origine Mali.* London: Tooke.

Laslett, P. (1965). *The World We Have Lost: England Before the Industrial Age.* London: Routledge.

Law, E. (1739). *An Essay on the Origin of Evil, Translated from the Latin.* Cambridge: Thurlbourne.

Leo XIII, Pope (1891). *Rerum Novarum.*

Lewis, C. S. (1969). "De Descriptione Temporum," in *Selected Literary Essays,* W. Hooper, (ed.). Cambridge: Cambridge University Press.

Locke, J. ([1689/90] 1967). *Two Treatises of Government.* P. Laslett, (ed.), 2nd edn. Cambridge: Cambridge University Press.

Malthus, T. R. (1798). *An Essay on the Principle of Population as it Affects the Future Improvement of Society, with Remarks on the Speculations of Mr Godwin, M. Condorcet, and Other Writers.* London: Johnson.

Malthus, T. R. (1800). *An Investigation of the Cause of the Present High Price of Provisions. By the Author of the Essay on the Principle of Population.* London: Johnson.

Malthus, T. R. (1803). *An Essay on the Principle of Population; or a View of its past and present Effects on Human Happiness; with an Inquiry into our Prospects respecting the future Removal or Mitigation of the Evils which it occasions.* London: Johnson.

Marciano, A. (2011). "Buchanan's Catallactic Critique of Robbins' Definition of Economics," *Journal of Economic Methodology,* 16(2), 125–138.

Munby, D. (1960). *God and the Rich Society: A Study of Christians in a World of Abundance.* Oxford: Oxford University Press.

Norman, E. R. (1976). *The Victorian Christian Socialists.* Cambridge: Cambridge University Press.

Paley, W. (1785). *The Principles of Moral and Political Philosophy.* London: Faulder.

Paley, W. (1802). *Natural Theology: Or, Evidences of the Existence and Attributes of the Deity, Collected from the Appearances of Nature.* London: Hatchard.

Preston, R. H. (1976). "Introduction Thirty-five Years Later; 1941–1976," in William Temple, *Christianity and Social Order,* p. 5. London: SPCK.

Robbins, K. (1993). *History, Religion and Identity in Modern Britain.* London: Hambledon Press.

Smith, A. ([1776] 1976). *An Inquiry into the Nature and Causes of the Wealth of Nations* Oxford: Oxford University Press, 2 vols.

Sumner, J. B. (1816). *A Treatise on the Records of the Creation; with Particular Reference to the Jewish History; and the Consistency of the Principle of Population with the Wisdom and Goodness of the Deity.* London: Hatchard.

Sutherland, L. S. and Mitchell, L. G. (eds.) (1986). *History of the University of Oxford: Vol. V The Eighteenth Century.* Oxford: Oxford University Press.

Temple, W. (1908). *The Economic Review* 18.

Temple, W. (1942). *Christianity and Social Order.* London: Penguin.

Temple, W. (1976). *Christianity and Social Order, Foreword by the Rt Hon. Edward Heath, MBE MP, Introduction by the Rev. Canon Ronald H. Preston.* London: Shepheard-Walwyn.

Thompson, E. P. (1963). *The Making of the English Working Class.* London: Gollancz.

Thompson, F. J. (1945). *Lark Rise to Candleford.* Oxford: Oxford University Press.

Waterman, A. M. C. (1983a). "The Ideological Alliance of Political Economy and Christian Theology, 1798–1833," *Journal of Ecclesiastical History*, 34(2), 231–244.

Waterman, A. M. C. (1983b). "Malthus as a Theologian: The *First Essay* and the Relation between Political Economy and Christian Theology," in *Malthus: Past and Present*, J. Dupâquier, E. Grebenik and A. Fauve-Chamoux (eds.). London: Academic Press.

Waterman, A. M. C. (1991). *Revolution, Economics and Religion: Christian Political Economy 1798–1833.* Cambridge: Cambridge University Press.

Waterman, A. M. C. (1996). "Why William Paley was 'the First of the Cambridge Economists'," *Cambridge Journal of Economics*, 20, 673–686.

Waterman, A. M. C. (2003). "Romantic Political Economy: Donald Winch and David Levy on Victorian Literature and Economics," *Journal of the History of Economic Thought*, 25(1), 91–103.

Waterman, A. M. C. (2006). "New Light on Malthus: The Kanto Gakuen Collection," *Research in the History of Economic Thought and Methodology*, 24(Part 1), 141–151.

Waterman, A. M. C. (2008). "Political Economy: The English School," *The New Palgrave Dictionary of Economics*, 2nd edn. London: Palgrave Macmillan.

Waterman, A. M. C. (2016). "*Rerum Novarum* and Economic Thought," *Faith and Economics*, 67(Spring), 29–56.

Waterman, A. M. C. (2017a). "William Paley 1743–1805," in *The Palgrave Companion to Cambridge Economics*, Robert Cord, (ed.). London: Palgrave Macmillan.

Waterman, A. M. C. (2017b). "Pope Francis on the Environmental Crisis," *The Independent Review*, 21(3), 375–398.

Waterman, A. M. C. (2019/20). "The Evolution of 'Orthodoxy' in Economics from Adam Smith to Paul Samuelson," *The Independent Review*, 24(3), 325–345.

Whately, R. (1831). *Introductory Lectures in Political Economy, Being Part of a Course Delivered in Easter Term MDCCCXXXI.* London: B. Fellowes.

Wordsworth, W. (1950). *Poetical Works*, T. Hutchinson, (ed.). new edn. Revd., E. de Selincourt. Oxford: Oxford University Press.

https://doi.org/10.1142/9789811273148_0011

Chapter 11

Economic Liberty and Zionism

Zev Golan

Jerusalem Institute for Market Studies
Primo Levi, Jerusalem, Israel
zevgolan@hotmail.com

Abstract

This chapter will show that Zionism has been mischaracterized as a socialist movement. It will focus on several of Zionism founders and important innovators and their plans for a relatively market-based economy, including Herzl in *The Jewish State*, Jabotinsky with his commitment to individualism and entrepreneurship, and Louis Brandeis' promotion of stock-based investments and loans rather than charity. Since the death of Herzl, an incentive-based Zionism has existed alongside a philanthropic, collectivist Zionism and has been responsible for many of Israel's major accomplishments, most recently the economic accomplishments of Benjamin Netanyahu.

Keywords: Zionism, Herzl, Jabotinsky, Brandeis, Ahimeir, Menachem Begin, Weizmann, Netanyahu, Jubilee, Philanthropy, *Kibbutz*

1. Introduction

In the virtual world, virtually every Jewish website with a description of Theodor Herzl says he envisioned a socialist utopian state.[1] Not surprisingly, what has been said of Herzl is what many believe about Zionism — it is or is supposed to be a socialist utopia.[2]

But there was always a stream of economic liberty and personal liberty running through Zionism, and the fact is it began with Herzl. This stream contributed greatly to the proverbial blooming of the desert. It could have contributed more, had it been allowed to.

This chapter will show the vibrancy of the idea of economic liberty in the pre-state Zionist movement and in Israel, and refute the apparently popular myth that Israel was built solely by dint of the socialist–Zionist movement's work. The chapter will focus on the most important and well-known personalities who propounded or fought for liberty, or who formulated policy based on their knowledge that markets are more efficient and more moral than a planned economy without competition or private initiative.

2. Herzl

It is a shame that Herzl was characterized as a socialist utopian, since he was neither. He called the idea of turning Jews into peasant farmers in an age of agricultural machinery "absurd" and thought the real utopians were those who believed that humanity could be perfected. Herzl wrote that

---

[1] Even by Israel's Foreign Ministry: https://mfa.gov.il/MFA/AboutIsrael/History/Zionism/Pages/Binyamin%20Ze-ev%20Herzl-%20Father%20of%20Zionism.aspx (26 April 2021).
[2] Many people think Zionism is identical to the socialist *kibbutzim*. But those *kibbutzim* that once took their children to be raised separately from their parents long ago gave up that practice, the *kibbutzim* have been bailed out by Israeli taxpayers countless times at a cost of billions of dollars, they now allow the possession of private property, and have been or are now being privatized. Today, they are symbolized by the shopping malls they erect on previously agricultural land, as they engage in land speculation and capitalist marketing in order to turn a profit and survive. The *kibbutzim* have contributed much to the Zionist dream and Israel, but whatever their contribution, without non-socialist donors and then taxpayers to foot the bill they would not have been able to keep going.

"universal brotherhood is not even a beautiful dream."[3] His dream was for a publicly traded company to implement Zionist goals, and his world-changing book, *The Jewish State*, was essentially a business plan.

Herzl opens the introduction to *The Jewish State* with praise for "the spirit of enterprise." "All our material welfare has been brought about by men of enterprise," he writes, and adds, "I feel almost ashamed of writing down so trite a remark." But he does write it down, specifically in order to counter the socialist notion that there are a limited number of goods in the world and when someone profits, someone else necessarily loses. The spirit of enterprise, Herzl says, creates new commodities.[4]

Thus, at the basis of modern political Zionism lies a commitment to economic and political liberty.

Herzl's idea as put forth in *The Jewish State* was that a company would run the Zionist enterprise, organize the transfer of Jews to Eretz Israel (the Land of Israel) and build the country. On the one hand, it was to be a private company. But on the other hand, he planned for the company to run things pretty firmly. This is why he stresses that "individual enterprise must never be checked by the Company with its superior force."[5] He expected to raise capital from banks in the form of investments rather than charity. His preferred method was "direct subscription," in other words, selling shares to the public. He knew that entrepreneurs are attracted by the prospect of doing business and wanted them to profit. He hoped entrepreneurs would move to Eretz Israel because they saw it as a good business opportunity. And he was far from an attitude of resentment that typifies some of the anti-capitalist rallies of our time; he hoped to see wealthy individuals build mansions so "it will soon become fashionable over there to live in beautiful modern houses."[6] Indeed, Herzl recognized what he called the importance of "private property, which

---

[3] Theodor Herzl, *The Jewish State*, available on Project Gutenberg, http://www.gutenberg. org/files/25282/25282-h/25282-h.htm#The_Jewish_State, leaves 88, 153.

[4] *Ibid.*, leaf 73. In the preface to *The Jewish State*, Herzl also takes pains to refute the charge he expected to be leveled at him, that he was a utopian. He argues for the practicality of his plan and specifies the conditions under which it will be practical. As noted, the entire book is essentially a thorough business plan.

[5] *Ibid.*, leaf 116.

[6] *Ibid.*, leaf 109.

is the economic basis of "independence," and planned for it to be "developed freely and be respected by us."[7]

When he described the building of the country, those mansions and beautiful homes and roads and factories, he wrote of the Company's ability to move large numbers of workers to where they would be needed, and he took pains to explain why according to his plan the workers would go willingly. He said they would be enticed by good working conditions — he touted a seven-hour work day as his great planned innovation — and though initially some salaries were to be paid in kind, there would be cash paid for overtime to allow for reward and to create savings. Also, Herzl advocated a version of what is now called Welfare to Work, or Work for Welfare; he modeled his plan on the French Assistance par le Travail. He expected industrialists to contact "labor agencies" (today's manpower agencies) to connect them to unskilled laborers who were available to work limited periods.[8]

Interestingly, given the disrepute in which socialist politicians and parties in Israel, historically and today, have held many of the aforementioned ideas, Herzl also expressed extreme distaste for "that objectionable class of men — professional politicians."[9]

In 1902, Herzl published his novel *Altneuland*, which describes a rebuilt Eretz Israel. Here, too, Herzl argues:

> Money is an extraordinary thing, if it did not already exist we would have to invent it. No, we have not [followed socialist dogma] and abolished the differences between mine and yours. We are not crazy. We have not thrown overboard the incentive to work, to try harder to invent and to develop. Remarkable talent deserves proper reward, and special effort high recompense. Wealth stimulates the ambitious and nurtures rare abilities. Profit encourages entrepreneurship and creates new opportunities. If free entrepreneurs accumulate great profits by honest endeavor it is absolutely Kosher. Our new society did not embrace equality. Each person is rewarded according to their work and effort; we have not abolished competition, though we insist on fair opportunity for all, as in sports.[10]

[7] *Ibid.*, leaf 116.
[8] *Ibid.*, leaves. 117, 103, 105–107.
[9] *Ibid.*, leaf 144.
[10] Selected citations from the book, in Doron (2007). Brackets in Doron.

In the years between the publication of these two books, Herzl of course organized the Zionist Congress and ignited the Zionist revolution. Herzl put much of his efforts in those years into organizing an investment bank. He explained that "the national movement must liberate itself from the kindness of philanthropists and charitable institutions"[11] and wrote:

> Just as we [Zionists] replaced Zionist pleading with Zionist statesmanship so we must replace in our settlement work the reliance on alms and charity by a strictly businesslike approach. Charity has impoverished both givers and takers. Charity seekers have climbed to the top [of our enterprise] and our work lost what is most essential: individual responsibility. Those who seek help from rich patrons will not build the economic status of the Jews nor improve their moral standing .... [Because] he who receives alms degenerates [and] patrons only create ingrates.[12]

At Herzl's urging, the Second Zionist Congress in 1898 passed a resolution calling for the establishment of the financial institution he sought. The Jewish Colonial Trust was incorporated the next year, and its subsidiary, the Anglo-Palestine Company, was founded in 1902. This became the Anglo-Palestine Bank the next year and opened its first branch in Jaffa. The bank was headed by a Russian banker chosen by Herzl, Zalman Levontin. Today, the Anglo-Palestine Bank is known as Bank Leumi, and Levontin is known to most Israelis, the products of state education, only as the name of a street in Tel Aviv.

Herzl died in 1904, and the movement fell under the influence and later the control of those who essentially opposed much of Herzl's work. Herzl's political Zionism ran into the pragmatists' misnamed "practical Zionism," Ahad Haam's cultural Zionism and Chaim Weizmann's synthetic Zionism, not to mention the socialist Zionism of Eastern European Jews who divided their commitment between Zionism and socialism. Weizmann won the day, his synthetic Zionism being a dilution of Herzl's grand political solutions by practical, cultural and socialist goals.

---

[11] Theodor Herzl, "Otsar Hityashvut Hayehudim," http://benyehuda.org/herzl/herzl_024. html (26 April 2021) [Hebrew] (my translation).

[12] *Ibid.*, trans. in Doron (2007). Brackets in Doron.

Weizmann and his socialist allies took over Zionism and founded the charity-based Settlement Fund (Keren Hayesod). They undermined Levontin's support for private settlements and enterprises, entrusting the settlement effort to a bureaucratic Settlement Department headed by Arthur Ruppin, a communist sympathizer, and to other avowed leftists. This group also directed all of Zionism's scarce resources to collectivist settlement and to a vicious class warfare against the successful private sector.[13]

Weizmann had to work hard to ensure Zionism would reflect his views, for there were strong personalities and forces in the movement promoting a different kind of Zionism, one that championed the individual, industry, liberty and grand political solutions. Herzl's ally Max Nordau, for instance, in 1919 advocated the immediate transfer of hundreds of thousands of Jews from Europe to Eretz Israel in order to save their lives, and he was sent into retirement by Weizmann and other supporters of gradual agricultural colonization (one dunam at a time) and a more restrictive immigration policy.

It has been argued that there have ever since Herzl been two strains in Zionism: a grand Zionism and a miniature Zionism. Dr. Moshe Cohen, who made this argument in the 1950s, felt that Vladimir (Ze'ev) Jabotinsky and others represented the grand Zionism of Herzl, and Weizmann and the socialists represented a reduced version of Zionism, which through political skill and the development of vested economic interests managed the movement, while the great strides were made by those loyal to Herzl's vision (Cohen, 1954: 58).

3. Brandeis

At about the time Nordau was being sidelined for his desperate efforts to save Europe's Jews, American Zionism was headed by Louis Brandeis, a Supreme Court Justice since 1916. Brandeis became a Zionist around 1910 and seriously involved himself in the movement a few years later. Under his leadership the number of American Jews supporting the Zionist

---

[13] Doron, D. (2007). Arthur Ruppin believed trade was nothing more than a redistribution of wealth and opposed competition and an increased number of shops or cafés. See Plessner, Y. (1993), p. 151.

movement went from some 20,000 to 200,000.[14] Brandeis helped raise large sums of money for Zionist activity, and he was a firm believer the money should be used efficiently. He wanted to see the funds he and others raised used to create sustainable industry and life, not communities that would need to subsist on future charity.

Explaining, for instance, why the Zionist Organization was raising money to extend a loan to those in Eretz Israel, Brandeis said:

> The colonies were in great need, not in need of charity, but of capital, capital to operate their plantations, capital to continue that life of self-support and self-respect which had won the admiration of all who are acquainted with their story and their struggle. We in America, the Zionist Provisional Committee and others, undertook to raise a loan for those planters, to be repaid when better conditions would enable them to market their products.[15]

Brandeis believed that even land improvement, including the draining of swamps, should not be financed by philanthropy, since in the long term it would be profitable. Given that in the short term such work would not allow the payment of interest on loans, Brandeis favored issuing stock to finance such endeavors (Plessner, 1993: 63).

When Weizmann and his associates established the Keren Hayesod fund, it formalized some of the difficulties Brandeis was having working in the same movement as Weizmann. This fund was supposed to give 20 percent of the money it raised to the Jewish National Fund (JNF), spend 25 percent on social welfare, education and immigration, and give the rest to national institutions and various projects. Brandeis opposed combining charity and investments in one fund and wanted a separate investment fund to ensure the economic independence of the Jews of Eretz Israel. Weizmann came to the United States to confront his nemesis. The result of the confrontation was that Weizmann's opponents took early retirement: the Zionist organization lost such luminaries as Brandeis,

---

[14]Feldberg, M. (August 2011). "Louis D. Brandeis and American Zionism," The Jewish Federations of North America, http://www.jewishfederations.org/page.aspx?id=53583.
[15]Louis Brandeis, speech to Knights of Zion, Chicago, January 2, 1916, in Brandeis, (1942), p. 86.

Felix Frankfurter, Nathan Straus, Rabbi Abba Hillel Silver, Judge Julian Mack and others (Fraenkel, 2004).

Brandeis, while afterwards distancing himself from the official movement, helped establish the investment fund he dreamed of. He and Rabbi Silver put together the Palestine Development League (later, the Palestine Economic Corporation) "for the social economic up building (sic) of Palestine so that it may be populated within a comparatively short time by a preponderance of self-supporting Jews" (Libo and Skakun, 2011).

In 1920, Brandeis argued against appointing inefficient people to high positions simply because they were respected or needed to be rewarded for past accomplishments:

> Unless our people recognize that the greatest public service they can perform in Palestine is to earn there an honest living and not be dependent upon the Organization, we shall not accomplish our work. The highest work that can be done for Palestine is to earn a living in Palestine; to put the Jewish mind and Jewish determination and Zionist idealism and enthusiasm into the problem of earning a living in Palestine; thus, setting an example for others to earn a living. That is real patriotism. A young woman who was in Palestine some time ago said that to make a good soup in Palestine was a contribution to the cause. I agree with her. But it is not a contribution to have someone else make a soup for you. It is not a contribution to get paid for making plans for a good soup. What we have to do is to make it possible for men to earn a living in Palestine. That is a very difficult thing. It cannot be done by subsidizing people.[16]

Brandeis' organization supported private enterprise as well as non-collectivist settlements and created the Palestine Mortgage and Credit Bank to loan funds to small businessmen and the middle class,[17] helping

---

[16]Louis Brandeis, statement to American delegation at the London Conference of the Zionist Actions. Committee, July 14, 1920, in *Brandeis on Zionism*, pp. 123–124.

[17]Fraenkel, "Louis D. Brandeis." But Brandeis shared the feeling that the emphasis in Eretz Israel should be on agriculture, and warned, "The utmost vigilance should be exercised to prevent the acquisition by private persons of land, water rights, or other natural resources or any concessions for public utilities," adjuring that "In other ways as well as this the possibility of capitalistic exploitation must be guarded against." Urofsky, (2009), p. 521. See also the following footnote. Since the creation of the state of Israel the state

enable the establishment of cities such as Herzliya and Natanya (the latter named for the American businessman Nathan Straus).

Although the Mack-Brandeis group had not found majority favor with the larger decision-making groups in Palestine (seeking to develop Palestine economically first, with a more capitalist, or American view), the Palestine Economic Corporation saw many of the financial needs for the Jewish homeland met via such ideology.[18]

While Brandeis's priority was to efficiently build Eretz Israel and make the Jewish national home there sustainable, other Zionists were moving in opposite directions. The Hashomer Hatzair movement wrote in its journal in 1922:

We see the weight of the national idea lying not in the nation of today, even if it is building our country with its money, but in us, as the last generation of the Diaspora and the first of redemption .... The nation of today is merely fulfilling its last purpose by furnishing its pioneers with money .... (Yevin, 1933)

---

monopolies in the areas Brandeis wanted to keep out of private hands have been the most exploitative enterprises in Israel. To this day there is no land market, water market or market for public utilities; each of these state monopolies has the highest-paid employees in the country and Israelis pay high prices for all the goods and services they provide.

[18] The Center for Online Jewish Studies, referencing Albright, W. F. *et al.* (1947). *Palestine: A Study of Jewish, Arab and British Policies*, Vol. 1. New Haven: Yale University Press, pp. 343–346, http://cojs.org/the_development_of_the_jewish_national_home-_important_points_from_albright-_et_al-_palestine-_a_study_of_jewish-_arab_and_british_policies-_vol-_i-_yale_university_press-_1947/ (26 April 2021).

As a lawyer and then jurist, Brandeis was known as a liberal and famous for his positions against monopolies and business. But he was also opposed to Roosevelt's New Deal expansion of presidential powers, Roosevelt's attempts to pack the Supreme Court and the centralization of business by government. Even his earlier rulings for free speech essentially limited state intervention in people's lives. He opposed government ownership except for public utilities and took the same attitude toward Jewish Eretz Israel; in the 1918 Pittsburgh Platform which he wrote, he called for "ownership and control by the whole people of the land, of all natural resources and of all public utilities" (Urofsky, *Brandeis*, pp. 304, 527). Far from a capitalist view, this was also far from what most of the socialist Zionists wanted, as it would have excluded the government from all other business.

Hashomer Hatzair was not alone, nor exceptionally extreme. The socialist–Zionist leader and future prime minister David Ben-Gurion wrote in 1925:

> The changes in the Yishuv as private money comes in … put the workers' enterprise and influence in future Zionist and community work in this country in great peril, and they obligate us to focus and increase the socialist power among the workers of Eretz Israel and the worldwide Zionist movement.[19]

And Hashomer made his goal clear. In 1931, the same year that the Zionist Congress rejected Jabotinsky's proposal to declare the goal of Zionism to be the establishment of a Jewish state, Hashomer's platform declared that "a Jewish state … with all the attributes of governance — would try to impose a colonial regime on the country, a regime of constant oppression of the Hebrew workers and abrogation of the rights of the Arab population," and Hashomer called instead for "constant class warfare and capturing the government."[20]

4. Jabotinsky

Jabotinsky was *persona non grata* in the Zionist establishment for many reasons. First of all because he established the Jewish Legion of the British army during World War I, while many Zionist establishments were against what they called Jewish militarism. Secondly, because he wanted to declare the goal of Zionism to be statehood while they either were afraid to do so or truly did not want a state. Thirdly, because he was the Supreme Commander of the activist Irgun that did not take orders from the Labor parties running the political Zionist movement. Fourthly, because he encouraged the doomed Jews of Europe to immigrate illegally to Eretz Israel while the Zionist leadership preferred, in all the years before the Holocaust, to accept the few thousand legal certificates given them each year by the British. And finally, and arguably mostly, because he wrote and spoke on behalf of markets.

---

[19]David Ben-Gurion, on behalf of the Actions Committee of Ahdut Ha'avoda, letter to Dr. Zemora, Jerusalem, 13 February 1925 (copy in author's files).
[20]Hashomer Hatzair, 1931, Third World Conference platform, clause 13.

Jabotinsky wrote that there was no essential difference between socialism and communism. The only difference Jabotinsky could see was that communism wants to move faster. Jabotinsky wrote that both want to impose their social agenda by force. A minority of the public is supposed to set the agenda and order society according to its wishes.

Jabotinsky argued that the very idea of a proletariat leads to communism, and everything on the way to communism is merely a temporary compromise. Once one accepts class distinctions as basic, he is on the road to communism. Jabotinsky decried the labeling of anyone who did not accept the primacy of the working class as a "reactionary." He said the opposite is true. The only means of assuring working-class rule is by being reactionary, because the ideals of equality for all, freedom of speech, majority rule, freedom of association and unions are all opposed to it. Therefore, the only way for the working class to attain or maintain power is by force.

Jabotinsky wrote of "wishing to combat poverty and seeking to eliminate it," and argued "there is no tie and no bridge between this desire and a 'proletarian' class outlook" (Jabotinsky, 1933). Workers should not automatically be defined as the "poor." When Jabotinsky wrote, workers were already better off than most poor. The Histadrut labor union monopoly in pre-state Eretz Israel (and later, Israel), and the unions of Jabotinsky's time, he noted, "own much public capital, banks, warehouses, hospitals, newspapers, libraries and clubs, and their political influence is as great as any other" (Jabotinsky, 1933).

Jabotinsky disagreed with the Marxist view that private property is evil. The Marxists and socialists Jabotinsky opposed believed that private property was based on the exploitation of the workers and needed to be fought. Jabotinsky said, "the success of our project, as everyone knows, depends on including private property. And the nature of private property is also known to all: it goes where it can profit. Whether this is good is irrelevant, terms such as good and evil are irrelevant; this is simply the nature of things." Jabotinsky mocked the leftists who went to the Diaspora and promised investors a nice profit if they would put their money into Eretz Israel, then went to the working public in Eretz Israel and urged holy war against the profits of evil (Jabotinsky, 1933).

Perhaps Jabotinsky was most violently attacked by the socialist Zionists of the 1930s for an article he wrote called, "Yes, Break It." They unfairly attacked him for calling to break strikes, which was not the subject of the article. Jabotinsky called to break the monopoly of the Histadrut over labor in Eretz Israel. (Regarding strikes, Jabotinsky favored a form of national arbitration that would protect both employee and employer (Jabotinsky, 1933; Finkelstein, 2003; Gazit, 2011).)

Jabotinsky was, as is clear from the above, solidly in the anti-socialist camp. Jabotinsky rejected attempts by socialist Zionists or other socialists to find support for their programs in the Bible. He wrote, "The Bible is full of social protest ... But socialism is not only a protest, socialism is a concrete program to solve a social problem by means of law, and this kind of program is not found in the Bible" (Jabotinsky, 1930).

Jabotinsky was quite emphatic on this point, explaining that the intent of socialism is to prevent a problem from arising while the Bible allows freedom and deals with the results: "The biblical program has nothing in common with a prophylactic system that prevents any possibility of inequality, exploitation, competition and economic struggle before they happen. The Bible seeks to preserve economic freedom but also tries to adjust it with mini-reservations and medicines" such as, Jabotinsky wrote, the Sabbath, tithing, the gleanings and corners of the field that were left for the poor and the jubilee. These biblical laws, Jabotinsky stressed, come to adjust rather than prevent economic freedom (Jabotinsky, 1930).

His views on these matters were of great importance for the Zionist movement. They were an alternative to socialist Zionism. As such, they allowed many non-socialists to find a home in Zionism and then in Zion. They assured that most of the tens of thousands of members of Jabotinsky's youth movement, Betar, would absorb and later espouse views favoring markets. Many of these people were the builders of Israeli cities, industries and homes.

Another characteristic of Jabotinsky that influenced his followers and Zionism, and that bolstered his students' market views, was his commitment to individualism. "Every individual is a king," he wrote. In one rather funny poem, he writes of a young woman he is trying to flirt with, who asks him his philosophical views. He makes short shrift of various thinkers and explains that he is neither a socialist nor a capitalist. Using Nietzschean terminology, he says an overman has no stamp on his forehead, and he tells her, "Before you stands a free man without any stamp" (Jabotinsky, 1958).

Indeed, Jabotinsky's own economic program was not what we would call pure capitalism. He based it on the idea that play characterizes humankind in its search for material as well as spiritual benefits. Man's imaginative abilities, which allow for progress, are displayed not only in what we think of as leisure activities but most importantly in the attempt to accumulate wealth. Only a market economy allows for play and competition, and therefore state involvement should be minimized.[21] The state's role is not to own the means of production or manage production, which would crush man's creative talents and his rights, but to enact social legislation and provide five basic needs, the levels of which, according to Jabotinsky, are relative to each society: housing, food, clothing, education and health. In Jabotinsky's vision, every person who wants to benefit from the state's largesse in these areas is entitled to, without showing need. Essentially he believed in a welfare state; he hailed economic competition as one of the "firm fundamentals of human life" while seeking to provide a soft landing ground for those who would fall in the ensuing fray because pure liberalism and capitalism are "unrestrained wildness and the competitiveness of abandon."[22] His most famous economic idea was to reinstate the biblical jubilee. According to the Bible, in the jubilee year loans are to be forgiven, land returned to its owners and slaves set free. According to Jabotinsky, "Economic life should be preserved ... with full freedom for changes. People will continue to consult, plan, struggle, compete; some will become rich, some will become poor; life will maintain its character as a wrestling ring, where one can lose or win, display initiative and fail or succeed."[23] But every 50 years the game should start again.

As noted, Jabotinsky's influence on the Zionist movement was great. Yet because he was officially marginalized by the establishment, and most of his followers remained without power for many years, his criticism of socialism, and his glorification of the individual, had more of an impact than his own economic program, which no one was ever in a position to attempt to implement. In addition, Jabotinsky proclaimed a policy of "One Flag," meaning he was going to raise only one flag, the Zionist flag, until the realization of Zionism's goal, the establishment of a Jewish state with a Jewish majority in Eretz Israel. He insisted that any other flag raised alongside Zionism — such as socialism or capitalism — would distract the activists from their goal and delay its attainment. Thus, he explained

---

[21] Jabotinsky (1958), pp. 49–56. The summary in this paragraph is based on Uri Heitner, "The Political and Social Thought of Jabotinsky," November 2010 [Hebrew], https://heitner.wordpress.com/2010/11/page/3/ (26 April 2021).

[22] Jabotinsky (1930), pp. 37–40; "Chapters in the Social Philosophy of the Bible" (1933), in *Nation and Society*, as cited by Heitner.

[23] Jabotinsky (1958), also cited by Heitner.

the benefits of his economic proposals but never actually pursued them as policy.

Jabotinsky's impact was felt when his students provided employees to factories that did not want to work with the Histadrut. They farmed, did guard duty and built communities in distant areas where the Histadrut was not supplying laborers. They provided a model of a "proud, generous and fierce"[24] Jew who defended his own honor and that of his people, and they fought for these ideas in their own labor union (the Nationalist Histadrut), their own underground militia (the Irgun), their own newspapers (*Hayarden, Herut* and others) and their own political movement (Herut, later Likud). These movements not only promoted Jabotinsky's views but they provided a home for people who were in accord with these views, who would have found no outlet for their own views or channels to express them, without the Jabotinskyite base. Among these people were or are Abba Ahimeir, the founder of the first underground in Eretz Israel, Brit Habirionim; Menachem Begin, Commander of the Irgun and Prime Minister of Israel; and Benjamin Netanyahu, the current Prime Minister.

Professor Benzion Netanyahu, the father of the current prime minister, worked with Jabotinsky and was active in the movement from the 1930s. In the early 1930s he pointed out that "productive capital made its way to lands owned by the Jewish National Fund only to a low degree, almost not at all, compared to the same type of capital that made its way to privately held land." Netanyahu explained the lack of investment in land not privately owned by noting "there is almost no possibility of exploiting the increase in value of [JNF]-owned land" (Netanyahu, 1934; Gazit and Golan, 2010).

At the same time that Netanyahu senior was seeing and writing about the harm being caused the Zionist enterprise by the socialist approach of its leadership, Jabotinsky's young followers were suffering hunger and beatings because of that approach. The Histadrut labor union, whose monopoly Jabotinsky wanted to break, managed all the employment offices in the country. Often, non-socialists were not given work, and this applied equally to communists and to the followers of Jabotinsky, who were members of Jabotinsky's Revisionist party or his Betar youth movement. The Histadrut's determination to maintain its labor monopoly led it to physically attack Revisionist workers. Such instances include the destruction of a Revisionist workers dormitory in Rehovot and the beating

---

[24] A verse from Jabotinsky's *Betar* anthem.

of Revisionist employees of the Frumin factory.[25] This further exacerbated the already tense relations between socialists and non-socialists in the Zionist movement. The worst fighting took place when Jabotinsky's movement was accused of the 1933 murder of Labor leader Haim Arlosoroff in Tel Aviv.

5. Abba Ahimeir

One of the three members of Jabotinsky's movement in Eretz Israel who was actually accused of that murder — the charge against him being incitement — and who was acquitted in court, as were the other followers of Jabotinsky who were accused of the actual deed, was the journalist Abba Ahimeir. Though found innocent, Ahimeir was immediately charged with incitement against the British, a charge of which he was convicted.

Ahimeir started his intellectual life as a teenaged Tolstoyan, moved toward communism and then saw the horrors of the Russian Revolution. For a time he even looked to fascism as the only political force capable of stopping Bolshevism, until "at the beginning of 1929 Jabotinsky appeared and completely cured me of that youthful illness" (Ahimeir, 1955). Ahimeir had written during the early 1920s for Labor Zionist newspapers, but by the end of the decade he was writing for Jabotinsky. He became the leader of the "maximalist" wing of the party and was one of the founders of the Brit Habirionim organization, a forerunner of the real undergrounds that waged war during the 1940s. Moshe Svorai, the last surviving member of Brit Habirionim, who passed away in December 2011 at the age of 97, recalled meeting Ahimeir in the early 1930s and "in that conversation, Ahimeir set himself a goal — to shatter the little faith a youth like me had in socialist ideas and prove to me that Hebrew youth should devote their lives to the sacred task of liberating their land" (Svorai, 1988).

Ahimeir himself recalled, in his final speech, shortly before his own death in 1962, that the difference between his underground and the Irgun

---

[25]Niv (1965), pp. 192–194 [Hebrew]. The Revisionists were not the only victims of Histadrut force. For instance, when the Manufacturers' Association sent its members a letter in 1937 reminding them that any Jew who comes to the country is eligible for work regardless of his party affiliation, the Histadrut threatened to take action if the policy were implemented. In 1938, Histadrut agents forcibly expelled workers from a construction site operated by Yetzira and beat workers who belonged to a different union. See Plessner (1993), p. 160.

and Lehi was that Brit Habirionim "had several goals. First, to fight a war against the foreign occupier, and indeed, the British saw it as dangerous. Second, to fight a war against socialism in whatever form," and the organization's third goal, he said, was to fight against the idea that it was enough to complacently read Jabotinsky and vote for him in Zionist elections, whereas a more active approach was necessary. Ahimeir credited the success of the Irgun and Lehi to their focusing only on one goal, the liberation of the country from the British.[26]

6. The Fighting Underground

The members of Betar and Brit Habirionim eventually became members of the Irgun underground, and no love was lost between them and the communal socialist leadership. The Irgun itself had been founded in 1931 — before it became associated with Jabotinsky — when Abraham T'homi, who was not a Revisionist, left the Hagana because he wanted to create an army that was not under the control of the Histadrut as the Hagana was. T'homi and a group of Jabotinsky's Betar members, who were also dissatisfied with putting what was supposed to be a non-political army under the control of a socialist labor union, and who wanted the army to be free of Labor's instructions to always be only on the defense, came together and founded the Irgun. Thus, to the list of Zionist developments linked to those who believed in some degree of economic, political or individual liberty, must be added the creation of the fighting underground.

Given Jabotinsky's insistence on raising only one flag, the Irgun did not get involved in economic issues or arguments over how to best develop the economy of a future state. But its anti-socialist stance was bolstered when it got a new commander in chief in 1943 — Menachem Begin. In September 1940, Begin, who was escaping from the Germans, had been arrested by the Soviets for his Zionist activity,[27] and his feelings toward the Soviets and their ideology were undoubtedly informed by the long months he spent in Soviet prisons and labor camps. In any case,

---

[26] Cited in "The History of the Brit" [Hebrew], *Beit Aba*, http://www.beitaba.com/index. php?dir=site&page=content&cs=26&langpage=heb.

[27] Ironically, he was accused of being an agent of British imperialism.

the Irgun under his leadership fought only to eject the British from Eretz Israel in order to establish an independent Jewish state.

In 1940, Abraham Stern left the Irgun to found the even fiercer Stern Group underground, known in Hebrew as Lehi. Stern believed as did Jabotinsky and Begin in raising only one flag. Thus, in the 1930s he refused to attend performances by an Eretz-Israeli theater that insisted on mounting only socialist shows, and he opposed aiding the labor movements in other countries, not so much because he hated socialism as because these were distractions from the Zionist cause (Golan, 2011). In Warsaw, he offered the anti-socialist Abba Ahimeir a column in an Irgun newspaper, but he rejected Ahimeir's proposed name for the column, "Anti-Marxist Musings," because he felt this, too, would detract from the Zionist effort and alienate some potential supporters(Ahimeir, 1949).

According to Moshe Cohen, the Irgun and Stern Group represented the grand Zionism of Herzl and Jabotinsky, in contrast to the miniature Zionism of Weizmann and the establishment. Of course, the Irgun and Stern Group were no more libertarians than were Herzl and Jabotinsky. But while the establishment organization and its military wing, the Hagana, sought accommodation with the British occupiers of Eretz Israel, the Irgun and Stern Group fought for freedom. When Menachem Begin visited the United States after his election as prime minister in 1977, the press was quite antagonistic to the Israeli nationalist and former "terrorist." His young American Jewish supporters distributed flyers comparing him to George Washington, since both had fought guerrilla wars with England to free their countries. For historical reasons the Hebrew freedom movement, or movement of liberation, was not focused on freedom from taxation without representation or from the billeting of soldiers in one's home; the Jews who fought were concerned with liberty for the nation and homeland, and were willing to delay discussion of what that meant for individuals. They fought a one-track war to eject the British from the Jewish homeland and attain self-government. The socialist Hagana militia and leadership sometimes cooperated with them and at other times hunted them down, kidnapped them and turned them over to the British for prison or hanging.

There was a major difference between the Irgun and Stern Group. T'homi and the later Irgun commanders intended the Irgun to be, as its Hebrew name states, a "National Military Organization." Stern intended his group to be a revolutionary movement whose tasks would never end. So he listed among his 18 goals not only ejecting the British but also establishing a society without poverty where everyone would find employment. Significantly, Stern did not say how these goals should be attained. His movement was open to socialists and capitalists, religious and secular, Jews and Arabs.[28]

The Irgun and Sternists fought for a state. When it was established, they joined its army and supported its institutions. These institutions were dominated by the socialist-Zionist establishment. The first prime minister was David Ben-Gurion. If you ask Israelis today what Ben-Gurion did before that, they don't know; but one cannot understand the economic development of Israel without knowing that Ben-Gurion had been general secretary of the Histadrut almost from its founding — he was its second leader, from 1921 to 1935. Moreover, Ben-Gurion's successor as general secretary, David Remez, was Israel's first minister of transportation and then minister of education; Remez's successor became the first Speaker of the Knesset; his successor as general secretary became a minister of agriculture and later minister of defense; and that person's successor became a minister of labor. The eight leaders of the Histadrut who followed have so far accounted for two ministers of transportation, one minister of justice and interior, and one minister of defense. Yehoshua Yevin, a partner of Abba Ahimeir's in the 1930s and a writer for the Irgun and Stern Group afterward, wrote in the 1950s that the Histadrut was essentially running a state within a state (Yevin, 1950–1951). Ben-Gurion forbade Sternists to teach in Israeli schools for fear they might influence the youth, and Irgunists and Sternists were not accorded the status of war heroes in the fight for Israel, so as not to compete with the mythic heroes of the Hagana. Thus, the mirage that all Zionist achievements were socialist, which had rested earlier on the *kibbutzim*, was now reinforced regarding the establishment of the state (Golan, 2011: 154, 225; Lebel, 2007: 237).

---

[28]By the late 1940s there were a good number of young socialists in the Stern Group. When the Soviet Union expressed an interest in the group's anti-British activities, the leadership made deliberate efforts to get closer to the Soviets. As the underground war against Britain came to an end, one of the organization's leaders, Nathan Yalin-Mor, propounded views that were either socialist or nearly socialist. When the underground disbanded, over half the members who voted expressed support for either socialism or anti-imperialist activities in other countries. As time passed, most of these members drifted away from such views and back toward their Jewish roots. Yalin-Mor and others drifted further toward the left. See Golan (2011), pp. 206–211, 220–221.

7. Private Capital Built the Country

As we have seen previously, this does not reflect the truth that private capital and industry and those committed to personal and national liberty made major contributions to Zionism from its inception.

From 1918 to 1929, 73 percent of the money invested in Eretz Israel was private. In the years 1930–1937, 84 percent was private. Private investments dropped during World War II, but overall during the British Mandate, public funds (raised by the Zionist Organization, PICA, the Joint Distribution Committee, etc., gifts to Hadassah hospital, funds used to absorb German refugees, and donations to political parties) totaled only about 20 percent of the money used to develop the Yishuv (Rabushka, 2001). Professor Yakir Plessner, a former deputy governor of the Bank of Israel, points out that during the wave of immigration known as the Fourth Aliya (1924–1929), the Keren Hayesod spent £163,500 a year on agricultural settlement, while estimating the cost of settling one family at £1,500–1,800; in other words, it was essentially financing 90–110 families a year (Plessner, 1993: 72). From the end of World War I through 1937, the two Zionist funds, Keren Hayesod and the JNF, were spending over half the money they distributed on agriculture, though by 1925, 83 percent of the Jews in Palestine lived in cities. But the two funds allocated a mere 9 percent of their funds to trade, industry, urban settlement and direct investment combined. The 1930s saw such important industries as Vulcan (foundries), Phoenicia (glass), Ata (textiles) and the Discount Bank established, all the result of private initiative. Indeed, Phoenicia was forced into receivership though it had no debt and was bought by the Histadrut in 1940; Vulcan was bought by the Histadrut the following year; and in the 1950s the new Israeli government in effect nationalized other productive private industries that built the country (Plessner, 1993: 153, 151, 165). Moshe Novomeski's Palestine Potash company, for example, which had been financed mostly by Novomeski's own money and an investment by Brandeis' PEC in 1930, became the Dead Sea Works of the state's Israel Chemicals (Plessner, 1993: 72),[29] and Pinchas Rutenberg's Palestine Electric Corporation was bought by the state and became the state electric monopoly Israel still has today.

---

[29] Israel Chemicals was later sold to the Israel Corporation and then sold to the Ofer family, one of the so-called oligarchic families dominating Israel's economy today.

In the early 1950s, inflation soared to 66 percent, while the government capped interest rates, making private savings unattractive. The government set up a state Investment Center not only to encourage and direct investment but to prevent whatever it considered undesirable investments. The government subsidized the investments it favored, and the years 1953–1958 saw only three offerings on the local capital market; so the government issued indexed bonds. The result of all this was what Plessner calls the "*de facto* nationalization" of the capital market (Plessner, 1993: 77–78).

Professor Yair Aharoni writes that the result of the socialist policies was big government and an economy built on protection, cronyism and ever-increasing corruption. Investment dropped, as noted, and taxes had to rise and transfer payments rose with them. Gross taxation went from 28 percent in the early 1960s to 50 percent by the 1980s. With the government directing savings and credit, business became dependent on the government for credit as well as for tax breaks and cash grants. The largest businesses accumulated their own capital, making government dependent on them for its success. Aharoni calls the result an "almost total identity between political and economic power" (Aharoni, 1993: 13).

Israel's leaders sought charity rather than investment. Herzl, Brandeis and Jabotinsky must have turned over in their graves as Israeli leaders ran around the world pleading for assistance. The Zionists had been doing it all along, the endeavors Brandeis was unable to prevent, but in the 1950s Israel's efforts to get German reparations brought the art and the results to new nadirs. The deal Israel worked out brought the reparations to the government's coffers rather than to individual Holocaust survivors, thus reinforcing the growth of big government rather than the private sector (Arad, 2010). Coincidentally or not, from the time that Israel turned to the United States for huge infusions of foreign aid following the 1973 war, economic growth essentially stopped; over the next 25 years it would average only 1.5 percent annually.

Aharoni attributes Israel's slow weaning from socialism partly to Soviet anti-Semitism, the worldwide failure of socialist economies, a decreasing importance attached to all ideology and Israel's alliance with the United States (Aharoni, 1993: 1–2, 18–19). Undoubtedly, another reason Israel moved away from socialism, to whatever extent it may have done so, was the electoral victory of Menachem Begin in 1977.

8. Menahem Begin

Once out of the underground, as the leader of a national political party, Begin was able to, and had to, raise more than one flag. He professed his commitment to individual liberty and markets from the very first Knesset. Begin declared, "Once, at a time when liberal thought blossomed, there was a saying that the authorities of the state should be limited to those of a night watchman. That time has passed, but every free man prays in his heart that we won't have to say it has passed forever."[30]

Begin opposed the statist economy then in formation and his reference to the results of socialist land policy recall the analysis of Benzion Netanyahu two decades earlier: "Not only in industrial production, but also in agricultural production, private initiative is the least expensive and most efficient system," said Begin, citing figures showing that agricultural production was 50 percent higher in the private farms of the Sharon than in the *kibbutzim* of the Bet She'an and Gilboa regions (Fuksman-Shaal, 2008: 27).

Moshe Fuksman, Director of the Knesset Museum, who has collected many of Begin's remarks on the economy, notes that Begin believed an individual's rights were his to begin with, not granted him by the state. Begin referred to the rights to life, liberty, work and the pursuit of happiness. Fuksman cites Begin's own explanation that his approach was based on the Bible's statement that man, and therefore all persons of all religions, nationalities and races, are created in God's image (Fuksman-Shaal, 2008: 26).

Fuksman quotes Begin's warnings about what happens when a government is responsible for people's jobs or, put another way, when people are dependent on the state for their living: the result is a form of slavery. Similarly, any attempt by a government to do away with the natural differences between individuals and enforce sameness would lead "not to the calm of freedom but the fears of a slave." Begin felt that the differences between individuals are no longer based on birth, property or political position (as in feudal, post-French Revolution industrial, and communist societies, respectively) but on a person's talents and efforts; as long as

---

[30] Menahem Begin, Knesset speech, 7 February 1950, cited in Fuksman-Shaal, M. (2008). "The Economic Revolution in Israel — From Socialism to a Free Market," *Hauma*, 174, 25 [Hebrew].

people are free to compete the differences between them will encourage them to improve their lot, and the society as a whole will improve with them (Fuksman-Shaal, 2008: 27–29; Begin, 1951: 30).[31]

Begin believed as Jabotinsky had in the government's responsibility to provide the five basic needs of which Jabotinsky spoke, but Begin argued they should be provided only to those who work or who are unable to work through no fault of their own (Fuksman-Shaal, 2008: 31). Fuksman lists the main points of Begin's economic agenda: Ending government foreign currency controls; ending monopolies and even private cartels; cutting taxes; reducing bureaucracy; privatizing state- and Histadrut-owned enterprises; reducing the budget deficit; ending automatic wage indexation, to be replaced with productivity-based wage hikes; and reaching an agreement on voluntary arbitration of labor disputes (Fuksman-Shaal, 2008: 32–33).

Begin's Herut party joined with the classically Liberal party in 1965. The Liberals were an incarnation of the General Zionists, which from the 1930s through 1961 offered a semi-capitalist alternative to Mapai's policies. They sought to separate the Histadrut and the governing socialist political parties from the provision of health and social welfare services in Israel; but to this end they called for the provision of such services by the state. Otherwise they called for reducing state (and Histadrut) involvement in the economy. They were supported mostly by the middle class. The General Zionists won seven seats in Israel's first Knesset, but catapulted to 20 seats in the 1951 elections as they bitterly attacked the government's economic policies. The government co-opted them and after they joined the coalition their electoral appeal began to fade. In 1961 they joined with the Progressives to form the Liberal party.[32]

Herut, the Liberals and several small parties and movements formed the Likud bloc in 1973 (later the Likud party). Likud won the 1977 elections, partly because of delayed dissatisfaction with Labor's management of the 1973 war, and also because of dissatisfaction with the "protection, cronyism and ever-increasing corruption" cited earlier. Begin won with

---

[31] Cited in Fuksman.

[32] Goldstein, p. 295 [Hebrew]; Knesset website, Knesset Elections Results, http://www. knesset.gov.il/description/eng/eng_mimshal_res.htm (26 April 2021). Some of the prominent leaders are these parties included Daniel Auster, Eliahu Berligne, Peretz Bernstein, Itzhak Greenbaum, Israel Rokach and Likud finance ministers Simcha Ehrlich and Moshe Nissim.

the support of the country's poor and middle class, and especially the discriminated-against Sephardic Jews from Arab countries.

Begin changed the country's economic agenda. Arguably, his two major economic policies were the cancellation of state controls over foreign currency, so that Israelis could for the first time buy and own foreign currency, and Project Renewal. The first policy liberalized the economy but led in the immediate term to runaway inflation, labor disputes and near chaos. Fuksman believes Begin underestimated the power of the bureaucrats and state- or party-backed monopolies, which prevented the hoped-for further liberalization of the economy and interfered with Begin's every move (Fuksman-Shaal, 2008: 35).[33] Plessner disagrees, and believes inflation was already in progress and the monetary system was "increasingly out of control" even before Begin's moves; these moves, Plessner writes, only exacerbated the problems, since Begin refrained from making the major institutional changes in the economy that would have reformed labor relations and freed the private sector from its dependence on the government (Plessner, 1993: 220–223).

The second economic policy innovation was more successful; instead of politicians trying to "buy" the poor Sephardim with bribes for votes or with jobs for the few, they tried to empower them. Begin involved the poor in the renewal of their own neighborhoods, seeking their ideas, input and assistance, and money raised from abroad went to specific projects rather than the government's general coffers.

Perhaps Begin fell victim not only to the Labor-controlled economy but also to political events. Egyptian President Anwar Sadat came to Jerusalem six months after Begin's election and Begin spent two hard years negotiating peace accords with him. This was followed by the at-first successful battles in Lebanon against the PLO, then the local and international outrage over the Christian massacre of refugees in Lebanon on Israel's watch, and the traumatic destruction of the Israeli city of Yamit in the Sinai before the Sinai was given to Egypt. Begin's economic agenda had to take a back seat. This problem has plagued almost all Israeli prime

---

[33] Indeed, the Histadrut at the time represented almost every employee in the country, including state employees at a time when the state ran the economy; to get medical coverage most Israelis had to join the Histadrut. Strikes were so rife and the country so unable to function that one of Begin's finance ministers, Yigal Hurwitz, called to the state employees demanding raises and those who supported them, "madmen, come down from the roofs."

ministers. They spend most of their time on foreign rather than domestic policy.

9. Recent History: Private Initiatives

Following the economic problems of the 1980s and then the economic stabilization plan of 1985, which moved even the Labor party toward markets, the idea of economic liberty in Israel has been carried mainly by private individuals and their non-profit organizations and a few public officials. Though the socialist system — its state- and labor-owned industries, *kibbutz* settlements, even its newspapers and bureaucracy — was essentially bankrupt and could not survive on its own anymore, bureaucracies and special interests, as well as the adherents of ideologies, did not acknowledge this. So the newspapers and parliamentary halls of Israel became a battleground for the minds of the public and the hearts of policymakers. Israel's state-backed think tanks have always promoted various forms of collectivist economics. Several private think tanks have offered an alternative: Daniel Doron's Israel Center for Economic and Social Progress, Robert Loewenberg's Institute for Advanced Strategic and Political Studies, and Robert and Corinne Sauer's Jerusalem Institute for Market Studies. The analysis and micro-economic studies published by these think tanks, as well as the cadres of young economists trained by them who are now teaching, employed in local industry or making policy in the government, allowed policymakers who understood the need for market-based policy to enact it.[34]

---

[34] In addition, a number of individuals, organizations and websites promote capitalism or explore liberal economic thought. Some of these are: the students of Ayn Rand in Israel, an organization associated with the Ayn Rand Institute, which manages a website called Anochi; a website called Kav Yashar; blogs called Hakapitalist Hayomi, Hazir Kapitalisti, and Al kalkala Vehofesh; Professor Noah Nissani's website; Uriel Lynn, a former member of Knesset from the Likud's Liberal wing and now president of the Federation of the Israeli Chambers of Commerce; and some political movements that have supported various aspects of liberty, such as Rafael Eitan's Tsomet party and the Shinui party (neither are represented today in the Knesset), the Tenua Haliberalit Hahadasha (founded in 2011, non-parliamentary) and Moshe Feiglin's Manhigut Yehudit section in the Likud. Their role in educating the public deserves mention. Eitan's Tsomet party once ran on a flat tax platform and Eitan, as minister of agriculture, opened the dairy sector to competition and market forces.

10. Netanyahu

One such political figure is the former prime minister, Benjamin Netanyahu. Netanyahu is the son of Benzion Netanyahu; he grew up in the Jabotinsky movement; and he inherited the leadership of Menachem Begin's Herut/Likud party.

In August 2011, Netanyahu explained to the Knesset his affinity for Jabotinsky's economic outlook:

He said that ownership, and I quote, was "something that is organically inherent in the very idea of civilian freedom."

So beyond the duty that a country has to take care of its citizens' basic needs, Jabotinsky clearly wrote, "An economy must be free. The state should stop poverty, but cannot limit success and the pursuit of happiness, which is the result of success." "Struggle and ambition," he said — and by ambition, he meant entrepreneurship — "an effort that is the result of an individual's talent and competition in all fields: these add flavor to life and without them, life is not worth living."

Jabotinsky believed in a competitive market. In other words, he believed that not only was competition desirous from an economic standpoint, but it was also just as it is part of an individual's freedom of action, and above all else, Jabotinsky believed in the freedom of the individual. The truth is that competitive markets contributed more to extricating people from the cycle of poverty and increasing the standard of living than any other economic method in human history ....

At the same time, however, it is important to define what a competitive market is, because in an open economy, as the result of competition, a state of lack of competition can be created. What begins as a competitive market can later be closed off by monopolies and cartels. In this situation, a government must encourage competition. By encouraging competition, I mean, first and foremost, in the private sector — which carries everything else, let there be no mistake. It, the companies, creates most of the added value. Businesspeople are an integral part of our economy. They fund security, and they finance the elementary needs.

The government does not create money; it consumes money, and the main added value comes from the private sector. We want to ensure that it operates from a competitive place, rather than from a lack of competitiveness. Therefore, the government must encourage competition, but there is no need, nor does it make sense to limit entrepreneurship and individual competitiveness. On the contrary, if a need exists, it is the need to fight against those who are trying, through various means, to unfairly limit competition. Limiting competition almost always is at the expense of the citizen — in the guise of higher prices, shortages and substandard service.[35]

During Netanyahu's first term as prime minister in the late 1990s, he privatized or set in motion the privatization of the state-owned banks and told the US Congress that Israel no longer wanted economic aid and would work to reduce it. Netanyahu was replaced as prime minister by Labor's Ehud Barak, who reversed course, and then by the Likud's Ariel Sharon, who appointed Netanyahu his finance minister. In that position, and apparently with Sharon's full backing, Netanyahu freed the economy of its socialist chains. His policies were much criticized from the right and left — he gave the bankrupt Histadrut pension funds and the Histadrut-dominated ports too much taxpayer money, or, alternately, he left the poor to suffer the results of his liberalization — but he essentially saved the economy, which was almost bankrupt and faced an imminent reduction of its credit rating. He cut taxes, bailed out the socialist institutions but ensured they would from then function on economic bases and no longer drain the public coffers, sold state-owned enterprises and cut foreign aid to Israel. Under his stewardship, foreign investment poured into Israel as aid became less important, growth soared, and Israel was in a good position to weather the economic crises that have afflicted most of the world's advanced economies over the past years.

Brandeis wrote in his dissent asserting the right of civilized men to be let alone by the government, when he warned of "insidious encroachment" by well-meaning men of zeal, that "Experience should teach us to be most on our guard to protect liberty when the Government's purposes are beneficent ...."[36] Given that four of the five sectors providing what the pro-market side of Zionism has referred to as basic needs (housing, education, health and food; excluding only clothing) are even now dominated in Israel by state monopolies or cartels, ending state

---

[35] Benjamin Netanyahu, speech to the Knesset, 1 August 2011, http://www.pmo.gov.il/PMOEng/Communication/PMSpeaks/speechjabu010811.htm [August 2011].

[36] Louis Brandeis, dissent, *Olmstead v. United States*, 277 U.S. 438, 479 (1928), 478–479, http://scholar.google.com/scholar_case?case=5577544660194763070&q=277%2BU.S.%2B438&hl=en&as_sdt=1002#r[12] (26 April 2021).

intervention in these markets would cost taxpayers nothing, allow further tax cuts, reduce bureaucracy, lower prices and free Israelis to display the entrepreneurship so praised by Herzl, Jabotinsky and Begin, as well as freeing Israelis from the burdens of big government, big business and big labor.

11. Conclusion

History is not at an end. The fight for liberty is one of the noblest human endeavors and the Zionist liberation movement is one of the noblest political movements in history. Its image was for a time hijacked by those who essentially to some extent opposed liberty — both national and individual liberty. If Israel is to succeed politically it will have to succeed economically, and act boldly in both spheres to protect the property, lives and liberty of Israelis.

My purpose has not been to portray Zionism as committed to the ideas of Milton Friedman or Friedrich Hayek. Zionism's times and concerns were different. The point is that a commitment to individual political, religious and economic liberty was part of the Zionist plan from the beginning and has contributed greatly to its success, and will of necessity be drawn on to ensure its future success.

References

Aharoni, Y. (1993). "The Israeli Economy: A Retrospective View," *IASPS Policy Studies*, 16, 1–2, 13, 18–19.

Ahimeir, A. (1955). "From the Notebook of a Fascist," *Herut*, 15 August.

Ahimeir, A. (1949). "Twarda and Gilboa: Two Meetings with Yair," *Herut*, 27 May.

Albright, W. F. *et al.* (1947). *Palestine: A Study of Jewish, Arab and British Policies*, Vol. 1. New Haven: Yale University Press.

Arad, B. (2010). "Holocaust Survivors Benefits in Israel," JIMS Position Paper, pp. 3–4 [Hebrew].

Begin, Menahem (1951). *Life View, National View*. Tel Aviv: Betar.

Brandeis, L. (1942). "Speech to Knights of Zion," 2 January 1916, *Brandeis on Zionism*. Washington: ZOA.

Cohen, M. (1954). Crisis of Leadership, *Sulam* 58.

Doron, D. (2007). "Theodor Herzl's Vision Betrayed," *Jerusalem Post*, 21 May.

Feldberg, M. (2002). "Louis D. Brandeis and American Zionism," The Jewish Federations of North America, http://www.jewishfederations.org/page. aspx?id=53583.

Finkelstein (Harel-Harari), K. (2003). "A Solution to Public Sector Strikes — Using the Agreed Arbitration Institute Efficiently," *IASPS Policy Studies*, 55.

Fraenkel, J. (2004). "Louis D. Brandeis 1856–1941: Patriot, Judge, and Zionist," www.doingzionism.org.

Fuksman-Shaal, M. (2008). "The Economic Revolution in Israel — From Socialism to a Free Market," *Hauma*, 174, 25.

Gazit, Y. (June 2011). "Mandatory Labor Arbitration," JIMS Position Paper.

Gazit, Y. and Golan, Z. (June 2010). "Building New Communities in Israel's Periphery," JIMS Position Paper.

Golan, Z. (2011). *Stern: The Man and His Gang*. Tel Aviv: Yair, pp. 21–22.

Goldstein, A. "The Decline of the General Zionists and the Failure of a Liberal Alternative," *Studies in the Revival of Israel*, 16, 295.

Heitner, Uri (Nov. 2010). The Political and Social Thought of Jabotinsky, https://heitner.wordpress.com/2010/11/page/3/ [26 April 2021].

Jabotinsky, Z. (1933). "Class," *Betar*, 1, 123–130, Ch. 3.

Jabotinsky, Z. (1958). "Introduction to Economic Thought," in *Nation and Society (Selected Essays)*, E. Pedatsur (ed.). Tel Aviv: Shilton Betar.

Jabotinsky, Z. (1930). "The Jubilee Idea," *Nation and Society (Selected Essays)*, E. Pedatsur (ed.). Tel Aviv: Shilton Betar, 37.

Jabotinsky, Z. (1958). *Tirgumin, Shirei Zion, Shirei Chol*. Jerusalem: Eri Jabotinsky.

Knesset website, Knesset Elections Results.

Lebel, U. (2007). *The Road to the Pantheon*. Jerusalem: Carmel, 237.

Libo, K. and Skakun, M. (2011). "Clash of the Titans: Stephen S. Wise vs. Abba Hillel Silver," Part 2, The Center for Jewish History, http://cjh.org/p/52.

Netanyahu, Benjamin (1 August 2011). Knesset speech. http://www.pmo.gov.il/PMOEng/Communication/PMSpeaks/speechjabu010811.htm [August 2011].

Netanyahu, B. (1934). "More on the Essence of the JNF," *Betar*, 2, 392–396.

Niv, D. (1965). *Battles of the Irgun Zvai Leumi*, Vol. 1. Tel Aviv: Mossad Klausner.

Plessner, Y. (1993). *The Political Economy of Israel*. Albany: SUNY.

Rabushka, A. (2001). "On Economic Freedom," *Globes*. 28 January.

Svorai, M. (1988). "The Jerusalem Cell," in *Hinenu Sicaricim*, Joseph Ahimeir and Shmuel Shatzky (eds.). Tel Aviv: Nitzanim.

Urofsky, M. (2009). *Louis D. Brandeis: A Life*. New York: Pantheon.

Yevin, Y. (1950–1951). "The Histadrut State Has an Outlet to the Sea," *Sulam*, 21.

Yevin, Y. (1933). The Incarnations of Hashomer Hatzair, *Betar*, Vol. 1.

Chapter 12

Jewish Economic Theory and Reflections on Practice

Robert M. Sauer

Royal Holloway, University of London, London, UK
robert.sauer@rhul.ac.uk

Abstract

In this chapter, I question the plausibility of the standard theory that Judaism impacts the belief system of American Jews in such a way that it explains their voting tendencies in the US political elections. The fundamental problem with the conventional wisdom is that Judaism is not clearly a set of principles that endorses income redistribution and other social programs that are flagships of the progressive movement in America. In fact, the opposite can also be coherently argued, i.e., that Judaism is a system of thought that aligns itself with the basic principles of economic liberalism.

Keywords: Judaism, Religion, Economics, Voting Behavior, Economic Liberalism

1. Introduction

A central paradox that is often noted in American politics is that, on average, American Jews tenaciously refuse to be part of any empirical regularity that links higher income levels with more conservative, or economically liberal political positions. Many different sources of data indicate that American Jews earn per capita almost twice as much as non-Jews. Yet, they are between 33 and 50 percent less likely than American Catholics and Protestants to identify themselves as politically conservative or supporters of the free market (Windmueller, 2003).

One of the most popular answers as to why this might be the case refers to the impact Judaism has on the belief system of American Jews, and Judaism's emphasis on aggressively pursuing social justice (Fuchs, 1956). The conventional wisdom is that Judaism not only motivates Jews to be highly educated and succeed professionally but to also aggressively support progressive social policies and other forms of government intervention for shaping an ideal society.

In this chapter, I question the plausibility of the standard theory. In my view, the fundamental problem with the conventional wisdom is that it is not at all clear that Judaism is a set of principles that endorses income redistribution and other social programs that are flagships of the progressive movement in America. In fact, the opposite can also be coherently argued, i.e., that Judaism is a system of thought that aligns itself with the basic principles of economic liberalism.

As just one example of the harmony rather than the discord between Judaism and economic liberalism, which is elaborated upon later on, consider the Jewish commandment of Tzedakah. Tzedakah, which means justice, requires every Jew to donate at least 10 percent of their annual income to help support the poor. But Tzedakah does not proscribe a public policy of involuntary taxation and non-contingent monetary handouts for the unemployed.

Rather, Maimonides, the great medieval Jewish philosopher and codifier of Jewish law, holds that the most praiseworthy and effective means of fulfilling the commandment of Tzedakah is through offering an impoverished person a business partnership, a business loan or a job. Therefore, one might think that Jews would be located on the "Right" when it comes to Wisconsin-style welfare reform. The Prime Minister of Israel, Benjamin Netanyahu, apparently understood this connection well. Speaking on the benefits of workfare reform in Israel, Netanyahu was once quoted in the press as saying that it is not enough to be a Thatcherite; a Jew should go even further and be a Maimonidite.

The rest of this chapter is organized as follows. In Section 2, I analyze survey data that helps empirically establish that American Jews have a tendency to shun economic liberalism at the political level. In Section 3, I posit five axioms that begin to lay the foundations for a general Jewish economic theory. Section 4 develops the public policy implications of this new Jewish economic theory. After ruling out Judaism as a plausible explanation for Jewish political persuasions in America, Section 5 considers an alternative hypothesis that has nothing to do with Judaism *per se*. Section 6 of the chapter summarizes and concludes.

2. The Political Preferences of American Jews

Is it true that American Jews overwhelmingly identify with a political agenda of government intervention in the economy and progressive social programs? One way to address this question is to examine data on voting outcomes from surveys of American Jewry, sponsored by the American Jewish Committee. Table 1 displays the percentage of the Jewish vote that went to the Democratic and Republican candidates in presidential elections between 1916 and 2004. The data after 2004 do not change the basic results.

The table indicates that American Jews have heavily supported the Democratic candidate in the overwhelming majority of presidential elections since 1924. The only elections in which there was less than a 20 percent spread in favor of the Democrats was 1916, 1920 and the race between Reagan, Carter and Anderson in 1980. The average percentage of American Jews voting for the Democratic candidate during this time period is 70.5 percent, while the average percentage voting for the Republican candidate is 24.5 percent.

Are American Jews moving away in recent years from their traditionally heavy support of the Democratic Party? In order to help detect movements over time, I fit a polynomial trend through the voting percentage data reported in Table 1. Figure 1 displays the raw data and the estimated trends.

As the estimated trends (fitted values) starkly illustrate, there was a widening gap in favor of the Democrats after the 1920 elections. Subsequent to the elections in 1944, the trends reversed direction. The percentage going to the Democrats and the percentage going to the Republicans began to slowly converge, even if the Democrats still commanded the overwhelming majority of the Jewish vote. However, the modest gains of the Republicans ceased starting in 1992. The recent trends indicate a return to wider gaps in favor of the Democrats.

Table 1:   American Jewish Voting Percentages, 1916–2004

Year	Republican	Democrat
1916	45	55
1920	43	19
1924	27	51
1928	28	72
1932	18	82
1936	15	85
1940	10	90
1944	10	90
1948	10	75
1952	36	64
1956	40	60
1960	18	82
1964	10	90
1968	17	81
1972	35	65
1976	27	71
1980	39	45
1984	31	67
1988	35	64
1992	11	80
1996	16	78
2000	19	79
2004	24	76
Average	24.5	70.5

Data on a range of other political preference measures tell a similar story. American Jewish support for increased government spending on education is quite high and on an upward trend. Between the years 1970 and 1982, 65 percent of American Jews favored greater public spending on education, while between 1991 and 2002, the figure was 82 percent. Support for greater levels of public welfare spending grew from 18 percent in the 1970s to 26 percent in the 1990s. There is also relatively little heterogeneity in the political preferences of American Jews.

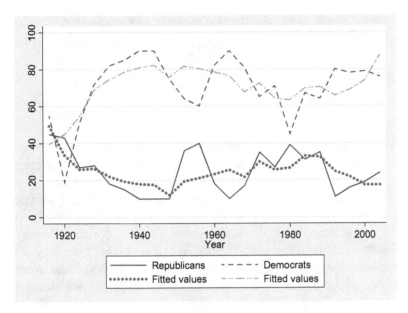

Figure 1: American Jewish Voting Trends, 1916–2004

Jewish support for the American liberal agenda is mostly unaffected by income level, education, religiosity or place of residence (see Greenberg and Wald, 2001).

But perhaps American Jews are not any different from "similar" American non-Jews in their aversion to a free market political agenda. A comparison of this type is rather important because American Jews have socioeconomic characteristics that are, on average, different from the American population as a whole. These socioeconomic characteristics might be highly correlated with political preferences, irrespective of religious affiliation.

The distinctiveness of American Jews in terms of socioeconomic characteristics can be empirically documented by analyzing data from the General Social Surveys (GSS) conducted by the National Opinion Research Center at the University of Chicago. According to these surveys, American Jews are the most educated ethnic group in the United States. Their average number of years of education is 15.7 as opposed to 13.2 for the American population as a whole. Further, 62 percent of American Jews are college graduates, compared to only 23 percent among

Table 2:   Political Preferences of Similar Jews and Non-Jews

	Jews (Percent)	Non-Jews (Percent)
Identify as Democrats	60	39
Supported Democratic Candidates for the House	76	54

all Americans. American Jews also work in occupations with higher occupational prestige rankings. The Jewish occupational prestige average is 51.9 compared to 43.2 for non-Jews.

Higher levels of education and employment in more prestigious occupations result in American Jews exceeding all other ethnic/racial groups in the US in terms of household income. In 1986 dollars, the average household income of Jews is $58,900, 70 percent higher than the average income of all American households. Jewish per capita income averages $27,500, which is 95 percent higher than the per capita income of American non-Jews.

Therefore, in order to more firmly establish a "Jewish affiliation effect," above and beyond the effect of education, occupation and income on attitudes toward economic liberalism, it is necessary to control for all of these other factors. Accordingly, Table 2 compares political preferences between Jews and non-Jews who are all white, college-educated, urban and middle-aged.

The 21 percent difference between Jews and non-Jews in identification as Democrats and the 22 percent difference in votes cast for Democratic candidates for the House of Representatives, after controlling for a number of important socioeconomic characteristics, strongly suggest an independent role for religious affiliation.[1]

3. Jewish Economic Theory

The simple empirical analysis of the political preferences of American Jews, performed in Section 2, suggests that there is a statistical basis for

---

[1] A more thorough identification of the Jewish affiliation effect on voting behavior (or political preferences in general) could be accomplished via regression analysis. Of course, one has to worry about endogeneity problems. Nonetheless, the basic story is unaffected when performing standard OLS regressions.

claiming that Jews have a strong distaste for economic liberalism. This is quite a paradox since it is also well known that Jews have benefited a great deal over the centuries from the operation of free markets and competitive capitalism.

Milton Friedman, in his 1972 address to the Mont Pelerin Society, (Friedman, 1988) appealed to basic economic theory to explain why Jews, as well as other minorities, generally derive great benefits from free market systems. Friedman said, "Wherever there is a monopoly, whether it be private or governmental, there is room for the application of arbitrary criteria in the selection of the beneficiaries of the monopoly — whether these criteria be the color of skin, religion, national origin or what not. Where there is free competition only performance counts. The market is color blind. No one who goes to the market to buy bread knows or cares whether the wheat was grown by a Jew, Catholic, Protestant, Muslim or atheist; by whites or blacks."

Friedman also made the empirical observation that Jews can be disproportionately found working in industries and professions that are characterized by free entry, as opposed to industries and professions that require government licensing or franchise. Examples range from Jewish representation in international banking during the time that the Church restricted these activities among Christians, to more recent Jewish representation in retail trade, law, medicine and accounting. When government permission is required to enter into a particular industry or profession, Jews will be discriminated against and suffer the consequences of anti-Semitism. When there is free entry, well-functioning capital markets and the potential for entrepreneurship, the rules of the "color" blind market will benefit all.

Perhaps the key to understanding why Jews have a political aversion to free market policies, despite the great personal benefit derived from free markets, lies in the cognitive dissonance produced by the support for socialism inherent in Judaism? On those thinkers that tried to link Judaism and socialism in the past, Rabbi Meir Tamari, a prominent Jewish scholar and former economist with the Bank of Israel writes, "the widespread identification of Jewish social thinking with that of socialism is, however, the product of either ignorance of the source material, or willful distortion." Tamari further states, in *The Challenge of Wealth*, "Socialism that denies private property and wealth creation is irreconcilable with Jewish theology." Tamari believes that private property and wealth accumulation are the cornerstones of Jewish economic theory (Tamari, 1995).

Admittedly, there has been very little work by orthodox Jewish scholars on the relationship between socialism, capitalism and Judaism.[2]
However, I believe, from my reading of the relevant literature, that it is
possible to posit five basic axioms of Jewish economic theory from which
many economic policy implications can be deduced. Although not
exhaustive, my five axioms represent, to the best of my knowledge, the
first attempt to formulate a parsimonious list of basic principles which
help systematize the foundations of Jewish economic theory.

3.1 *Participation in the creative process*

The first axiom of Jewish economic theory that I posit is "Man is created
in G-d's image." In Judaism, this statement is interpreted as meaning that
G-d is the creator of the world, and Man is the creator in the world. Man
was given a divine essence in order to be a partner with G-d in the act of
creation (Babylonian Talmud Shabbat 10a). The Midrash says, "All that
was created during the six days that God created the world still requires
work" (Freedman and Simon, 1983, Genesis Rabba 11:6). G-d gave Man
an incomplete world, and Man is supposed to help perfect it through
domination of material resources, work and innovation.

In Genesis 1:28, where G-d says to Adam and Eve: "Be fruitful, and
multiply, and replenish the earth, and subdue it: and have dominion over
the fish of the sea, and over the fowl of the air, and over every living thing
that moved upon the earth," the Rabbis interpreted these words as a commandment for Man to develop and improve the incomplete world. G-d
created wheat but Man must work and innovate and produce bread out of
the grain. Along these lines, the Midrash recalls the story of Rabbi Akiva
who placed grain and bread before a General and asked him which one he
would prefer to eat (Singer *et al.*, 1901–1906, Tanhuma Tazriah 19). In
Judaism, work, creative activity and innovation are the avenues through
which the divine image is expressed.

3.2 *Protection of private property*

The second axiom of Jewish economic theory that I posit is that private
property rights are essential and must be protected. Man was given the

---

[2]The chief Rabbi of Great Britain, Jonathan Sacks, has also written on Judaism and economics and has come to similar conclusions as Tamari (see Sacks, 1985). See also Lifshitz
(2004).

potential to create, but the Jewish sages clearly recognized that Man will only dominate the material world, work and innovate if there is the ability to appropriate the fruits of one's labor. To motivate Man to fulfill the commandment to participate in the act of creation, the granting and uncompromising protection of private property was recognized to be essential.

Note that two of the Ten Commandments directly relate to the safeguarding of private property; "you shall not steal" and "you shall not covet anything that belongs to your neighbor." The prohibition against stealing not only includes outright robbery but also various forms of theft by deception and unethical business practices, like the use of false weights in a transaction. The second prohibition goes further and prohibits Jews to covet the possessions of others, even if there is no unlawful acquisition of property. The punishment for violation of the commandments is quite harsh, demonstrating the overriding importance of private property in the Jewish tradition. In fact, the flood in the time of Noah is understood by the Rabbis as a punishment for sins against private property.

The protection of private property is sacred even in the case of war (Singer *et al.*, 1901–1906, Bava Kama 60b). The prophet Samuel, in his famous speech on the dangers of monarchy, warns against the constant temptation of kings to expropriate persons and property for public purposes (Tsumura, 2007, I Samuel 8). In this context, the Torah also warns against the evil inclination of kings to overtax the people.

3.3 *The accumulation of wealth*

The third axiom of Jewish economic theory that I posit is that the accumulation of wealth is a virtue not a vice. Man is obligated to participate in the creative process, does not face incentive incompatibility problems related to the lack of protection of private property, and is blessed when the outcome of honest labor is the accumulation of wealth.

The Talmud teaches, "One who benefits from his own labour is greater than one who fears heaven" (Singer, *et al.*, 1901–1906, Berachot 8a; Telushkin, 1991, Avot 4:1). In the Torah, productive and virtuous workers are repeatedly rewarded with great wealth. The Torah describes in great detail the riches of the patriarchs, Abraham, Isaac and Jacob. Wealth, accumulated honestly, is a signal of great effort, skill and success in partnering with G-d in the creative process. The wealthy individual has been unusually successful in elevating the material world and in expressing the divine image.

The Talmud sages regard the refusal to attempt to benefit from one's labor and accumulate wealth as dangerous behavior that can lead to craziness.[3] A particularly strong statement against idleness can be found in the writings of Maimonides. Maimonides claims that "whomsoever has in his heart that he shall indulge in the study of Torah and do no work but rather be sustained from charity, defames the Lord's name, cheapens the Torah, extinguishes the light of faith, causes himself ill and removes himself from the world to come" (Twersky, 1972, Mishneh Torah Laws of Oaths and Vow 8:13). Maimonides' statement is aimed at individuals who choose religious learning over working. Considering that learning Torah is itself a religious obligation, one can easily infer how much stronger his words would be for someone who chooses only leisure, whether that individual be rich or poor.[4]

Consider also the Jewish view on the lack of wealth, or poverty. Rabbi Jonathan Sacks writes that the consensus among rabbinical sources is clear; poverty is an "unmitigated evil, worse than 50 plagues." Even for the sake of helping the poor, impoverishing oneself and living an ascetic lifestyle is prohibited. In the Mishneh Torah, Maimonides regards asceticism as foolish (Maimonides, 2003). Moreover, the Rabbis forbid individuals to give more than a fifth of their possessions to charitable causes, regardless of their level of wealth (Boruchovich, 2015, Karo, Shulchan Aruch, Yoreh De'ah 249:1). This is for fear that, by giving too much, one may eventually become impoverished.

The praiseworthiness of wealth accumulation in no way implies that Judaism is not interested in the plight of the poor. All individuals are required to help the poorest members of society through charitable gifts. But the gift-giving obligation, called Tzedakah, is more subtle than, and should not be confused with, income redistribution. Income redistribution

---

[3] Some opinions place religious study, which is also a commandment, above the obligation to work. The idea of "Torah as a trade" is present in the literature and a minority of opinions recommend that scholars should be subsidized by the community to be able to continue their learning. However, this is only applicable to Torah scholars and is not considered idleness. For laymen, "Torah is not a trade" and work is the virtue that will better enhance their moral development.

[4] Schnall (2001) reviews "work related statements" in Jewish sources and finds that 84 percent reflect a "high esteem of work and craft," and that most of the statements reflect an intrinsic value placed on labor rather than having value merely as a vehicle for sustenance.

aims at reducing income inequalities because income disparities are seen as unfair or immoral. This is not the Jewish view.

3.4 *Caring for the needy*

The fourth axiom of Jewish economic theory that I posit is the obligation to care for the needy through charitable giving. The Torah mentions the commandment to give charity (Tzedakah, literally justice) in parashat Re'eh: "You should not harden your heart or shut your hand from your needy brother" (Kaplan, 1981, Deuteronomy 15:7–8). The role of Man in the world is not only to work, create, innovate, accumulate wealth and elevate the material world but also to care for those in need. As Maimonides explains in the *Guide for the Perplexed*, "we do perform an act of Tzedakah when we fulfill those duties towards our fellow men which our moral conscience imposes upon us; e.g., when we heal the wounds of the sufferer" (Maimonides, 1956).

In order to understand the Jewish view of charity, it is useful to recognize that in Judaism behavior is regulated by two kinds of commandments; commandments that fall under the heading of Man to G-d and commandments that fall under the heading of Man to Man. For example, dietary restrictions are commandments in the Man to G-d category. These are moral principles. Regulations on proper business transactions are examples of commandments in the Man to Man category. These are considered to be legal principles. Charity belongs to the first category of commandments, making it a moral principle, not a legal one.

This distinction is very important because where legal principles are at issue, property rights can be violated to comply with the law. For example, if one causes damages to another individual, he is obliged to relinquish part of his property rights and pay just compensation. If he does not comply, the judges can seize his property to fully compensate the injured party. Because charity is defined as a moral principle these types of rules of expropriation do not fully apply. The implication is that in a society with large income disparities, one cannot take from the wealthy to redistribute to the poor. The poor cannot legally claim damages and expropriate the property of the wealthy.

In the past, during times of widespread poverty in Jewish communities, Rabbis have been known to dispatch charity collectors who compelled community members to give at least 10 percent, but no more than 20 percent, of their income to charity. This might be seen as contradicting the aforementioned argument. However, this ruling does not constitute a Jewish endorsement of forced income redistribution for reasons of what is commonly thought of today as "social justice."

The goal of the Rabbis in these cases was not to achieve an optimal distribution of income within the community, because income disparities are immoral. Rather, the goal was to achieve an optimal level of individual religiosity (see Lifshitz, 2004). In Judaism, economic disparities reflect fundamental differences among individuals in preferences, motivations and abilities, an unavoidable heterogeneity. The Torah says, "For the poor shall never cease out of the land" (Kaplan, 1981, Deuteronomy 15:11). Eradicating income inequality is impossible and not the goal in Judaism. It is the absolute standard of living of the poor that is at issue. Not their relative position *vis-à-vis* the wealthy. The commandment of Tzedakah is about shoring up one's character, or one's individual morality, by caring for the poor through voluntary, limited gift-giving.

3.5 *Limited government*

The fifth axiom of Jewish economic theory that I posit is the inefficiency of government and the dangers of concentrated power. The Torah repeatedly warns about the evil nature of government and bureaucracy. The main warning is issued in the book of Samuel when the Israelites request a king. "Fine: if you want a king, I will give you a king. You have rejected me; therefore, I will give you a merely human king and all the bureaucracy that such a monarch entails. But know this: when you bitterly complain to me after your king's bureaucracy reduces not only the size of your wealth, but also the size of your household, my ears will be deaf to your cries. You have rejected my decentralized political order; consequently, I will reject your bitter complaints at the burdens of the centralized political order entailed by the human bureaucracy for which you lust" (Tsumura, 2007, I Samuel 8:7–18).

Rabbi Sacks has compared the words of the prophet Samuel to Friedrich Hayek's warning in *The Road to Serfdom* (Hayek, 1944). Simply stated, when governments play an important role in allocating resources in society, when they map out a plan of how the economy should be run, we will face ever-increasing degrees of oppression, in order to meet the goals of the plan. To effectively combat these natural evils of government design and control, Judaism prescribes that kings should have strictly limited tasks. The monarchy's functions are to be clearly defined and constrained by Jewish law.

As an example of the constraints placed on government behavior in Judaism, consider that kings were not permitted to take control of people's lives by dictating where they could not live or what types of jobs they should take. Moreover, taxation cannot be confiscatory, arbitrary or discriminatory. There is also no basis for taxation as a means of redistributing income.

4. Policy Implications

Although I have alluded to several economic policy implications in the discussion of the five axioms of Jewish economic theory, in this section I will explicitly assess two economic policies that are of central importance throughout the world today and are quite controversial. First, I will offer a Jewish analysis of flat-rate tax systems. Second, I will examine, from the Jewish perspective, recent initiatives in welfare reform. In both cases, I will point out the connection between these policies and the axioms of Jewish economic theory that was posited above.

4.1 *A flat-rate tax system*

The flat tax first appears in the Torah in the book of Genesis. When Abraham arrives in the kingdom of Salem he agrees to "give him (the King) a tenth of everything." (Kaplan, 1981, Genesis 14:18–20) The same flat-rate tax appears again in the book of Leviticus when the Mosaic Law is announced. A flat tax of 10 percent, called tithing, is to be levied on all individuals in order to support the priests in charge of the Temple (Kaplan, 1981, Leviticus 27:30–32 and Singer *et al.*, 1901–1906, Malachi 3:10).

The priests were performing a moral service for the community and the community was deemed to be responsible for their support and well-being. The Torah apparently saw the service of the priests in the Temple as a public good. Under normal circumstances, no one could be excluded from benefiting from the service of the priests, and the service could be spiritually "consumed" by one person without diminishing the amount consumed by others. As is widely accepted throughout the economic ideological spectrum, the provision of public goods usually requires public financing.

After the destruction of the Temple and the cessation of the priestly service, Jews were still obligated to give (to tithe) a minimum of 10 percent of their income to charitable causes. The tithing of 10 percent applied to every member of the community regardless of their level and source of income. Even the poorest individuals who are sustained by charitable giving are obligated to tithe 10 percent of their receipts. This is consistent with the understanding of Tzedakah discussed in the fourth axiom. Tzedakah is an issue of individual morality which is not aimed at reducing income inequalities. Moreover, since Jewish tithing does not contain a threshold income level under which individuals do not have to give (pay taxes), one could say that the Jewish flat-tax position is stricter than most flat-tax systems in effect in Eastern Europe today.

Of course, Judaism is also concerned with fairness. Why is it that the flat-rate tax is considered to be fair? In Judaism, fairness is understood as equal treatment in a process, where an individual's income or wealth does not imply special consideration. Equal treatment in the process is the important aspect of fairness, not equal outcomes at the end of the process. Since all individuals face the same tax rate in a flat-rate tax system, they are treated in the same way regardless of their income or wealth. Note that a flat-rate tax system still results in unequal outcomes. Individuals with higher incomes are treated the same way as those with lower incomes, but they pay more taxes in absolute terms.

In stark contrast to flat tax systems, progressive tax systems punish individuals who accumulate more wealth. A wealthy person keeps less of every extra dollar earned in a progressive system. But, as discussed in the third axiom, the accumulation of wealth is a virtue, not a vice. Progressive tax systems are, therefore, not consistent with Jewish economic theory.

Another considerable advantage of flat tax systems from the Jewish perspective is that they limit the scope of government, and are less conducive to corruption. Flat tax systems, strictly applied, reduce the power of politicians and lobbyists to choose winners and losers through politically based tax exemptions. Support for a strict flat universal tax rate policy follows naturally from the fifth axiom of limited government and the dangers of concentrated power.

Because in a flat-rate tax system, as in all tax systems, paying taxes is not on a voluntary basis, the flat tax does violate one's property rights. This contradicts the second axiom on the importance of protecting private property rights. However, a flat tax rate of 10 percent is quite low, and the lower the rate, the less is the violation.[5] Therefore, it might be that the flat

---

[5] Russia and Ukraine have flat rates of 13 percent on personal income. This is the lowest flat-rate tax among the countries in the former Soviet bloc that have adopted the flat tax system since the beginning of the 1990s.

tax is fixed at the relatively low level of 10 percent in the Torah because it minimizes the extent of the expropriation of private property.

Finally, to the extent that a low universal flat-rate tax is growth enhancing, and there is much speculation that these tax systems have done wonders for Eastern European economies, the flat tax creates new employment opportunities enabling differentially more individuals to participate in the creative process (the first axiom).

4.2 *Welfare reform*

Passage of the US Social Security Act of 1935 created the welfare program known as Assistance to Families with Dependent Children (AFDC). AFDC was mainly a monetary hand-out program and was the primary avenue for public assistance to low-income families and single mothers in the US for more than 60 years.

AFDC was considered by many to be a failure, as it became increasingly characterized by long-term use of public assistance, or welfare dependency, and increasing rates of welfare take-up. Around the time substantial welfare reforms were implemented in 1996, reforms embodied in the Personal Responsibility and Work Opportunity Reconciliation Act (PRWORA), there was a spectacular drop in welfare caseloads and a sharp increase in the labor force participation rate of single mothers.

However, despite the apparent success of the reforms contained in PRWORA, there is no consensus that the new mode of public assistance is desirable. Under PRWORA, public assistance was substantially decentralized. The federal government reduced its involvement in welfare administration by offering block grants to individual states, and allowing them to determine eligibility for public assistance as well as what the types of cash support programs they preferred. Work requirements for the receipt of benefits, time limits on benefits and outright denial of benefits to individuals who were deemed "work-ready" also became possible for the first time.

How are these rather radical changes to public assistance in the US to be viewed through the lens of Judaism? One of the most important aspects of PRWORA, as mentioned earlier, was the passing of responsibility for welfare implementation from the federal government to the states. There is certainly no contradiction with the principles of Judaism whenever governmental activity is decentralized. This was discussed in the context of the fifth axiom on limited government and the dangers of concentrated power.

Particularly relevant in this context is the fact that the Torah teaches that individuals are first obligated to give charity to their family members, then to their neighbors, then residents of the same city, and so on. These concentric circles of charitable contributions are a clear illustration of the importance Judaism places on the role of decentralization in the specific context of the fight against poverty. It is also suggests that the passing of the baton in PRWORA from the federal to the state level is not only praiseworthy, but does not go far enough. From the Jewish perspective, states should consider further devolving responsibility for welfare implementation to the city and the local level.

A second important and controversial aspect of PRWORA is the ability to deny benefits to individuals who are deemed work-ready. This aspect of welfare reform is patently not immoral from the Jewish perspective. It does not contradict the fourth axiom on caring for the needy. In Judaism, there are explicit criteria for being defined as needy. The Mishnah states that, "Someone who has 200 zuz [an ancient coin], may not take the stray or forgotten sheaf or the unharvested corner or the poor tithe." In today's currencies, 200 zuz is roughly equivalent to the amount of money a person would needs for a year's subsistence. It is an absolute, not a relative definition of poverty.

In defining a needy person, the Mishnah also takes into account potential future earnings (human capital) and asset levels. One who is able to generate income even with a very small amount of physical capital is not considered poor and is not permitted to receive public charity.[6] Judaism is not more progressive, but rather quite a bit stricter than PRWORA in determining who is eligible to receive welfare benefits.

A third important and perhaps defining aspect of PRWORA is the requirement to work in order to continue receiving public assistance. This includes work that welfare recipients may deem as being beneath their dignity. In the Jewish view, a poor person is required to go to all reasonable lengths to avoid a situation of dependence on the community. This is illustrated by sayings such as "make your Shabbat like a week-day rather than accept charity," and "better to flay a dead animal in the market place (for a living) than to accept charity."

It is fully acceptable from the Jewish perspective to require welfare recipients to accept any type of job in order to continue receiving

---

[6]In Judaism, only food can be given without checking the claim. In the case of clothing or money, each claim must be verified in order not to waste communal money.

assistance. According to the Talmud, "One should despise arrogance in his work. When considering a job position, do not convince yourself that certain jobs are beneath your dignity, with the result that you remain unemployed. Instead, take the job for its pay." Living off of donations is not the correct solution to poverty; every effort to find a job or a trade should be made by the indigent.

As mentioned briefly in the introduction, Maimonides identifies a Jewish hierarchy in caring for the poor. The highest levels of charity are offering a loan, a business partnership, or a job to the needy. Unconditional monetary handouts are the lowest form, "it is better to lend to a poor person than to give him alms, and best of all is to provide him with capital for business" (Shabbat 63a). The logic behind the hierarchy of giving is that one who is suffering should be aided, but at the same time, put back on the path of expressing the divine image through participation in the creative process, the accumulation of wealth and the ability to care for others who might be in need.

5. The Legacy of European Anti-Semitism

The axioms of Jewish economic theory that I have proposed, and the religious support of flat-rate tax systems and welfare reforms, clearly demonstrate that Judaism is highly consistent with many of the tenets of economic liberalism. It is, therefore, extremely doubtful that Judaism is the underlying reason for the Jewish political preferences that I empirically described earlier.

So what might explain the general distaste for economic liberalism among the Jews if it is not the religion? In Milton Friedman's address to the Mont Pelerin Society in 1972, an interesting alternative explanation was briefly raised. The alternative hypothesis is that anti-Semitism in Europe led the Jews to politically align with the secular Left after the French Revolution, and the effects of this alignment are still being acutely felt today. In this section, I expand on this idea.

Until the end of the eighteenth century, Jews in Europe were almost completely excluded from politics and any sort of participation in the social sphere of the nations in which they lived. The Jews mostly resided in segregated communities, or ghettos, and in these ghettos all social, political and economic decisions rested with the rabbinical establishment. Rabbis were the religious scholars, economists, judges, psychologists and administrators. Eventually, a substantial number of Jews pushed for a break with the ghetto tradition and better integration with the non-Jewish world. This led to what is known as the Haskalah movement.

The Haskalah movement can be considered the Jewish version of the Enlightenment. The Haskalah and Enlightenment doctrines shared the goal of shedding traditional religious values which were considered irrational, superstitious and tyrannical. The Age of Enlightenment ultimately led to a reshaping of the European political spectrum into a secular Left and a religious Right after the French Revolution in 1796. At the same time, as a result of the Haskalah movement, many Jews were eager to integrate and participate in politics at the national level.

It was the Left's adoption of the concept of the secular citizen that enabled Jews to find a national political home. In contrast, the religious Right was only permitting Christians to participate in their political parties. Moreover, while France, Britain and the Netherlands granted equal rights to Jews during the course of the nineteenth century, in Central and Eastern Europe, Jews still remained second class citizens devoid of any political influence. The exclusivist practices of the pro-capitalist religious Right and the institutionalized discrimination against Jews in Central and Eastern Europe pushed many Jews to join leftist revolutionary camps. In Russia and most other European countries, Jews became dominant in the leadership of the Socialist and Communist parties.

The secularization of the Jews during the Haskalah, the emergence of a secular Left around the time of the French Revolution and the exclusion of Jews from the religious, pro-capitalist parties on the Right, may very well be responsible for the historical distaste among Jews for economic liberalism at the political level. The strong distaste for free market policies may have remained deeply ingrained in the psyche of the Jews who emigrated from Europe to America. Anti-Semitism in Europe as an explanation for the political preferences of Jews today in America seems to me to be a more plausible explanation than the principles of the Jewish religion.

6. Conclusion

In this chapter, I have explored the relationship between Judaism and the political preferences of American Jews. After examining data on the voting patterns of American Jews and comparing Jewish voting patterns to those of non-Jews with similar socioeconomic characteristics, I conclude that there is empirical support for a "Jewish affiliation effect." The data suggest that American Jews have a differentially strong distaste for economic liberalism.

A natural question that arises in this context is whether or not the eschewing of free market political positions among Jews is somehow a function of the basic principles of Judaism. In order to answer this question, I attempt to formalize Jewish economic theory with only a small number of axioms that can plausibly capture the essence of Judaism's approach to economics. The axioms and the policy implications that logically derive from them are, perhaps surprisingly, highly consistent, rather than discordant, with economic liberalism.

For example, Judaism can be interpreted to support universal and low flat-rate tax systems as well as rather strict welfare-to-work welfare reforms. Although future research could certainly refine or expand upon the axioms, as well as examine additional policy implications, it seems highly unlikely that Judaism *per se* explains today's political preferences among American Jews. The alternative hypothesis that is expanded upon, that current Jewish political preferences are a legacy of Jewish secularization and European anti-Semitism, seems to be a much more plausible explanation.

If it is true that the current distaste among American Jews for free market political positions is due to the lingering effect of European anti-Semitism, then one might predict that the Jewish affiliation effect will disappear over time. That is, as the horrifying circumstances of Jewish history in Europe fade further into the past, we may see a convergence in the distribution of political preferences between Jews and similar non-Jews. On the other hand, the recent resurgence of anti-Semitism in Europe could delay or reverse any convergence. Future research might be able to more rigorously assess the strength of this alternative explanation and explore the Jewish affiliation effect in other countries such as Israel, the UK and France.

References

Boruchovich, S. Z. (2015). *The Shulchan Aruch*. Kehot Publication Society.
Friedman, M. (1988). "Capitalism and the Jews," *The Freeman Ideas on Liberty*, 38(10), 1–15.
Freedman, H. and Simon, M. (Trans.) (1983). *Midrash Rabbah: Genesis*. Vols. 1–2. London: Soncino Press.

Fuchs, L. (1956). *The Political Behavior of American Jews*. Glencoe, IL: Free Press.

Greenberg, A. and Wald, K. D. (2001). "Still Liberal After All These Years? The Contemporary Political Behavior of American Jewry," in *Jews in American Politics*, S. Maisel and Ira N. Forman (eds.), pp. 167–199. Lanham, MD: Rowman & Littlefield.

Hayek, F. A. (1944). *The Road to Serfdom*. London: Routledge Press.

Kaplan, A. (1981). *The Living Torah: The Five Books of Moses and the Haftarot*. New York, Jerusalem: Moznaim Publishing Corporation.

Lifshitz, Y. Y. (2004). "Foundations of a Jewish Economic Theory," Azure, Shalem Center.

Maimonides (2003). *Mishneh Tora*. New York: Moznaim Publishing Corp.

Maimonides (1956). *The Guide for the Perplexed*, M. Friedlander. (trans.) New York: Dover.

Sacks, J. (1985). "Wealth and Poverty a Jewish Analysis," The Social Affair Unit, Big Blog Company.

Schnall, D. J. (2001). *By the Sweat of Your Brow: Reflections on Work and the Workplace in Classic Jewish Thought*. New York: KTAV Publishing House, Inc.

Singer, I. *et al.* (eds.) (1901–1906). "TANḤUMA, MIDRASH." *The Jewish Encyclopedia*. New York: Funk & Wagnalls.

Singer, I. *et al.* (eds.) (1901–1906). "Baba Kamma." *The Jewish Encyclopedia*. New York: Funk & Wagnalls.

Singer, I. *et al.* (eds.) (1901–1906). "Malachi, Book of." *The Jewish Encyclopedia*. New York: Funk & Wagnalls.

Singer, I. *et al.* (eds.) (1901–1906). "Berakot." *The Jewish Encyclopedia*. New York: Funk & Wagnalls.

Tamari, M. (1995). *The Challenge of Wealth*. New Jersey: Jason Aroson, Inc.

Telushkin, J. (1991). *Jewish Literacy*. New York: William Morrow and Co.

Tsumura, D. T. (2007). *The First Book of Samuel*. Eerdmans.

Twersky, I. (1972). *A Maimonides Reader*. Behrman House. Inc.

Windmueller, S. F. (2003). "Are American Jews Becoming Republican?: Insights into Jewish Political Behavior," Jerusalem Viewpoints, 509.

Index

persistence, 5, 101, 103–104

persistence, *see* long-run development, 98

persistent diversity, 24

philanthropy, 299

Physics, 136

Physiology, 136–137

Plessner, Yakir, 311–312, 315

pluralism, 148, 151, 153, 256, 263, 265

polarization, 29

political culture, 246, 253, 264

political economy, 29, 32, 43–44, 51

political elites, 44

political Islam, 111, 113, 115–119, 122–123

political power, 47–48

polygamy, 105

polymorphic cultural distribution, 10

polymorphic cultural equilibrium, 7

population dynamic, 4, 6–7, 9–11, 19

poverty, 317

power legitimacy, 67

power legitimization, 67

prayer, 189, 191, 198–199, 201, 203, 206, 214, 229

preference endogeneity, 2

preferences, 2–3, 9, 29, 32, 50

prestige-biased cultural transmission, 40

printing, 102, 104–105

private property, 295, 303

privatization, 294, 318

professional/managerial, 138–141

project renewal, 315

proletariat, 303

prosocial, 187, 191, 193, 204, 210, 233

protestant, 68, 99, 194, 196, 202, 212, 216–217, 222–223, 228, 231

protestant missions, 100, 102, 105

public good, 39, 42, 48, 112–115, 117–118, 121–122, 124–128

public health, 106

public reason, 246, 262–263, 265–266

public sphere, 104–105

Pulitzer Prizes, 137

Q

quantity/quality trade-off, 13

R

radicalization, 31, 40, 51

radio, 143

Rawls, John, 262, 265

redistribution, 112, 114–118, 128

reinforcement learning, 60

religion, 2, 4

religiosity, 15–16, 63, 65, 111, 113–116, 118–119, 124–128

religious, 17

religious activities, 16

religious affiliation, 3, 12

religious awakenings, 4

religious beliefs, 5, 32, 35, 43, 48, 51

religious blending, 22

religious capital, 3, 5

religious club, 40, 51

religious community, 19, 29

religious coping, 64, 66, 69, 72, 79–80

religious denominations, 68, 75

religious diversity, 21

religious education, 35

religious goods, 117–118, 128

religious group, 14, 21, 38

religious identity, 17, 189, 204, 234

religious institutions, 47, 67

religious leader, 5, 32–33, 35, 37–40, 51

religious minorities, 11

religious norms, 113, 127

Printed in the USA
CPSIA information can be obtained
at www.ICGtesting.com
LVHW080825011123
762556LV00006B/146